THE BIGGEST TRIVIA BOOK EVER

And That's a Fact!

Includes 5,000 mind-bending trivia questions (and even their answers)

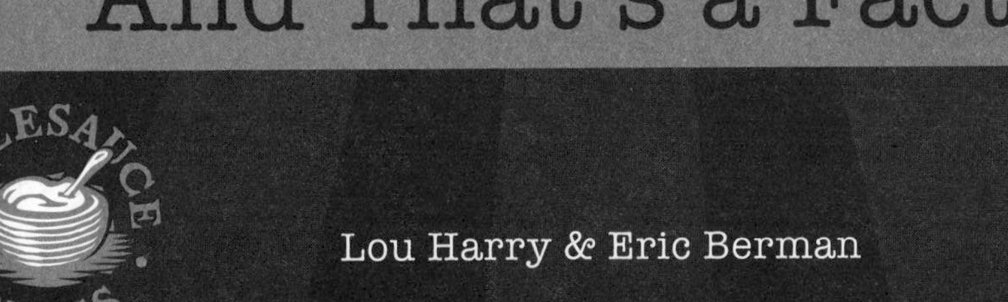

Lou Harry & Eric Berman

The Biggest Trivia Book Ever And That's a Fact!

13-Digit ISBN: 9781604332711
10-Digit ISBN: 1604332719

This book may be ordered by mail from the publisher. Please include $4.95 for postage and handling. Please support your local bookseller first!

Books published by Cider Mill Press Book Publishers are available at special discounts for bulk purchases in the United States by corporations, institutions, and other organizations.
For more information, please contact the publisher.

Applesauce Press is an imprint of
Cider Mill Press Book Publishers
"Where good books are ready for press"
12 Port Farm Road
Kennebunkport, Maine 04046

Visit us on the Web!
www.cidermillpress.com

Design by Tilly Grassa, TGCreative Services
All illustrations courtesy of Anthony Owsley
Printed in China

1 2 3 4 5 6 7 8 9 0
First Edition

Dedication

To Kenny, Kyle, Jay, Mel, Trent, Lauren, Justin and Taylor: The next-generation. –L.H.

To Christine and Christian, whose love is anything but trivial. –E.B.

Acknowledgments

Thanks to Cindy, Emily, Katie, Maggie, and Jonah Harry; Kat and Conner Falls; Sydney Vigran; Larry Graber; Ed Wenck; Dave O'Brian; Beth; and Joe and Tilly for their help in pulling this beast together.

CONTENTS

CHAPTER 1

The Natural World

ANIMALS

1) True or false: **The duckbill platypus has poison-tipped spurs behind each leg.**

Match the animal to the name for its habitat:

2) Penguin
3) Beaver
4) Wolf
5) Hare

a) Lodge
b) Down
c) Lair
d) Rookery

Match the animal to its young:

6) Elephant
7) Fox
8) Horse
9) Goat

a) Kid
b) Foal
c) Cub
d) Calf

10) True or false: **There are more than 10,000 species of mammals in the world.**

11) *Are mammals warm-blooded or cold-blooded?*

12) Can an aardvark move its ears independently of each other?

TOUGH TRIVIA CHALLENGE

13) Does an aardvark have more claws on its front feet or its back feet?

1. true, 2.d, 3.a, 4.c, 5.b, 6.d, 7.c, 8.b, 9.a, 10. false—the number ranges from 4,500-5,000. 11. Warm-blooded. 12. yes. 13. back—it's got four on each front foot and five on each back

Match the scientific name to the species that it includes.

14) Edentata d × f
15) Carnivora e ✓
16) Proboscidea f × d
17) Marsupialia a ✓
18) Rodentia b ✓
19) Primates c ✓

a) Kangaroo
b) Rat
c) Man
d) Elephant
e) Dog
f) Armadillo

20) True or false: **All aardvarks weigh less than 100 lbs.** F ✓

21) **True or false:** An African buffalo's horns can help it float in water. F

22) True of false: **An African buffalo keeps all of its hair until it dies.** T ×

23) **TRUE OR FALSE:** THE AFRICAN WILD DOG RUNS ON ITS TOES. T ✓

24) True or false: **The African wild dog always has a black-tipped tail.** F ✓

25) **True or false:** Each African wild dog has a different pattern in its coat. F ✓

26) True or false: The shape of an American bison's face can help you figure out its age.

27) How many toes are there on each paw of an African wild dog?

28) True or false: **The fennec is the smallest of all foxes.**

29) **True or false:** The Arctic fox has fur on both the top and bottom of its paws.

TOUGH TRIVIA CHALLENGE

33) Which usually has a shorter tail, the American bison or the European bison?

30) True or false: The Arctic fox can sleep on ice.

31) True or false: An armadillo's front legs are about twice as long as its back legs.

32) True or false: A badger cannot run.

14. f, 15. e, 16. d, 17. a, 18. b, 19. c, 20. false, 21. true, 22. false—its hair thins out over time, leaving patches of skin, 23. true, 24. false—it's always white-tipped, 25. true, 26. true, 27. four, 28. true, 29. true, 30. true, 31. false—they are about the same size, 32. false, 33. American

TOUGH TRIVIA CHALLENGE

34) True or false: The Arctic fox has pointed ears.

35) Which tends to be smaller, a black bear or a polar bear?

36) How many toes does a black bear have on each paw?

37) True or false: A black bear's teeth are completely grown by its first birthday.

38) True or false: Grizzly bears have no lips.

39) WHICH CAN GROW TALLER, A GRIZZLY BEAR OR A KODIAK BEAR?

40) WHICH ARE LONGER, A BADGER'S FORECLAWS OR ITS HIND CLAWS?

41) True or false: Because of its relatively small ears, grizzly bears cannot hear very well.

42) Which tends to have a shorter coat, the black bear or the grizzly bear?

43) Koalas and wallabies are *diprotodonts,* which means...

a) Their feet and hands are different shapes

b) They have shorter front limbs than back limbs

c) They are marsupials with two incisor teeth in their lower jaw

d) They eat eucalyptus

44) True or false: Polar bears eat mostly meat.

45) Is a polar bear's skin white?

46) When running, do a hare's hind legs ever go in front of its forelegs?

47) Which has a longer hind leg, a hare or a rabbit?

48) True or false: The term "hairlip" comes from the shape of a hare's lip.

34. false—they are curved, 35. a black bear, 36. five, 37. false—they grow slowly through its lifetime, 38. false, 39. Kodiak—it can reach over 12 feet on its hind legs, 40. foreclaws, 41. false, 42. black bear, 43. c, 44. true, 45. no—it's black, 46. yes, 47. hare, 48. true

49) True or false: The hands of a koala each have two thumbs.

50) True or false: Young camels have more incisor teeth than adult camels.

51) True or false: If a camel is starving, its hump may slide to one side.

52) TRUE OR FALSE: A CAMEL HAS NO EYELASHES.

53) True or false: A beaver's tale can store fat.

54) Which is usually taller, a leopard or a cheetah?

55) What color are the backs of a cheetah's ears?

56) True or false: A cheetah can retract its claws all the way into its paws.

TOUGH TRIVIA CHALLENGE

57) About how many muscle units are in an elephant's trunk?
a) 1,000
b) 10,000
c) 100,000
d) 1,000,000

58) True or false: Leopards have hair on their tongues.

59) Is a snow leopard bigger or smaller than a regular leopard?

60) Which has a spine that curves upward, an African or an Asian elephant?

61) The tongue of an adult giant anteater is about:

a) 9 inches long
b) 24 inches long
c) 48 inches long
d) 64 inches long

62) True or false: The anteater's nostrils are near its eyes.

63) TRUE OR FALSE: THE ANTEATER WALKS ON ITS CLAWS.

64) True or false: *All of an anteater's claws are the same size.*

49. true, 50. true, 51. true, 52. false, 53. True, 54. Cheetah, 55. black, 56. false, 57. c, 58. true, 59. smaller, 60. Asian, 61. b, 62. false—they are at the end of its snout, 63. false, 64. false

65) True or false: **Elephants cannot run faster than 20 mph.**

66) Which are heavier, male anteaters or female anteaters?

67) **How many vertebrae in a giraffe's neck?**

a) 7
b) 70
c) 700
d) 7,000

68) True or false: A giraffe's front legs are almost twice as long as its hind legs.

69) WHAT COLOR IS A GIRAFFE'S TONGUE?

A) RED
B) BLACK
C) PINK
D) TAN

70) What color are a giraffe's eyes?

a) Green
b) Blue
c) Brown
d) Black

TOUGH TRIVIA CHALLENGE

71) The giant panda's "false thumb" is actually...

a) A chunk of fatty tissue
b) A large wrist bone
c) Excess skin
d) A claw

72) Can the giant panda see well at night?

73) **True or false:** **Giraffes don't have eyelashes.**

74) Does a hedgehog have cheekbones?

75) **TRUE OR FALSE:** A HEDGEHOG'S SPINE IS HOLLOW.

TOUGH TRIVIA CHALLENGE

79) How many pointed teeth does an adult hedgehog have?

a) 0
b) 12
c) 24
d) 36

76) True or false: **A pygmy hippo can weigh as much as 600 lbs.**

77) How many toes does a hippo have?

78) **True or false:** A hippo can gallop up to 30 mph.

80) True or false: **A hyena has retractable claws.**

81) True or false: A hyena's stomach can digest bones.

65. false, 66. male, 67. a, 68. false—they are only slightly longer, 69. b, 70. c, 71. b, 72. yes, 73. false, 74. yes, 75. true, 76. true, 77. four, 78. true, 79. d, 80. false, 81. true

82) True or false:

A hippo can't wag its tail.

83) ARE MALE OR FEMALE HYENAS HEAVIER?

84) Which has longer horns, a male or female ibex?

85) Are jaguar claws retractable?

TOUGH TRIVIA CHALLENGE

88) Are male wild goat horns smooth or ridged?

86) True or false: The canine teeth of a jaguar are used primarily for eating.

87) In bright light, do a jaguar's pupils shrink to a dot or to a slit?

89) PROPORTIONATELY. WHICH HAS LONGER FRONT LEGS. A CHEETAH OR A JAGUAR?

90) Which is bigger, an adult male kangaroo or adult female kangaroo.

91) How many digits are on a kangaroo's hand?

92) An aardwolf feeds mostly on...

a) Rabbits
b) Termites
c) Hyenas
d) Lizards

93) True or false: A red kangaroo can reach 40 mph.

94) Do female opossums have pouches?

95) HOW MANY TOES DOES AN OPOSSUM HAVE ON EACH FOOT?

96) The lion is the second largest cat. What's the first?

97) What is usually longer, a meerkat's body or its tail?

TOUGH TRIVIA CHALLENGE

98) Opossums have the most teeth of any marsupial. How many does each have?

a) 44
b) 50
c) 62
d) 84

82. false, 83. females, 84. male, 85. yes, 86. false—they are for killing, 87. dot, 88. ridged, 89. cheetah, 90. male, 91. five, 92. b, 93. true, 94. yes, 95. five, 96. tiger, 97. body, 98. b

99) A lion's skull can weigh up to...

a) 2 lbs
b) 4 lbs
c) 6 lbs
d) 12 lbs

100) True or false:
Most mongoose species are herbivores.

TOUGH TRIVIA CHALLENGE

101) Meerkats are different from other mongooses because...
a) They only have four toes on each foot
b) They have opposable thumbs
c) They are primarily found in Asia
d) They do not dig

102) True or false:
A pronghorn signals danger by raising its white rump hairs.

103) Which of the following is not a common fur color for a puma:
a) Red-brown
b) Blue-grey
c) Yellow
d) Black

104) TRUE OR FALSE:
ALL ZEBRAS HAVE THE SAME STRIPE PATTERN.

105) Which is usually longer, a ring-tailed coati or a kinkajou?

106) Is the tip of a raccoon's striped tail always dark or always light?

107) True or false: The antelope is the largest living deer.

108) HOW LONG DOES IT TAKE FOR A RED DEER TO GET TWELVE POINTS ON ITS ANTLERS?

A) 2 YEARS
B) 4 YEARS
C) 6 YEARS
D) 8 YEARS

109) True or false: Red deer are born with white spots that fade away.

110) True or false: The red fox has a scent gland on its tail.

111) Which has a longer horn, the Sumatran rhino or the white rhino?

99. c, 100. false—omnivores, 101. a, 102. true, 103. c, 104. false, 105. ring-tailed coati, 106. always dark, 107. false—it's the moose, 108. c, 109. true, 110. true, 111. white rhino

112) Which is larger, the Sumatran rhino or the Indian rhino?

113) Which has more horns, the Sumatran rhino or the Indian rhino?

114) True or false: Rhino ears can only be moved together.

115) How many hooves on a rhino's foot?

116) TRUE OR FALSE: SHREWS EAT FOOD ADDING UP TO 80–90% OF THEIR BODY WEIGHT EVERY WEEK.

117) Is a Tasmanian devil a mammal, a marsupial, or a rodent?

118) True or false: The Tasmanian devil has no whiskers.

119) True or false: The Tasmanian devil's tail can only move side to side.

120) On what continent are Tasmanian devils found?

121) TRUE OR FALSE: TASMANIAN DEVILS WILL SOMETIMES TAKE OVER THE FORMER NESTS OF WOMBATS.

TOUGH TRIVIA CHALLENGE

122) A Tasmanian devil's jaw can open:

a) 20-30 degrees

b) 30-50 degrees

c) 50-70 degrees

d) 75-80 degrees

123) True or false: The smallest tiger species is the Sumatran tiger.

124) How many claws does a tiger have on each forepaw?

125) True or false: **Small cats can't roar because of its hyoid bone.**

126) True or false: Tiger teeth can be up to 10 inches long.

127) Which is larger, a gray wolf or a red wolf?

128) Does a wolf have more teeth on its upper jaw or its lower jaw?

112. Indian, 113. Sumatran, 114. false, 115. three, 116. false—they eat that every day, 117. marsupial, 118. false, 119. false, 120. Australia, 121. true, 122. d, 123. true, 124. five, 125. true, 126. false—five inches is about the maximum, 127. gray, 128. lower

129) A COW CAN'T PRODUCE MILK UNTIL IT...

A) HAS A CALF
B) IS OVER 390 LBS.
C) BOTH OF THE ABOVE
D) NONE OF THE ABOVE

130) When hand-milked, about how many squirts does it take to produce a gallon of milk from a cow?

a) 12
b) 120
c) 345
d) 450

131) True or false: Azaleas are poisonous to cats.

132) True or false: cats have 32 muscles in each ear

133) True or false: Tigers can easily walk on hot surfaces.

134) TRUE OR FALSE: DOGS SHOULDN'T EAT GRAPES.

135) True or false: There is a real disease called cat scratch fever.

136) How long do Irish wolf hounds usually live?

a) 6-8 years

b) 8-10 years

c) 10-12 years

d) 12-15 years

TOUGH TRIVIA CHALLENGE

137) Which tends to have the longest ears, a wombat, a bandicoot, or a bilby?

138) True or false: The fastest herbivore on Earth is the cheetah.

139) True or false: Turkey eggs can have two yolks.

140) True or false: Aardvark means "earthpig" in Afrikaans.

141) True or false: More than a million wildebeests have been known to herd in Tanzania and Kenya.

142) TRUE OR FALSE:
THERE IS NO MALE FOUR-HORNED ANIMAL.

143) True or false: The American antelope can shed its horns every year.

129. a, 130. c, 131. true, 132. true, 133. false—they have soft footpads to better walk quietly in the jungle, 134. true, 135. true, 136. a, 137. a bilby, 138. false—the North American pronghorn is faster, 139. true, 141. true, 142. false—the male four-horned antelope has a quartet of them, 143. true

144) True or false: The smallest camel species is the vicuna.

145) True or false: Musk—considered the most powerful scent in the world—is produced by the female musk deer.

146) Which African country has the most hippopotamuses?

a) South Africa
b) Congo
c) Zambia
d) Egypt

147) DO HIPPOS HAVE SWEAT GLANDS?

148) True or false: A skunk's skin is striped.

149) Does a woodchuck chuck wood?

150) Which sleeps for more hours a day, a horse or a squirrel?

151) Which sleeps for more hours a day, a ferret or a pig?

152) Which sleeps for more hours a day, a dog or a tiger?

153) Porcupines are
a) Nearsighted
b) Hard of hearing
c) Both
d) Neither

154) Are porcupine quills darker at the tip or at the base?

155) ABOUT HOW MANY QUILLS DOES A PORCUPINE HAVE?
A) 300
B) 3,000
C) 30,000
D) 300,000

156) True or false: When attacked, a porcupine may swing its tail back and forth.

144. True, 145. false—it's the male, 146. c, 147. no, 148. true, 149. no, 150. a squirrel, 151. a ferret, 152. a dog, 153. a, 154. at the tip, 155. c, 156. true

GEOLOGY

157) Which is closer to the Earth's surface, the mantle or the outer core?

158) About how deep is the Earth's crust?
a) 2 miles
b) 4 miles
c) 10 miles
d) 25 miles

159) About how deep is the Earth's magma layer?
a) 100 miles
b) 1,000 miles
c) 1,800 miles
d) 2,400 miles

160) True or false: The Earth's inner core is estimated to be about the size of the Moon.

161) About how many different kinds of minerals are there on Earth?
a) 1,000
b) 1,200
c) 1,500
d) 2,000

162) About how much shorter are mountains estimated to get every 1,000 years?

a) 30 feet

b) 3 feet

c) 30 inches

d) 3 inches

163) WHAT IS BETWEEN TOPSOIL AND BEDROCK?

A) SUBSOIL

B) MIDSOIL

C) SECONDARY SOIL

D) LIGHTSOIL

164) What discovery helped date the age of the Earth?

a) Gravity

b) Radioactivity

c) Nuclear power

d) Atomic power

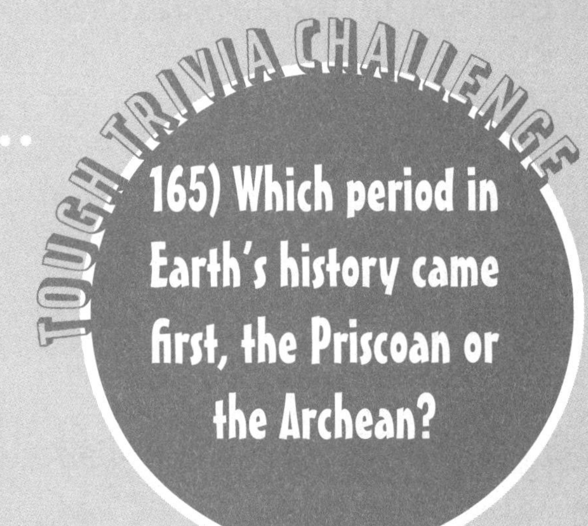

166) True or false: The ozone layer developed during the Proterozoic period.

167) True or false: It's calculated that the Earth reverses its polarity every half a million years.

157. the mantle, 158. d, 159. c, 160. true, 161. d, 162. d, 163. a, 164. b, 165. Priscoan—between 4.6 and 3.8 billion years ago, 166. true, 167. true

168) What is the equatorial circumference of the Earth?

a) About 24,000 miles
b) About 32,000 miles
c) About 40,000 miles
d) About 48,000 miles

169) DOES THE EARTH CONTAIN MORE MAGNESIUM OR SODIUM?

170) Does the Earth contain more aluminum or potassium?

171) Does the Earth contain more silicon or iron?

172) METEOROLOGIST ALFRED WEGENER PROPOSED IN 1911 THAT THE CONTINENTS ALL WERE ONCE ONE LARGE LAND MASS. WHAT COUNTRY WAS WEGENER FROM?

TOUGH TRIVIA CHALLENGE

173) What scale tells whether a mineral can scratch another?

a) The Taft-Hartley Hardness Scale
b) Mohs' Hardness Scale
c) The Washington/Kruxton Hardness Scale
d) The Mueller Scale

174) What continent does the Nubia Plate largely include?

175) Which of the following is not one of the major tectonic plates?

a) Nazca Plate

b) Pacic Plate

c) Arctic Plate

d) Indian Plate

176) True or false: Gravimetry measures gravitational force.

177) What is the name given to the supercontinent that existed in the late Paleozoic and early Mesozoic era?

a) Painglass

b) Pangaea

c) Penniless

d) Prinus

178) True or false: Panthalassa is the name given to the global ocean that surrounded the land in the previous question.

179) TRUE OR FALSE: EARLY SEISMOGRAPHS USED A PENDULUM TO DRAW ON GLASS OR PAPER.

168. a, 169. sodium, 170. potassium, 171. silicon, 172. Germany, 173. b, 174. Africa , 175. c, 176. true, 177. b, 178. true, 179. true

TOUGH TRIVIA CHALLENGE

180) What was the developer of the Richter magnitude scale's first name?
a) Chris
b) Andy
c) Charles
d) Francis

181) True or false: Earthquakes under 2.0 on the Richter scale are perceivable by most people.

182) How much more powerful is a 6.0 on the Richter scale then a 5.0?
a) 1 time
b) 5 times
c) 10 times
d) 100 times

183) True or false: The 1995 earthquake in Kobe, Japan, is thought to be the one in recorded history in which the most people died.

184) How long did it take for plants to start growing again after the eruption of Mount St. Helens?
a) Days
b) Weeks
c) Months
d) Years

185) TRUE OR FALSE: SEAQUAKES CAUSE MOST TSUNAMIS.

186) True or false: There's a 37-mile-long magma chamber under New York City.

187) True or false: Earthquakes come before all volcano eruptions.

188) Where is Old Faithful?

a) Nebraska
b) North Dakota
c) Washington
d) Wyoming

TOUGH TRIVIA CHALLENGE

189) Modern skyscrapers should be able to withstand what level of earthquake as recorded on the Richter scale?

a) 8.5
b) 8.7
c) 8.9
d) 9.3

190) Which is not one of the places where you can find a geyser.

a) United States
b) Ethiopia
c) Spain
d) Chile

191) Everest is called Sagarmatha in Nepalese. What does that mean?

a) King of the mountains
b) King of the heavens
c) King of the hills
d) King of the Earth

192) How many of the 14 "eight-thousanders" (mountains over 8,000 meters high) are located in the Himalayas?

180. c, 181. true, 182. c, 183. false, 184. c, 185. true, 186. false—but there is one under Yellowstone National Park, 187. true, 188. d, 189. a, 190. c, 191. b, 192. ten

TOUGH TRIVIA CHALLENGE

193) Black smokers—undersea hot springs—eject water as hot as...

a) 120°F
b) 430°F
c) 660°F
d) 800°F

194) From what country was the first woman to reach Everest's peak?

a) England
b) Thailand
c) Japan
d) Australia

195) True or false: Snow slides are often deliberately caused on mountains in order to avoid future avalanches.

196) About what percent of the land mass of the Earth is covered in ice?

a) 5%
b) 10%
c) 15%
d) 18%

197) True or false: George Everest was the first person to reach the top of the mountain that would be named after him.

198) What is the only continent without mountain glaciers?

199) About how much of an iceberg is typically above the water level?

a) One-quarter

b) One-half

c) One-sixth

d) One-ninth

TOUGH TRIVIA CHALLENGE

200) Which is more likely to have some trees, a veldt or a plain?

201) TRUE OR FALSE: THE FIZZING SOUND A MELTING ICEBERG MAKES IS KNOWN AS "BERGIE SELTZER."

202) Which is larger, a medium or a growler iceberg?

203) Which is larger, a Bergy Bit or a small iceberg?

204) Do tabular icebergs have steep or sloped sides?

205) What does the letter in an iceberg's name refer to?

a) Its weight

b) Its height

c) Its depth

d) Its place of origin

193. c, 194. c, 195. true, 196. b, 197. false—Everest was a British surveyor, 198. Australia, 199. d, 200. veldt, 201. true, 202. medium, 203. small, 204. steep, 205. d

BODIES OF WATER

206) What percentage of the Earth is covered by water?

a) 48%
b) 63%
c) 71%
d) 82%

207) Which ocean has the most islands?

208) Is the average depth of the Pacific Ocean over or under 10,000 feet?

209) IS THE DEEPEST PART OF THE PACIFIC OCEAN MORE OR LESS THAN 35,000 FEET?

210) Is the deepest part of the Atlantic Ocean more or less than 35,000 feet?

211) Is the deepest part of the Indian Ocean more or less than 30,000 feet?

212) **True or false: The hotter and dryer the climate, the greater the salt content in the ocean.**

TOUGH TRIVIA CHALLENGE

213) How many square miles is the Indian Ocean?

a) 15 million
b) 20 million
c) 29 million
d) 43 million

214) What is the average salt content of the oceans?

a) 1%
b) 3.5%
c) 4.8%
d) 6%

215) IN THE OPEN SEA, ABOUT HOW FAR CAN SUNLIGHT REACH UNDERWATER?

A) 1,280 FEET
B) 2,480 FEET
C) 3,280 FEET
D) 4,680 FEET

216) True or false: The unit used to measure ocean current is the sverdrup.

217) Where are the strongest tidal currents found?

a) Florida's Atlantic coast
b) Japan's Pacific coast
c) Finland
d) Chile

206. c, 207. Pacific, 208. over, 209. more, 210. less, 211. less, 212. true, 213. c, 214. b, 215. c, 216. true, 217. c

218) About how long is the U.S. continental coastline?

a) 100,000 miles
b) 200,000 miles
c) 250,000 miles
d) 350,000 miles

TOUGH TRIVIA CHALLENGE

219) True or false: Kansai International Airport in Japan is on an articial island.

220) How high do most waves get?

a) About 4 feet
b) About 6 feet
c) About 8 feet
d) About 10 feet

221) True or false: About half of the world's population lives within 60 miles of an ocean.

222) IS THE ATLANTIC OCEAN GROWING OR SHRINKING?

223) What is the largest island on Earth?

224) The Great Barrier Reef is off what Australian coast?

a) Southwest
b) Southeast
c) Northwest
d) Northeast

225) About how many islands are in the Great Barrier Reef?

- **a) 100**
- **b) 300**
- **c) 600**
- **d) 1,000**

226) True or false: A bathysphere is a deep-sea submersible lowered on a cable.

227) True or false: Sponges have no organs.

228) TRUE OR FALSE: SPONGES HAVE NO NERVE CELLS.

229) True or false: Corals and jellyfish are from the phylum Cnidaria.

230) True or false: Jellyfish can be up to fifteen feet long.

218. c, 219. true, 220. d, 221. true, 222. growing, 223. Greenland, 224. d, 225. c, 226. true, 227. true, 228. true, 229. true, 230. false—they can grow as big as six feet long

231) True or false: The Yangtze is the longest river in Asia.

232) **Parasitic worms in whales can be up to how long?**

a) 5 feet
b) 10 feet
c) 20 feet
d) 30 feet

TOUGH TRIVIA CHALLENGE

233) Do allochthonous rivers gain or lose water as they flow?

234) WHEN WAS THE SAINT LAWRENCE SEAWAY COMPLETED?

A) 1930S
B) 1940S
C) 1950S
D) 1960S

235) About what percentage of the Earth's surface is covered by lakes?

a) .5%
b) 1%
c) 2%
d) 4%

236) True or false: Most salt lakes originally were filled with fresh water.

237) Where is the largest reservoir in the world?

a) United States
b) Ghana
c) China
d) Brazil

238) Which is larger, a brook or a stream?

239) Which is larger, a creek or a stream?

240) Which is larger, a tributary or a branch?

241) DOES A WATERWAY BEGIN OR END AT THE HEAD?

242) If a river is flowing west is the northern bank the right bank or the left bank?

243) What is the place where a fresh waterway empties into a salt-water body?

a) Estuary
b) Basin
c) Lock
d) Rift

231. true, 232. d, 233. lose, 234. c, 235. c, 236. true, 237. b, 238. stream, 239. creek, 240. tributary, 241. begin, 242. right bank, 243. a

244) Which is larger a channel or a sound?

245) What is the average daily water usage per person in industrialized countries?

a) 8 gallons
b) 18 gallons
c) 28 gallons
d) 38 gallons

246) TRUE OR FALSE: A 100-YEAR FLOOD IS A FLOOD THAT HAPPENS EVERY 100 YEARS.

247) The Cuyahoga River in Ohio was so polluted that it caught fire.

248) In what state is Siesta Beach considered by some to be the best beach in the U.S.?

249) In what state are Wildwood, North Wildwood, and Wildwood Crest beaches?

250) In what state is Kauapea Beach?

251) In what state is Ocracoke Island Beach?

252) In what state is Wildcat Beach?

253) True or false: New Smyrna Beach is right next to Old Smyrna Beach.

254) In what state is Poipu Beach?

255) In what state is Sanibel Island?

256) In what state is South Padre Island?

257) In what state is Catalina Island?

258) IN WHAT NEW ENGLAND STATE IS OLD ORCHARD BEACH?

259) In what Pacic state is Cannon Beach?

244. sound, 245. d, 246. false—it's a flood level that has a one-percent chance of being matched or exceeded in a given year, 247. true—multiple times, 248. Florida, 249. New Jersey, 250. Hawaii, 251. North Carolina, 252. California, 253. false, 254. Hawaii, 255. Florida, 256. Texas, 257. California, 258. Maine, 259. Oregon

260) In what state is Malibu Beach?

261) In what state is Galveston Beach?

TOUGH TRIVIA CHALLENGE

262) The ancient Egyptians called the Nile River Ar, which means what?
a) Water
b) Black
c) Flowing
d) Danger

263) In what state is Panama City Beach?

264) In what state is Cape Hatteras?

265) Oval Beach is located in what Midwest state?

266) Is the Nile shorter or longer than 4,000 miles?

267) True or false: The Nile touches Ethiopia, Kenya, and Zaire.

268) Is Cairo on the banks of the Nile?

269) True or false: More than half of the Nile is in Egypt.

270) IS EGYPT AT THE SOURCE OR THE MOUTH OF THE NILE?

271) The Nile is formed from the White Nile and the Blue Nile. Which one comes from Ethiopia?

272) Which is longer, the White Nile or the Blue Nile?

273) Is the Nile more likely to flood in August or February?

274) Which of the following is not a damn on the Nile?

a) Sennar Dam
b) Aswan High Dam
c) Owen Falls Dam
d) East Cairo Dam

275) Which has a higher average discharge of water, the Amazon or the Nile?

260. California, 261. Texas, 262. b, 263. Florida, 264. North Carolina, 265. Michigan, 266. longer, 267. true, 268. yes, 269. false, 270. mouth, 271. Blue Nile, 272. White Nile, 273. August, 274. d, 275. the Amazon

276) True or false: There are no crocodiles in the Nile.

277) True or false: During the wet season, the Amazon can be 40 miles wide.

278) True or false: No bridges cross the Amazon.

279) WHICH OF THE FOLLOWING DOES THE AMAZON NOT FLOW THROUGH.

A) BRAZIL
B) COLOMBIA
C) CHILE
D) BOLIVIA

280) Does the Amazon end farther east than its beginning or farther west?

281) True or false: There are piranhas in the Amazon River.

282) True or false: There are places on the Mississippi River that are more than 180 feet deep.

283) True or false: The name Mississippi comes from a Greek word.

284) TRUE OR FALSE: THE PONTCHARTRAIN CAUSEWAY IS THE LONGEST BRIDGE OVER WATER IN AMERICA.

285) In what state is the source of the Mississippi?

286) Does the Mississippi River only flow in the U.S.?

287) Which of the following states doesn't have the Mississippi River running through it?

a) Mississippi

b) Missouri

c) Indiana

d) Maryland

288) Which is closer to the source of the Mississippi, Genoa Wisconsin or Hannibal, Missouri?

289) Do any railroad tunnels go under the Mississippi River?

276. false, 277. false—the Amazon can grow to be just over 20 miles wide, 278. true, 279. c, 280. east, 281. true, 282. true, 283. false, 284. true, 285. Minnesota, 286. yes, 287. d, 288. Genoa, 289. no

290) The Savanna-Sabula Bridge connects Savanna, Illinois to the island of Sabula, which is part of what state?

TOUGH TRIVIA CHALLENGE

291) True or false: The John James Audubon Bridge is the longest cable-stayed bridge in the Western Hemisphere.

292) True or false: Amerigo Vespucci was the first European to reach the Mississippi River.

293) True or false: The Mississippi River was once the border between the Spanish Empire and the British Empire.

294) Was Mark Twain's *Life on the Mississippi* published before or after *The Adventures of Huckleberry Finn?*

295) True or false: American swimmer Mark Spitz swam the length of the Mississippi River.

296) TRUE OR FALSE: WATER SKIING WAS INVENTED ON THE MISSISSIPPI RIVER.

297) True or false: The Yangtze River ows primarily north.

298) True or false: The Three Gorges Dam is 300 feet high.

299) True or false: The Three Gorges Dam is the world's largest hydro-electric power station.

300) True or false: The Yangtze River is named after Emperor Yangtze.

301) True or false: The Yangtze River flows into the Pacific Ocean.

302) True or false: The rainy season on the south side of the Yangtze River is May and June.

303) TRUE OR FALSE: THE FINLESS PORPOISE CAN BE FOUND IN THE YANGTZE RIVER.

304) True or false: The Yangtze River flows through four countries.

305) In what country is the source of the Ob River?

306) In what country is the source of the Yellow River?

290. Iowa, 291. false—it is second to the Baluarte bridge in Mexico, 292. false—it was Hernando de Soto, 293. true, 294. before, 295. false—but Martin Strel did, 296. true, 297. false, 298. false—it's 600 feet, 299. true, 300. false, 301. false, 302. true, 303. true, 304. false, 305. Russia, 306. China

307) In what country is the source of the Yenisei River?

308) WHICH IS LONGER, THE MISSOURI RIVER OR THE VOLGA RIVER?

309) Which Great Lake is the source of the St. Lawrence River?

TOUGH TRIVIA CHALLENGE

310) Which is longer, the Irtish River or the Lena River?

311) True or false: **The Rio Grande River flows into the Pacific Ocean.**

312) True or false: The source of the Euphrates River is in Turkey.

313) Which is longer, the Rio Grande River or the Euphrates River?

314) True or false: The Ganges is one of the ten longest rivers in the world.

315) Is the Colorado River only in Colorado?

316) True or false: The Hoover Dam is the only dam on the Colorado River.

317) IS THE PILCOMAYO RIVER IN ASIA OR SOUTH AMERICA?

318) Does the Columbia River begin in Canada or the United States?

319) Is the Peace River in Canada or Australia?

320) Does the Tigris River flow through Iraq?

321) Which is larger, Lake Victoria or Lake Superior?

322) HOW MANY OF THE FIVE LARGEST LAKES IN THE WORLD ARE GREAT LAKES?

323) Is Great Bear Lake in Canada or Asia?

324) True or false: Some geographers consider the Caspian Sea to be a lake.

325) True or false: Lake Huron has more than twice the square mileage of Lake Erie.

307. Russia, 308. Missouri, 309. Lake Ontario, 310. Irtish, 311. false, 312. true, 313. Rio Grande, 314. false, 315. no, 316. false, 317. South America, 318. Canada, 319. Canada, 320. yes, 321. Superior, 322. three, 323. Canada, 324. true, 325. true

326) True or false: Lake Titicaca is in Ecuador.

327) True or false: The Great Salt Lake in Utah is over 200 feet deep in places.

328) True or false: There are no islands on the Great Salt Lake.

329) TRUE OR FALSE: THE GREAT SALT LAKE IS ABOUT 75 MILES LONG.

330) True or false: Few fish live in the Great Salt Lake.

331) True or false: It is estimated that over 100 billion brine flies make their home at the Great Salt Lake.

TOUGH TRIVIA CHALLENGE

332) The Great Salt Lake is a remnant of what prehistoric lake?
a) Lake Neanderthal
b) Lake Bonneville
c) Lake Saltcatrine
d) Lake Salmanar

333) Toledo, Ohio, is on what Great Lake?

334) Traverse City, Michigan, is on what Great Lake?

335) BUFFALO, NEW YORK, IS ON WHAT GREAT LAKE?

TOUGH TRIVIA CHALLENGE

336) The Straits of Mackinac connect which two Great Lakes?

337) Toronto, Ontario, is on what Great Lake?

338) Thunder Bay, Ontario, is on what Great Lake?

339) Duluth, Minnesota, is on what Great Lake?

340) Rochester, New York, is on what Great Lake?

341) Green Bay, Wisconsin, is on what Great Lake?

342) Which of the Great Lakes is at a lower elevation than the others?

343) THE ST. MARYS RIVER CONNECTS WHICH TWO GREAT LAKES?

326. false, 327. false, 328. false, 329. true, 330. true, 331. true, 332. b, 333. Erie, 334. Michigan, 335. Erie, 336. Michigan and Huron, 337. Ontario, 338. Superior, 339. Superior, 340. Ontario, 341. Michigan, 342. Ontario, 343. Superior and Huron

344) Georgian Bay is part of what Great Lake?

345) True or false: There are more than 30,000 islands in the Great Lakes.

346) True or false: The largest island in the Great Lakes, Manitoulin Island, is in Lake Huron.

347) Which Great Lake is entirely within the United States?

348) THE NAMES OF WHICH TWO GREAT LAKES COME FROM FRENCH WORDS?

349) True or false: The combined Great Lakes are larger than New York and New Jersey combined.

350) The "Graveyard of the Great Lakes"—named because of the many shipwrecks there—is located in what lake?

351) Is the Bay of Fundy on the Atlantic or Pacific coast?

352) Which of the following does not border the Bay of Bengal?

a) Bangladesh
b) Sri Lanka
c) Mongolia
d) India

TOUGH TRIVIA CHALLENGE

355) The SS *Edmund Fitzgerald* sank in Lake Superior in what year?

a) 1945
b) 1955
c) 1965
d) 1975

353) True or false: The Dead Sea is below sea level.

354) True or false: The Bay of Bengal is part of the Mediterranean Sea.

356) Did any of Christopher Columbus's ocean trips take him to the Gulf of Mexico?

357) What are the five states that border the Gulf of Mexico?

358) WHICH HAS MORE GULF OF MEXICO COASTLINE, THE U.S. OR MEXICO?

359) How far from the U.S. coast was the Deepwater Horizon oil platform when it exploded in 2010?

a) 30 miles
b) 40 miles
c) 60 miles
d) 80 miles

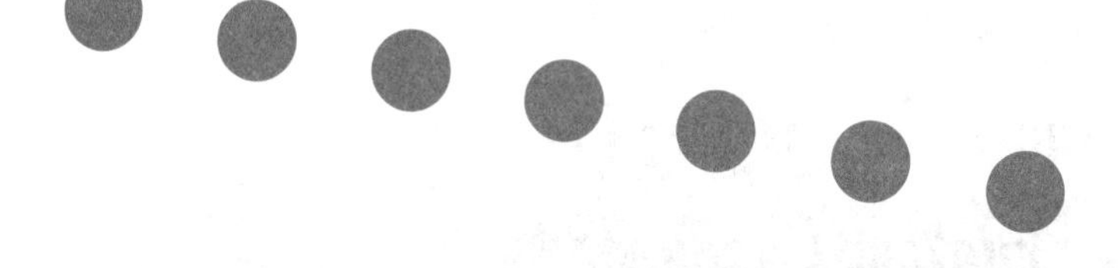

344. Huron, 345. true, 346. true, 347. Michigan, 348. Superior and Huron, 349. true, 350. Superior, 351. Atlantic, 352. c, 353. true, 354. false, 355. d, 356. no, 357. Texas, Louisiana, Mississippi, Alabama, and Florida, 358. U.S., 359. b

360) The Gulf of Aqaba is connected to what sea?

361) Is the Suez Canal at the northwest or southeast end of the Gulf of Suez?

362) Which is larger, the Persian Gulf or the Gulf of California?

363) WHICH IS LARGER, THE ENGLISH CHANNEL OR THE GULF OF ST. LAWRENCE?

364) Which is larger, the U.S.'s Lake Michigan or Canada's Great Bear Lake?

365) Which is larger, the Caspian Sea or Lake Huron?

366) Which is larger Africa's Lake Victoria or the U.S.'s Lake Superior?

367) True or false: Baikal in Russia is the world's deepest lake.

368) The Great Salt Lake covers how many square miles?

a) 170
b) 1,700
c) 17,000
d) 170,000

TOUGH TRIVIA CHALLENGE

369) True or false: The Gulf of Mexico covers more than 15 times the area of the English Channel.

MOUNTAINS

370) MOUNT EVEREST IS THE EARTH'S HIGHEST MOUNTAIN. WHICH SIDE OF THE NEPAL/CHINESE BORDER IS IT ON?

371) What country named Mount Everest?

a) The United States
b) China
c) Nepal
d) England

372) True or false: The people of Nepal called Mount Everest Chomolungma.

373) True or false: Mount Everest is considered the most difficult mountain in the world to climb.

374) True or false: More than 2,000 people have climbed Mount Everest.

375) True or false: More than 1,000 people have died trying to climb Mount Everest.

376) True or false: Mauna Kea in Hawaii is actually a bigger mountain then Mount Everest...if you measure it from its base, which is below sea level.

360. Red Sea, 361. Northwest, 362. Persian Gulf, 363. Gulf of St. Lawrence, 364. Lake Michigan, 365. Caspian Sea, 366. Lake Superior, 367. true, 368. b, 369. true, 370. Nepal, 371. d, 372. true, 373. false, 374. true, 375. false—200, 376. true

377) Of the two main climbing routes up Mount Everest, which is the easiest to climb, the southeast ridge from Nepal or the northeast ridge from Tibet?

378) TRUE OR FALSE: THE OLDEST CLIMBER TO REACH THE TOP OF EVEREST WAS 92 YEARS OLD.

TOUGH TRIVIA CHALLENGE

379) Two days before Edmund Hilary and Tenzing Norgay made it to the top of Everest in 1953, Tom Bourdillon and Charles Evans were almost first, but they ran out of oxygen and turned back around. How close were they to the top?

a) 3000 ft.
b) 1500 ft.
c) 900 ft.
d) 300 ft.

380) True or false: a black jumping spider was found on Everest at about 22,000 ft.

381) True or false: The highest peak in the Adirondacks is Mt. Milly.

382) In 1978, Reinhold Messner and Peter Habeler were the first to make it to the top of Everest without supplemental ______________.

383) True or false: The Appalachians stretch from Quebec to Alabama.

384) In 2005, what did French pilot Didier Delsalle land on Everest?

385) On what continent are the Andes?

386) On what continent is the Hamersley Range?

387) On what continent are the Jura Mountains?

388) On what continent are the San Bernardino Mountains?

389) ON WHAT CONTINENT ARE THE KUNLUN MOUNTAINS?

390) Which is higher: Dome Fuji Peak in Antarctica or K2 in Pakistan?

391) Which is higher: Kilimanjaro in Tanzania or Mt. McKinley in the U.S.

392) True or false: The Sassafras Mountains are in South Dakota.

393) TRUE OR FALSE: MT. SHASTA IN CALIFORNIA IS AN EXTINCT VOLCANO.

TOUGH TRIVIA CHALLENGE

394) Which is higher: Adam's Peak in Sri Lanka or Boundary Peak in the U.S.?

377. the southeast, 378. false—he was 76 years old, 379. d, 380. true, 381. false—it's Mt. Marcy, 382. oxygen, 383. true, 384. a helicopter, 385. South America, 386. Australia, 387. Europe, 388. North America, 389. Asia, 390. K2, 391. Mt. McKinley—but only by about 1,000 ft., 392. false—they are in South Carolina, 393. true, 394. Boundary Peak—it's the highest point in Nevada

METEOROLOGY

395) Which weather pattern features warmer water, El Nino or La Nina?

396) According to the Beaufort Wind Scale, how fast does the wind have to be blowing for it to be considered a violent storm?

a) 10-20 mph
b) 30-48 mph
c) 50-60 mph
d) 64-72 mph

397) According to the Beaufort Wind Scale, how fast does the wind have to be blowing for it to be considered a light breeze?

1-2 mph
4-7 mph
9-11 mph
12-16 mph

398) **True or false:** George Washington used a thermometer and a weather vane to gauge the weather and made note of the measurements in his diary.

399) **True or false:** Hailstones have been reported heading to Earth at over 150 mph.

400) ACCORDING TO THE SAFFIR-SIMPSON HURRICANE SCALE, WHAT CATEGORY IS A HURRICANE WITH WINDS 131-155 MPH?

A) CATEGORY 2

B) CATEGORY 3

C) CATEGORY 4

D) CATEGORY 12

401) Which high cloud type indicates that it's raining?

a) Cirrus

b) Cirrocumulus

c) Cirrostratus

d) None of the above

402) True or false: George Washington's original Inauguration Day was postponed because of bad weather conditions.

403) Which gets more hail, Nebraska or Maine?

404) Which gets more hail, Colorado or Oregon?

405) True or false: In 2003, a hailstone was found that had a circumference over 18 inches.

395. El Nino, 396. d, 397. b, 398. true, 399. false—but they have reached 90 mph, 400. c, 401. c, 402. true, 403. Nebraska, 404. Colorado, 405. true

406) TRUE OR FALSE: IN 1947, THE TEMPERATURE IN THE YUKON TERRITORY REACHED −81°F?

407) True or false: Temperature in Libya once reached 136°F.

408) True or false: No one has ever been stuck by lightning more than five times.

409) Which is higher, the stratosphere or the mesosphere?

410) Which is higher, the troposphere or the ionosphere?

411) TRUE OR FALSE: THE OZONE LAYER IS BETWEEN THE STRATOSPHERE AND THE MESOSPHERE.

412) How high above the Earth does the ionosphere begin?

a) 10 miles

b) 30 miles

c) 50 miles

d) 75 miles

413) Is the area between a cold air mass and a warm air mass called a cold front or a warm front?

414) What is the calm area at the center of a hurricane called?

415) True or false: **The Earth's atmosphere is over 50 miles thick.**

416) Is the troposphere higher at the poles or at the equator?

417) True or false: **Vilhelm Bjerknes developed the theory of cold and warm fronts.**

418) TRUE OR FALSE: WE CAN LEARN ABOUT CLIMATE CONDITIONS IN THE PAST FROM LOOKING AT THE RINGS OF TREES.

419) True or false: **Temperatures drop about 8°F for every 328 ft one goes up a mountain.**

420) True or false: There was once a 160-day heat wave in Australia.

TOUGH TRIVIA CHALLENGE

421) Are you more likely to get struck by lightning in Central Africa or the Australian outback?

406. true, 407. true, 408. false—Roy C. Sullivan got hit seven times, 409. mesosphere, 410. ionosphere, 411. true, 412. c, 413. A cold front, 414. the eye, 415. true, 416. equator, 417. true, 418. true, 419. false—the drop is much greater, 420. true, 421. Central Africa

• • NATURAL DISASTERS • •

422) True or false: **Small earthquakes happen every day on Earth.**

423) Has there ever been an earthquake on Earth that measured 9.7 on the Richter scale?

424) WHAT IS THE TERM FOR THE LINE WHERE AN EARTHQUAKE IS MORE LIKELY TO HIT?

425) Where was the strongest earthquake ever recorded?

a) France
b) Chile
c) United States
d) China

426) The earthquake location where the earth first moved is called what?

427) Which did more damage, the San Francisco earthquake of 1906 or the aftermath—which included looting and an ill-fated plan to dynamite buildings to create firebreaks.

428) True or false: Of the top-10 earthquakes ever recorded, none took place in Europe or Africa.

429 The color-coded map that is used to determine how far-reaching an earthquake impacts is called what?

a) ShakeMap

b) QuakeMap

c) RichterMap

d) VibraMap

430) In what state did the strongest U.S. earthquake occur?

a) California

b) New Mexico

c) Hawaii

d) Alaska

TOUGH TRIVIA CHALLENGE

431) How strong on the Richter scale was the earthquake that hit Haiti in 2010?

a) 5.5

b) 6.2

c) 7.0

d) 7.4

432) WHAT SHAPE IS THE PACIFIC RING OF FIRE, WHICH INCLUDES ABOUT THREE-QUARTERS OF ALL THE EARTH'S DORMANT VOLCANOES?

A) TRIANGLE

B) CIRCLE

C) OVAL

D) HORSESHOE

433) How hot can volcanic lava get?

a) Up to 2,300°F

b) Up to 1,800°F

c) Up to 1,200°F

d) Up to 900°F

434) Are there more volcanoes on the Earth's surface or beneath the ocean?

435) Hurricanes form in the Atlantic. What name is given to a similar storm in the Pacific?

422. true, 423. no, 424. fault line, 425. b, 426. the epicenter, 427. the aftermath, 428. true, 429. a, 430. d, 431. c, 432. d, 433. a, 434. beneath the ocean, 435. typhoon

436) What American city was burned to the ground in 1871 in a fire allegedly started by a cow?

a) Atlanta
b) Chicago
c) Cincinnati
d) San Francisco

437) WHAT HURRICANE DEVASTATED NEW ORLEANS IN 2005?

A) HUGO
B) KATRINA
C) RITA
D) WILMA

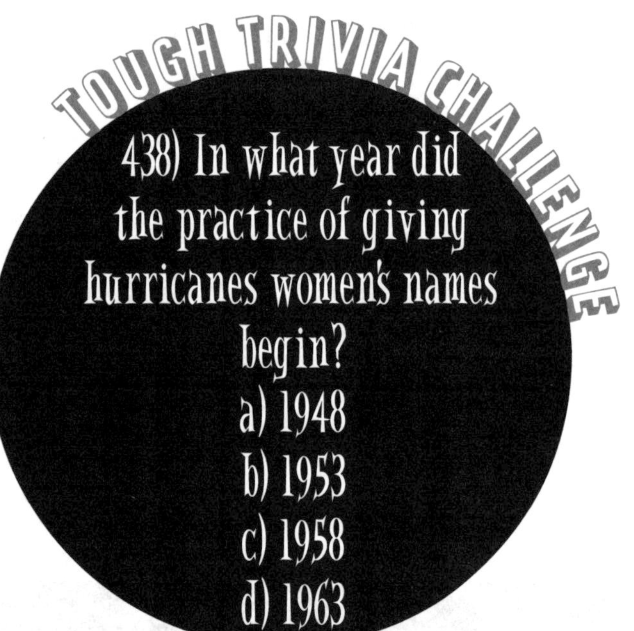

TOUGH TRIVIA CHALLENGE

438) In what year did the practice of giving hurricanes women's names begin?

a) 1948
b) 1953
c) 1958
d) 1963

439) What hurricane struck New Jersey in 2011, the first to hit that state in more than a century?

a) Andrew
b) Ike
c) Irene
d) Wilma

440) What is the largest number of hurricanes to form in a single year?

a) 12
b) 23
c) 26
d) 28

441) WHAT WAS THE FIRST HURRICANE TO BE GIVEN A MALE NAME?

A) ALLAN
B) ARNOLD
C) BILL
D) BOB

442) What Japanese word translates as "harbor wave"?

WHY WE DON'T NAME HURRICANES AFTER VERBS...

443) If there are so many hurricanes in one year that all the names are used up, what is used instead?

a) Letters
b) Numbers
c) Greek letters
d) Nothing

436. b, 437. b, 438. b, 439. c, 440. d, 441. d, 442. tsunami, 443. c

FIRE

444) True or false: Earth is the only planet we know of where fire can burn.

445) Which will be bluer, a fire with low oxygen or one with high oxygen?

446) WHICH CAUSED MORE DEATHS, THE GREAT CHICAGO FIRE OR WISCONSIN'S PESHTIGO FIRE (WHICH HAPPENED ON THE SAME DAY)?

447) True or false: The deadliest fire in the U.S. was on a steamship.

TOUGH TRIVIA CHALLENGE

448) When was the first fire engine company founded?

a) 1678
b) 1772
c) 1798
d) 1801

449) Which has more people killed by fires each year, Russia or the United States?

450) Which has more people killed by fires each year, Finland or the United States?

451) What was the first volunteer fire company, founded by Ben Franklin, called?

a) Union Fire Company
b) First Union Company
c) First Anti-Fire Brigade of the United States
d) The U.S. Fire and Emergency Company

452) TRUE OR FALSE: A BOEING 747 WAS USED TO DROP 20.000 GALLONS OF FIRE RETARDANT ON A LOS ANGELES WILDFIRE.

453) True or false: City blocks were dynamited to block the spread of fires caused by the San Francisco earthquake in 1906.

454) Who burned the Temple in Jerusalem in the year 70 CE?

a) The Greeks
b) The Romans
c) The Chinese
d) The Dutch

TOUGH TRIVIA CHALLENGE

455) In what year did Shakespeare's Globe Theatre burn?

a) 1590
b) 1613
c) 1692
d) 1714

444. true, 445. high, 446. the Wisconsin fire, 447. true, 448. a, 449. United States, 450. Finland, 451. a, 452. true, 453. true, 454. b, 455. b

456) True or false: In 1972 there was a fire in the Empire State Building caused by a plane that crashed into it.

TOUGH TRIVIA CHALLENGE

457) In 1941, the Terminal Hotel burned in what city?
a) Charlotte
b) Cleveland
c) Atlanta
d) Baltimore

458) TRUE OR FALSE: A NINETEENTH-CENTURY SHIP, THE CUTTY SARK, CAUGHT FIRE WHILE BEING RESTORED BY A LONDON MUSEUM.

459) Who has a higher risk of death by fire, teenagers or people over 65?

460) London experienced major fires in 982, 989, 1212, and 1666. Which is considered the Great Fire of London?

461) What Las Vegas hotel caught fire in 1980, killing 87?
a) The Sands
b) The Flamingo
c) The Horseshoe
d) The MGM Grand

462) True or false: The inventor of the fire hose was Dutch.

463) What city had the first full-time paid fire department in the U.S.?

a) Philadelphia
b) Boston
c) Washington, D.C.
d) Cincinnati

464) True or false: George Washington was a volunteer firefighter.

465) WHICH IS A MORE COMMON CAUSE OF DEATH IN A FIRE, BURNING OR SMOKE INHALATION?

466) True or false: **"Two-alarm fire" is a universal term meaning the same for every fire company in America.**

467) Is an accelerant more likely to be used by a firefighter or an arsonist?

456. false—that happened, but it was in 1945, 457. c, 458. true, 459. people over 65, 460. the fire in 1666, 461. d, 462. true, 463. d, 464. true, 465. smoke inhalation, 466. false, 467. arsonist

TOUGH TRIVIA CHALLENGE

468) About how much air is usually in a firefighter's SCBA?
a) About 5-8 minutes worth
b) About 10-12 minutes worth
c) About 15-20 minutes worth
d) About 30-45 minutes worth

469) True or false: A Class C fire is an electrical fire.

470) TRUE OR FALSE: A CLASS D FIRE ALWAYS INVOLVES BODILY INJURY.

471) What does GPM stand for in firefighting?

472) In firefighter terminology, is Side B to the left or right of Side A?

473) TRUE OR FALSE: A CLASS K FIRE INVOLVES COOKING OIL.

TREES

474) True or false: More than half of Idaho is covered in trees.

475) TRUE OR FALSE: THE OLDEST LIVING TREE, A BRISTLECONE PINE, IS OVER 4,600 YEARS OLD.

476) *In what month is Arbor Day?*

TOUGH TRIVIA CHALLENGE

477) The first Arbor Day was celebrated in what year?

a) 1444
b) 1792
c) 1872
d) 1914

478) A deciduous tree...

a) Produces cones
b) Loses all leaves and needles in a year
c) Lives for ten years
d) Produces single-colored leaves

479) Fill in the blank in Joyce Kilmer's famous poem: "I think that I shall never see/a ______________ as lovely as a tree."

468. d, 469. true, 470. false, 471. gallons per minute, 472. left, 473. true, 474. false, 475. true, 476. April, 477. c, 478. b, 479. poem

480) True or false: A wild fig tree in South Africa has roots going down 400 feet.

481) The state tree of New York, Wisconsin, Vermont, and West Virginia has the Latin name *Acer saccharin*. What is it better known as?

a) Sugar Maple
b) Elm
c) Douglas Fir
d) Tulip Poplar

482) IS A TULIP POPLAR A TULIP, A POPLAR, BOTH, OR NEITHER?

TOUGH TRIVIA CHALLENGE

483) Texas Governor James Hogg requested that a certain tree be planted by his grave instead of a headstone. It became his state tree 13 years later. What is this "nutty" tree?

484) This kind of pine tree, the state tree of Montana, is also the name of a chain of steak houses.

TOUGH TRIVIA CHALLENGE

485) About how much CO2 does a large tree clean from the atmosphere each year?

a) 10 lbs.
b) 140 lbs.
c) 220 lbs.
d) 330 lbs.

486) True or false: The Wollemi pine can only be found in Wollemi National Park in Australia.

487) True or false: There are more than 300 varieties of trees growing on the Purdue University campus.

488) What do coniferous trees produce instead of flowers?

489) True or false: The coco-de-mer nut can weigh up to 45 lbs.

490) WHEN DOES MOST ROOT GROWTH OCCUR IN NORTH AMERICAN NATIVE TREES?

A) EARLY SPRING
B) LATE SPRING
C) LATE SUMMER
D) WINTER

491) In Norse mythology, animals and giants live in Yggdrasil, a giant ______________ tree.

a) Ash
b) Fir
c) Pine
d) None of the above

492) In Greek legend, who was Daphne trying to get away from when she turned into a laurel tree?

a) Zeus
b) Apollo
c) Poseidon
d) Athena

TOUGH TRIVIA CHALLENGE

493) An oak tree can produce about how many acorns in a single year?

a) 1,000
b) 5,000
c) 10,000
d) 50,000

494) Do all oaks produce acorns?

495) True or false: There are more than 100 species of pine tree?

496) Do roots tend to group deeper or wider?

497) True or false: Ferns sometimes grow on other trees.

498) Is the bark cambium the inner or outer layer of a tree's bark?

480. true, 481. a, 482. neither, 483. pecan, 484. ponderosa pine, 485. d, 486. true, 487. true, 488. cones, 489. true, 490. b, 491. a, 492. b, 493. d, 494. yes, 495. true, 496. wider, 497. true, 498. inner

499) Does cinnamon come from the tree bark of young saplings or mature trees?

500) DOES THE THICK AND FIBROUS BARK OF THE SEQUOIA MAKE IT MORE OR LESS LIKELY TO CATCH FIRE?

501) True or false: If a tree is dioecious, like the yew, that means its male and female flowers grow on different trees.

502) True or false: Bats pollinate some trees.

503) How many seed compartments are there in an apple?

TOUGH TRIVIA CHALLENGE

504) True or false: The Chile pine is also known as the monkey puzzle.

506) What do carotenoids do?
a) Give berries their color
b) Help trees grow
c) Strengthen roots
d) None of the above

507) The nutmeg tree produces two spices. One, obviously, is nutmeg. What is the other?
a) Marjoram
b) Anise
c) Mace
d) Sage

508) Mango trees originally only grew in...
a) Southern Africa
b) Australia
c) Hawaii
d) Southeast Asia

• • PLANTS • • •

509) WHICH OF THE FOLLOWING IS NOT A KIND OF DAFFODIL:

A) FLEINDRE
B) MERRYWEATHER
C) CHEERFULNESS
D) MARIEKE

510) True or false: No wild plant produces a black flower.

511) True or false: **Daffodils grow to face the sun.**

512) True or false: Daffodils grow from bulbs.

513) True or false: Sometimes tulip bulbs are substituted for onions in recipes.

514) True or false: Dandelion greens are a source of vitamin A.

515) True or false: Flowering plants are as old as the Earth.

TOUGH TRIVIA CHALLENGE

516) True or false: The *titan arum* can produce flowers over 9 feet high.

499. young saplings, 500. less likely, 501. true, 502. true, 503. Five, 504. true, 505. a, 506. a, 507. c, 508. d, 509. b, 510. true, 511. true, 512. true, 513. true, 514. true, 515. false, 516. true

517) Are there more species of flowering plants or ferns?

518) WHICH CAME FIRST: FLOWERING PLANTS OR FERNS?

519) Which came first: Flowering plants or dinosaurs?

520) True or false: Amber is tree resin that has been fossilized.

521) Some types of bamboo can grow more than three feet a day.

522) True or false: Only about 100 plants are used by humans for food.

523) Which state is the largest producer of Christmas trees in the U.S.?

524) Which state is the second largest producer of Christmas trees in the U.S.?

TOUGH TRIVIA CHALLENGE

525) Poison ivy irritates the skin because it produces...
a) Urushiol
b) Uniroyal
c) Univerlol
d) Uriac oil

526) True or false: Bamboo can grow more than 100 feet high.

TOUGH TRIVIA CHALLENGE

527) What tree does the drug quinine come from?

a) Elm

b) Oak

c) Weeping willow

d) Cinchona

528) TRUE OR FALSE: MOST TEA COMES FROM THE SAME KIND OF PLANT.

529) TRUE OR FALSE: ORCHIDS ARE A MEMBER OF THE ASPARAGUS FAMILY.

530) True or false: A double coconut palm once had a seed weighing 60 lbs.

531) True or false: The spice saffron comes from the root of the saffron flower.

532) True or false: It takes about 75,000 saffron plants to produce a pound of saffron.

533) True or false:

Bamboo is a tree.

517. flowering plants, 518. ferns, 519. dinosaurs, 520. true, 521. true, 522. false, 523. Oregon, 524. North Carolina, 525. a, 526. true, 527. d, 528. true, 529. true, 530. true, 531. false—from the stigma, 532. true, 533. false—it's a grass

534) True or False:
Apple seeds contain cyanide.

535) True or false: Kudzu vines can grow a foot a day.

536) How many seeds in a nut?

537) True or false: Cinnamon comes from tree bark.

538) TRUE OR FALSE: EACH KIWI CONTAINS EXACTLY 124 SEEDS.

539) A lotus is a single if it has fewer than 25 petals. How many petals does it need to be considered a double?

540) True or false:
The lotus is a waterlily.

541) Are lotus seeds edible?

542) True or false: Vanilla is a member of the asparagus family.

543) True or false: **A pineapple is a berry.**

544) True or false:
The peanut is actually a legume.

TOUGH TRIVIA CHALLENGE

545) True or false: An adult *grammatophyllum speciosum* orchid can produce as many as 10,000 blooms.

546) Are shrubs perennials?

547) TRUE OR FALSE: MOSSES DON'T HAVE A VASCULAR STRUCTURE TO TRANSPORT FLUIDS AND NUTRIENTS.

548) How many years does a plant have to live for it to be called a perennial?

549) Does a succulent plant retain water?

550) Is horticulture the study of garden plants or forest plants?

551) Is pomology the study of ferns or fruits?

552) True or false: **Orchids can be found growing naturally on every continent.**

534. true, 535. true, 536. one, 537. true, 538. false—usually between 600-1000, 539. more than 50—in between, it's a semi-double, 540. false, 541. yes, 542. true, 543. true, 544. true, 545. true, 546. yes, 547. true, 548. two, 549. yes, 550. garden plants, 551. fruits, 552. false—not Antarctica

CHAPTER 2

Sports

..BASEBALL..

553) Five men have hit 60 or more homers in a season: Babe Ruth, Roger Maris, Mark McGwire, Sammy Sosa, and Barry Bonds. Place them in order of how many career homers they hit.

554) In 2010, what Phillies ace became the second pitcher to throw a postseason no-hitter?

a) Joe Blanton
b) Roy Halladay
c) Cole Hamels
d) Cliff Lee

555) Who threw the only no-hitter in a World Series?

a) Sandy Koufax
b) Don Larsen
c) Allie Reynolds
d) Cy Young

556) Who dismissed Giants manager Mel Ott with the phrase, "Nice guys finish last," before replacing him as manager?

557) IN WHAT CITY DID THE TEXAS RANGERS PLAY BEFORE MOVING TO TEXAS?

553. Bonds, Ruth, Sosa, McGwire, Maris, 554. b, 555. b, 556. Leo Durocher, 557. Washington

558) Where did the Baltimore Orioles play before moving to Baltimore?

559) Where did the Oakland A's play immediately before moving to Oakland?

560) Where did the Atlanta Braves play immediately before moving to Atlanta?

561) Where did the Minnesota Twins play before moving to Minnesota?

562) Where did the Los Angeles Dodgers play before moving to Los Angeles?

563) Where did the Washington Nationals play before moving to Washington?

564) True or false: The Atlanta Braves were once known as the Eagles.

565) TRUE OR FALSE: THE LOS ANGELES DODGERS WERE ONCE KNOWN AS THE ROBINS.

566) True or false: The Philadelphia Phillies were once known as the Blue Jays.

TOUGH TRIVIA CHALLENGE

567) What Cleveland Indians star holds the career record for doubles?

a) Albert Belle
b) Lou Boudreau
c) Kenny Lofton
d) Tris Speaker

568) What team was once known as the Colts?

a) Baltimore Orioles
b) Boston Red Sox
c) Chicago Cubs
d) New York Yankees

569) What team was once known as the Colt .45s?

a) Arizona Diamondbacks
b) Houston Astros
c) Kansas City Royals
d) Texas Rangers

570) EFFA MANLEY IS THE ONLY WOMAN IN THE HALL OF FAME. WHAT ROLE DID SHE PLAY IN THE GAME?

A) OWNER

B) UMPIRE

C) INVENTOR OF THE BOX SCORE AND SEVERAL STATISTICS, INCLUDING RBI

D) COMPOSER OF "TAKE ME OUT TO THE BALL GAME"

573) Each of these men hit a famous home run to clinch the pennant or World Championship. Which one was not a walk-off homer?

a) Bobby Thomson

b) Bill Mazeroski

c) Bucky Dent

d) Joe Carter

571) True or false: Connie Mack managed the A's for 50 years.

574) What pitching feat has been achieved by, among others, Charlie Robertson, Len Barker, Dallas Braden, and David Wells?

572) What three brothers played the outeld together for two innings in 1963?

a) Felipe, Matty, and Jesus Alou

b) Ken, Clete, and Cloyd Boyer

c) Joe, Dom, and Vince DiMaggio

d) Ed, Jim, and Tom Delahanty

558. St. Louis, 559. Kansas City, 560. Milwaukee, 561. Washington, 562. Brooklyn, 563. Montreal, 564. false, 565. true, 566. true, 567. d, 568. c, 569. b, 570. a, 571. true, 572. a, 573. c, 574. a perfect game

575) What happens if a base runner is hit by a batted ball?

a) Batter is awarded first base
b) Batter is called out
c) Runner is called out
d) Do-over

576) What team was the first—and so far, only—team to lose the first three games of a postseason series, yet come back to win?

a) Boston Red Sox
b) Chicago Cubs
c) New York Mets
d) New York Yankees

TOUGH TRIVIA CHALLENGE

577) What pitcher won 31 games in 1968, the most in 37 years, but only 41 more in the rest of his career?

a) Ron Bryant
b) Don Drysdale
c) Bob Gibson
d) Denny McLain

578) WHAT HALL OF FAMER WAS NICKNAMED "THE SPLENDID SPLINTER"?

A) JOE DIMAGGIO
B) SANDY KOUFAX
C) MICKEY MANTLE
D) TED WILLIAMS

579) True or false: If the catcher drops strike three, the batter can run to first unless there are less than two outs and a runner on first.

580) In standard scorer's notation, what number represents the shortstop?

581) What team was the first to win the World Series after finishing last the previous season?

a) 1914 Braves
b) 1969 Mets
c) 1991 Twins
d) 1997 Marlins

582) Donora, Pennsylvania, with a population of less than 5,000, is nonetheless the hometown of Ken Griffey Sr. and Jr., and what Hall of Famer?

a) Harry Heilmann
b) Stan Musial
c) Al Simmons
d) Willie Stargell

583) Since 1928, the record for striking out the most times in a career has been held in succession by four Hall of Fame outfielders. Can you name all four?

TOUGH TRIVIA CHALLENGE

584) What player, the career leader in triples, was nicknamed for his hometown?

a) Cap Anson
b) Wahoo Sam Crawford
c) Pea Ridge Day
d) Vinegar Bend Mizell

585) Which of these cities has never been home to a Major League baseball team?

a) Altoona, PA
b) Norfolk, VA
c) Providence, RI
d) Toledo, OH

586) The New York Yankees have won more World Championships than any other team. What team ranks second?

a) Cardinals
b) Dodgers
c) Giants
d) Red Sox

575. c, 576. a, 577. d, 578. d, 579. true, 580. 6, 581. c, 582. b, 583. Babe Ruth, Mickey Mantle, Willie Stargell, Reggie Jackson, 584. b, 585. b, 586. a

TOUGH TRIVIA CHALLENGE

587) What outfielder twice finished third in the National League in stolen bases before retiring to become a prominent evangelist?

a) Billy Graham
b) Billy North
c) Billy Sunday
d) Billy Williams

588) Match the team to its current home.

1) Citi Field
2) Minute Maid Park
3) PNC Park
4) U.S. Cellular Field

a) Chicago White Sox
b) Houston Astros
c) New York Mets
d) Pittsburgh Pirates

589) Match the team to its former stadium.

1) Briggs Stadium
2) Candlestick Park
3) Hubert H. Humphrey Metrodome
4) Shea Stadium

a) Detroit Tigers
b) Minnesota Twins
c) New York Mets
d) San Francisco Giants

590) Who was the first National Leaguer to hit 40 homers in a season?

a) Rogers Hornsby
b) Stan Musial
c) Mel Ott
d) Bill Terry

591) Each of these men holds both the single-season and career record in the category given, with one exception. Which one?

a) Barry Bonds, home runs
b) Rickey Henderson, stolen bases
c) Pete Rose, hits
d) Nolan Ryan, strikeouts

592) WHO WON A BATTING CHAMPIONSHIP IN 1968 WITH A .301 AVERAGE, THE LOWEST AVERAGE EVER TO WIN THE TITLE?

A) CURT FLOOD
B) BROOKS ROBINSON
C) FRANK ROBINSON
D) CARL YASTRZEMSKI

593) Who coined the phrase, "It ain't over till it's over"?

a) Yogi Berra
b) Dizzy Dean
c) Satchel Paige
d) Casey Stengel

594) The leftfield wall in what ballpark is known as "The Green Monster"?

a) Coors Field
b) Dodger Stadium
c) Fenway Park
d) Yankee Stadium

595) True or false: Babe Ruth's real first name was George.

596) TRUE OR FALSE: SPARKY ANDERSON'S REAL FIRST NAME WAS GEORGE.

587. c, 588. 1c, 2b, 3d, 4a; 589. 1a, 2d, 3b, 4c; 590. a, 591. c, 592. d, 593. a, 594. c, 595. true, 596. true

597) True or false: Tom Seaver's real first name was George.

598) True or false: Casey Stengel's real first name was George.

599) Which pitcher never struck out 20 men in a single game?

a) Roger Clemens
b) Randy Johnson
c) Nolan Ryan
d) Kerry Wood

600) Who is the only player to win the batting championship in three different decades?

a) George Brett
b) Ty Cobb
c) Tony Gwynn
d) Ted Williams

601) How many no-hitters did Nolan Ryan pitch?

a) 4
b) 5
c) 6
d) 7

602) How many no-hitters did Roger Clemens pitch?

a) 0
b) 1
c) 2
d) 3

603) Who was the first National Leaguer to hit 50 homers in a season?

a) George Foster
b) Ralph Kiner
c) Willie Mays
d) Hack Wilson

604) Who drew the most walks in a season?

a) Willie McCovey
b) Babe Ruth
c) Barry Bonds
d) Ted Williams

605) TRUE OR FALSE:

IN 1921, BABE RUTH HIT 59 HOME RUNS BY HIMSELF, MORE THAN ANY AMERICAN LEAGUE TEAM OTHER THAN HIS OWN.

606) WHAT DISABILITY WAS SHARED BY BROWNS OUTFIELDER PETE GRAY AND ANGELS PITCHER JIM ABBOTT?

A) BLINDNESS
B) DEAFNESS
C) MUTENESS
D) ONE ARM

607) A farming accident as a youth gave Hall of Fame pitcher Mordecai Brown what nickname?

a) Gimpy
b) Lefty
c) Stumpy
d) Three Finger

608) What is Prince Fielder's real first name?

a) Cecil
b) Henry
c) Jaden
d) Prince

TOUGH TRIVIA CHALLENGE

609) True or false: Hank Aaron and Lou Gehrig have the same first and middle names.

597. true, 598. false—it was Charles, 599. c, 600. a, 601. d, 602. a, 603. d, 604. c, 605. false—but was true in 1920, when he hit 54, 606. d, 607. d, 608. d, 609. true—Henry Louis

Match the nickname to the player:

610) The Count
611) The Duke of Flatbush
612) The Duke of Tralee
613) The Red Baron
614) The Sultan of Swat

a) Roger Bresnahan
b) John Montefusco
c) Babe Ruth
d) Duke Snider
e) Rick Sutcliffe

TOUGH TRIVIA CHALLENGE

615) True or false: Hall of Fame second baseman Ryne Sandberg was named after Yankees relief pitcher Ryne Duren.

616) Who was the first Rookie of the Year?

617) In 1997, Jackie Robinson's #42 was retired by every MLB team except the Yankees, who were allowed to let what player to continue wearing it?

a) Derek Jeter
b) Mariano Rivera
c) Alex Rodriguez
d) Bernie Williams

618) What did Ted Williams do in his final at-bat?

a) Single
b) Double
c) Triple
d) Homer

TOUGH TRIVIA CHALLENGE

619) Who won the first Cy Young Award?

620) True or false: Joe DiMaggio once collected eight hits in a single game.

MATCH THE PLAYER TO HIS UNIFORM NUMBER.

621) Mickey Mantle

622) Willie Mays

623) Pete Rose

624) Babe Ruth

a) 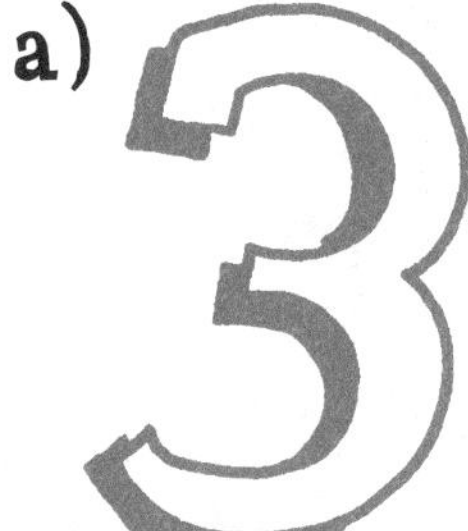

b) 7

c) 14

d) 24

625) What Hall of Famer homered in his first career at-bat, and never hit another?

a) Luis Aparicio
b) Rabbit Maranville
c) Hoyt Wilhelm
d) Cy Young

626) True or false: Since 1900, no team has scored 30 runs in a single game.

610. b, 611. d, 612. a, 613. e, 614. c, 615. true, 616. Jackie Robinson, 617. b, 618. d, 619. Don Newcombe, 620. false, 621. b, 622. d, 623. c, 624. a, 625. c, 626. false

627) WHAT IS THE RECORD FOR RUNS SCORED IN ONE INNING?

A) 5
B) 17
C) 25
D) 35

628) Who won the longest MLB game ever played, 26 innings?

a) Braves
b) Cubs
c) Dodgers
d) No one—it was a tie

629) True or false: Statistics from a forfeited game do not count.

TOUGH TRIVIA CHALLENGE

630) After his retirement, Jackie Robinson became an executive for what coffee company?

a) Chock Full o' Nuts
b) Folger's
c) Maxwell House
d) Starbucks

631) What is the official score of a forfeited game?

a) 1-0
b) 2-0
c) 9-0
d) 0-0

632) True or false: No one is credited as the winning or losing pitcher in a forfeited game.

633) True or false: a pitcher once retired the side in order for 12 straight innings, and still lost the game.

634) True or false: Babe Ruth once pitched a no-hitter.

635) What nickname was shared by Jim Hunter, Bill Klem, and George Metkovich?

a) Catfish
b) Piano Legs
c) Rabbit
d) Thumper

TOUGH TRIVIA CHALLENGE

MATCH THE NICKNAME TO THE PLAYER.

636) The Bird — a) Harry Brecheen
637) The Cat — b) Mark Fidrych
638) The Hat — c) Bill Skowron
639) Moose — d) Harry Walker

Match the nickname to the player.

640) The Big Cat — a) Randy Johnson
641) The Big Hurt — b) Walter Johnson
642) Big Mac — c) Christy Mathewson
643) Big Papi — d) Mark McGwire
644) Big Poison — e) Johnny Mize
645) Big Six — f) David Ortiz
646) The Big Train — g) Frank Thomas
647) Big Unit — h) Paul Waner

Match the nickname to the player.

648) Little Napoleon — a) Dom DiMaggio
649) Little Poison — b) Gary Matthews Jr.
650) The Little Professor — c) John McGraw
651) Little Sarge — d) Lloyd Waner

627. b, 628. d, 629. false, 630. a, 631. c, 632. true, 633. true, 634. false, 635. a, 636. b, 637. a, 638. d, 639. c, 640. e, 641. g, 642. d, 643. f, 644. h, 645. c, 646. b, 647. a, 648. c, 649. d, 650. a, 651. b

TOUGH TRIVIA CHALLENGE

Match the middle name to the player.

652) Centennial
653) Glee
654) Julius Caesar
655) True

a) Mordecai Brown
b) Cal McLish
c) Paul Waner
d) Cy Young

656) How many Hall of Fame pitchers have losing records?

a) 0
b) 1
c) 2
d) 3

657) Which of these men did not manage both the Yankees and Mets?

a) Yogi Berra
b) Joe Girardi
c) Dallas Green
d) Joe Torre

658) True or false: Joe Torre, who reached 14 straight postseasons as a manager, never played a postseason game as a player.

659) WHO IS THE ONLY MAN TO PLAY OR MANAGE THE BROOKLYN DODGERS, NEW YORK GIANTS, NEW YORK METS AND NEW YORK YANKEES?

MATCH THE OWNER TO HIS TEAM.

660) Gene Autry	a) Angels
661) George W. Bush	b) A's
662) Charles Comiskey	c) Braves
663) Charlie Finley	d) Cubs
664) George Steinbrenner	e) Rangers
665) Ted Turner	f) Red Sox
666) Phil Wrigley	g) White Sox
667) Tom Yawkey	h) Yankees

668) Place these managers in order of their career wins: Sparky Anderson, Bobby Cox, Leo Durocher, Tony LaRussa, Joe Torre.

669) True or false: **The 2011 Texas Rangers are the first team to come within one strike of winning the World Series and not win it.**

670) **True or false:** There was no World Series in 1994 because of a players' strike.

TOUGH TRIVIA CHALLENGE

671) What unusual feat has been achieved by Bill Wambsganss, Johnny Neun, and Mickey Morandini, among others?

652. a, 653. c, 654. b, 655. d, 656. c, 657. b, 658. true, 659. Casey Stengel, 660. a, 661. e, 662. g, 663. b, 664. h, 665. c, 666. d, 667. f, 668. LaRussa, Cox, Torre, Anderson, Durocher, 669. false—1986 Boston Red Sox also did this, 670. true, 671. unassisted triple play

TOUGH TRIVIA CHALLENGE

672) Who was the only non-Yankee manager to win the American League pennant between 1949 and 1964?

a) Lou Boudreau
b) Leo Durocher
c) Eddie Dyer
d) Al Lopez

673) Who was the first manager to win the World Series with teams from both leagues?

674) Who was the first African-American manager to win the World Series?

675) TRUE OR FALSE: THE 1972 WORLD SERIES BETWEEN THE A'S AND REDS AND THE 1984 WORLD SERIES BETWEEN THE TIGERS AND PADRES FEATURED THE SAME TWO MANAGERS.

676) What comedy team immortalized the routine "Who's on First?"

a) Abbott and Costello
b) Laurel and Hardy
c) The Marx Brothers
d) The Three Stooges

677) True or false:
There was no World Series from 1942–45 because of World War II.

MATCH THE WORLD SERIES-WINNING MANAGER TO THE TEAM.

678) Anaheim Angels
679) Arizona Diamondbacks
680) Atlanta Braves
681) Baltimore Orioles
682) Boston Braves
683) Boston Red Sox
684) Chicago Cubs
685) Chicago White Sox
686) Cincinnati Reds
687) Cleveland Indians
688) Detroit Tigers
689) Florida Marlins
690) Kansas City Royals
691) Los Angeles Dodgers
692) Milwaukee Braves
693) Minnesota Twins
694) New York Giants
695) New York Mets
696) New York Yankees
697) Oakland A's
698) Philadelphia A's
699) Philadelphia Phillies
700) Pittsburgh Pirates
701) St. Louis Cardinals
702) San Francisco Giants
703) Toronto Blue Jays

a) Joe Altobelli
b) Bruce Bochy
c) Lou Boudreau
d) Bob Brenly
e) Frank Chance
f) Bobby Cox
g) Alvin Dark
h) Leo Durocher
i) Terry Francona
j) Cito Gaston
k) Joe Girardi
l) Ozzie Guillen
m) Fred Haney
n) Whitey Herzog
o) Dick Howser
p) Davey Johnson
q) Tom Kelly
r) Tommy Lasorda
s) Connie Mack
t) Charlie Manuel
u) Jack McKeon
v) Lou Piniella
w) Mike Scioscia
x) Mayo Smith
y) George Stallings
z) Chuck Tanner

672. d, 673. Sparky Anderson, 674. Cito Gaston, 675. true, 676. a, 677. false, 678. w, 679. d, 680. f, 681. a, 682. y, 683. i, 684. e, 685. l, 686. v, 687. c, 688. x, 689. u, 690. o, 691. r, 692. m, 693. q, 694. h, 695. p, 696. k, 697. g, 698. s, 699. t, 700. z, 701. n, 702. b, 703. j

704) What double-play combination was immortalized in a poem as "the saddest of possible words"?

TOUGH TRIVIA CHALLENGE

706) WHO HAS THE MOST CAREER VICTORIES AS A MANAGER WITHOUT EVER PLAYING IN THE MAJORS?

A) WALTER ALSTON
B) JIM LEYLAND
C) JOE MCCARTHY
D) EARL WEAVER

705) What team did that double-play combination play for?

Match the positions to the players' names in the comedy routine "Who's on First?"

707) Because	a) Pitcher
708) I Don't Care	b) Catcher
709) I Don't Know	c) First base
710) Today	d) Second base
711) Tomorrow	e) Third base
712) What	f) Shortstop
713) Who	g) Left field
714) Why	h) Center field
715) Never specified	i) Right field

HALL OF FAMER, YES OR NO?

716) Elmer Flick?

717) Bill Klem?

718) Dave Parker?

719) Tommy Henrich?

720) Gene Mauch?

721) Eppa Rixey?

722) Bruce Sutter?

723) Ron Santo?

724) Ken Holtzman?

725) Don Drysdale?

726) Maury Wills?

727) Roger Maris?

728) Hack Wilson?

729) Chuck Klein?

730) Mule Haas?

731) Moose Haas?

732) Moose Skowron?

733) Bob Moose?

734) Old Hoss Radbourne?

735) Tim Keefe?

736) Kid Nichols?

737) Catfish Hunter?

704. Tinker to Evers to Chance, 705. Chicago Cubs, 706. c, 707. h, 708. f, 709. e, 710. b, 711. a, 712. d, 713. c, 714. g, 715. i, 716. yes, 717. yes, 718. no, 719. no, 720. no, 721. yes, 722. yes, 723. yes, 724. no, 725. yes, 726. no, 727. no, 728. yes, 729. yes, 730. no, 731. no, 732. no, 733. no, 734. yes, 735. yes, 736. yes, 737. yes

FOOTBALL

738) What team won the first two Super Bowls?

a) Chicago Bears
b) Dallas Cowboys
c) Green Bay Packers
d) Pittsburgh Steelers

739) What is the only team in the Super Bowl era to go undefeated?

a) Baltimore Colts
b) Indianapolis Colts
c) Miami Dolphins
d) New England Patriots

740) What team was the first to go 0-16 in a season?

a) Detroit Lions
b) Indianapolis Colts
c) Kansas City Chiefs
d) Tampa Bay Buccaneers

Match the team to its stadium.

741) Arrowhead Stadium	a. Kansas City Chiefs
742) Candlestick Park	b. San Francisco 49ers
743) FedEx Field	c. Tennessee Titans
744) LP Field	d. Washington Redskins

745) What was Brett Favre's first NFL team?

a) Atlanta Falcons
b) Green Bay Packers
c) Minnesota Vikings
d) New York Giants

TOUGH TRIVIA CHALLENGE

749) In Canadian football, a team can score one point by kicking the ball untouched into the other team's end zone. What is this play called?

a) Blanc
b) Bleu
c) Rouge
d) Verde

746) True or false: No Super Bowl has ever gone into overtime.

Match the coach with his team.

750) Bill Cowher	a. Chicago Bears
751) George Halas	b. Dallas Cowboys
752) Tom Landry	c. Oakland Raiders
753) John Madden	d. Pittsburgh Steelers

747) What Chicago Bears great was nicknamed "Sweetness"?

a) Dick Butkus
b) Walter Payton
c) Brian Piccolo
d) Gale Sayers

754) Who are the only brothers to both be drafted with the #1 pick?

748) What did WFL stand for?

755) Which city has never been home to an NFL franchise?

a) Akron, OH
b) Hammond, IN
c) Racine, WI
d) Wichita, KS

738. c, 739. d, 740. a, 741. a, 742. b, 743. d, 744. c, 745. a, 746. true, 747. b, 748. World Football League, 749. c, 750. d, 751. a, 752. b, 753. c, 754. Peyton and Eli Manning, 755. d

TOUGH TRIVIA CHALLENGE

756) Match the franchise to the now-defunct league.

1) AFL a. Barcelona Dragons
2) USFL b. Boston Breakers
3) WFL c. Honolulu Hawaiians
4) WLAF d. New York Titans

757) Who was the NFL's first black player?

a) Jim Brown
b) Tony Dungy
c) Fritz Pollard
d) Jackie Robinson

758) WHAT OAKLAND RAIDERS OWNER WAS COMMISSIONER OF THE AFL?

759) What quarterback "guaranteed" a Super Bowl victory for the underdog New York Jets, and then delivered?

760) True or false: The Pittsburgh Steelers are the only team to win three straight Super Bowls.

761) What quarterback threw 420 touchdown passes, 2nd-most in NFL history, but never won a Super Bowl?

a) Dan Marino
b) Warren Moon
c) Fran Tarkenton
d) Johnny Unitas

762) PRO BOWL RECEIVER ART MONK IS A SECOND COUSIN OF WHAT JAZZ LEGEND?

Match the nickname to the player.

763) Hollywood a. Thomas Henderson
764) Snake b. Ed Jones
765) Too Mean c. Harvey Martin
766) Too Tall d. Ken Stabler

767) Who led the NFL in rushing yards every year but one from 1957 to 1965?

768) The original Cleveland Browns left Cleveland and are now what team?

769) What school won a share of the 1990 National Championship after being saved from defeat when the officials mistakenly awarded the team a fifth down?

a) Alabama
b) Colorado
c) Louisiana State
d) USC

770) Future President Ronald Reagan played what Notre Dame football legend in a movie?

a) Grover Cleveland Alexander
b) George Gipp
c) Paul Hornung
d) Knute Rockne

TOUGH TRIVIA CHALLENGE

771) What former skier is the only placekicker in the Pro Football Hall of Fame?

a) Ray Guy
b) Mark Moseley
c) Jan Stenerud
d) Matt Stover

772) What award is given to the top college football player in the nation?

773) True or False: **Carl Weathers, who played Apollo Creed in the Rocky movies, was once a professional football player.**

774) What team reached four straight Super Bowls, but lost them all?

a) Buffalo Bills
b) Indianapolis Colts
c) Kansas City Chiefs
d) Minnesota Vikings

756. 1d, 2b, 3c, 4a, 757. c, 758. Al Davis, 759. Joe Namath, 760. false—no team has, 761. a, 762. Thelonious Monk, 763. a, 764. d, 765. c,
766. b, 767. Jim Brown, 768. Baltimore Ravens, 769. b, 770. b, 771. c, 772. Heisman Trophy, 773. true, 774. a

775) WHAT, APPROPRIATELY, WAS THE NICKNAME OF NFL KICKER LOU GROZA?

A) THE FOOT
B) THE LEG
C) THE SHOE
D) THE TOE

776) What team has won five Super Bowls and never lost one?

a) Dallas Cowboys
b) Oakland Raiders
c) Pittsburgh Steelers
d) San Francisco 49ers

777) What comedian was a commentator on Monday Night Football from 2000-2002?

a) George Carlin
b) Dennis Miller
c) Pete Barbutti
d) Jeff Foxworthy

778) How many yards is it from the goal line to the back of the end zone?

a) 5
b) 10
c) 15
d) 17

779) HOW WIDE IS A FOOTBALL FIELD?

A) 33-1/3 YARDS
B) 50 YARDS
C) 53-1/3 YARDS
D) 66-2/3 YARDS

780) What school won the first Rose Bowl?

a) Michigan
b) Ohio State
c) UCLA
d) USC

Match the coach to the school where he coached the most games.

781) Bear Bryant	**a. Alabama**
782) Woody Hayes	**b. Michigan**
783) Joe Paterno	**c. Ohio State**
784) Bo Schembechler	**d. Penn State**

785) How many schools are in the Big Ten Conference?

a) 8

b) 10

c) 11

d) 12

TOUGH TRIVIA CHALLENGE

787) USC's Roy Riegels and the Minnesota Vikings' Jim Marshall are both notorious for committing what blunder?

788) Astroturf was originally developed for use in what stadium?

789) The answer to the previous question wasn't the first field to have it installed though. That was Franklin Field, then home to what team?

786) Then Atlanta Falcons' quarterback Michael Vick got in trouble for being involved in what illegal sport?

a) Bear bating

b) Cockfighting

c) Dog fighting

d) Dwarf tossing

775. d, 776. d, 777. b, 778. b, 779. c, 780. a, 781. a, 782. c, 783. d, 784. b, 785. d, 786. c, 787. running toward the wrong end zone, 788. the Astrodome, 789. Philadelphia Eagles

TOUGH TRIVIA CHALLENGE

790) Joe Namath quit pro football over a dispute with commissioner Pete Rozelle over a bar that Namath invested in. What was the bar named?

a) Bachelors
b) Bachelors II
c) Bachelors III
d) Bachelors IV

791) True or false: A New York Giants quarterback was a contestant on the reality show The Bachelor?

792) DID THE GIANTS QUARTERBACK AND HIS PICK GET MARRIED?

793) How long has Pat Patriot been the fictional mascot of the New England Patriots?

a) Since 1950
b) Since 1961
c) Since 1972
d) Since 1976

794) WHAT IS THE NAME OF THE PITTSBURGH STEELERS' MASCOT?

A) STEELY MCIRON
B) STEELY MCSTEEL
C) STEELY MCBEAM
D) STEELY MCSTUDS

795) Comic character Tank McNamara is a former NFL...

a) Quarterback
b) Defensive lineman
c) Center
d) Kicker

796) What was William Perry's nickname?

a) The Refrigerator
b) The Toaster
c) The Burner
d) The Microwave

MATCH THE RUSHER TO THE TEAM.

797) Atlanta Falcons
798) Baltimore Colts
799) Carolina Panthers
800) Chicago Bears
801) Cleveland Browns
802) Dallas Cowboys
803) Denver Broncos
804) Detroit Lions
805) Green Bay Packers
806) Indianapolis Colts
807) Jacksonville Jaguars
808) Kansas City Chiefs
809) Minnesota Vikings
810) New England Patriots
811) New Orleans Saints
812) New York Giants
813) New York Jets
814) Oakland Raiders
815) Philadelphia Eagles
816) Pittsburgh Steelers
817) St. Louis Cardinals
818) St. Louis Rams
819) San Francisco 49ers
820) Tampa Bay Buccaneers
821) Tennessee Titans
822) Washington Redskins

a) Joseph Addai
b) Mike Alstott
c) Jamal Anderson
d) Tiki Barber
e) Rocky Bleier
f) Jim Brown
g) Larry Brown
h) Tony Canadeo
i) Sam Cunningham
j) Terrell Davis
k) Frank Gore
l) Steven Jackson
m) Chris Johnson
n) Maurice Jones-Drew
o) Napoleon Kaufman
p) Deuce McAllister
q) Freeman McNeil
r) Stump Mitchell
s) Lenny Moore
t) Christian Okoye
u) Walter Payton
v) Don Perkins
w) Adrian Peterson
x) Barry Sanders
y) Steve Van Buren
z) DeAngelo Williams

790. c, 791. true, 792. no, 793. b, 794. c, 795. b, 796. a, 797. c, 798. s, 799. z, 800. u, 801. f, 802. v, 803. j, 804. x, 805. h, 806. a, 807. n, 808. t,
809. w, 810. i, 811. p, 812. d, 813. q, 814. o, 815. y, 816. e, 817. r, 818. l, 819. k, 820. b, 821. m, 822. g

MATCH THE QUARTERBACK TO THE TEAM.

823) Atlanta Falcons
824) Baltimore Ravens
825) Buffalo Bills
826) Chicago Bears
827) Cincinnati Bengals
828) Cleveland Browns
829) Dallas Cowboys
830) Denver Broncos
831) Detroit Lions
832) Green Bay Packers
833) Indianapolis Colts
834) Jacksonville Jaguars
835) Kansas City Chiefs
836) Los Angeles Rams
837) Miami Dolphins
838) New England Patriots
839) New Orleans Saints
840) New York Giants
841) New York Jets
842) Pittsburgh Steelers
843) St. Louis Cardinals
844) St. Louis Rams
845) San Diego Chargers
846) San Francisco 49ers
847) Tampa Bay Buccaneers
848) Washington Redskins

a) Troy Aikman
b) Ken Anderson
c) Terry Bradshaw
d) Tom Brady
e) John Brodie
f) Marc Bulger
g) John Elway
h) Joe Flacco
i) Dan Fouts
j) Josh Freeman
k) David Garrard
l) Pat Haden
m) Eric Hipple
n) Jim Kelly
o) Bill Kenney
p) Neil Lomax
q) Sid Luckman
r) Peyton Manning
s) Dan Marino
t) Matt Ryan
u) Mark Sanchez
v) Phil Simms
w) Brian Sipe
x) Bart Starr
y) Joe Theismann
z) Dave Wilson

MATCH THE RECEIVER TO THE TEAM.

849) Arizona Cardinals
850) Atlanta Falcons
851) Baltimore Colts
852) Carolina Panthers
853) Cincinnati Bengals
854) Cleveland Browns
855) Dallas Cowboys
856) Denver Broncos
857) Detroit Lions
858) Green Bay Packers
859) Houston Texans
860) Indianapolis Colts
861) Kansas City Chiefs
862) Miami Dolphins
863) Minnesota Vikings
864) New England Patriots
865) New Orleans Saints
866) New York Giants
867) New York Jets
868) Oakland Raiders
869) Philadelphia Eagles
870) Pittsburgh Steelers
871) San Diego Chargers
872) San Francisco 49ers
873) Seattle Seahawks
874) Washington Redskins

a) Raymond Berry
b) Fred Biletnikoff
c) Troy Brown
d) Dwight Clark
e) Cris Collinsworth
f) Marques Colston
g) Donald Driver
h) Mark Duper
i) Larry Fitzgerald
j) Antonio Gates
k) Marvin Harrison
l) Michael Irvin
m) Andre Johnson
n) Calvin Johnson
o) Steve Largent
p) Ozzie Newsome
q) Pete Retzlaff
r) Rod Smith
s) Steve Smith
t) Charley Taylor
u) Otis Taylor
v) Amani Toomer
w) Wesley Walker
x) Hines Ward
y) Roddy White
z) Sammy White

823. t, 824. h, 825. n, 826. q, 827. b, 828. w, 829. a, 830. g, 831. m, 832. x, 833. r, 834. k, 835. o, 836. l, 837. s, 838. d, 839. z, 840. v, 841. u, 842. c, 843. p, 844. f, 845. i, 846. e, 847. j, 848. y, 849. i, 850. y, 851. a, 852. s, 853. e, 854. p, 855. l, 856. r, 857. n, 858. g, 859. m, 860. k, 861. u, 862. h, 863. z, 864. c, 865. f, 866. v, 867. w, 868. b, 869. q, 870. x, 871. j, 872. d, 873. o, 874. t

BASKETBALL

875) True or false: Basketball was invented by the head of the P.E. department at a school in Massachusetts when he was asked to create a game to be played in winter.

876) True or false: Peach baskets were the first basketball baskets.

877) True or false: Basketball was first played with a tennis ball.

878) TRUE OR FALSE: IN EARLY WOMEN'S BASKETBALL, PLAYERS HAD TO STAY IN ASSIGNED AREAS OF THE COURT.

879) True or false: In early women's basketball, there were a limited number of dribbles a player could do.

880) True or false: The Buffalo Germans won 111 games in a row from 1908-1911.

881) True or false: No college offered women's varsity basketball until 1950.

TOUGH TRIVIA CHALLENGE

882) How many teams have won two NCAA championships in a row?

883) What basketball position did Bill Russell play?

884) True or false: **Wilt Chamberlain once scored 100 points in a single game.**

885) What college team did John Wooden coach from 1963-1975?

a) NYC
b) UCLA
c) LSU
d) USC

886) What position did Oscar Robertson play?

887) WHAT TEAM DID ISIAH THOMAS AND DENNIS RODMAN BOTH PLAY FOR?

888) What division is the Milwaukee Bucks in?

889) What division is the Golden State Warriors in?

875. true, 876. true, 877. false—a soccer ball, 878. true, 879. true, 880. true, 881. false, 882. seven, 883. center, 884. true, 885. b, 886. guard, 887. Detroit Pistons, 888. Central, 889. Pacific

890) What division is the Portland Trail Blazers in?

891) What division is the Dallas Mavericks in?

892) WHAT DIVISION IS THE MIAMI HEAT IN?

Match the NBA player to the country where he was born:

893) Pau Gasol	a) Nigeria
894) Yao Ming	b) Germany
895) Hakeem Olajuwon	c) Congo
896) Dirk Nowitzki	d) China
897) Dikembe Mutombo	e) Spain
898) Manu Ginobili	f) Argentina

899) Did the American Basketball Association last more or less than a decade?

900) What colors were the ABA basketball?

901) What is it called when a player dribbles, holds the ball, and then dribbles again?

902) Is the WNBA's Tulsa Shock in the Western or Eastern conference?

904) Is the WNBA's Chicago Sky in the Western or Eastern conference?

905) What team did Shaquille O'Neal and Kobe Bryant play for together?

TOUGH TRIVIA CHALLENGE

903) WHEN WERE THE HARLEM GLOBETROTTERS FOUNDED?

A) 1927

B) 1945

C) 1955

D) 1968

906) Was the first professional basketball league created before or after 1900?

907) The National Basketball Association was formed by a merger of the National Basketball League and...

a) The Basketball League of Teams

b) The Basketball Association of America

c) The American Basketball Association

d) The North American Gamesmen's League

908) What is the diameter of a basketball rim?

a) 14 inches

b) 16 inches

c) 18 inches

d) 20 inches

890. Northwest, 891. Southwest, 892. Southeast, 893. e, 894. d, 895. a, 896. b, 897. c, 898. f, 899. less, 900. red, white, and blue, 901. double dribble, 902. Western, 903. a, 904. Eastern, 905. Los Angeles Lakers, 906. before, 907. b, 908. c

909) True or false: The backboard was added to the game to prevent interference from spectators.

910) What is basketball fandom in Indiana known as?
A) Hoosier Hoopla
B) Hoosier Hysteria
C) Hoosier Hallelujah
D) Hoosier Hijinks

911) True or false: Kareem Abdul-Jabber has the most NBA career games played.

912) True or false: Reggie Miller played more NBA games than Julius Erving.

913) True or false: Shaquille O'Neal played more NBA games than Moses Malone.

914) True or false: Hakeem Olajuwan played more NBA games than Mark Jackson.

TOUGH TRIVIA CHALLENGE

915) Which of the following did not play in the ABA?
a) Louie Dampier
b) Byron Beck
c) Freddie Lewis
d) Jim Kimball

916) True or false: Elvin Hayes played more NBA games than Karl Malone.

917) Who had more NBA field goals in a single season, Kareem Abdul-Jabbar or Wilt Chamberlain?

918) WHO HAD MORE NBA FIELD GOALS IN A SINGLE SEASON, MICHAEL JORDAN OR BOB MCADOO?

919) Who had more NBA field goals in a single season, Elgin Baylor or George Gervin?

920) Who had more free throws in a single NBA season, Jerry West or Wilt Chamberlain?

TOUGH TRIVIA CHALLENGE

921) In what year was the first NCAA men's basketball championship?

a) 1903
b) 1916
c) 1939
d) 1952

922) Who had more free throws in a single NBA season, Michael Jordan or Oscar Robertson?

923) Who had more free throws in a single NBA season, Moses Malone or Charles Barkley?

924) WHO HAD MORE OFFENSIVE REBOUNDS IN A SINGLE NBA SEASON, MOSES MALONE OR CHARLES BARKLEY?

925) *Who had more offensive rebounds in a single NBA season, Jayson Williams or Hakeen Olajuwon?*

926) Who had more offensive rebounds in a single NBA season, Dennis Rodman or Shaquille O'Neal?

909. true, 910. b, 911. false, 912. true, 913. false, 914. false, 915. d, 916. false, 917. Wilt Chamberlain, 918. Michael Jordan, 919. Elgin Baylor, 920. Jerry West, 921. c, 922. Michael Jordan, 923. Moses Malone, 924. Moses Malone, 925. Jayson Williams, 926. Dennis Rodman

927) Who had more defensive rebounds in a single NBA season, Kareem Abdul-Jabbar or Elvin Hayes?

928) Who had more defensive rebounds in a single NBA season, Truck Robinson or Dennis Rodman?

929) Who had more defensive rebounds in a single NBA season, Dave Cowens or Kevin Garnett?

930) True or false: As of the 2010 season, John Stockton held the seven of the top ten positions for most assists in a single NBA season.

931) True or false: As of the 2010 season, Wilt Chamberlain and Bill Russell occupy all of the top ten slots for highest average rebounds per NBA game in a single season.

932) What future U.S. senator led Princeton to the Final Four?

933) WHO HAD A HIGHER NBA CAREER AVERAGE OF STEALS PER GAME. MICHAEL JORDAN OR ALLEN IVERSON?

934) Which two teams did Kareem Abdul-Jabbar play for?

935) Who had a higher NBA career average of steals per game, Alvin Robertson or Mookie Blaylock?

936) Who had a higher NBA career average of steals per game, Maurice Cheeks or Michael Ray Richardson?

937) Who had the higher number of average blocks in a single NBA season, Manute Bol or Hakeem Olajuwon?

938) Who had the higher number of average blocks in a single NBA season, Mark Eaton or David Robinson?

939) WHICH TEAM DID ALONZO MOURNING NOT PLAY FOR?

A) MIAMI
B) CHARLOTTE
C) NEW JERSEY
D) PHILADELPHIA

927. Kareem Abdul-Jabbar, 928. Dennis Rodman, 929. Dave Cowens, 930. true, 931. true, 932. Bill Bradley, 933. Michael Jordan, 934. Milwaukee and Los Angeles, 935. Alvin Robertson, 936. Michael Ray Richardson, 937. Manute Bol, 938. Mark Eaton, 939. d

940) Which team did Dikembe Mutombo not play for?

a) Houston

b) San Francisco

c) Atlanta

d) Denver

TOUGH TRIVIA CHALLENGE

941) Which team did Manute Bol not play for:

a) Washington Bullets

b) Golden State

c) Cleveland

d) Philadelphia

942) True or false: Patrick Ewing's middle name is Aloysius.

943) In what year was Patrick Ewing drafted by the New York Knicks?

a) 1980

b) 1983

c) 1985

d) 1989

944) What team did Ben Wallace not play for?

a) Detroit

b) Golden State

c) Cleveland

d) Chicago

945) Was Shaquille O'Neal taller or shorter than 7 feet?

946) Was Dwight Howard a first-round draft pick?

947) WHAT TEAM DID SHAQUILLE O'NEAL NOT PLAY FOR?

A) ORLANDO
B) MIAMI
C) CLEVELAND
D) TORONTO

948) Where did Jermaine O'Neal begin his NBA career, Portland or Indianapolis?

949) True or false: Patrick Ewing played his entire NBA career with the New York Knicks.

950) WHAT ARE THE MEASUREMENTS OF AN NBA BACKBOARD?

A) 6 FT. BY 3.5. FT.
B) 5 FT. BY 2.5 FT.
C) 5.5 FT. BY 3 FT.
D) 6.5 FT. BY 4 FT.

951) True or false: There was an NBA player with the first name Cincinnatus.

940. b, 941. c, 942. true, 943. c, 944. b, 945. taller, 946. yes, 947. d, 948. Portland, 949. false, 950. a, 951. true—Cincinnatus Powell, who played 1967-1975

952) Is an ofcial NBA basketball more or less than 30 inches in circumference.

953) True or false: A college basketball player once scored 116 points in a single game.

954) Has anyone ever scored 100 points in an NCAA Division I game?

955) True or false: Bill Russell won 11 NBA Championships.

956) True or false: Until 1913, the bottom of the basketball net was closed.

957) True or false: It was against the rules to slam dunk between 1967 and 1976.

958) IN WHAT YEAR WAS THE THREE-POINT FIELD GOAL INTRODUCED?

A) 1980
B) 1986
C) 1992
D) 1995

959) True or false: **The three-point line is 16.5 feet from the center of the basket.**

960) How many schools participated in the first NCAA tournament?

a) 8
b) 16
c) 32
d) 64

961) HOW MANY TEAMS HAVE WON THREE NCAA CHAMPIONSHIPS IN A ROW?

962) What NBA legend is the only three-time NCAA Most Outstanding Player in the Final Four?

a) Kareem Abdul-Jabbar
b) Wilt Chamberlain
c) Michael Jordan
d) Shaquille O'Neal

963) What college did Kobe Bryant play for?

964) What school has won the most NCAA championships?

952. less, 953. true, 954. yes—Frank Selvy for Furman University, 955. true, 956. true, 957. true, 958. b, 959. false—19 ft. 9 inches, 960. a, 961. one, 962. a, 963. none, 964. UCLA

965) Has any team won the NIT one year and the NCAA the next?

TOUGH TRIVIA CHALLENGE

966) Who was named the Most Outstanding Player of the Final Four two years in a row—even though his team lost the championship the second year?

a) Bob Cousy
b) John Havlicek
c) Jerry Lucas
d) Jerry West

967) UCLA WON THE NCAA CHAMPIONSHIP EVERY YEAR EXCEPT ONE FROM 1964–73. HOW DID THEY FARE IN 1966?

A) NATIONAL RUNNER-UP
B) LOST IN FINAL FOUR
C) LOST IN REGIONAL FINAL
D) DID NOT MAKE THE TOURNAMENT

TOUGH TRIVIA CHALLENGE

968) Has any team won the NIT and NCAA in the same year?

MATCH THE PLAYER TO HIS COLLEGIATE ALMA MATER.

969) Auburn
970) California
971) Central Arkansas
972) Cincinnati
973) Connecticut
974) Georgetown
975) Gonzaga
976) Houston
977) Indiana
978) Indiana State
979) Kansas
980) Kentucky
981) Louisiana State
982) Louisiana Tech
983) Marquette
984) Memphis
985) Michigan State
986) Navy
987) North Carolina
988) Oklahoma
989) San Francisco
990) Santa Clara
991) Syracuse
992) Texas
993) UCLA
994) Wake Forest

a) Kareem Abdul-Jabbar
b) Ray Allen
c) Carmelo Anthony
d) Charles Barkley
e) Larry Bird
f) Wilt Chamberlain
g) Tim Duncan
h) Kevin Durant
i) Blake Griffin
j) Allen Iverson
k) Magic Johnson
l) Michael Jordan
m) Jason Kidd
n) Karl Malone
o) Steve Nash
p) Hakeem Olajuwon
q) Shaquille O'Neal
r) Scottie Pippen
s) Oscar Robertson
t) David Robinson
u) Rajon Rondo
v) Derrick Rose
w) Bill Russell
x) John Stockton
y) Isiah Thomas
z) Dwyane Wade

965. no, 966. c, 967. d, 968. yes—CCNY in 1950, 969. d, 970. m, 971. r, 972. s, 973. b, 974. j, 975. x, 976. p, 977. y, 978. e, 979. f, 980. u, 981. q, 982. n, 983. z, 984. v, 985. k, 986. t, 987. l, 988. i, 989. w, 990. o, 991. c, 992. h, 993. a, 994. g

SOCCER

995) What soccer team has the same name as a U.S. kitchen cleanser and plays at the Amsterdam Arena?

996) True or false: Juventus is an Italian soccer team.

997) Which soccer team was founded first, FC Barcelona or FC Liverpool?

998) True or false: Manchester United is based in France.

999) TRUE OR FALSE: DF VALENCIA IS BASED IN BRAZIL.

1000) True or false: Werder Bremen is based in Germany.

1001) Who is older, Chelsea's Salomon Kalou or Arsenal's Marouane Chamakh?

1002) True or false: Handling of the soccer ball was banned in 1869.

1003) Did Peru play in the first World Cup?

1004) What are the 1815 rules that helped popularize soccer known as?

a) The Harvard Rules

b) The Oxford Rules

c) The Cambridge Rules

d) The Liverpool Rules

1005) Where was the first World Cup?

a) Brazil

b) Uruguay

c) England

d) Japan

1006) DID NEW ZEALAND PLAY IN THE FIRST WORLD CUP?

1007) Did Mexico play in the first World Cup?

1008) Did the United States play in the first World Cup?

1009) Did Finland play in the first World Cup?

1010) Who won the first World Cup?

995. Ajax, 996. true, 997. Liverpool, 998. false, 999. false—it's in Spain, 1000. true, 1001. Chamakh, 1002. true, 1003. yes, 1004. c, 1005. b, 1006. no, 1007. yes, 1008. yes, 1009. no, 1010. France, 1011. thirteen

1012) True or false: The oldest player ever to compete in a World Cup finals match was 52 years old.

1013) TRUE OR FALSE: THE WORLD CUP WAS HELD DESPITE WORLD WAR II.

1014) True or false: The first Women's World Cup was held in 2000.

1015) True or false: Cameroon has competed in the World Cup.

1016) Which has won more World Cup championships, Brazil or Germany?

1017) True or false: Germany has finished in the World Cup in the top two more often than Italy.

1018) Has Sweden ever been in the World Cup top two?

1019) Has Hungary ever been in the World Cup top two?

1020) WHICH HAS BEEN IN THE WORLD CUP TOP THREE MORE OFTEN, GERMANY OR BRAZIL?

1021) Has Croatia ever made it into the World Cup top three?

1022) Has Chile ever made it into the World Cup top three?

1023) Has New Guinea ever made it into the World Cup top three?

1024) True or false: No team has ever won two consecutive World Cups.

1025) TRUE OR FALSE: ARGENTINA WENT 48 YEARS BETWEEN WINNING SPOTS IN THE WORLD CUP TOP TWO.

1026) True or false: The World Cup has never been won by a host team.

1027) True or false: Host team South Africa was defeated in the first round of the 2010 World Cup.

1028) True or false: Canada played three World Cup matches in which they didn't score a goal.

1029) True or false: Antonio Carbajal played in five World Cup tournaments.

1012. false—40 years old, 1013. false, 1014. false—in 1991, 1015. true, 1016. Brazil, 1017. true, 1018. yes, 1019. yes, 1020. Germany, 1021. yes, 1022. yes, 1023. no, 1024. false—Italy and Brazil both did it, 1025. true, 1026. false, 1027. true, 1028. true, 1029. true

1030) True or false: The youngest player ever to compete in a World Cup tournament was 15 years old.

1031) Did Pele play in the 1958 World Cup finals?

1032) TRUE OR FALSE: OLEG SALENKO OF RUSSIA SCORED FIVE GOALS IN A WORLD CUP MATCH.

1033) True or false: Geoff Hurst of England scored three goals in a World Cup finals match.

1034) True or false: A World Cup match was once won by nine goals.

1035) True or false: In the 2010 World Cup tournament, Greece's coach was 71 years old.

TOUGH TRIVIA CHALLENGE

1036) Did Germany score more goals in the 2010 World Cup tournament or the 2006 World Cup tournament?

1037) HAS THERE EVER BEEN A PLAYER TO WIN SEPARATE WORLD CUP TOURNAMENTS AS A PLAYER AND AS A COACH?

1038) True or false: Peleé played for Brazil his entire soccer career.

1039) True or false: Pelé's real name is Edson.

1040) In Brazil, Pelé was known as:

a) The King

b) The Duke

c) The Bishop

d) The Prince

1041) In what year did Pelé retire from soccer?

a) 1977

b) 1982

c) 1986

d) 1990

1042) True or false: Pelé appeared in the World War II film Escape to Victory.

1043) Where was the term "soccer" first used, the United States or England?

1030. false—he was 17, 1031. yes—Brazil vs. Sweden, 1032. true, 1033. true, 1034. true—it has actually happened multiple times, 1035. true, 1036. 2010, 1037. yes—Brazil's Mario Zagallo and West Germany's Franz Beckenbauer, 1038. false, 1039. true, 1040. a, 1041. a, 1042. true, 1043. England

1044) True or false: Soccer is also known as association football.

1046) TRUE OR FALSE: EACH SOCCER TEAM FIELDS TEN PLAYERS AT A TIME.

1047) True or false: A four-day war between Honduras and El Salvador in 1969 is known as The Soccer War.

TOUGH TRIVIA CHALLENGE

1045) Which was not a team in the Xtreme Soccer League?

a) Chicago Storm
b) Milwaukee Wave
c) Cleveland Mashers
d) Detroit Ignition

1048) True or false: Iran once beat the U.S. in a World Cup match.

1049) Are soccer players allowed to wear watches during games?

1050) How many minutes in a standard soccer half?

1051) A SOCCER PLAYER IS "BOOKED" IF HE OR SHE HAS:

A) A RED CARD
B) A YELLOW CARD
C) A BLUE CARD
D) A WHITE CARD

1052) True or false: Since 1984, professional soccer players have been allowed to compete in the Olympics.

HOCKEY

1053) True or false: A fighting penalty in hockey is four minutes.

1054) True or false: The first hockey puck was square.

1055) True or false: Hockey pucks are frozen before put in play.

1056) HOW MANY TOTAL PLAYERS ARE ON THE ICE FOR ONE TEAM AT ONE TIME (WITH NO PENALTIES)?

1057) True or false: An NHL hockey puck is made of vulcanized rubber?

1058) How many places on the rink can a face-off occur?

1059) Which usually has longer blades, a goaltender's skates or a forward's?

1060) Is "fast ice" colder or warmer?

1044. true, 1045. c, 1046. false—fields eleven, 1047. true, 1048. true—in 1998, 1049. no, 1050. forty-five, 1051. b, 1052. true, 1053. false—five minutes, 1054. true, 1055. true, 1056. six, 1057. true, 1058. nine, 1059. goaltender, 1060. colder

1061) Is "fast ice" smoother or rougher?

1062) True or false: Overtime periods are played with one less player on the ice per team.

1063) HOW MANY RED LINES ARE THERE ON A HOCKEY RINK?

1064) True or false: There are three officials in an NFL hockey game—two referees and a linesman.

1065) Which of the following was not one of the original six NHL franchises?
a) Boston Bruins
b) New York Islanders
c) Montreal Canadiens
d) Toronto Maple Leafs

1066) Who did the U.S. team defeat in 1980 to win the Olympic Gold medal?

1067) IS THE NHL HALL OF FAME IN THE U.S. OR CANADA?

1068) True or false: There is a regulation size ice rink in the Hockey Hall of Fame.

TOUGH TRIVIA CHALLENGE

1069) Which Montreal Canadien was also a member of Parliament and did color commentary for the 1980 "Miracle" game?
a) Gordie Howe
b) Ken Dryden
c) Bernie Parant
d) Bobby Orr

TOUGH TRIVIA CHALLENGE

1070) Who was not a 2011 inductee in the Hockey Hall of Fame?

a) Mark Howe
b) Myles Strong
c) Joe Nieuwendyk
d) Ed Belfour

1071) What team was in the NHL in 1917 before moving to St. Louis, and then disbanding, only to see a new team of the same name begin play in 1992?

1072) True or false: Gordie Howe played over 1,700 games.

1073) Who played more games, Wayne Gretzky or Dave Andreychuk?

1074) Who played more games, Mark Messier or Dean Prentice?

1075) Who played more games, Rod Brind'Amour or Scott Stevens?

1076) What team has won the most NHL championships?

a) Boston Bruins
b) Detroit Red Wings
c) Montreal Canadiens
d) Toronto Maple Leafs

1061. smoother, 1062. true, 1063. three—center and two end lines, 1064. false—there's one referee and two linesmen, 1065. b, 1066. Finland, 1067. Canada, 1068. false, 1069. b, 1070. b, 1071. Ottawa Senators, 1072. true, 1073. Dave Andreychuk, 1074. Mark Messier, 1075. Scott Stevens, 1076. c

MATCH THE NATIONAL HOCKEY LEAGUE TROPHY TO THE ACHIEVEMENT IT HONORS.

1077) Jack Adams
1078) Lady Byng
1079) Calder
1080) Hart
1081) William M. Jennings
1082) James Norris
1083) Presidents
1084) Maurice "Rocket" Richard
1085) Art Ross
1086) Conn Smythe
1087) Vezina

a) Best combination of skill and sportsmanship
b) Best defenseman
c) Best goalie
d) Coach of the Year
e) Fewest goals allowed
f) Most goals scored
g) Most points, regular season (team)
h) Most points, regular season (player)
i) Most Valuable Player (regular season)
j) Most Valuable Player (Stanley Cup playoffs)
k) Rookie of the Year

Match the team with the city where it used to play.

1088) Calgary Flames
1089) Carolina Hurricanes
1090) Colorado Avalanche
1091) Dallas Stars
1092) New Jersey Devils
1093) Phoenix Coyotes

a) Atlanta
b) Bloomington, Minnesota
c) Denver
d) Hartford
e) Quebec City
f) Winnipeg

TOUGH TRIVIA CHALLENGE

1094) The Cougars, the last non-NHL team to win the Stanley Cup, represented what Canadian city?
a) Calgary
b) Edmonton
c) Saskatoon
d) Victoria

1095) Which team did Wayne Gretzky never play for?

a) Edmonton Oilers
b) Los Angeles Kings
c) Phoenix Coyotes
d) New York Rangers

1096) WHAT ARENA IS HOME TO THE NEW YORK RANGERS?

1097) Who is the only person to win the Stanley Cup as a player and an owner?

1098) Who was the "Stanley" the Stanley Cup is named for?

a) A player
b) An owner
c) A silversmith
d) A Canadian governor-general

1099) There was no winner of the 1919 Stanley Cup. Why not?

a) Flu epidemic
b) Player strike
c) World War I
d) The Cup wasn't created till 1920

1100) WHICH OF THESE HOCKEY LEAGUES NEVER COMPETED FOR THE STANLEY CUP?

A) EAST COAST HOCKEY LEAGUE
B) NATIONAL HOCKEY ASSOCIATION
C) PACIFIC COAST HOCKEY ASSOCIATION
D) WESTERN CANADA HOCKEY LEAGUE

1077. d, 1078. a, 1079. k, 1080. i, 1081. e, 1082. b, 1083. g, 1084. f, 1085. h, 1086. j, 1087. c, 1088. a, 1089. d, 1090. e, 1091. b, 1092. c, 1093. f, 1094. d, 1095. c, 1096. Madison Square Garden, 1097. Mario Lemieux, 1098. d, 1099. a, 1100. a

BOWLING

1101) How many inches tall is a bowling pin?

1102) True or false:

If a bowling ball bounces out of the gutter and knocks over a pin, the pin counts for the bowler.

1103) How much does a bowling pin weigh?

a) 1-2 lbs
b) 2-3 lbs
c) 3-4 lbs
d) 4-5 lbs

TOUGH TRIVIA CHALLENGE

1104) What is the distance in inches between the center of pin one and the center of pin 12?

1105) In a bowling pin rack, which pin is number 7?

a) The rear right
b) The rear left
c) The center
d) The second pin in the third row

1106) AN EARLY VERSION OF BOWLING APPEARS IN A FAMOUS STORY BY WASHINGTON IRVING ABOUT A MAN WHO FALLS ASLEEP AND WAKES UP 20 YEARS LATER. WHAT'S THE NAME OF THE STORY?

TOUGH TRIVIA CHALLENGE

1107) In what year was the first rubber bowling ball introduced?

a) 1877
b) 1890
c) 1905
d) 1922

1108) Bowling transitioned from human pinsetters to automatic devices in the...

a) 1980s
b) 1970s
c) 1960s
d) 1950s

1109) True or first: **Early television included such programs as *Make That Spare, Celebrity Bowling,* and *Bowling for Dollars.***

1110) What is a perfect score in bowling?

1111) How many open frames in a row does it take to have a buzzard?

1101. fifteen, 1102. false—it's considered "illegal pinfall", 1103. c, 1104. 36 inches, 1105. b, 1106. "Rip Van Winkle", 1107. c, 1108. d,
1109. true, 1110. 300, 1111. three

1112) HOW MANY STRIKES IN A ROW ARE CONSIDERED A TURKEY?

1113) Bedposts is a nickname for what in bowling?

1114) WHAT *SPLIT* IS REFERRED TO AS THE GOLDEN GATE?

1115) Is bowling an Olympic sport?

1116) For a right-handed bowler, which way does a hook break, left or right?

TOUGH TRIVIA CHALLENGE

1117) About how wide is a bowling alley gutter?
a) 6 inches
b) 8 inches
c) 9 ½ inches
d) 11 inches

1118) For a left-handed bowler, which way does a hook break, left or right?

BOXING

1119) In boxing, which is heavier: lightweight or bantamweight?

1120) In boxing, which is heavier: featherweight or flyweight?

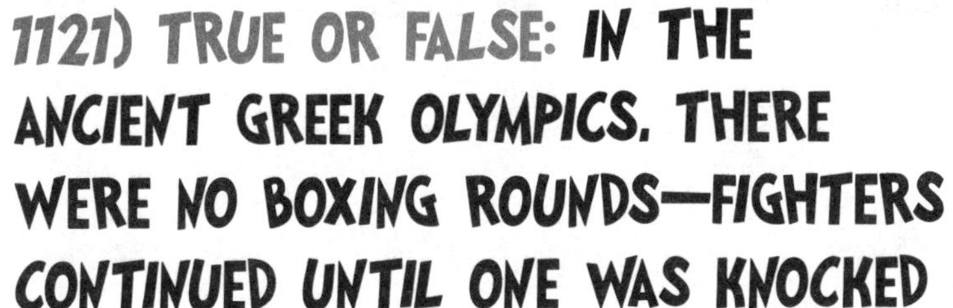

1121) TRUE OR FALSE: IN THE ANCIENT GREEK OLYMPICS, THERE WERE NO BOXING ROUNDS—FIGHTERS CONTINUED UNTIL ONE WAS KNOCKED OUT OR GAVE UP.

1122) True or false: In 1988, bare-knuckle boxer John L. Sullivan had a match that lasted 75 rounds.

1123) True or false: Boxing didn't become a modern Olympic sport until 1964.

1124) In 1947, lightweight boxer Glen Smith died during a fight with Sam Baroudi. What happened the next year in a fight between Baroudi and Ezzard Charles?

1112. three, 1113. a 7-10 split, 1114. 4-6-7-10, 1115. no, 1116. left, 1117. c, 1118. right, 1119. lightweight, 1120. featherweight, 1121. true, 1122. true, 1123. false—it became one in 1904, 1124. Baroudi died from a punch that led to a brain hemorrhage

TOUGH TRIVIA CHALLENGE

1125) The first televised boxing match was between Joe Louis and Billy Conn in what year?

a) 1946
b) 1948
c) 1952
d) 1963

1126) True or false: Boxing legends Jake LaMotta and Rocky Graziano learned to fight in the same reform school.

1127) TRUE OR FALSE: SUGAR RAY ROBINSON WON 69 OF HIS 85 AMATEUR BOUTS BY KNOCKOUTS.

1128) One of the first closed-circuit television events was a broadcast of the Ken Overlin-Billy Soose middleweight championship fight in 1941. Where did the event take place?

a) Madison Square Garden
b) Carnegie Hall
c) Shea Stadium
d) Atlantic City Convention Hall

1129) True or false: All major title fights were frozen from 1941 to 1951 because of World War II.

1130) Gene Tunney beat Jack Dempsey for the world heavyweight championship in 1926. Who won when they fought again in 1927?

1131) IN WHAT ROUND DID JOE LOUIS KNOCK OUT MAX SCHMELING IN THEIR 1938 BOUT?

1132) The movie made about boxer James J. Braddock was called...

a) *A Cinderella Story*
b) *Cinderella Man*
c) *Punching Cinderella*
d) *Cinderella's Fight*

1133) Where was the 1938 Joe Louis-Max Schmeling ght held?

a) Madison Square Garden
b) Yankee Stadium
c) Shea Stadium
d) Staples Center

1134) George Forman became the oldest heavyweight champion ever at what age?

a) 36
b) 38
c) 42
d) 45

1135) True or false:

Idi Amin, future leader of Uganda, was a boxing champion.

1125. a, 1126. true, 1127. true, 1128. a, 1129. false—they were frozen until 1946, 1130. Tunney won again, 1131. first round, 1132. b, 1133. b, 1134. d, 1135. true

1136) A fish is named after which heavyweight champ?

1137) How long did Mike Tyson's 1995 bout against Peter McNeeley last?

a) Two hours, twelve minutes
b) One hour, twelve minutes
c) Twelve minutes
d) One minute, nine seconds

1138) What was Muhammad Ali's former name?

1139) Who fought title bouts against George Foreman and Larry Holmes and won both?

a) Evander Holyfield
b) Muhammad Ali
c) George Foreman
d) Sugar Ray Leonard

1140) TRUE OR FALSE: **JOE LOUIS WAS HEAVYWEIGHT CHAMPION FOR OVER 11 YEARS.**

1141) True or false: Rocky Marciano never lost a fight.

1142) What long-shot underdog shocked the boxing world by knocking out Mike Tyson, ending his run as heavyweight champ?

1143) True or false: **Heavyweight champ Jersey Joe Walcott was from New Jersey.**

1144) When Howard Cosell repeatedly screamed, "Down goes Frazier!" who had knocked Joe Frazier down?

1145) On July 2, 2011, the defeat of David Haye meant that all five of the world sanctioning bodies recognized as heavyweight champion one of two brothers with what last name?

1146) A FAMOUS PHOTO SHOWS MUHAMMAD ALI STANDING OVER AND TAUNTING WHAT EX-HEAVYWEIGHT CHAMP, WHOM HE HAD JUST KNOCKED OUT IN THE FIRST ROUND?

TOUGH TRIVIA CHALLENGE

1147)
In what state did that title fight take place?
a) Maine
b) Massachusetts
c) South Dakota
d) Wyoming

1136. Jack Dempsey 1137. d, 1138. Cassius Clay, 1139. a, 1140. true, 1141. true, 1142. James "Buster" Douglas, 1143. true, 1144. George Foreman, 1145. Klitschko (Vitali and Wladimir), 1146. Sonny Liston, 1147. a

1148) Who came first, Sugar Ray Leonard or Sugar Ray Robinson?

TOUGH TRIVIA CHALLENGE

1149) Which heavyweight champ was the father and namesake of a Pro Bowl linebacker for the Cowboys and 49ers?

1150) Sugar Ray Robinson's success prompted what musician to change his name to avoid confusion, using his middle name professionally?

1151) Is the band Sugar Ray named after Sugar Ray Leonard, Sugar Ray Robinson, or neither?

1152) WHICH WELTERWEIGHT CHAMPION IS A MEMBER OF THE CONGRESS OF THE PHILIPPINES?

1153) What boxer has won championships in four different weight classes, including the heavyweight championship in 2003?

1154) True or false: Boxer Roy Jones Jr. played eight games for the NBA's Charlotte Bobcats.

1155) TRUE OR FALSE: THE HOLIDAY BOXING DAY CELEBRATES THE FIRST PROFESSIONAL HEAVYWEIGHT FIGHT.

MATCH THE MOVIE ABOUT BOXING OR BOXERS TO THE STAR.

1156) *The Fighter*
1157) *Golden Boy*
1158) *The Great White Hope*
1159) *The Hurricane*
1160) *Million Dollar Baby*
1161) *On the Ropes*
1162) *The Quiet Man*
1163) *Raging Bull*
1164) *Rocky*
1165) *Somebody Up There Likes Me*

a) Robert DeNiro
b) William Holden
c) James Earl Jones
d) Paul Newman
e) Meg Ryan
f) Sylvester Stallone
g) Hilary Swank
h) Mark Wahlberg
i) Denzel Washington
j) John Wayne

MATCH THE BOXER TO HIS NICKNAME.

1166) The Ambling Alp
1167) The Bayonne Bleeder
1168) The Big Bear
1169) The Black Hercules
1170) The Brockton Blockbuster
1171) The Brown Bomber
1172) Butterbean
1173) The Cincinnati Cobra
1174) Gentleman Jim
1175) The Greatest
1176) Hurricane
1177) The Manassa Mauler
1178) The Raging Bull
1179) Slapsie Maxie
1180) Smokin' Joe
1181) The Wild Bull of the Pampas

a) Muhammad Ali
b) Primo Carnera
c) Rubin Carter
d) Ezzard Charles
e) Jim Corbett
f) Jack Dempsey
g) Eric Esch
h) Luis Firpo
i) Joe Frazier
j) Jake LaMotta
k) Sonny Liston
l) Joe Louis
m) Rocky Marciano
n) Ken Norton
o) Max Rosenbloom
p) Chuck Wepner

1148. Robinson, 1149. Ken Norton (Sr.), 1150. Ray Charles, 1151. Leonard, 1152. Manny Pacquiao, 1153. Roy Jones Jr., 1154. false, 1155. false, 1156. h, 1157. b, 1158. c, 1159. i, 1160. g, 1161. e, 1162. j, 1163. a, 1164. f, 1165. d, 1166. b, 1167. p, 1168. k, 1169. n, 1170. m, 1171. l, 1172. g, 1173. d, 1174. e, 1175. a, 1176. c, 1177. f, 1178. j, 1179. o, 1180. i, 1181. h

RUGBY

1182) True or false: Rugby is named after Sir. John Rugby of Derbyshire.

1183) In rugby, how many points do you score for a try?

1184) How many points do you score for a conversion kick?

1185) HOW MANY POINTS DO YOU SCORE FOR A PENALTY KICK?

1186) Which of the following is not a rugby position?

a) Flanker

b) Hooker

c) Eightman

d) Center

1187) In rugby, is the 5-meter line a solid line or a broken line?

1188) Which of these countries has not won a Rugby World Cup?

a) South Africa

b) England

c) Australia

d) United States

TOUGH TRIVIA CHALLENGE

1189) Is the 22-meter line a solid line or a broken line?

1190) When was the first Rugby World Cup played?

a) 1922

b) 1947

c) 1973

d) 1987

1191) Is the 10-meter line a solid line or a broken line?

1192) Is the 15-meter line a solid line or a broken line?

1193) HOW MANY PLAYERS FROM EACH TEAM GATHER IN A SCRUM?

1194) Should the ball hit the ground before it is kicked in a drop kick?

1195) True or false: **Numbers on rugby jerseys tell you what position is being played.**

1196) True or false: There are no kicking tees in rugby.

1182. false—it's named for an English town and school, 1183. five, 1184. two, 1185. three, 1186. d, 1187. broken, 1188. d, 1189. solid,
1190. d, 1191. solid, 1192. broken, 1193. eight, 1194. yes, 1195. true, 1196. false

..FISHING..

1197) TRUE OR FALSE: ARCHEOLOGISTS HAVE FOUND ANCIENT FISHHOOKS USED ON THE NILE.

1198) True or false:
The first sport-fishing handbook, *The Complete Angler*, was written in 1714.

1199) Ledger rods are also known as ________

a) Flat rods
b) Spinning rods
c) Feeder rods
d) Resting rods

TOUGH TRIVIA CHALLENGE

1200) Sections of a fishing rod are connected using ______.

a) Ferulles
b) Ferrises
c) Felanges
d) Falafels

1201) Most modern salt water rods divide into how many sections?

1202) HICH IS USUALLY SHORTER, A SURFCASTING ROD OR A BOAT ROD?

1203) True or false: **The largest number hook is the largest hook.**

1204) Which of the following is not one of the three main types of reels?

a) Spinning

b) Conventional

c) Rotational

d) Fly

1205) Which of the following is not one of the purposes of a boom?

a) To prevent tangles

b) To offer extra bait coverage

c) To help spread the trace away from the main line

d) To minimize excess line

1206) Which is better for surface fishing, a carp float or a loaded giant crystal float?

1197. true, 1198. false—it goes back to 1652, 1199. c, 1200. a, 1201. four, 1202. boat rod, 1203. false—the bigger the number the smaller the hook, 1204. c, 1205. d, 1206. carp float

1207) Which has more stretch, a mono line or a braded line?

1208) Which is better for tying together two lines of unequal diameter, a blood knot or a surgeon's knot?

TOUGH TRIVIA CHALLENGE

1209) Which of the following is not a kind of float?
a) Drift beater
b) Loafer
c) Big bear
d) Peacock

1210) WHICH IS BETTER FOR TYING A LINE THAT IS GOING TO BE CARRYING A WEIGHT. A RAPALA KNOT OR A SHOCKLEADER KNOT?

1211) True or false: Dog biscuits can be used for bait for carp fishing.

1212) True or false: Canned corn can be used as fishing bait.

1213) Peelers make good bait. These are crabs that...
a) Are very young
b) Are close to shedding their shells
c) Are missing legs
d) None of the above

1214) Are vertical jigs used in surface or deepwater shing?

1215) Which of the following is not a type of lure?

a) Ernie

b) Burt

c) Hornet spinner

d) Professor spoon

1216) WHICH OF THE FOLLOWING IS NOT A TYPE OF LURE?

A) ZALT ZAM

B) TAIMENLIPPA SPINNER SPOON

C) ACE LARGE FLAT FLIPPER

D) DEUCE DOUBLE FLAT SPINNER

1217) Which of the following is not a type of fishing fly?

a) Adam's Parachute

b) Dads' Demoiselle

c) Hare's-ear Nymph

d) Captive Contessa

TOUGH TRIVIA CHALLENGE

1218)
Who said, "Be patient and calm—for no one can catch a fish in anger"?
a) Aristotle
b) Herbert Hoover
c) James Cameron
d) Lady Gaga

1207. mono line, 1208. surgeon's knot, 1209. c, 1210. shockleader knot, 1211. true, 1212. true, 1213. a, 1214. deepwater, 1215. b, 1216. d, 1217. d, 1218. b

GOLF

1219) True or false: James II of Scotland banned golf.

1220) TRUE OR FALSE: THE FAMED ST. ANDREWS LINKS IN SCOTLAND WAS THE FIRST COURSE TO HAVE 18 HOLES.

1221) What is the maximum number of strokes for a hole in golf?

1222) True or false: If a golfer gets angry and breaks off the head of a club, he or she can replace it with a new club during the round.

1223) Who was the first foreign player to win the Masters?

a) Gary Player
b) Jack Nicklaus
c) Arnold Palmer
d) Mickey Wright

1224) True or false:

Golf was intended to stand for "Gentlemen only, Ladies forbidden."

1225) What was golf's World Cup called before its name was changed?

a) Canada Cup

b) North American Cup

c) British Cup

d) None of the above

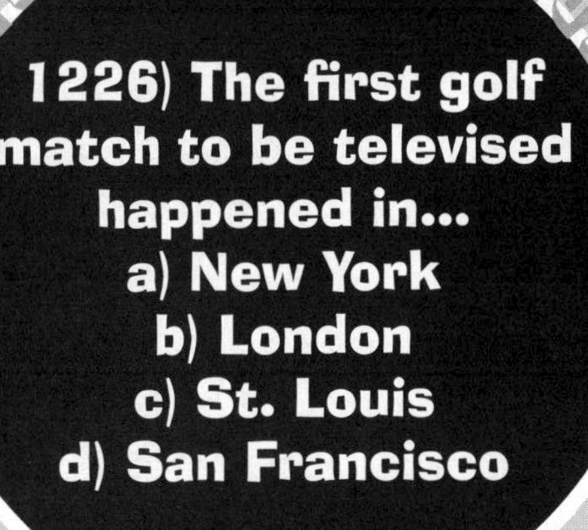

TOUGH TRIVIA CHALLENGE

1226) The first golf match to be televised happened in...

a) New York

b) London

c) St. Louis

d) San Francisco

1227) HOW MANY CLUBS IS A PLAYER ALLOWED TO CARRY IN A ROUND?

1228) Does an umbrella count as a club carried?

1229) What is the maximum number of balls a golfer may carry?

1230) Is there a time limit for a golfer to complete a stroke?

1231) If all balls are not on the green, who takes the next shot?

1219. true, 1220. false, 1221. there is no maximum—the ball must be holed, 1222. false, 1223. a, 1224. false—that's a popular myth, 1225. a, 1226. c, 1227. fourteen, 1228. no, 1229. there is no maximum number, 1230. no, 1231. the one farthest from the hole

1232) IF A BALL FALLS OFF A TEE BEFORE IT IS HIT, DOES IT COUNT AS A STROKE?

1233) What are your choices if the ball you hit accidentally bounces off another player, a caddie, or equipment?

1234) Is a sand trap rake considered a movable obstacle?

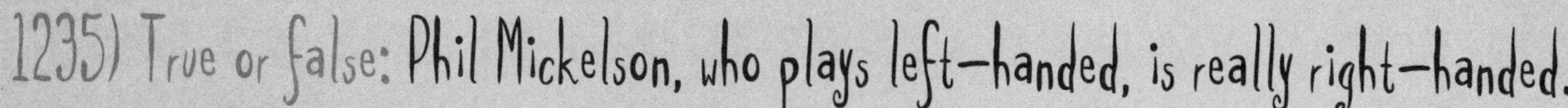

1235) True or false: Phil Mickelson, who plays left-handed, is really right-handed.

1236) How many dimples on a regulation golf ball?
a) 150-212
b) 250-289
c) 330-500
d) 550-600

TOUGH TRIVIA CHALLENGE

1237) The highest golf course in the world is in what country?
a) Tibet
b) Peru
c) Canada
d) Dubai

TOUGH TRIVIA CHALLENGE

1238) **True or false: Golf balls used to be packed with pebbles.**

1239) What month is national golf month?

1240) Which of the following is not a layer of a standard golf ball?

a) Polyurethane
b) Synthetic rubber
c) Surlyn
d) Foamcore

1241) Chi Chi Rodriguez was born where?

a) Guatamala
b) Chile
c) Puerto Rico
d) El Salvador

1242) What year did Tiger Woods turn pro?

a) 1990
b) 1996
c) 1999
d) 2001

1243) What college did Tiger Woods attend?

a) Stanford
b) Tufts
c) University of Maryland
d) University of Pennsylvania

1244) What golfer has a lemonade/iced tea drink named after him?

1232. no, 1233. you can either play it where it lies or take the shot over again, 1234. yes, 1235. true, 1236. c, 1237. b, 1238. false—with feathers, 1239. August, 1240. d, 1241. c, 1242. b, 1243. a, 1244. Arnold Palmer

1245) TIGER WOODS' REAL FIRST NAME IS:

A) EARL
B) ELDRICK
C) VINCENT
D) TIGER

TOUGH TRIVIA CHALLENGE

1246) What French golfer needed only a six on the par-4 18th hole to win the 1999 British Open, but hit shots into the rough and the water to register a seven and lose the tournament in a playoff?

1247) The Masters is played in what city?

1248) Who called golf a good walk spoiled?

a) Ben Hogan
b) Bobby Jones
c) Sam Snead
d) Mark Twain

1249) What color jacket do Masters champions wear?

1250) What is the term for scoring two below par on a hole?

1251) What is the term for scoring three below par on a hole?

1252) What is the term for scoring two above par on a hole?

1253) What is the term for scoring three above par on a hole?

1254) WHAT NAME IS GIVEN TO A GOLF ROUND WHERE THE PURSE IS DIVIDED NOT BASED ON THE NUMBER OF STROKES, BUT THE NUMBER OF HOLES WON?

1255) What golfer was nicknamed the Golden Bear?

1256) What golfer was nicknamed Super Mex?

1257) WHAT GOLFER IS MARRIED TO FORMER MAJOR LEAGUE BASEBALL PLAYER AND MANAGER RAY KNIGHT?

1258) The climax of the movie *Tin Cup* takes place at what golf tournament?

1259) What golfer was nicknamed the Shark?

1260) Who was the youngest player to make an LPGA cut, at age 16?

1261) Who has the most wins of any female golfer?

1245. b, 1246. Jean van de Velde, 1247. Augusta, Georgia, 1248. d, 1249. green, 1250. eagle, 1251. albatross, 1252. double bogey, 1253. triple bogey, 1254. skins game, 1255. Jack Nicklaus, 1256. Lee Trevino, 1257. Nancy Lopez, 1258. U.S. Open, 1259. Greg Norman, 1260. Michelle Wie, 1261. Annika Sorenstam

1262) Who has the most PGA Tour wins?

a) Ben Hogan
b) Jack Nicklaus
c) Sam Snead
d) Tiger Woods

1263) American men's golfers compete with European golfers every other year for what trophy?

1264) What is the equivalent trophy for a similar competition among women's golfers?

1265) How many tournament wins does it take to earn a lifetime exemption for the PGA Tour?

a) 10
b) 15
c) 20
d) 25

1266) Who won a record 18 PGA Tour events in a single year?

a) Tommy Bolt
b) Ben Hogan
c) Byron Nelson
d) Tiger Woods

1267) TRUE OR FALSE: JACK NICKLAUS HOLDS OR SHARES THE RECORD FOR MOST WINS IN THE MASTERS, THE U.S. OPEN, THE BRITISH OPEN, AND THE PGA CHAMPIONSHIP

BADMINTON

1268) Is badminton an Olympic sport?

1269) True or false: badminton was developed in British India.

TOUGH TRIVIA CHALLENGE

1270) Which was not a founding member of the International Badminton Federation?

a) The Netherlands

b) New Zealand

c) Iceland

d) Denmark

1271) True or false: Badminton was once known as Goona.

1272) True or false: Badminton is named after Badminton House in Gloucestershire.

1273) IS A BADMINTON NET HIGHER OR LOWER THAN FIVE FEET AT THE EDGES?

1274) How long is a full badminton court?

a) 16 ft.

b) 18 ft.

c) 20 ft.

d) 22 ft.

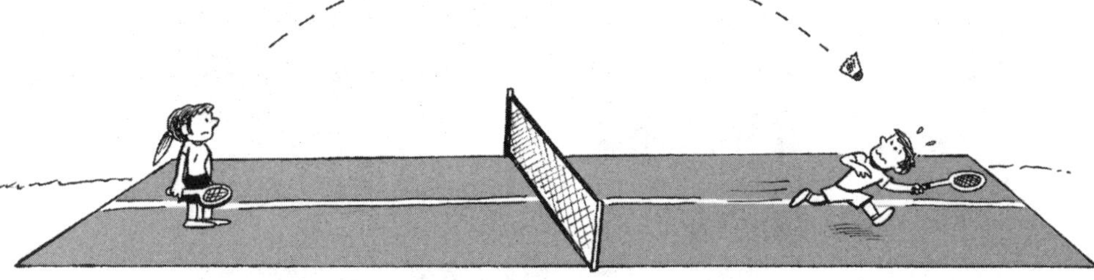

1262. c, 1263. Ryder Cup, 1264. Solheim Cup, 1265. c, 1266. c, 1267. false (3 British Open championships ties him for 11th), 1268. yes, 1269. true, 1270. c, 1271. false—poona, 1272. true, 1273. higher, 1274. c

TOUGH TRIVIA CHALLENGE

1275) How many overlapping feathers on a badminton shuttlecock?

1276) Is the serving side the only side that can score points in badminton?

1277) How many points does a badminton game go up to?

1278) In badminton, do you need a two-point lead to win a game?

1279) How many times is a shuttlecock allowed to bounce and still be playable.

1280) HOW MANY CHANCES IS A BADMINTON SERVER ALLOWED TO TRY TO GET THE SHUTTLECOCK OVER THE NET.

VOLLEYBALL

1281) True or false: **An early version of volleyball was called mintonette.**

1282) What was the first country besides the U.S. to embrace volleyball?

a) France
b) Mexico
c) Canada
d) England

1283) In what year was beach volleyball added to the Olympics?

a) 1984
b) 1988
c) 1992
d) 1996

1284) Is volleyball a sport in the Paralympics?

1285) HOW MANY PLAYERS ON EACH SIDE IN A VOLLEYBALL GAME?

1286) True or false: *According to a rule change in 2000, a ball is out of play if it hits the net, even if it goes over.*

1275. sixteen, 1276. no, 1277. twenty-one, 1278. yes, 1279. zero, 1280. one, 1281. true, 1282. d, 1283. d, 1284. yes, 1285. six, 1286. false

CRICKET

1287) How many players needed for a cricket team?

a) 7
b) 9
c) 11
d) 13

1288) True or false: The player with the bat in cricket is known as the batsman.

1289) In "Test Cricket"—the standard form of the game—how many innings does each team play?

a) 2
b) 4
c) 6
d) 8

1290) TRUE OR FALSE: THERE IS A FIVE-DAY LIMIT FOR A GAME OF TEST CRICKET.

1291) How many outs are needed to end an inning in cricket?

a) 3
b) 5
c) 7
d) 10

1292) True or false: in a 5-day cricket game, if the team that batted first is up by more than 200 runs, they can let the second team take the top of the next inning.

TOUGH TRIVIA CHALLENGE

1293) Is a cricket ball's leather covering thicker or thinner than a baseball's?

1294) True or false: A cricket bat is flat on both sides.

1295) How many wickets in a cricket match?

1296) How many stumps per wicket in cricket?

TOUGH TRIVIA CHALLENGE

1297) TRUE OR FALSE: THE FIRST INTERNATIONAL CRICKET GAME WAS BETWEEN ENGLAND AND FRANCE.

1298) True or false: Cricket was invented by a group of college students in 1957.

1299) What was the first year that a national cricket champion was declared in England?

a) 1890
b) 1922
c) 1943
d) 1957

1300) True or false: The governing body in the cricket world is known as Her Majesties Royal Cricket Association and Loyal Order of Batsmen.

1287. c, 1288. true, 1289. a, 1290. true, 1291. d, 1292. true, 1293. thicker, 1294. false, 1295. two, 1296. three, 1297. false—it was between the U.S. and Canada in 1844, 1298. false—no one knows when it was created, 1299. a, 1300. false—it's just the International Cricket Counsil

CYCLING

1301) The predecessors to bicycles were nicknamed what?

a) Rollers
b) Dashers
c) Wheelers
d) Runners

1302) True or False: A hardtail bike is one with no rear suspension.

1303) True or False: The Tour de France is held once every four years.

1304) True or False: Lance Armstrong finished every Tour de France he started.

1305) Which of the following is not the name of a top bicycle company?

a) Bianchi
b) Colnago
c) Cinzano
d) Pinarello

1306) Which of the following is not a common material for bike frames?

a) Aluminum
b) Steel
c) Tin
d) Carbon

1307) WHAT IS EDDY MERCKX'S NICKNAME?

A) THE SPOKE

B) THE CANNIBAL

C) MOUNTAIN MAN

D) THE TRAIN

1308) Lance Armstrong was only the second American to win the Tour de France. Who was the first?

a) Gary Fisher

b) Greg LeMond

c) Eric Heiden

d) David Blase

1309) Breaking Away is based on an annual Indiana University bike race. What is its name?

a) Tour de Indiana

b) Little 500

c) Hilly Hundred

d) Cream and Crimson

1301. d, 1302. true, 1303. false—it's held every year, 1304. false, 1305. c, 1306. c, 1307. b, 1308. b, 1309. b

1310) The leader's jersey in the Giro d'Italia is what color?

a) Pink
b) Purple
c) Yellow
d) Green

1311) On the typical bike, to get the highest pedal cadence, you'll shift to what front/rear sprocket combination?

a) Largest/largest
b) Largest/smallest
c) Smallest/smallest
d) Smallest/largest

MATCH THE JERSEY COLOR TO ITS TOUR DE FRANCE SIGNIFICANCE:

1312) YELLOW
1313) GREEN
1314) POLKA DOT
1315) WHITE

A. BEST YOUNG RIDER
B. KING OF THE MOUNTAINS
C. POINTS LEADER
D. RACE LEADER

1316) True or False: In a team time trial race, a team's finishing time is determined by the first team member to cross the finish line.

1317) In order to draft in a crosswind, cyclist use what kind of formation?

a) Echelon
b) Pace line
c) Flying Wedge
d) Spartacus

• • SKATEBOARDING • •

1318) In a bluntslide, is the tail side or the nose on a ledge?

1319) In a slob air move, do you grab the board with your front hand or your back hand?

1320) IN AN INDY AIR MOVE, DO YOU GRAB THE BOARD WITH YOUR FRONT HAND OR YOUR BACK HAND?

1321) True or false: In a frontside pop shuvit, you kick the tail of the board 180 degrees frontside.

1322) With a drop in, do you enter tranny from a tail stall or a wheelie?

1323) With a no comply, do you scoop and lift the board with your front foot or rear foot?

1310. a, 1311. d, 1312. d, 1313. c, 1314. b, 1315. a, 1316. false, 1317. a, 1318. tail side, 1319. front hand, 1320. back hand, 1321. true, 1322. tail stall, 1323. rear foot

1324) In a nose manual, do you wheelie on the front or the back wheels?

1325) In a Smith grind, are the front wheels or the back wheels below the rail?

1326) With a sweeper, do you footplant the rear foot or the front foot with a frontside sweep?

1327) TRUE OR FALSE: THE "DEATH BOX" REFERS TO THE VERY BOTTOM OF A SWIMMING POOL.

1328) What is another name for a kinked rail?

a) Dragon rail
b) Demon rail
c) Daniel's rail
d) Dummy rail

TOUGH TRIVIA CHALLENGE

1329) How many non-uniform pockets, at minimum, does a bowl have to have to be called an amoeba bowl?

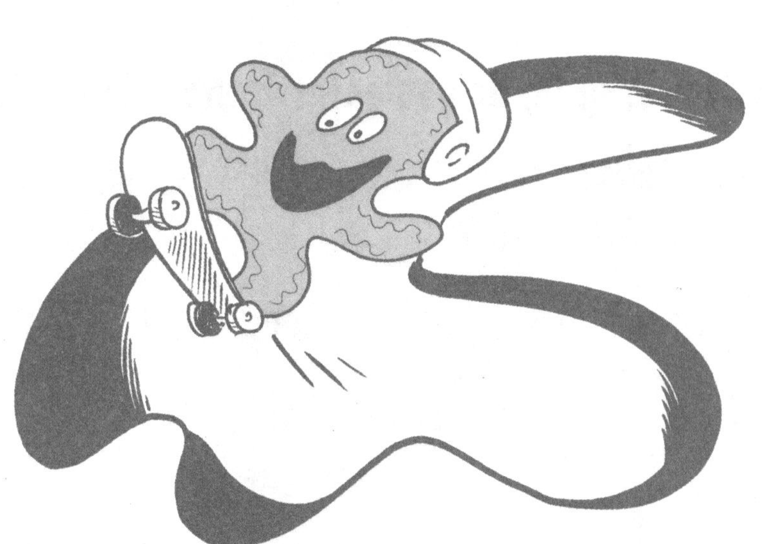

1330) Is a manual pad short and wide or long and thin?

1331) Does a volcano have a flat top or a curved top?

1332) DOES A SPEED WALL HAVE A TALL VERTICAL EXTENSION OR A SHORT VERTICAL EXTENSION?

1333) True or false: **Slalom boards are usually 1- times the size of a street board.**

1334) On a concave board, are the edges higher or lower than the center?

1335) If someone is right-footed, is the toe side the right side or the left side?

TOUGH TRIVIA CHALLENGE

1336)
True or false: The hardness of skateboard wheels is measured in megameters.

1337) Do goofy footers ride with the left foot forward or the right foot?

1338) Which relies on the friction of the grip tape to move, a sweep or a scoop?

1339) True or false: **For a time, skateboards were banned in Norway.**

1324. front, 1325. front, 1326. rear foot, 1327. false—it's the space just under the coping, 1328. a, 1329. four, 1330. short and wide, 1331. flat top, 1332. tall, 1333. false, 1334. higher, 1335. right side, 1336. false—durometers, 1337. right foot, 1338. scoop, 1339. true

1340) True or false: Drifters are also called power slides.

1341) IN A FAKIE, WHICH IS BACKWARD, YOUR BOARD, YOUR BODY, OR BOTH?

1342) A spacewalk combines a manual with a

a) Tic-tac
b) Bric-a-brac
c) Hard tack
d) Fric-n-frac

1343) How many rotates in a 900?

1344) How many rotations in a 1080?

1345) True or false: In most landings, your lead foot should be at about the middle of the board.

1346) True or false: Tony Hawk was born Switzerland.

1347) True or false: Tony Hawk was the first skater to land a 900.

1348) True or false: Tony Hawk's Big Spin was a ride created for Six Flags parks.

1349) What was the name of Tony Hawk's 2002-launched tour?

a) Big Bad Huck Finn
b) Boom Boom HuckJam
c) Bim Bam BoomJam
d) Born Bad BigJam

1350) Complete the title of the 1989 skateboarding movie *Gleaming the* ________.

1351) True or false: There's a skateboard move called an ollie north.

1352) When were polyurethane wheels developed?

a) 1950s
b) 1960s
c) 1970s
d) 1980s

1353) HOW WIDE ARE MOST STREET BOARDS?

A) 14–26 INCHES
B) 26–28 INCHES
C) 28–30 INCHES
D) 30–32 INCHES

1340. true, 1341. both, 1342. a, 1343. two and a half, 1344. three, 1345. false—it should be over the baseplate bolts, 1346. false, 1347. true, 1348. true, 1349. b, 1350. Cube, 1351. true, 1352. c, 1353. d

CHAPTER 3

Game Time

• BOARD & CARD GAMES •

TOUGH TRIVIA CHALLENGE

1354) On early Egyptian playing cards, which was not a symbol.

a) Cups
b) Coins
c) Swords
d) Crowns

1355) Which county added the joker to the playing card deck?

1356) On a Battleship game board, what is the highest letter?

1357) TRUE OR FALSE: BATTLESHIP WAS ORIGINALLY A PENCIL-AND-PAPER GAME CALLED BROADSIDES: THE GAME OF NAVAL STRATEGY.

1358) How many peg spaces are there in Battleship's submarine piece?

1359) How many peg spaces are there in a Battleship's aircraft carrier piece?

1354. d, 1355. U.S.A., 1356. j, 1357. true, 1358. three, 1359. five

1360) True or false: The 2010 updated version of Battleship includes islands.

1361) True or false: Blue box Boggle contains the same number of Ks as yellow box Boggle.

1362) True or false: Each side of a Boggle cube contains only one letter.

1363) True or false: It's possible to form the word Inconsequentially in Boggle.

1364) How many cube slots are there in a standard game of Boggle

1365) HOW MANY CUBES IN TRAVEL BOGGLE?

1366) True or false: There was a game called Body Boggle.

1367) True or false: There was a TV game show version of Boggle.

1368) True or false: Boggle was created by the same person who created Scrabble.

1369) HOW MANY SPACES ARE THERE ON THE CANDY LAND BOARD?

A) 72
B) 91
C) 112
D) 134

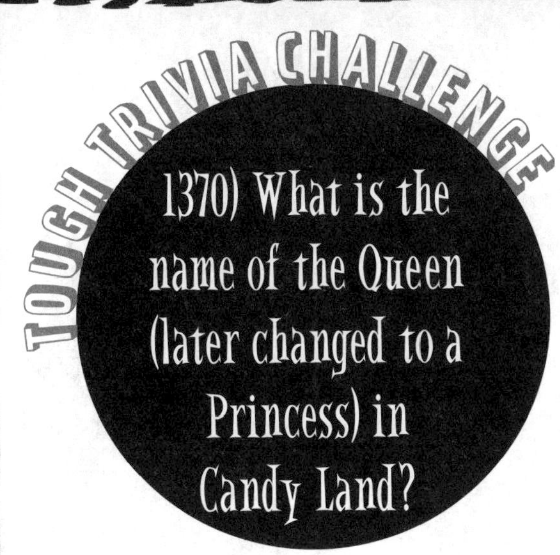

1371) True or false: In the 2004 update of Candy Land, the last space became a rainbow space rather than a specic color.

1372) True or false: Candy Land was developed while its creator was recovering from polio.

1373) True or false: The first version of Candy Land had no characters on the board.

1374) What was the Molasses Swamp changed to in the 2002 edition of Candy Land?

1375) True or false: Plumpy was removed from the 2002 edition of Candy Land.

1376) Which of the following was not a Candy Land spin-off:

a) Candy Land: Winnie-the-Pooh edition
b) Candy Land: VCR Board Game
c) Candy Land: Eat-n-Play Edition
d) Candy Land Castle Game

1377) True or false: The Sugar Gang was featured on pre-1982 versions of Candy Land.

1378) WHICH OF THE FOLLOWING IS NOT A KIND OF MILLE BORNES CARD?

A) HAZARD
B) REMEDY
C) BONUS
D) SAFETY

1360. true, 1361. false, 1362. false—there's a Qu side, 1363. true, 1364. sixteen, 1365. sixteen, 1366. true, 1367. true, 1368. false, 1369. d, 1370. Queen Frostine, 1371. true, 1372. true, 1373. true, 1374. Chocolate Swamp, 1375. true, 1376. c, 1377. false, 1378. c

1379) Which of the following is not a Mille Bornes hazard?
a) Flat tire
b) Out of gas
c) Accident
d) Broken window

TOUGH TRIVIA CHALLENGE

1380) Which of the following is not the value of a Distance card in Mille Bornes?
a) 25 kilometers
b) 50 kilometers
c) 150 kilometers
d) 200 kilometers

1381) Which of the following is not a Mille Bornes safety card?
a) Driving Ace
b) Evasive Maneuvers
c) Puncture Proof
d) Extra Tank

1382) How many cards are dealt to each player at the start of Mille Bornes?

1383) TRUE OR FALSE: OTHELLO WAS FORMERLY SOLD UNDER THE NAME REVERSI.

1384) Does a game of Othello start with four pieces in the center of the board or at the corners?

1385) In Othello, who makes the first move, light or dark?

1386) In Othello, can pieces placed in the corners be flipped?

1387) What does the name of the popular game Pente mean in Greek?

a) Pants
b) Five
c) Shape
d) People

1388) WHEN DID THE POKÉMON TRADING CARD GAME FIRST ENTER THE JAPANESE MARKET?

A) 1976
B) 1986
C) 1996
D) 2001

1389) How many cards do you draw at the begining of a basic game of Pokémon?

1390) How many pawns does each player get in a game of Sorry!

1391) What two numbers, between 1 and 12, are not featured on the cards in a game of Sorry!?

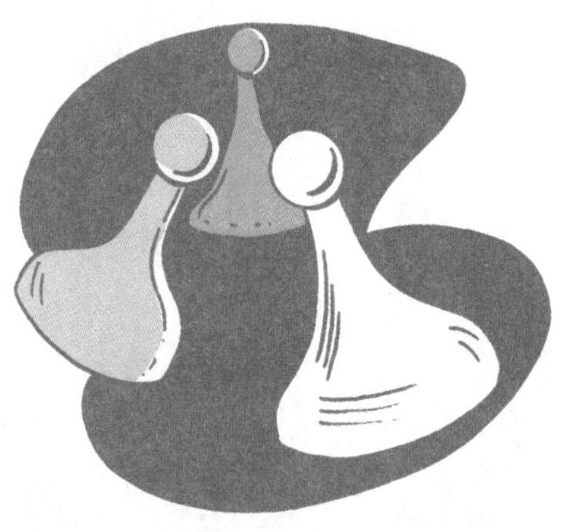

1392) What is your other choice, besides moving ten spaces forward, when you draw a ten card in Sorry!

1379. d, 1380. c, 1381. b, 1382. six, 1383. true, 1384. center of the board, 1385. dark, 1386. no, 1387. b, 1388. c, 1389. seven, 1390. four, 1391. six and nine, 1392. you can move back one space

1393) Of each player's 40 pieces in Stratego, how many are bombs?

1394) Of each player's 40 pieces in Stratego, how many are spies?

1395) How many spaces wide is a Stratego board?

1396) How many flags does each Stratego player have?

1397) In Stratego, what is higher ranked, a Colonel or a Major?

1398) IN STRATEGO, WHAT IS HIGHER RANKED, A MINER OR A LIEUTENANT?

1399) In Stratego, what is higher ranked, a Captain or a Scout?

1400) Uno was invented in...

a) 1771
b) 1849
c) 1901
d) 1971

TOUGH TRIVIA CHALLENGE

1401) The familiar version of Stratego was first published where?

a) England
b) France
c) The Netherlands
d) Italy

1402) True of false: There is one Draw Three card in a standard Uno game.

1403) Which is not the color of an Uno card?

a) Red
b) Orange
c) Green
d) Blue

1404) True or false: Uno was created by the same people who developed the Pizzeria Uno restaurant chain.

Match the Trivial Pursuit category to its color:

1405) Geography	a) Pink
1406) Entertainment	b) Blue
1407) Arts & Literature	c) Green
1408) Science and Nature	d) Orange
1409) Sports & Leisure	e) Brown
1410) History	f) Yellow

1411) True or false: Yahtzee is based on a similar game called Yacht.

1412) How many points do you get for a large straight in Yahtzee?

1413) How many points do you need to score in the upper section of Yahtzee in order to get a bonus?

1393. six, 1394. one, 1395. ten, 1396. one, 1397. colonel, 1398. lieutenant, 1399. captain, 1400. d, 1401. c, 1402. false, 1403. b, 1404. false, 1405. b, 1406. a, 1407. e, 1408. c, 1409. d, 1410. f, 1411. true, 1412. forty, 1413. sixty-three

1414) What is technically the minimum Yahtzee score?

TOUGH TRIVIA CHALLENGE

1416) What is the maximum Yahtzee score (without bonuses)?

1415) THE ODDS OF ROLLING FIVE OF A KIND ON YOUR FIRST YAHTZEE ROLE IS....

A) 1 IN 522
B) 1 IN 1296
C) 1 IN 2500
D) 1 IN 3725

1417) True or false: Yahtzee has been played on *Family Guy* and *South Park*.

1418) How many different dice sizes are there in Challenge Yahtzee?

1419) Which is a board game, Showdown Yahtzee or Triple Yahtzee?

1420) How many pair of pants in a game of Ants in the Pants?

1421) How many monkeys do you need to hook together to win a game of Barrel of Monkeys?

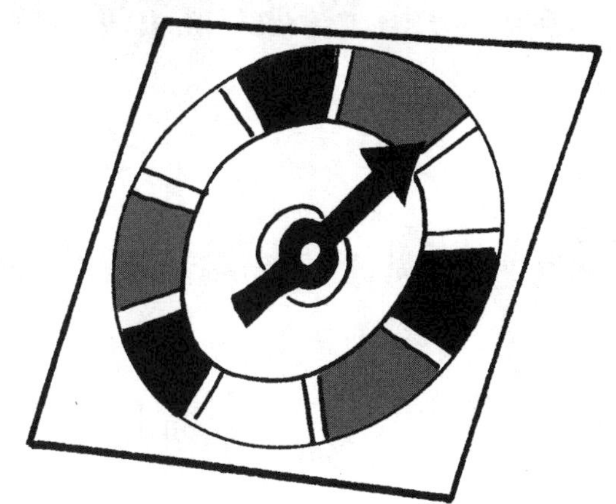

1422) What tells you how many spaces to move in Chutes and Ladders?

a) Dice

b) Tiles

c) A spinner

d) None of the above

1423) True or false: Chutes and Ladders is based on an Indian game called Snakes and Ladders.

1424) True or false: The spaces in Chutes and Ladders are lettered.

1425) What happens if you role a six in Chutes and Ladders?

1426) How many pieces are there in a total Cootie?

1427) True or false: The creator of Cootie originally designed the bug as a fishing lure.

1428) HOW MANY BUCKETS IN A GAME OF HI HO CHERRY O?

1414. five—if you put five ones in Chance and 0s in every other box, 1415. b, 1416. 375, 1417. True, 1418. two, 1419. Showdown Yahtzee, 1420. one, 1421. twelve, 1422. c, 1423. true, 1424. false—they're numbered, 1425. you move and then roll again, 1426. thirteen, 1427. true, 1428. four

1429) How many blocks in a game of Jenga?

a) 48 b) 54 c) 62 d) 72

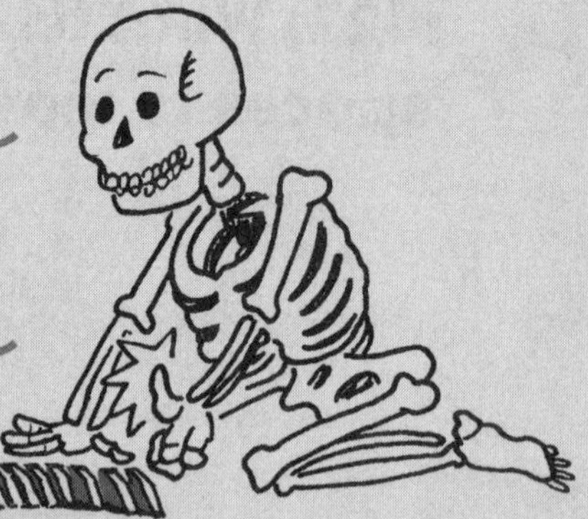

1430) True or false: Canasta is played with 152 cards.

1431) How many tiles in a standard set of dominoes?

a) 24

b) 28

c) 32

d) 36

1432) What is the highest number of dots on one standard domino?

1433) True or false: Dominoes are sometimes called bones.

1434) True or false: Domino spots are sometimes called Peps.

POINK!

GUT BUSTERS

1435) True or false: Chinese dominoes are different from European dominoes.

1436) In dominoes, what is a trey?

1437) OW MANY TILES IN A DOUBLE SIX SET OF DOMINOES?

1438) True or false: More than 700,000 dominoes were set up and toppled by one person in Singapore in 2003.

1439) True or false: A German man stacked more than 700 dominoes in 2003.

1440) TRUE OR FALSE: EUCRE IS PLAYED WITH 32 CARDS.

TOUGH TRIVIA CHALLENGE

1441) Which of the following is not a dominoes variation:

a) Blind Hughie
b) Fight Right
c) Matador
d) Sebastopol

1442) What is the highest hand in poker (with no wild cards)?

1443) What beats paper in Rock Paper Scissors?

1444) True or false: Sales of Twister took off after it was played on the *Tonight Show*.

1445) Which of the following games is not played by Bill and Ted against Death in Bill & Ted's Bogus Journey?

a) Twister
b) Battleship
c) Candy Land
d) Electronic football

1429. b, 1430. false—108, 1431. b, 1432. twelve, 1433. true, 1434. false—pips, 1435. true, 1436. a domino with three dots on at least one end, 1437. twenty-eight, 1438. false—it was 300,000, 1439. true, 1440. false—24, 1441. b, 1442. royal flush, 1443. scissors, 1444. true, 1445. c

1446) How many people can play Rock'em Sock'em Robots at one time?

1447) In Rock'em Sock'em Robots, one robot is blue. What color is the other?

1448) How many buttons are on each side of Rock'em Sock'em Robots?

1449) WHAT COLOR IS THE BOXING PLATFORM IN ROCK'EM SOCK'EM ROBOTS?

1450) True or false: In England, Rock'em Sock'em Robots was called Raving Bonkers.

1451) True or false: In Australia, Rock'em Sock'em Robots was called Pound 'em Buddies.

1452) True or false: Bingo is based on a game called Beano, where dry beans were used as markers.

1453) True or false: The N column in Bingo features numbers from 40-55.

1454) TRUE OR FALSE: THE LAST NUMBER IN BINGO IS 75.

1455) What is the person who announces letters and numbers in a Bingo game called?

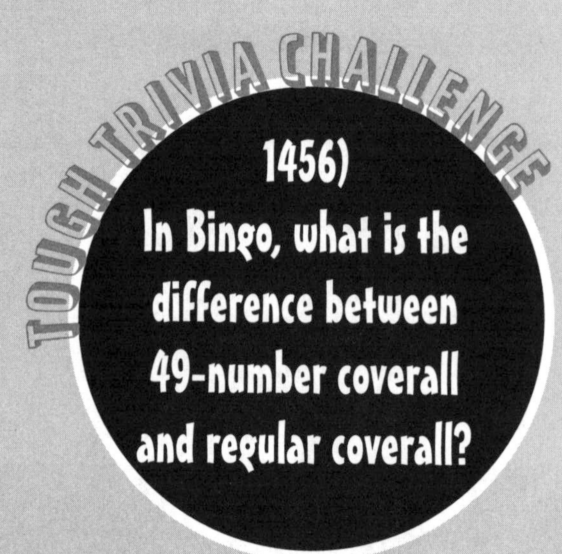

1457) What country is Rory's Story Cubes creator Rory O'Connor from?

1458) True or false: Rory O'Connor originally put his images on a Rubik's Cube.

1459) What is each story in a game of Rory's Story Cubes supposed to start with?

1460) In what country was the Settlers of Catan first published?

1461) Are players ever eliminated in the Settlers of Catan?

1462) WHAT IS CATAN?

A) AN ISLAND
B) A CONTINENT
C) A PLANET
D) A CAVERN

1463) What shape are the tiles in the Settlers of Catan?

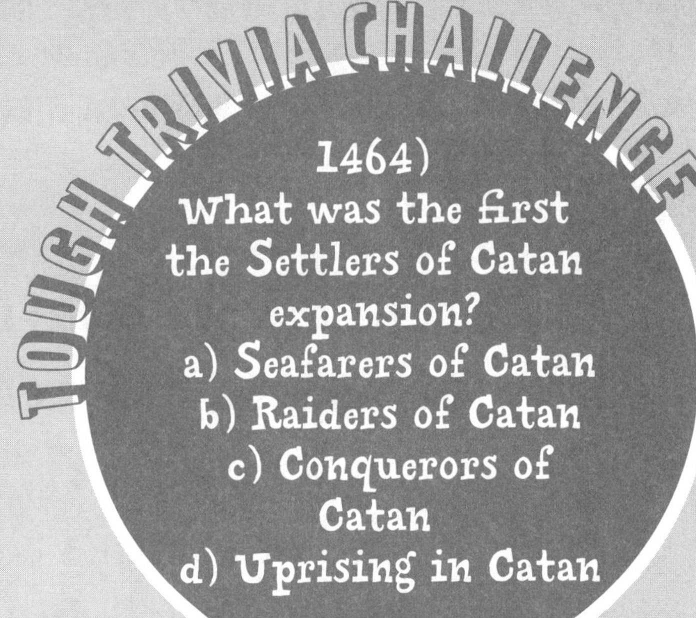

1465) Which of the following is not a resource in the Settlers of Catan?

a) **Brick**
b) **Lumber**
c) **Grain**
d) **Gold**

1466) How many dice are rolled in the Settlers of Catan?

1467) How many victory points do you need to win a game of the Settlers of Catan?

1446. two, 1447. red, 1448. two, 1449. yellow 1450. true, 1451. false, 1452. true, 1453. false, 1454. true, 1455. the caller, 1456. in 49-number coverall, if 49 numbers are called without a Bingo, nobody wins, 1457. Ireland, 1458. true, 1459. Once upon a time…, 1460. Germany, 1461. no, 1462. a, 1463. hexagon, 1464. a, 1465. d, 1466. two, 1467. ten

1468) True or false: There has been a novel published that is set on the island of Catan.

1469) Which of the following is not a Catan Histories game?

a) Settlers of the Stone Age
b) Struggle for Rome
c) Settlers of America
d) Settlers Down Under

1470) Does Dominion primarily use cards or dice?

1471) Which Dominion expansion came first, Prosperity or Seaside?

1472) Is Dominion: Intrigue a standalone game?

1473) Which is not a card from the Dominion base game?

a) Moneylender
b) Throne Room
c) Witch
d) Layabout

1474) Which is not a card from the Dominion: Intrigue game?

a) Baron
b) Saboteur
c) Wildebeast
d) Shanty Town

1475) WHICH IS NOT A CARD FROM THE DOMINION: SEASIDE GAME?

A) BAZAAR
B) TREASURE MAP
C) BERZERKER
D) PEARL DIVER

1476) Which is not a card from the Dominion: Alchemy game?

a) Apprentice
b) Poison
c) Scrying Pool
d) Philospher's Stone

1477) Which is not a card from the Dominion: Prosperity game?

a) Bishop
b) Counting House
c) Windfall
d) Royal Seal

1478) Which is not a card from the Dominion: Cornucopia game?

a) Farming Village
b) Fortune Teller
c) Horn of Plenty
d) Governor's Feast

1468. true, 1469. d, 1470. cards, 1471. seaside, 1472. yes, 1473. d, 1474. c, 1475. c, 1476. b, 1477. c, 1478. d

1479) Which is not a card from the Dominion: Hinterlands game?

a) Cartographer
b) Protector
c) Haggler
d) Spice Merchant

1480) IN TICKET TO RIDE, WHAT COLOR IS THE CABOOSE CARD?

1481) In Ticket to Ride, what color is the boxcar?

1482) True or false: All of the locations in the basic Ticket to Ride game are in the United States.

1483) In Ticket to Ride, how many extra points do you get for completing the longest route?

1484) True or false: Ticket to Ride: Europe includes Ferry routes.

1485) What year in the U.S.A. was featured in the second Ticket to Ride expansion?

a) 1874
b) 1910
c) 1922
d) 1941

1486) True or false: There's a board game called Hedbanz Game.

1487) Is the game Landslide about natural disasters or presidential politics?

1488) WAS THE GAME GIRL TALK FIRST RELEASED IN THE 1980S OR THE 1990S?

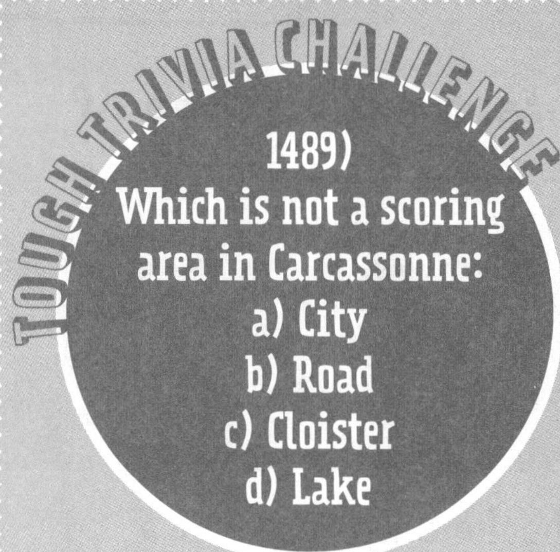

1489) Which is not a scoring area in Carcassonne:
a) City
b) Road
c) Cloister
d) Lake

1490) HOW MANY FOLLOWERS DOES EACH PLAYER HAVE IN CARCASSONNE?

1491) Which is not a Carcassonne expansion?
a) Carcassonne—Traders and Builders
b) Carcassonne—Thieves and Cutthroats
c) Carcassonne—The Tower
d) Carcassonne—Abbey and Mayor

1492) True or false: Ralph Querfurth won the world Carcassonne championship at least two times (as of this publication).

1493) How many ages make up a game of 7 Wonders?

1494) HOW MANY DISEASES HAVE BROKEN OUT IN THE WORLD IN A BASIC GAME OF PANDEMIC?

1495) True or false: You can win a game of Wits and Wagers without knowing the answer to a single question.

1496) Which of the following is not a LEGO game:
a) Heroica
b) Pirate Plank
c) Terror Ship
d) Ramses Return

1497) Is Dixit a card or dice game?

1498) What level do you need to get to in order to win a basic game of Munchkin?

1479. b, 1480. green, 1481. yellow, 1482. false, 1483. ten, 1484. true, 1485. b, 1486. true, 1487. presidential politics, 1488. 1980s, 1489. d, 1490. seven, 1491. b, 1492. false—he's won it at least four times, 1493. three, 1494. four, 1495. true, 1496. c, 1497. card, 1498. ten

1499) How many white checkers start out a game of Backgammon in white's home board?

1500) How many white checkers start out a game of Backgammon in red's home board?

1501) How many of each color checkers are used in a game of Backgammon?

1502) WHAT IS THE SECOND LOWEST NUMBER ON A BACKGAMMON DOUBLING CUBE?

1503) What is the highest number on a Backgammon doubling cube?

1504) If the loser of a game of Backgammon still has a checker in the winner's home board, is that a gammon or a backgammon?

1505) Can a Backgammon player pass his or her turn?

1506) True or false: In Backgammon, if you can only play one number, you have to use the highest usable dice role.

1507) TRUE OR FALSE: IN BACKGAMMON, YOU CAN ONLY HAVE FIVE CHECKERS ON A POINT.

1508) True or false: In Backgammon, if you have six consecutive points with at least two checkers of your color on each it's called a bammo.

1509) True or false: In Backgammon, if your role lands on a checker, both dice are to be rerolled.

1510) Was Apples to Apples introduced in the 1990s or the 2000s?

1511) Are the players in Apples to Apples dealt green apple cards or red apple cards?

1512) Are there more red or green cards in Apples to Apples?

1513) True or false: There is a Jewish edition of Apples to Apples.

1514) True or false: There is an HBO edition of Apples to Apples.

1499. five, 1500. two, 1501. fifteen, 1502. four, 1503. sixty-four, 1504. backgammon, 1505. no, 1506. true, 1507. false, 1508. false—it's called a prime, 1509. true, 1510. 1990s, 1511. red, 1512. red, 1513. true, 1514. false

1515) TRUE OR FALSE: **THERE IS A BIBLE EDITION OF APPLES TO APPLES**

1516) True or false: There is a Disney edition of Apples to Apples.

1517) True or false: **Sour Apples to Apples contains apple dice.**

1518) Was Pictionary launched in the 1980s or the 1990s?

1519) WHAT DOES AN O MEAN ON A PICTIONARY SPACE?

1520) *What does an A mean on a Pictionary space?*

1521) What does AP on a Pictionary space mean?

1522) True or false: **You are not permitted to use numbers in a Pictionary drawing.**

1523) HOW MUCH TIME DOES IT TAKE A PICTIONARY TIMER TO RUN OUT?

1524) What color Cranium spaces let players choose a category?

1525) Which of the following is not a Cranium category?

a) Word Worm

b) Fact Junkie

c) Creative Cat

d) Star Performer

1526) What is the Cranium version for kids called?

1527) TRUE OR FALSE: THERE'S A GAME CALLED CRANIUM KABOOKII.

1528) True or false: There's a game called Cranium Brainbuster.

1529) True or false: **There's a game called Cranium Scribblish.**

TOUGH TRIVIA CHALLENGE

1530) The game Arkham Horror is set in a town in what state?

a) Pennsylvania

b) Massachusetts

c) Michigan

d) North Carolina

1531) Arkham Horror is based on the writings of...

a) Edgar Allan Poe

b) H.P. Lovecraft

c) H.G. Wells

d) Jules Verne

1515. true, 1516. true, 1517. false—it has a spinning apple, 1518. 1980s, 1519. object, 1520. action, 1521. all play, 1522. true, 1523. one minute, 1524. purple, 1525. b—the category is Data Head, 1526. Cadoo, 1527. true, 1528. false, 1529. true, 1530. b, 1531. b

1532) IS ARKHAM HORROR A COMPETITIVE OR COOPERATIVE GAME?

1533) True or false: The game Puerto Rico was created in Puerto Rico.

1534) How many players can play Chinese Checkers at one time?

1535) How many points do you get in Balderdash if you guess the correct definition.

1536) How many points do you get in Balderdash if someone thinks your incorrect definition is correct?

1537) The game Axis and Allies is set during what war?

1538) How many players can play Guess Who? at one time?

1539) Has there been a TV game show based on Taboo?

1540) WHICH OF THE FOLLOWING OBJECTS IS NOT A PART OF MOUSE TRAP?

A) A BATHTUB
B) A BUCKET
C) A BOOT
D) AN ANVIL

1541) True or false: **Cheese pieces were added to Mouse Trap in the 1970s.**

1542) What does it say on a Mouse Trap space that would require a player to start operating the trap?

TOUGH TRIVIA CHALLENGE

1543) What do you have to do in order to play a shorter game of Scene It?

1544) Which comes first in Mouse Trap, the diver or the marble?

1545) True or false: Scene It was originally played with Super 8 movie film.

1546) Which is not an edition of Scene It:

a) *James Bond* edition

b) Turner Classic Movies edition

c) Sitcom edition

d) *Pirates of the Caribbean* edition

1547) Which is not an edition of Scene It:

a) *Glee* edition

b) *Seinfeld* edition

c) *Friends* edition

d) *Pretty Little Liars* edition

1532. cooperative, 1533. false—in Germany, 1534. six, 1535. three, 1536. one, 1537. World War II, 1538. two, 1539. yes, 1540. d, 1541. true, 1542. Turn Crank, 1543. fold the board, 1544. the marble, 1545. false, 1546. c, 1547. d

• DUNGEONS AND DRAGONS •

1548) When was Dungeons and Dragons first published?
a) 1968 b) 1974 c) 1979 d) 1987

1549) Who co-created Dungeons and Dragons?
a) Gary Gygax
b) Gary Varval
c) Gary Gilmore
d) Gary Coleman

1550) WHAT COMPANY NOW PUBLISHES DUNGEONS AND DRAGONS?
A) WIZARDS OF WESTFIELD
B) WIZARDS OF THE COAST
C) WIZARDS AND WARRIORS
D) WIZARDS OF WARRIOR PLACE

1551) Who leads a game of Dungeons and Dragons?
a) The oldest player
b) The Dungeon Master
c) The Cerberus
d) The Leading Troll

1552) Which is not a part of your character's Dungeons and Dragons ability score:

a) Strength
b) Fortitude
c) Wisdom
d) Charisma

1553) In the first edition of Dungeons and Dragons, which of the following was not a player class:

a) Monk
b) Bard
c) Cleric
d) Leader

1554) Which of the following was not a core race in the original Dungeons and Dragons:

a) Elf
b) Gnome
c) Sprite
d) Dwarf

1556) Absent magical curses, what is the minimum score for an ability?

1557) Absent magical enhancements, what is a character's maximum score for an ability?

1558) Was there a Dungeons and Dragons movie?

1548. b, 1549. a, 1550. b, 1551. b, 1552. b, 1553. d, 1554. c, 1555. non-player character, 1556. three, 1557. eighteen, 1558. yes

1559) In Dungeons and Dragons, what is a D20?

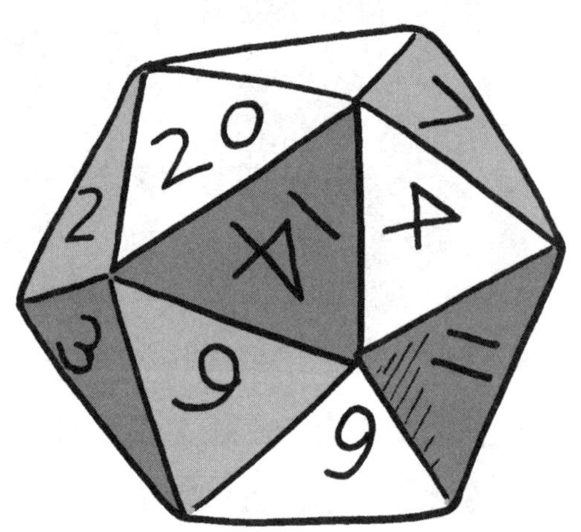

1560) What company originally published Dungeons and Dragons?

a) Avalon Hill
b) Hasbro
c) Milton Bradley
d) TSR

TOUGH TRIVIA CHALLENGE

1561) WHAT CHARACTER CLASS SHARES ITS NAME WITH THE LEAD CHARACTER IN THE TV SERIES *HAVE GUN, WILL TRAVEL?*

1562) CAN DEAD CHARACTERS IN D&D BE REVIVED?

1563) What Oscar-winner starred in the movie *Dungeons and Dragons*?

a) Daniel Day-Lewis
b) Anthony Hopkins
c) Jeremy Irons
d) Ben Kingsley

1564) True or false: the magazine for D&D enthusiasts is called *The Dungeon*.

1565) How many possible character alignments are there?

1566) What alignment is the polar opposite of "Lawful-Good"?

1567) What character class is always true neutral?

a) Bard
b) Cavalier
c) Cleric
d) Monk

1568) Which spell is easier to learn, magic missiles or fireballs?

1569) What character class is most useful against undead monsters?

a) Cavalier
b) Cleric
c) Fighter
d) Paladin

1570) WHAT THEN-LITTLE-KNOWN ACTOR PLAYED THE TROUBLED STUDENT IN A TV MOVIE VERSION OF THE RONA JAFFE NOVEL?

A) GEORGE CLOONEY
B) LEONARDO DICAPRIO
C) TOM HANKS
D) BRAD PITT

TOUGH TRIVIA CHALLENGE

1571) In what Rona Jaffe novel does a troubled college student become dangerously obsessed with a Dungeons and Dragons-like game?

a) Lizards and Labyrinths
b) Mazes and Monsters
c) Treasures and Trolls
d) Witches and Warriors

1572) A character's ability to withstand further attack is measured in what?

a) Damage points
b) Hit points
c) Life points
d) Vita points

1573) What kind of coin is more valuable than copper pieces but less valuable than silver pieces?

1559. a twenty-sided dice, 1560. d, 1561. paladin, 1562. yes, 1563. c, 1564. false—The Dragon, 1565. nine, 1566. Chaotic-Evil, 1567. d, 1568. magic missiles, 1569. b, 1570. c, 1571. b, 1572. b, 1573. electrum pieces

..SCRABBLE..

1574) How many A tiles are there in a game of Scrabble?

1575) True or false: Scrabble's original name was Lexicogs.

1576) True or false: Scrabble's creator was named Alfred Butts.

1577) TRUE OR FALSE: THE SAME INVENTOR CREATED A GAME CALLED ALFRED'S OTHER GAME.

1578) True or false: There is no Scrabble-acceptable two-letter word containing a V.

1579) What is the rule change in Duplicate Scrabble?

a) Players each get 14 letters
b) All players play with the same letters
c) Two boards are connected at a corner
d) There are twice as many letters in the game

1580) Is it possible to play Scrabble with Chinese letters?

1581) True or false: In French Scrabble, the X and the Y are each worth 10 points.

1582) How many spaces wide is a Scrabble board?

1583) Is Scrabble an acceptable Scrabble word?

1584) How many extra points do you get for using all seven of your letters in one play in Scrabble?

1585) TRUE OR FALSE: SCRABBLE TILES ARE MADE FROM THE WOOD FROM ELM TREES.

1586) True or false: **Scrabble was originally played without a board.**

1587) How many points is an M worth in a game of Scrabble?

1588) Which of the following words is impossible to get in Scrabble without using a blank?

a) Quagmire
b) Quizzical
c) Zipper
d) Albatross

1574. nine, 1575. false—it was Lexico, 1576. true, 1577. true, 1578. true, 1579. b, 1580. no, 1581. true, 1582. fifteen spaces, 1583. yes, 1584. fifty, 1585. false—they are made from Vermont maple, 1586. true, 1587. three, 1588. b—because there is only one z

1589) True or false: In determining which player goes first in Scrabble, a blank tile beats an A tile.

TOUGH TRIVIA CHALLENGE

1590) The highest possible opening word in Scrabble is Muzjiks. How many points would that word get you (keeping in mind that the opener uses a double word square)?

a) 98
b) 102
c) 112
d) 128

1591) Are there any acceptable Scrabble words that have two Qs in them?

1592) In Scrabble, are there more Ks or Fs?

1593) In Scrabble, are there more Ds or Bs?

1594) In Scrabble, are there more Ps or Us?

1595) In Scrabble, are there more Ys or Gs?

1596) How many Zs are there in a Scrabble game?

1597) Are there any acceptable Scrabble words containing a Q but no U?

1598) HOW MANY LETTERS ARE REPRESENTED JUST ONCE IN A SCRABBLE SET?

1599) How many tiles are there in a Scrabble set?

a) 100
b) 104
c) 130
d) 150

1600) True or false: A losing player at the World Scrabble Championship once accused his opponent of pocketing a G and demanded that officials strip-search him.

1601) True or false: the World Scrabble Championship is played in Washington every year.

1602) True or false: National Scrabble championship officials once disallowed a word because it was considered offensive, even though it was in the dictionary.

1603) TRUE OR FALSE: JEOPARDY! CHAMPION KEN JENNINGS IS ALSO A PAST WINNER OF THE NATIONAL SCRABBLE CHAMPIONSHIP.

1604) What documentary chronicles championship-level Scrabble players?

a) Spellbound
b)Word Freak
c) Word Wars
d) Wordplay

1589. true, 1590. d, 1591. yes, 1592. Fs, 1593. Ds, 1594. Us, 1595. Gs, 1596. one, 1597. yes, 1598. five, 1599. a, 1600. true, 1601. false, 1602. true, 1603. false, 1604. c

RISK

1605) The man who invented Risk, Albert Lamorisse, was a French film director who also made the award-winning film *The Red Balloon.* Which was released first, the game or the movie?

1606) What continent has the most territories?

1607) Which of the following is not a territory in Risk?

a) Yakutsk
b) Ukraine
c) Ural
d) Uganda

TOUGH TRIVIA CHALLENGE

1608) If you have six attacking armies and your opponent has six defending armies, who is more likely to win the overall battle?

1609) How many continents on the Risk board?

1610) Which of these is not on Risk cards given at the end of a successful turn?

a) Infantry
b) Cavalry
c) Aircraft
d) Artillary

1611) How many territory cards are there in Risk?

a) 36
b) 42
c) 56
d) 62

1612) IF TWO PLAYERS ARE PLAYING RISK. HOW MANY ARMIES DOES EACH PLAYER START WITH?

A) 30
B) 40
C) 50
D) 60

1613) How many extra armies do you get if you have all of Asia at the beginning of your turn?

1614) How many extra armies to you get if you have all of North America at the beginning of your turn?

1615) How many extra armies do you get if you have all of Australia at the beginning of your turn?

1616) How many routes are there for someone outside the continent to attack South America?

1617) HOW MANY ROUTES ARE THERE FOR SOMEONE OUTSIDE THE CONTINENT TO ATTACK AUSTRALIA?

1618) How many armies must you have on a country in order to attack a neighboring country?

1619) True or False: The current rules for two-player Risk weren't incorporated into the official game until 1975.

1620) Is Venezuela a territory in Risk?

1621) Is Quebec a territory?

1622) Is Italy a territory?

1623) Can Iceland attack Ukraine?

1624) Can Egypt attack Congo?

1625) TRUE OR FALSE: EVERY COUNTRY IN SOUTH AMERICA CAN ATTACK EVERY OTHER COUNTRY IN SOUTH AMERICA.

1626) Is the Middle East part or Africa or Asia in Risk?

1627) Can Afghanistan attack China?

1628) Castle Risk focuses only on what continent?

1605. the movie came out in 1956—the game came a year later, 1606. Asia, 1607. d, 1608. you have a 52% chance of winning the battle, 1609. eight, 1610. c, 1611. a, 1612. b, 1613. seven, 1614. five, 1615. two, 1616. two, 1617. one, 1618. two, 1619. true, 1620. yes, 1621. yes, 1622. no, 1623. no, 1624. no, 1625. false, 1626. Asia, 1627. yes, 1628. Europe

THE GAME OF LIFE

1629) True or false: An early version of the Game of Life was called the Checkered Game of Life?

1630) When was the contemporary version of the Game of Life first released?

a) 1950
b) 1960
c) 1970
d) 1980

1631) How many numbers on the Game of Life spinner?

1632) True or false: The $500 bills have been dropped from the Game of Life?

1633) CAN YOU BUY RENTER'S INSURANCE IN THE GAME OF LIFE?

1634) Can you buy flood insurance?

1635) Can you buy life insurance?

1636) True or false: In the 1960's edition, you could end up at the Poor Farm.

TOUGH TRIVIA CHALLENGE

1637) True or false: The original Game of Life cars were convertibles.

1638) In the early editions of the Game of Life, Art Linkletter appeared on its cover. Who was Art Linkletter?

a) A baseball player
b) A former governor
c) A New York real estate mogul
d) A TV game-show host

1639) What was added in the 1990s?

a) The option of staying single
b) Life Tiles, which rewarded good behavior
c) Gambling in retirement
d) The option to travel backward

1640) How many peg holes are there in a Game of Life car?

1641) WHAT IS THE LARGEST DENOMINATION OF CASH IN THE GAME OF LIFE?

1642) Which of the following was not featured in a special edition of the Game of Life?

a) Monsters, Inc.
b) Indiana Jones
c) The Wizard of Oz
d) The Chronicles of Narnia

1629. true, 1630. b, 1631. ten, 1632. true, 1633. no, 1634. no, 1635. yes, 1636. true, 1637. true, 1638. d, 1639. b, 1640. six (some editions have eight), 1641. $100,000, 1642. d

CLUE

1643) What is the name of the Colonel?

1644) True or false: In England, the game is known as Cluedo.

1645) WHAT COLOR PIECE IS MRS. PEACOCK?

TOUGH TRIVIA CHALLENGE

1646) What is the victim's name in the American version of Clue?

a) Mr. Boddy
b) Mr. Palid
c) Mr. Was
d) Mr. Goner

1647) TRUE OR FALSE: IN THE BRITISH EDITION OF CLUE. MR. GREEN IS REV. GREEN.

1648) True or false: In some editions of Clue the rope is made of string. In others, it's plastic.

1649) True or false: if you accuse another player of being the killer, his piece is automatically moved into the room you are in.

1650) How many possible murderer/location/weapon combinations are there in a standard game?

a) 124   b) 196   c) 224   d) 324

1651) Are you allowed to block a room to prevent another player from entering?

1652) True or false: When it was released in theaters, the movie Clue had different endings that could change from screening to screening.

1653) Which is not a room in Clue:

a) Dining Room
b) Laundry Room
c) Kitchen
d) Conservatory

1654) What was the extra murder weapon in the 50th anniversary edition of Clue?

a) A bottle of poison
b) A hand grenade
c) A blackjack
d) A submachine gun

TOUGH TRIVIA CHALLENGE

1655) Who is the victim in *The Simpsons* Clue?

a) Homer
b) Bart
c) Mr. Burns
d) Marge

1656) Which of the following was not a Clue variation?

a) Clue: Seinfeld Collectors Eidtion
b) Clue: The Office Edition
c) Clue: Futurama Edition
d) Clue: Harry Potter Edition

1657) Mrs. White's piece starts closest to what room?

a) Ballroom b) Hall c) Kitchen d) Lounge

1643. Colonel Mustard, 1644. true, 1645. blue, 1646. a, 1647. true, 1648. true, 1649. true, 1650. d, 1651. yes, 1652. true, 1653. b, 1654. a, 1655. c, 1656. c, 1657. a

1658) True or false: In Clue: Dungeons and Dragons, Mr. Green has been replaced by a lump of gelatinous ooze.

1659) A Clue-like game in which players wander a mansion trying to kill a character rather than find the murderer is called:

a) Kill Mr. Killer
b) Kill or Be Killer
c) Kill Dr. Killdare
d) Kill Dr. Lucky

1660) Which of these rooms does not have a secret passageway?

a) Billiard room
b) Conservatory
c) Kitchen
d) Study

1661) WHICH ROOM HAS THE MOST DOORS?

A) BALLROOM
B) DINING ROOM
C) HALL
D) LIBRARY

1662) Which player goes first?

a) Mr. Green
b) Col. Mustard
c) Miss Scarlet
d) Mrs. White

1663) What player goes last?

a) Mrs. Peacock
b) Prof. Plum
c) Miss Scarlet
d) Mrs. White

1664) What heading is on the pads included with the game for you to keep track of your deductions?

MONOPOLY

1665) True of false: According to the rules of Monopoly, you collect money from the center of the board when you land on Free Parking.

1666) WHAT ARE THE FIRST TWO PURCHASABLE PROPERTIES ON THE MONOPOLY BOARD?

1667) Name the four Monopoly railroads.

1668) In Monopoly, is "You've won second prize in a beauty contest" a Chance card or a Community Chest card?

1669) **True or false:** All of the properties in Monopoly are in Atlantic City, New Jersey.

TOUGH TRIVIA CHALLENGE

1670) The Rich Uncle Pennybags character, best known from Monopoly, also appeared on each of the following games except one. Which did he not appear on?

a) Advance to Boardwalk

b) Careers

c) Don't Go to Jail

d) Free Parking

1658. false, 1659. d, 1660. a, 1661. a, 1662. c, 1663. b, 1664. Detective Notes, 1665. false, 1666. Mediterranean and Baltic, 1667. Reading, B&O, Short Line, Pennsylvania, 1668. Community Chest, 1669. false—Marvin Gardens, which is actually spelled Marven Gardens, is in nearby Margate City, NJ, 1670. b

1671) Does a Monopoly game contain more or less than $12,000 in play money?

1672) True or false: Monopoly is available in more than 40 languages.

1673) True or false: **The longest recorded Monopoly game lasted more than 70 days.**

1674) TRUE OR FALSE: A JEWELER CREATED A VERSION OF MONOPOLY VALUED AT $12 MILLION.

1675) True or false: **In Spain, the Broadway space has been replaced with Paseo del Prado.**

1676) True or false: In France, the Boardwalk space has been replaced with the Eifel Tower.

1677) True or false: Escape maps were hidden in Monopoly sets that were sent to American prisoners or war during World War II.

1678) WHICH OF THE FOLLOWING WAS NOT ONCE A MONOPOLY PIECE:

A) LANTERN
B) PURSE
C) SLED
D) ROCKING HORSE

1679) True or false: The guy in Monopoly jail doesn't have an official name.

1680) *Was the dog one of the original Monopoly pieces?*

1681) Was the wheelbarrow one of the original Monopoly pieces?

1682) In what movie do characters play Monopoly with real money?

a) *Night of the Living Dead*

b) *Zombieland*

c) *Shaun of the Dead*

d) *Return of the Living Dead*

1683) True or false: The prize at the Monopoly World Championships is the real dollar equivalent of the amount of fake money in a Monopoly game box.

TOUGH TRIVIA CHALLENGE

1684) How much money is in a Monopoly game box?

a) $10,540

b) $14,500

c) $20,580

d) $26,665

1685) True or false: There's a version of Monopoly with a round board.

1686) How many spaces on a Monopoly board?

1687) HOW MANY PROPERTIES IN A MONOPOLY GAME?

1688) True or false: The cost of the luxury tax has changed in Monopoly.

1689) True or false: **The real B&O Railroad did not serve Atlantic City.**

1690) How much do you get for passing Go in regular Monopoly?

1671. more, 1672. true, 1673. true, 1674. false—it was worth $2 million, 1675. true, 1676. false, 1677. true, 1678. c, 1679. false—it's Jake the jailbird, 1680. no, 1681. no, 1682. b, 1683. true, 1684. c, 1685. true, 1686. forty, 1687. twenty-eight, 1688. true, 1689. true, 1690. $200

1691) How much do you get for passing Go in Monopoly Here and Now?

1692) TRUE OR FALSE: THE WORLD MONOPOLY TOURNAMENT HAS AIRED ON ESPN.

1693) True or false: **Atlantic City has never hosted the World Monopoly Tournament.**

1694) What kind of hat is a Monopoly playing piece?

1695) How many utilities are in a Monopoly game?

1696) How many hotels in a Monopoly game?

1697) How many houses in a Monopoly game?

1698) What color are the $20 bills?

1699) What color are the $1 bills?

1700) CAN YOU BUY PROPERTY WHILE YOU ARE IN JAIL?

1701) Which of the following can't you do with a Monopoly speed dice, introduced in 2007?

a) Move three additional spaces
b) Move to the next unowned property
c) Buy an undeveloped property from another player for the face value
d) Opt to use just one of the die and "get off the bus early"

1702) True or false: **Parker Brothers does not allow slot machines to use Monopoly logos and characters.**

1703) True or false: Rich Uncle Pennybags officially had his name changed to Mr. Monopoly by Parker Brothers.

1704) What is the only property you can land on by drawing the "Go Back 3 Spaces" card?

1705) TRUE OR FALSE: IF ALL THE HOUSES OR HOTELS IN THE BOX HAVE BEEN PURCHASED, YOU CAN USE PENNIES FOR HOUSES AND NICKELS FOR HOTELS (OR WHATEVER MARKERS YOU HAVE AVAILABLE).

1706) How much money does each player start with in Monopoly?

1707) If you roll nothing but sevens the entire game, what is the only property you will never land on?

1708) True or false: in British Monopoly, the Income Tax space is called "Super Tax."

1709) If you have three hotels and nine houses, and you are assessed for street repairs, how much money do you owe?

1691. $2 million, 1692. true, 1693. false, 1694. top hat, 1695. two, 1696. twelve, 1697. Thirty-two, 1698. blue, 1699. white, 1700. yes, 1701. c, 1702. false, 1703. true, 1704. New York Avenue, 1705. false, 1706. $1,500, 1707. Park Place, 1708. false—that's Luxury Tax, 1709. $705

1710) How many monopolies consist of just two properties?

1711) Which space on the board is landed on the most?
a) Go
b) Jail
c) Illinois Avenue
d) Boardwalk

1712) True or false: an economics professor trying to illustrate the virtues of a free market over monopolies published a game called Anti-Monopoly.

1713) TRUE OR FALSE: MONOPOLY WAS BANNED IN THE SOVIET UNION AS CAPITALISTIC.

1714) True or false: Attorney Clarence Darrow invented Monopoly.

1715) How many Monopoly properties can you reach by drawing a Chance card?

1716) What game company was first to mass-market Monopoly?
a) Hasbro
b) Ideal
c) Milton Bradley
d) Parker Brothers

1717) If you get out of jail by throwing doubles, do you get an extra turn?

1718) HOW MUCH DO YOU GET FOR SELLING A GET OUT OF JAIL FREE CARD BACK TO THE BANK?

1719) How many Monopoly properties are named after saints?

1720) Not counting the railroads and utilities, how many properties are named after neither states nor bodies of water?

1721) True or false: In the movie *The Sting*, Robert Redford switches a gangster's stash of cash with a sack of Monopoly money.

1722) In Whoville-opoly, how much do you get for passing Go?

a) $100
b) $200
c) $300
d) $200 plus 2

1723) True or false: if you land on Go instead of passing it, you get $400, not $200.

1724) Which property completes the monopoly if you own St. Charles Place and Virginia Ave.?

1725) Which property completes the monopoly if you own Marvin Gardens and Atlantic Ave.?

1726) WHICH PROPERTY COMPLETES THE MONOPOLY IF YOU OWN NORTH CAROLINA AND PENNSYLVANIA AVENUES?

1727) Which property completes the monopoly if you own Illinois and Indiana Avenues?

1728) Which property completes the monopoly if you own New York and Tennessee Avenues?

1710. two, 1711. c, 1712. true, 1713. true, 1714. false—Charles Darrow was the inventor, and there's evidence that he copied an earlier game, 1715. nine, 1716. d, 1717. no, 1718. nothing—you aren't allowed to do it (banks can't go to jail!), 1719. two, 1720. seven, 1721. false—it's just plain paper, 1722. d, 1723. false, 1724. States Avenue, 1725. Ventnor Ave., 1726. Pacific Avenue, 1727. Kentucky Avenue, 1728. St. James Avenue

PUZZLES

1729) HOW MANY SMALL SQUARES ARE THERE IN A STANDARD SUDOKU PUZZLES?

1730) What is the highest number in a standard Sudoku puzzle?

1731) True or false: **While its origins are vague, the modern Sudoku puzzle format is believed to have been created by Howard Garns of Indiana.**

TOUGH TRIVIA CHALLENGE

1732)
What company first popularized Sudoku puzzles in 1986?

a) Nikoli

b) Niki

c) Nikochi

d) Nihi

1733) How many numbers are used in Mini Sudoku?

1734) True or false: **When a Sudoku puzzle first appeared in the British newspaper *The Times*, it was called Su Doku.**

1735) True or false: The Sky One TV show *Sudoku Live* featured nine players on nine teams.

1736) TRUE OR FALSE: **KENKEN WAS INVENTED BY A MATH TEACHER.**

1737) In a crossword puzzle, which clues are usually listed first, the across clues or the down clues?

1738) True or false: A crossword creator is a cruciverbalist.

1739) Which tends to have more letter squares in a same-size puzzle, an American-style crossword grid or a British-style crossword grid.

TOUGH TRIVIA CHALLENGE

1740) Where was the first World Sudoku Championship held?

a) France
b) Japan
c) United States
d) Italy

1741) True or false: In a Japanese crossword puzzle, the corners are traditionally all white squares.

1742) TRUE OR FALSE: IN JAPANESE CROSSWORD PUZZLES, NO TWO SHADED SQUARES ARE NEXT TO OR ON TOP OF EACH OTHER.

1743) In most Spanish crossword puzzles, are accent marks used?

1744) In a crossword puzzle, what is used to indicate that the clue indicates a pun.

1745) What does an abbreviation in a clue indicate?

1746) When was the first crossword puzzle published?

a) 1654
b) 1712
c) 1890
d) 1910

1747) When was the first crossword puzzle book published?

a) 1840
b) 1894
c) 1924
d) 1946

1748) When did the *New York Times* begin publishing crossword puzzles?

a) 1942
b) 1955
c) 1960
d) 1964

1749) TRUE OR FALSE: THE FIRST 30 AMERICAN CROSSWORD PUZZLE TOURNAMENTS WERE HELD IN CROSSWORD, VIRGINIA.

1729. eighty-one, 1730. nine, 1731. true, 1732. a, 1733. six, 1734. true, 1735. true, 1736. true, 1737. across, 1738. true, 1739. American,
1740. d, 1741. true, 1742. true, 1743. no, 1744. a question mark, 1745. the answer is in abbreviated form, 1746. c, 1747. c, 1748. a,
1749. false—Stamford, Connecticut

1750) What puzzle popularizer founded the American Crossword Puzzle Tournament?

a) Will Geer
b) Will Pants
c) Will Shortz
d) Will Shertz

1751) True or false: **Word Search puzzles were first published in the 1860s.**

1752) Are more jigsaw puzzles made of wood or cardboard?

1753) True or false: All 1,000-piece jigsaw puzzles have the same pattern of pieces, only with different illustrations.

1754) True or false: **The company Ravensburger created a jigsaw puzzle of over 18,000 pieces.**

1755) True or false: Many 1,000-piece jigsaw puzzles actually have more than 1,000 pieces.

1756) True or false: **The oldest jigsaw puzzle—then called a dissected puzzle—was created by a Japanese toymaker.**

1757) TRUE OR FALSE: EARLY JIGSAW PUZZLES WERE ACTUALLY CUT BY A FRETSAW, NOT A JIGSAW.

1758) True or false: During the Great Depression, there were companies that issued weekly jigsaw puzzles.

PLAYGROUND & BACKYARD GAMES

1759) The Four Square World Championship is held in...

a) Maine

b) Minnesota

c) Maryland

d) Mississippi

1760) True or False: **Students at Manchester College played Four Square for 120 hours to set a world record in 2011.**

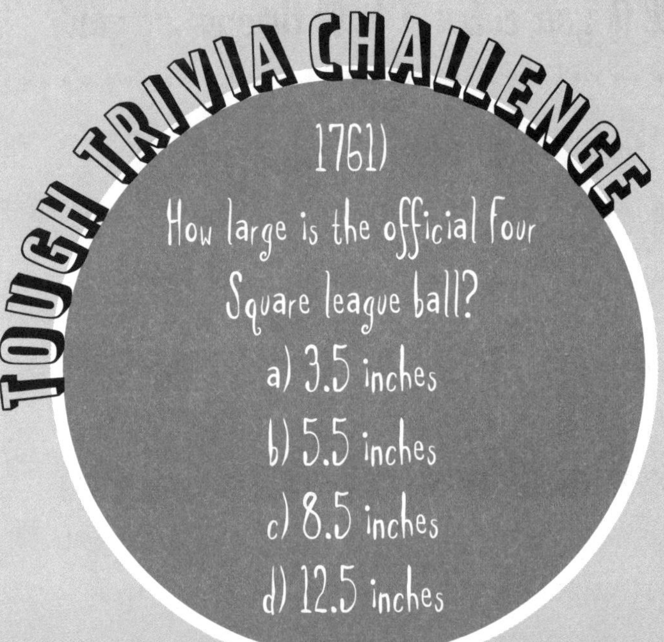

TOUGH TRIVIA CHALLENGE

1761) How large is the official Four Square league ball?

a) 3.5 inches

b) 5.5 inches

c) 8.5 inches

d) 12.5 inches

1762) In competitive Four Square, are you allowed to spin the ball on a serve?

1763) In Four Square, is a ball that bounces on a line in or out?

1764) Does the server in Four Square serve from the highest-ranking square to the second highest ranking square or to the lowest ranking square.

1765) In Four Square, do your feet have to stay in your square?

1766) IN HOPSCOTCH, DOES A MARKER THAT LANDS ON A LINE COUNT?

1767) In Chain Tag, what happens to the "It" person after he or she tags someone?

1750. c, 1751. false—1960s, 1752. cardboard, 1753. false, 1754. true, 1755. true, 1756. false—it was a London mapmaker, 1757. true, 1758. true, 1759. a, 1760. false—it was just 30 hours, 1761. c, 1762. yes, 1763. in, 1764. to the second highest ranking, 1765. no, 1766. no—it has to be completely in the numbered area, 1767. he or she holds hands with the new "It" person, forming a lengthening chain

1768) In Zombie Tag (aka Gang Up or Minion Tag), what happens to the "It" person after he or she tags someone?

1769) In Duck, Duck, Goose, do you get up and chase if you are tapped as a duck or if you are tapped as a goose?

1770) In Freeze Tag, how do you get unfrozen?

1771) WHERE ARE THE BALLS LINED UP AT THE BEGINNING OF A GAME OF DODGE BALL.

1772) What happens in Dodge Ball if you catch a ball thrown at you?

1773) True or false: In 2011, a game of Dodge Ball at the University of California, Irvine, included more than 4,400 players.

1774) True or false: Aggie, mica, and Cat's Eye are all types of marbles.

1775) What's another name for croquet hoops?

a) Archdoors
b) Wickets
c) Tunnels
d) Bats

1776) What happens in a standard game of croquet if your ball hits someone else's ball?

TOUGH TRIVIA CHALLENGE

1777) What other color balls does the team with the red balls use?

a) Yellow

b) Black

c) Blue

d) None of the above

1778) How many balls does each croquet team get?

1779) WHAT HAPPENS IN A STANDARD GAME OF CROQUET IF YOUR BALL GOES THROUGH THE CORRECT WICKET?

1780) How many wickets in a standard backyard game of croquet?

1781) Is it generally better to go first or last in croquet?

1782) Do you have to go through wickets in order in croquet?

1783) In croquet, the person whose turn it is is called the ______

a) Striker

b) Hitter

c) Pounder

d) Batter

1768. he or she stays it along with the tagged person, 1769. goose, 1770. when someone who has not been tagged tags you, 1771. center court, 1772. the thrower is eliminated, 1773. true, 1774. true, 1775. b, 1776. you get two more shots, 1777. a, 1778. four—two pairs, 1779. you get one more shot, 1780. nine, 1781. last, 1782. yes, 1783. a

1784) HOW MANY POINTS IS A RINGER IN HORSESHOES?

1785) How many points is a close shoe in horseshoes?

1786) How close does a horseshoe have to be to the stake to be a close shoe?

1787) How many points is a leaner in horseshoes?

1788) What's another name for a close shoe in horseshoes?

a) A neary

b) An incher

c) A shoe in count

d) An almost

TOUGH TRIVIA CHALLENGE

1789) How far from the stake is an adult foul line for backyard horseshoes?

a) 22 feet

b) 28 feet

c) 32 feet

d) 37 feet

1790) How many inches of steel rod should be above the ground to play horseshoes?

a) 10 inches

b) 14 inches

b) 20 inches

d) 30 inches

1791) True or false: Horseshoe stakes should be positioned straight up?

1792) WHEN DID HOOKED ENDS TAKE THE PLACE OF POINTED ENDS IN HORSESHOES?

A) 1874
B) 1927
C) 1955
D) 1974

1793) True or false: Bocce comes from the Latin meaning "boss."

1794) True or false: Romans sometimes used coconuts to play an early version of bocce.

1795) True or false: King Carlos IV of Spain is the only king to prohibit bocce playing.

1796) How many games in a bocce match?

1797) TRUE OR FALSE: IN CHAMPIONSHIP BOCCE, THREE PLAYERS ON EACH TEAM PLAY THE ENTIRE MATCH.

1798) Championship bocce games usually go to how many points?

1784. three. 1785. one. 1786. any part of is has to be six inches from the stake. 1787. One. 1788. c. 1789. d. 1790. b. 1791. false—they are supposed to lean toward the tosser. 1792. c. 1793. true. 1794. true. 1795. false—King Carlos V did, too. 1796. three. 1797. false—the first is three-on-three, the second is one-on-one, and the third is two-on-two, with no player playing more than twice. 1798. fifteen

1799) True or false: One team always gets zero in a round of bocce?

1800) What is the name of the small ball in bocce?

a) The Pellechia
b) The Pallendrome
c) The Palladium
d) The Pallino

1801) True or false: **In international bocce, there are punto, raffa, and volo shots.**

1802) What does the word bocce mean?

1803) Is bocce an Olympic sport?

TOUGH TRIVIA CHALLENGE

1804) How much does an official bocce ball weigh?
a) Between 300-500 grams
b) Between 500-700 grams
c) Between 700-900 grams
d) Between 900-1200 grams

1805) TRUE OR FALSE: **KICKBALL WAS ORIGINALLY CALLED KICK BASEBALL?**

1806) Kickball has been played since around...

a) 1857
b) 1917
c) 1928
d) 1954

1807) In early kickball, was there a pitcher?

1808) How many outs ended an inning in early kickball?

1809) WHAT COLOR IS A TRADITIONAL KICKBALL BALL?

1810) According to WAKA, how many players does a kickball team need?

a) Between 5 and 9
b) Between 6 and 10
c) Between 8 and 11
d) Between 5 and 16

TOUGH TRIVIA CHALLENGE

1811) Being a playground game, kickball rules adapt to location and region. But according to the World Adult Kickball Association, what should the distance be between the strike zone at home and second base?

a) 44 feet
b) 64 feet
c) 84 feet
d) 94 feet

1812) According to WAKA, how many innings is a full kickball game?

1813) How many points do you get in cornhole for landing a bag in the hole?

1814) How many points do you get in cornhole for landing a bag on the platform?

1815) How many points do you need to win a game of cornhole?

1816) How many bags do you throw in an inning of cornhole?

1817) IN CORNHOLE, DO YOU NEED TO WIN BY ONE OR TWO POINTS?

1818) How many rungs on each ladder in a game of ladder toss?

1819) In ladder toss, which is worth three points, the top rung or the bottom rung?

TOUGH TRIVIA CHALLENGE

1820) In cornhole, what is a "Carlton"?

a) When a bag hits the ground then roles or bounced onto the board.
b) When a bag knocks an opponent's bag into the hole
c) When all four bags land in a whole in an inning
d) When a team scores no points in an inning

1799. true—because only the highest-scoring team gets points. 1800. d, 1801. true, 1802. balls, 1803. no, 1804. d, 1805. true, 1806. b, 1807. no, 1808. outs didn't end an inning—it ended when all batters had one turn each, 1809. red, 1810. c, 1811. c, 1812. five, 1813. three, 1814. one, 1815. twenty-one, 1816. four, 1817. one, 1818. three, 1819. top, 1820. b

1821) In ladder toss (aka ladder golf and hillbilly golf), what are the strung-together balls called?

a) Boleros
b) Bojos
c) Bolas
d) Bohos

1822) WHAT ARE THE TWO WAYS OF GETTING A BONUS POINT IN LADDER TOSS?

1823) Wiffle Ball was invented in the...

a) 1920s
b) 1930s
c) 1950s
d) 1970s

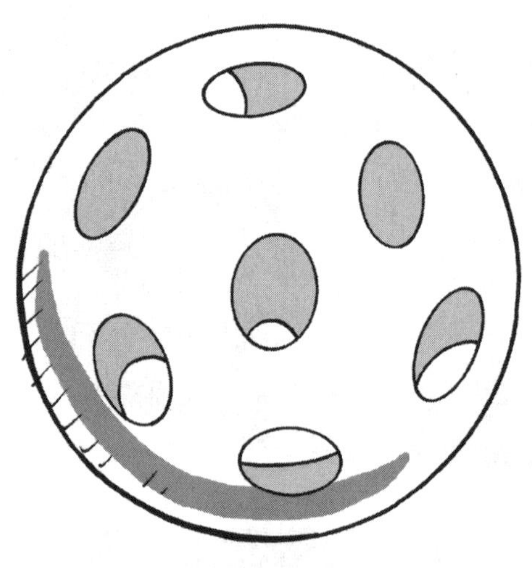

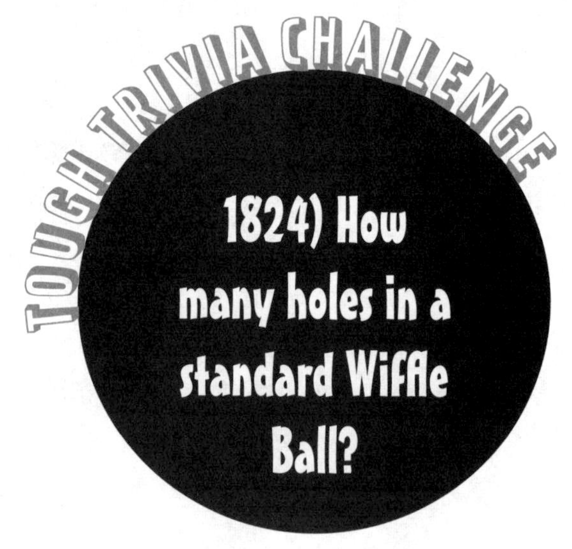

1825) What are the three basic pitches in Wiffle Ball?

1826) In Wiffle Ball, what happens if a ball is caught in the air in fair territory?

1827) How far is it from first to second base in an official Wiffle Ball game?

a) 18 feet
b) 22 feet
c) 28 feet
d) You don't need bases in an official Wiffle Ball game

VIDEO GAMES

1828) True or false: **The Atari was the first home video game system.**

1829) Atari is a term used when playing Parcheesi.

1830) What year did Space Invaders first invade arcades?

a) 1976
b) 1978
c) 1980
d) 1982

1832) What is the name of the addictive game developed by Russian programmer Alex Pajitnov in 1985?

TOUGH TRIVIA CHALLENGE

1831) Who was the exclusive seller of Atari's Pong game?
a) Wal-Mart
b) K-Mart
c) Sears
d) Macy's

1833) What year was the Nintendo Game Boy first released?

a) 1986 b) 1989 c) 1991 d) 1993

1821. c, 1822. one bolo on each rung or three bolos on the same rung, 1823. c, 1824. eight, 1825. curve, straight, slider, 1826. it's considered an out, 1827. d, 1828. false—it was the Magnavox Odyssey, 1829. false—it's a term used when playing Go, 1830. b, 1831. c, 1832. Tetris, 1833. b

1834) WHICH CAME FIRST, ASTEROIDS OR PAC-MAN?

1835) True or false: **The Entertainment Software Ratings Board began in 1989, the same year that the Sega Genesis system was launched.**

1836) Which came first, the Sims or Tamagotchi?

1837) Which came first Sony PSP or Nintendo's Wii?

1838) Which came first, Super Mario World or Super Mario Bros. 3?

1839) TRUE OR FALSE: **SUPER MARIO BROS. IS A SPIN-OFF FROM THE GAME DONKEY KONG.**

1840) For what computer was the first John Madden Football game designed?

1841) **True or false:** The original Guitar Hero was released for Playstation 1.

1842) What two colors are the arrow footpads on the standard Dance Dance Revolution arcade game?

1843) Which came first, Myst or Halo?

TOUGH TRIVIA CHALLENGE

1844) The Nintendo Entertainment System was first known as:

a) Famicom
b) Gencon
c) Playcom
d) Gamicon

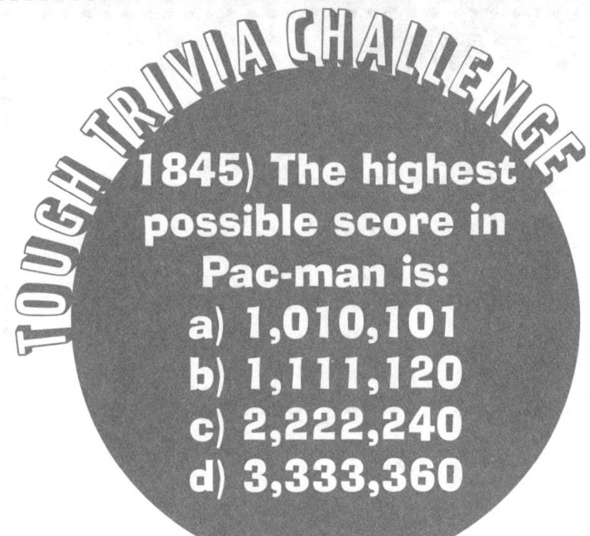

TOUGH TRIVIA CHALLENGE

1845) The highest possible score in Pac-man is:

a) 1,010,101
b) 1,111,120
c) 2,222,240
d) 3,333,360

1846) Which of the following is not a song on the main set list of the first Rock Band?

a) *"Ballroom Blitz"*
b) *"Philadelphia Freedom"*
c) *"Suffragette City"*
d) *"Won't Get Fooled Again"*

1847) True or false: A 1982 song called "Pac-Man Fever" actually became a top-10 record.

1848) Which of the following artists does not have a hit song of his or hers featured on the first Rock Band?

a) Red Hot Chili Peppers
b) Kiss
c) Madonna
d) The Police

1849) What color is Pac-Man?

1850) Was Abraham Lincoln one of the original world leaders in Civilization IV?

1834. Asteroids, 1835. false—it was 1994, the same year that the Sony PlayStation was launched in Japan, 1836. Tamagotchi, 1837. Sony PSP, 1838. Super Mario Bros. 3, 1839. true, 1840. Apple II, 1841. false—Playstation 2, 1842. pink and blue, 1843. Myst, 1844. a, 1845. d—and it was reached by a player in 1999, 1846. b, 1847. true, 1848. c, 1849. yellow, 1850. no

MATCH THE VILLAIN TO THE VIDEO GAME:

1851) GlaDOS
1852) Mother Brain
1853) Bowser
1854) Andrew Ryan
1855) Ganon
1856) Dr. Robotnik
1857) Dr. Wily
1858) Albert Wesker
1859) M. Bison
1860) Joker
1861) Covenant
1862) Lich King
1863) Grue
1864) Zeus
1865) Captain Qwark

a) Metroid games
b) Mega Man games
c) Portal
d) Resident Evil games
e) Zork
f) Sonic the Hedgehog games
g) Batman games
h) Zelda games
i) Ratchet and Clank games
j) BioShock
k) Mario games
l) God of War series
m) Halo
n) Street Fighter games
o) World of Warcraft

1866) In Sims, which gets you more money, being a Getaway Driver or a Con Artist?

1867) IN SIMS, WHICH GETS YOU MORE MONEY, BEING A BANK ROBBER OR A COUNTERFEITER?

1868) In Sims, which gets you more money, being a Smuggler or a Cat Burglar?

1869) Which of the following is not a Sims career track in the base game?

a) Business
b) Entertainment
c) Adventurer
d) Medical

1870) Where do the Sims live?

1871) True or false: In the first Sims game, children did not grow up into adults.

1872) TRUE OR FALSE: AFTER A SIM DIES, IT MAY HAUNT THE PLACE WHERE ITS LIFE ENDED.

1873) True or false: When it was released, the Sims became the bestselling game in PC history.

1874) What language do Sims speak?

1875) Which expansion came first: The Sims: House Party or The Sims: Vacation?

1876) Which expansion came first: The Sims: Superstar or The Sims: Hot Date?

1877) What game sold more copies for Atari, Missile Command or Pac-Man?

1878) Which sold more copies for Wii: Wii Fit or Mario Party 8?

1851. c, 1852. a, 1853. k, 1854. j, 1855. h, 1856. f, 1857. b, 1858. d, 1859. n, 1860. g, 1861. m, 1862. o, 1863. e, 1864. l, 1865. i, 1866. Getaway Driver, 1867. Counterfeiter, 1868. Smuggler, 1869. c, 1870. SimCity, 1871. true, 1872. true, 1873. true, 1874. Simlish, 1875. Sims: House Party, 1876. The Sims: Hot Date, 1877. Pac-Man, 1878. Wii Fit

1879) Which sold more for Wii: Wii Party or Wii Play?

1880) True or false: Over $2.5 billion in quarters were spent in Pac-Man video games.

1881) WHICH SOLD MORE FOR WII: WII SPORTS OR SUPER MARIO GALAXY?

1882) Which sold more for PlayStation: Tomb Raider II or Tom Raider?

1883) Which sold more for PlayStation 2: Final Fantasy X or Grand Theft Auto III?

1884) TRUE OR FALSE: THE WII WAS AVAILABLE IN WHITE, BLUE, OR RED IN ITS FIRST YEAR.

TOUGH TRIVIA CHALLENGE

1885) What was the code name for the Wii while it was in development?

a) Reaction
b) Revolution
c) Recreator
d) Recreationator

1886) Which of the following is not a Super Mario game for Wii?

a) Super Mario Galaxy 2
b) Super Mario All-Stars
c) Super Paper Mario
d) Super Mario Indestructible

COMPLETE THE TITLE OF THESE WII GAMES:

1887) Active Life: Extreme ________
1888) Alien ______ Bowling League
1889) AMF Bowling World _______
1890) Are You Smarter Than a 5th Grader: Make the ____
1891) Backyard Sports: Sandlot _______
1892) Batman: The Brave and the ______
1893) Big Brain ________: Wii Degree
1894) Bratz: Girlz Really _____!
1895) Cabela's Big Game ________
1896) Call of Duty: Black ____
1897) Celebrity Sports _________
1898) Doctor Fizzwhizzle's Animal ______
1899) Donkey Kong Jungle ______
1900) Kidz Bop Dance _____
1901) Kirby's Return to ___________
1902) Legend of Zelda; Skyward ______
1903) Mario and Sonic at the ________ Games
1904) MySims: Sky _______
1905) Pet Pals: Animal _______
1906) Pirates vs. _______: Dodgeball

1907) Which of the following is not a Tony Hawk game for Wii?

a) Tony Hawk's Downhill Jam

b) Tony Hawk: Shred

c) Tony Hawk: Ride It Alone

d) Tony Hawk's Proving Ground

1908) Which Wii game was released first in the U.S., Super Swing Golf or Madden NFL 07?

1879. Wii Play, 1880. true, 1881. Wii Sports, 1882. Tomb Raider II, 1883. Grand Theft Auto III, 1884. false—just white, 1885. b, 1886. d, 1887. Challenge, 1888. Monster, 1889. Lanes, 1890. Grade, 1891. Sluggers, 1892. Bold, 1893. Academy, 1894. Rock, 1895. Hunter, 1896. Ops, 1897. Showdown, 1898. Rescue, 1899. Beat, 1900. Party, 1901. Dreamland, 1902. Sword, 1903. Olympic, 1904. Heroes, 1905. Doctor, 1906. Ninjas, 1907. c, 1908. Madden NFL 07

1909) Which Wii game was released first in the U.S., Brunswick Pro Bowling or MySims?

1910) Which came first for Wii, LEGO Indiana Jones: The Original Adventures or LEGO Star Wars: The Complete Saga.

1911) What does a white bird drop in Angry Birds?

1912) THE DESIGNER OF ANGRY BIRDS IS FROM:

A) ENGLAND
B) FINLAND
C) CONGO
D) ECUADOR

1913) Which came first for Wii: LEGO Batman or LEGO Harry Potter?

1914) In Angry Birds, what is a player trying to hit with the birds?

1915) What color are the birds at the initial levels of Angry Birds?

1916) How many smaller birds can the blue bird separate into in Angry Birds?

1917) HOW MANY LEVELS IN EACH CHAPTER OF THE INITIAL RELEASE OF ANGRY BIRDS?

1918) What country invades the U.S. in Call of Duty: Modern Warfare 3?

1919) True or false: According to Portal 2, the game is set in Arizona.

1920) What is the player character in Portal promised as a prize when all of the puzzles are solved?

1921) What is the name of the player character in Portal?

a) Krell b) Chell c) Shell d) Mell

TOUGH TRIVIA CHALLENGE

1922) In Portal, what does GLaDOS stand for?

a) Genetic Lifeform and Disk Operating System

b) Generic Living Duck Outreach Sergeant

c) General Losers Don't Often Stay

d) Genetic Lizard Defense Online Strategy

1923) True or false: The Legend of Zelda was originally released as the Hyrule Fantasy: Legend of Zelda.

1924) IN ZELDA, HOW MANY FRAGMENTS OF THE TRIFORCE OF WISDOM MUST BE COLLECTED?

1925) True or false: Zelda takes place in the land of Hyrule.

1926) What is the boy hero in the Legend of Zelda named?

1927) True or false: Rovio, maker of Angry Birds, also made the game Desert Sniper?

1928) Who is the villain of The Legend of Zelda?

a) Ganon

b) Gamon

c) Gambon

d) Grammion

1929) What is Zelda's nursemaid's name?

a) Impanima

b) Impa

c) Ooompa

d) Yolanda

1930) TRUE OR FALSE: A FILM VERSION OF THE LEGEND OF ZELDA WAS MADE IN CHINA BUT NEVER RELEASED IN THE U.S.

1909. Brunswick Pro Bowling, 1910. LEGO Star Wars: The Complete Saga, 1911. eggs, 1912. b, 1913. LEGO Batman, 1914. Pigs, 1915. Red, 1916. three, 1917. twenty-one, 1918. Russia, 1919. false—Michigan, 1920. cake, 1921. b, 1922. a, 1923. true, 1924. eight, 1925. true, 1926. Link, 1927. true, 1928. a, 1929. b, 1930. false

CHAPTER 4

Celebrities

ALSO KNOWN AS

1931) Stefani Germanotta is better known as whom?

1932) Is Issur Danielovitch Demsky better known as Kirk Douglas or Michael Douglas?

1933) True or false: Actor Stewart Granger was born under the name James Stewart, but had to change it because it was already taken.

1934) True or false: Actor Michael Keaton was born under the name Michael Douglas, but had to change it because it was already taken by another actor?

TOUGH TRIVIA CHALLENGE

1935) What is Michael J. Fox's middle name?

a) James
b) Jefferson
c) Jonathan
d) Andrew

1936) What actress, born Dianne Hall, was the mother in the *Father of the Bride* movies?

1937) Alexandra Molinsky is better known as what comedian?

1931. Lady Gaga, 1932. Kirk Douglas, 1933. true, 1934. true, 1935. d, 1936. Diane Keaton, 1937. Joan Rivers

Match the initials to the name.

1938) F.W. a) Author Andrews
1939) G.K. b) Author Chesterton
1940) I.F. c) Comedian Fields
1941) I.M. d) Lyricist Gilbert
1942) K.C. e) Rapper Hammer
1943) K.D. f) NBA star Jones
1944) K.T. g) Singer Lang
1945) M.C. h) Wide receiver McDufe
1946) N.C. i) Author Naipaul
1947) O.J. j) Singer Oslin
1948) S.J. k) Architect Pei
1949) U.L. l) Humorist Perelman
1950) V.C. m) Journalist Stone
1951) V.S. n) Quarterback Tittle
1952) W.C. o) Shortstop Washington
1953) W.S p) Store-owner Woolworth
1954) Y.A. q) Artist Wyeth

Match the initials to the name.

1955) L.A. a) Clothier Bean
1956) L.B. b) Defensive end Greenwood
1957) L.C. c) Movie producer Mayer
1958) L.L. d) Record producer Reid

1959) Frederick Austerlitz is better known as what famous dancer?

1960) True or false: Betty Jo Perske is better known as Betty White?

1961) LESLIE L. KING JR. IS BETTER KNOWN AS WHAT FORMER U.S. PRESIDENT?

Match the initials to the name.

1962) P.D. a) Circus impresario Barnum
1963) P.G. b) Author James
1964) P.J. c) Actress Soles
1965) P.K. d) Author Travers
1966) P.L. e) Author Wodehouse
1967) P.T. f) Confectioner Wrigley

1968) Allen Stuart Konigsberg is better known as what writer/actor/director?

MATCH THE FIRST NAME AND MIDDLE INITIAL TO THE LAST NAME.

1969) Alice B.
1970) Angus T.
1971) Ann B.
1972) Arthur C.
1973) Ben E.
1974) David O.
1975) Edward G.
1976) Edward R.
1977) George C.
1978) George M.
1979) Jaye P.
1980) John C.
1981) Michael C.
1982) Michael J.
1983) Michael W.
1984) William H.

a) Clarke
b) Cohan
c) Davis
d) Fox
e) Hall
f) Jones
g) King
h) Macy
i) Morgan
j) Murrow
k) Reilly
l) Robinson
m) Scott
n) Selznick
o) Smith
p) Toklas

1985) John Mellencamp's first four albums were recorded under what name?

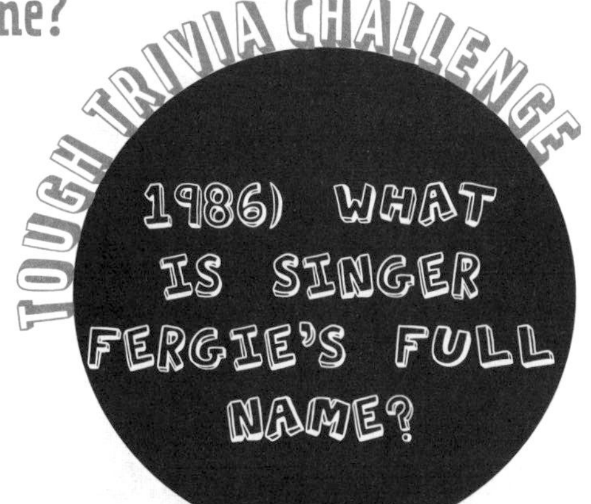

1987) What is writer William Sydney Porter better known as?

a) O. Henry
b) Mark Twain
c) Stephen King
d) R. L. Stein

1938. p, 1939. b, 1940. m, 1941. k, 1942. f, 1943. g, 1944. j, 1945. e, 1946. q, 1947. h, 1948. l, 1949. o, 1950. a, 1951. i, 1952. c, 1953. d, 1954. n, 1955. d, 1956. c, 1957. b, 1958. a, 1959. Fred Astaire, 1960. false—it's actress Lauren Bacall, 1961. Gerald Ford, 1962. b, 1963. e, 1964. c, 1965. f, 1966. d, 1967. a, 1968. Woody Allen, 1969. p, 1970. f, 1971. c, 1972. a, 1973. g, 1974. n, 1975. l, 1976. j, 1977. m, 1978. b, 1979. i, 1980. k, 1981. e, 1982. d, 1983. o, 1984. h, 1985. Johnny Cougar, 1986. Stacy Ferguson, 1987. a

MATCH THE FIRST INITIAL AND MIDDLE NAME TO THE LAST NAME.

1988) A. Bartlett	a) Abraham
1989) C. Thomas	b) Boyle
1990) E. Howard	c) Carroll
1991) E. Jean	d) Fitzgerald
1992) F. Murray	e) Giamatti
1993) F. Scott	f) Hoover
1994) G. Gordon	g) Howell
1995) H. Ross	h) Hunt
1996) J. Edgar	i) Liddy
1997) M. Emmet	j) Perot
1998) R. Dean	k) Pickens
1999) R. Emmett	l) Stone
2000) T. Boone	m) Taylor
2001) T. Coraghessan	n) Tyrrell
2002) W. Clement	o) Walsh

2003) Samuel Clemens is better known as whom?

2004) Reginald Dwight is better known as what singer?

2005) True or false: Comedian W.C . Fields' given names were Warren Corbett.

2006) True or false: C.C. Sabathia's given names are Carsten Charles.

2007) True or false: O.J. Simpson's given names are Oliver Jameson.

MATCH THE INITIALS TO THE NAME.

2008) A.A.
2009) A.C.
2010) A.E.
2011) A.J.
2012) A.M.
2013) A.P.

a) NBA star Green
b) Confederate general Hill
c) Poet Housman
d) Actress Michalka
e) Author Milne
f) Journalist Rosenthal

2014) TRUE OR FALSE: THE C IN J.C. PENNEY STANDS FOR CASH.

2015) True or false: James Hoffa, whose disappearance in 1975 remains a mystery to this day, had the middle name Riddle.

2016) True or false: Leonard Slye is better known as Roy Rogers?

MATCH THE INITIALS TO THE NAME.

2017) T.C.
2018) T.D.
2019) T.E.
2020) T.J.
2021) T.R.
2022) T.S.

a) Poet Eliot
b) TV character Hooker
c) Pastor Jakes
d) Actor Knight
e) Military hero Lawrence
f) Artist Steele

2023) True or false: Writer C.S. Lewis's given names were Clive Staples.

Match the initials to the name.

2024) B.A.
2025) B.B.
2026) B.D.
2027) B.F.
2028) B.J.
2029) B.L.
2030) B.O.

a) TV character Baracus
b) Singer King
c) Comic strip character Plenty
d) Psychologist Skinner
e) TV character Stryker
f) Singer Thomas
g) Actor Wong

1988. e, 1989. g, 1990. h, 1991. c, 1992. a, 1993. d, 1994. i, 1995. j, 1996. f, 1997. o, 1998. m, 1999. n, 2000. k, 2001. b, 2002. l, 2003. Mark Twain, 2004. Elton John, 2005. false—William Claude, 2006. true, 2007. false—Orenthal James, 2008. e, 2009. a. 2010. c, 2011. d, 2012. f, 2013. b, 2014. true, 2015. true, 2016. true, 2017. f, 2018. c, 2019. e, 2020. b, 2021. d, 2022. a, 2023. true, 2024. a, 2025. b, 2026. g, 2027. d, 2028. f, 2029. e, 2030. c

TOUGH TRIVIA CHALLENGE

2031) TRUE OR FALSE: HARRY S. TRUMAN'S MIDDLE NAME WAS SHIPPE.

2032) Phineas Taylor and James Anthony were the given names of what famous pair of businessmen?

2033) True or false: J.K. Rowling's given names are Joanne Kathleen.

2034) William Henry McCarty Jr. is better known as what western outlaw?

2035) True or false: Baroness Karen von Blixen-Finecke wrote under the pen name Virginia Woolf?

Match the initials to the name.

2036) J.A.
2037) J.B.
2038) J.C.
2039) J.D.
2040) J.G.
2041) J.J.
2042) J.K.
2043) J.M.
2044) J.P.
2045) J.R.
2046) J.S.
2047) J.T.

a) Producer Abrams
b) Composer Bach
c) Author Ballard
d) Author Barrie
e) TV character Ewing
f) Pitcher Happ
g) Financier Morgan
h) Scientist Priestley
i) Author Rowling
j) Author Salinger
k) Actor Walsh
l) Congressman Watts

2048) TRUE OR FALSE: MARION MORRISON IS BETTER KNOWN AS JOHN WAYNE.

2049) Norma Jean Baker is better known as whom?

2050) What was Princess Diana's maiden name?

2051) True or false: Michael Igorevitch Peschkowsky is better known as director Mike Nichols?

Match the initials to the name.

2052) C.B.	a) TV character Cregg
2053) C.C.	b) Director DeMille
2054) C.J.	c) Author Lewis
2055) C.P.	d) Pitcher Sabathia
2056) C.S.	e) Author Snow

2057) WHAT WAS MUHAMMAD ALI'S BIRTH NAME?

2031. false—it stood for itself, 2032. Barnum and Bailey, 2033. false—she has no middle name, 2034. Billy the Kid, 2035. false—Isak Dinesen, 2036. f, 2037. h, 2038. l, 2039. j, 2040. c, 2041. a, 2042. i, 2043. d, 2044. g, 2045. e, 2046. b, 2047. k, 2048. true, 2049. Marilyn Monroe, 2050. Spencer, 2051. true, 2052. b, 2053. d, 2054. a, 2055. e, 2056. c, 2057. Cassius Clay

2058) What was Kareem Abdul-Jabbar's birth name?

2059) Who changed his name to Chad Ochocinco?

2060) What basketball player changed his name to Metta World Peace?

2061) True or false: Benny Kubelsky is better known as comedian Jack Benny.

2062) Dino Crocetti and Joseph Levitch are better known as what comedy team?
a) Martin and Lewis
b) Laurel and Hardy
c) Burns and Allen
d) None of the above

2063) True or false: Nathan Birnbaum is better known as comedian George Burns.

Match the initials to the name.

2064) D.A. a) Hijacker Cooper
2065) D.B. b) Running back Dozier
2066) D.H. c) Director Griffith
2067) D.J. d) Comedian Hughley
2068) D.L. e) Author Lawrence
2069) D.W. f) Filmmaker Pennebaker

2070) Natalia Zakharenko is better known as whom?

2071) True or false: Writer P.G. Wodehouse's given names were Pelham Grenville.

TOUGH TRIVIA CHALLENGE

2073) True or false: The given name of W.S. Gilbert (of Gilbert and Sullivan) was Wyndham Sheridan.

2072) True or false: Ellas Otha Bates is better known as The Big Bopper.

2074) True or false: *Legend of Sleepy Hollow* author Washington Irving wrote his book *History of New York* under the name Diedrich Knickerbocker.

Match the initials to the name.

2075) E.B.	a) Poet Cummings
2076) E.C.	b) Author Doctorow
2077) E.E.	c) Author Forster
2078) E.F.	d) Lyricist Harburg
2079) E.G.	e) Stockbroker Hutton
2080) E.J.	f) Actor Marshall
2081) E.L.	g) Cartoonist Segar
2082) E.M.	h) Racecar driver Viso
2083) E.Y.	i) Author White

MATCH THE INITIALS TO THE NAME.

2084) H.B.	a) Condiment maker Heinz
2085) H.G.	b) Journalist Kaltenborn
2086) H.H.	c) Journalist Mencken
2087) H.J.	d) Author Munro
2088) H.L.	e) TV character Pufnstuf
2089) H.R.	f) Actor Warner
2090) H.V.	g) Author Wells

2058. Lew Alcindor, 2059. Chad Johnson, 2060. Ron Artest, 2061. true, 2062. a, 2063. true, 2064. f, 2065. a, 2066. e, 2067. b, 2068. d, 2069. c, 2070. Natalie Wood, 2071. true, 2072. false—Bo Diddley, 2073. false—it was William Schwenck, 2074. true, 2075. i, 2076. g, 2077. a, 2078. e, 2079. f, 2080. h, 2081. b, 2082. c, 2083. d, 2084. f, 2085. g, 2086. d, 2087. a, 2088. c, 2089. e, 2090. b

WHAT'S MY JOB

2091) David Cameron: British prime minister or Google executive?

2092) John Lasseter: Arizona congressman or head of Pixar?

2093) David Petraeus: CIA director or building designer?

2094) Gerry Adams: Former Spice Girl or Irish resistance leader?

2095) ISABEL ALLENDE: CHILEAN WRITER OR WORLD-RENOWNED CHEF?

2096) Dave Barry: Humor writer or founder of Amazon.com?

2097) Christopher Buckley: Magazine editor or Republican presidential candidate?

2098) Mark Burnett: *Survivor* producer or syndicated radio host?

2099) Van Cliburn: Pianist or silent movie actor?

2100) Chuck Close: Former astronaut or photo-realist painter?

2101) Jon Corzine: U.S. senator or Olympic bobsledder?

2102) Freeman Dyson: Physicist or infomercial pitchman?

2103) IRA GLASS: RADIO BROADCASTER OR JUGGLER?

2104) Seymour Hersh: Investigative reporter or convicted embezzler?

2105) Daniel Handler: Former New York City Mayor or children's book author?

2106) Arianna Huffington: Website cofounder or cast member of *Desperate Housewives*?

2107) Judith Jameson: Choreographer or fashion designer?

2108) Richard Bachman: Pseudonym for Stephen King or chairman of Southwest Airlines?

2109) Susan Lucci: Governor of Ohio or soap opera actress?

2110) Keith Lockhart: Conductor of the Boston Pops or last American in space?

2111) Angela Merkel: Chancellor of Germany or Nobel-prize-winning chemist?

2112) Janet Napolitano: U.S. secretary of homeland security or Canadian folksinger.

2113) Sam Walton: Baseball player or founder of Wal-Mart?

2114) Jay Gould: American railroad developer or star of TV show *All in The Family*?

2091. British prime minister, 2092. head of Pixar, 2093. CIA director, 2094. Irish resistance leader, 2095. Chilean writer, 2096. humor writer, 2097. magazine editor, 2098. Survivor producer, 2099. pianist, 2100. photo-realist painter, 2101. U.S. senator, 2102. physicist, 2103. radio broadcaster, 2104. investigative reporter, 2105. children's book author, 2106. website cofounder, 2107. choreographer, 2108. pseudonym for Stephen King, 2109. soap opera actress, 2110. conductor, 2111. chancellor, 2112. U.S. secretary of homeland security, 2113. founder of Wal-Mart, 2114. American railroad developer, 2115. advertising executive

2116) CARL SAGAN: SCIENTIST AND TV HOST OR HOCKEY MVP?

2117) Lord Kelvin: Scientist or British politician?

2118) Jim Morrison: Rock musician or Harry Truman's vice president?

2119) Arthur Schopenhauer: Physician or philosopher?

2120) John Wesley: Methodist minister or founder of Harvard?

2121) JOHN MAYNARD KEYNES: ECONOMIST OR ECOLOGIST?

2122) Alfred North Whitehead: Beatles manager or mathematician?

2123) William Wallace: The "Guardian of Scotland" or director of *The Wizard of Oz*?

2124) Emiliano Zapata: Mexican revolutionary leader or J-Lo's first husband?

2125) Ansel Adams: Astronomer or photographer?

2126) Yoshiro Mori: Prime minister of Japan or star or *The King and I*?

2127) Stephen Ambrose: Historian or jockey?

2128) Joan Baez: First lady of Spain or folk singer.

2129) ELIZABETH BLACKWELL: FIRST WOMAN TO FLY IN SPACE OR FIRST WOMAN TO GRADUATE FROM MEDICAL SCHOOL.

2130) Dian Fossey: Gorilla researcher or fashion designer?

2131) Enrico Fermi: Scientist or chef?

2132) Howard Hughes: Reclusive billionaire or magazine publisher?

TOUGH TRIVIA CHALLENGE

2133) Yuri Gagarin: Cosmonaut or Soviet politician?

2134) SANDRA DAY O'CONNOR: SUFFRAGETTE OR SUPREME COURT JUSTICE?

2135) Leni Riefenstahl: German filmmaker or founder of the American Kennel Club.

2136) Mel Tillis: Country singer or Georgia governor?

2137) Robert Merrill: Three-time Indy 500 winner or opera singer?

2116. scientist and TV host, 2117. scientist, 2118. rock musician, 2119. philosopher, 2120. Methodist minister, 2121. economist, 2122. mathematician, 2123. Guardian of Scotland, 2124. Mexican revolutionary leader, 2125. photographer, 2126. Prime minister of Japan, 2127. historian, 2128. folk singer, 2129. first woman to graduate from medical school, 2130. gorilla researcher, 2131. scientist, 2132. reclusive billionaire, 2133. cosmonaut, 2134. Supreme Court justice, 2135. German filmmaker, 2136. country singer, 2137. opera singer

2138) Bob Love:
Chicago Bulls basketball player or peace activist?

2139) Greg Louganis:
Diving champion or Greek revolutionary?

2140) Rubin "Hurricane" Carter:
Meteorologist or boxer?

2141) John Updike:
Plymouth Rock pilgrim or 20th-century American writer?

2142) HENRY LUCE:
FOUNDER OF *TIME* MAGAZINE OR LAS VEGAS-BASED MAGICIAN?

2143) Alan Turing: Mathematician or notorious embezzler?

2144) Jack Welch:
Chairman of GE or creator of the War of the Worlds hoax?

2145) Billy Mays:
Commercial pitchman or baseball star?

2146) Charles Addams: Cartoonist or signer of the Declaration of Independence?

2148) Pat Garrett: College basketball coach or killer of Billy the Kid?

2149) August Wilson: Playwright or creator of the standardized calendar.

2150) Marcel Duchamp: Artist or French prime minister?

2151) Henry Highland Garnet: Abolitionist or New York mayor?

2152) George Best: British soccer star or "fifth Beatle"?

2153) Ambrose Burnside: Civil War general or New England poet?

2154) Joseph Lister: Dictionary developer or founder of antiseptic medicine?

2155) Modest Mussorgsky: Early fashion model or composer?

2156) Thomas Nast: Illustrator or adventurer?

2157) Geraldo Rivera: Motel owner or TV talk-show host?

TOUGH TRIVIA CHALLENGE

2158) Ned Kelly: Australian outlaw or Texas governor?

2138. Chicago Bulls player, 2139. diving champion, 2140. boxer, 2141. 20th-century American writer, 2142. founder of *Time*, 2143. mathematician, 2144. chairman of GE, 2145. commercial pitchman, 2146. cartoonist, 2147. political philosopher, 2148. killer of Billy the Kid, 2149. playwright, 2150. artist, 2151. abolitionist, 2152. British soccer star, 2153. Civil War general, 2154. founder of antiseptic medicin[illegible] c[illegible]poser, 2156. illustrator, 2157. TV t[illegible] s[illegible]w nost, 2158. Australian outlaw

IBSEN: INVENTOR OF THE CRAYON OR PLAYWRIGHT.

2160) WILHELM CONRAD RONTGEN: X-RAY PIONEER OR SOVIET PRISONER/AUTHOR?

TOUGH TRIVIA CHALLENGE

2161) Donald Neilson: *Saturday Night Live* regular or armed robber?

2162) Margaret Mead: Ethnologist or inventor of Jell-O?

2163) Brian Jones: Rolling Stones guitarist or member of Monty Python's Flying Circus?

2164) David Koresh: Cult leader or Internet pioneer?

2165) Aileen Wuornos: French new wave film director or serial killer?

2166) John Gotti: Mobster or Los Angeles mayor?

2167) ANNA QUINDLEN: COLUMNIST/NOVELIST OR INFOMERCIAL SPOKESPERSON?

2168) Jeff Bezos: Amazon.com founder or early TV clown?

2169) Bobby Fischer: Kennedy relative or chess champion?

2170) Brian Wilson: Leader of Irish revolutionary organization or leader of the Beach Boys?

2171) Judith Jamison: Dancer/choreographer or candy manufacturer?

2172) IAN FLEMING: JAMES BOND AUTHOR OR INVENTOR OF THE NASAL STRIP?

2173) Pierre Omidyar: Middle Eastern political leader or founder of eBay?

2174) Lon Chaney: Olympic wrestler or horror movie star?

TOUGH TRIVIA CHALLENGE

2175) Sergey Brin: Cofounder of Google or "Barbarian of Serbia"?

2176) Sam Kinison: Comedian or early motion-picture pioneer?

2177) Gareth Edwards: Rugby player or modern dancer?

2178) Ken Follett: Sports announcer or bestselling novelist?

2179) Tina Weymouth: Bass player/Talking Heads cofounder or Prime Minster of England

2180) Steve Allen: Original host of *The Tonight Show* or World Series of Poker champion?

2159. playwright, 2160. X-ray pioneer, 2161. armed robber, 2162. ethnologist, 2163. Rolling Stones guitarist, 2164. cult leader, 2165. serial killer, 2166. mobster, 2167. columnist/novelist, 2168. Amazon.com founder, 2169. chess champion, 2170. leader of the Beach Boys, 2171. dancer/choreographer, 2172. James Bond author, 2173. founder of eBay, 2174. horror movie star, 2175. cofounder of Google, 2176. comedian, 2177. rugby player, 2178. bestselling novelist, 2179. bass player/Talking Heads cofounder, 2180. original host of *The Tonight Show*

2181) ELIZABETH ARDEN:
PRINCIPAL IN THE MOVIE *GREASE* OR BEAUTY INDUSTRY PIONEER?

2182) Rowan Atkinson: Mr. Bean alter ego or founder of Bloomingdale's?

2183) Shirley Bassey:
Singer or congresswoman?

2184) Barbara Billingsley:
Creator of the Post-It note or 50s TV mom?

2185) Victor Borge:
Pianist or Antarctic explorer?

2186) CARLA BRUNI:
MOBSTER OR MODEL/FIRST LADY OF FRANCE?

2187) Stephen Decatur: War of 1812 naval ofcer or founder of Illinois?

2188) Hank Greenberg: Baseball player or creator of the Snickers Bar?

2189) Gene Krupa:
Track and field star or drummer?

2190) Hugh Lofting:
Dr. Doolittle writer or star of *House*?

2191) Nancy Lopez:
Golfer or New Mexico congresswoman?

2192) James Edward Oglehorpe:
Founder of Savannah, Georgia, or conflicted Wall Street inside trader?

2193) BARRY GOLDWATER:
CONSERVATIVE POLITICAL ICON OR STEAMBOAT INVENTOR?

2194) Hal Roach:
Movie producer or drug lord?

2195) Tom Mix: Animal rights activist or movie cowboy?

2196) Soupy Sales: TV comedian or Campbell's cofounder?

2197) Don Shula: Legendary acting coach or football coach?

2198) Jodie Sweetin: *Full House* actress or inventor of aspartame.

2199) Madame C.J. Walker: Hair care entrepreneur or World War II historian?

2200) Douglas Wilder: Virginia governor or inventor of the microwave?

2201) David Foster Wallace: Novelist or attempted presidential assassin?

2202) Harlan Fiske Stone: Fast-food pioneer or Supreme Court Chief Justice?

2203) Charles Q. Dawes: *Survivor* winner or U.S. vice president?

2204) Eddie Rickenbacker: Racecar driver or German fighter pilot?

2205) Johnnie Cochran: Lawyer or original cast member of *The Electric Company*?

2206) Melvil Dewey: Muppeteer or developer of library organization system?

2181. beauty industry pioneer, 2182. Mr. Bean alter ego, 2183. singer, 2184. 50s TV mom, 2185. pianist, 2186. model/First Lady of France, 2187. War of 1812 naval officer, 2188. baseball player, 2189. drummer, 2190. *Dr. Doolittle* writer, 2191. golfer, 2192. founder of Savannah, Georgia, 2193. conservative political icon, 2194. movie producer, 2195. movie cowboy, 2196. TV comedian, 2197. football coach, 2198. *Full House* actress, 2199. hair care entrepreneur, 2200. Virginia governor, 2201. novelist, 2202. Supreme Court Chief Justice, 2203. U.S. vice president, 2204. racecar driver, 2205. lawyer, 2206. developer of library organization system

2207) CLIVE BARNES:
CHEF OR THEATER CRITIC?

2208) Bella Abzug: American politician or German tycoon?

2209) Bob Kane:
Batman creator or fictional newspaper publisher?

2210) Jeb Magruder:
Civil War general or Watergate conspirator?

2211) Paul Erdos:
Novelist or mathematician?

2212) PAUL KRUGMAN:
ACTOR OR ECONOMIST?

2213) Charles Guiteau:
Assassin or French president?

2214) Andrew Wyeth: Artist or signer of the Declaration of Independence?

2215) Bill Rancic:
Reality-show contestant or singer?

2216) Allen Drury:
Novelist or TV host?

2217) Conchita Martinez:
Member of congress or tennis player?

2218) Tara Conner: Miss USA or Olympic gold medalist?

2219) Jacques Chirac:
French president or pirate?

2220) MIYOSHI UMEKI:
JAPANESE NOVELIST OR OSCAR-WINNING ACTRESS?

2221) Vincent Gallo:
Actor-director or chemist?

2222) Melvin Belli: Attorney or mobster?

2223) Stephan Pastis: Cartoonist or Linkedin.com founder?

2224) Craig Newmark: Craigslist founder or hotel-chain owner?

2225) AISHWARYA RAI: ACTRESS OR NOBEL MEDICINE PRIZE WINNER?

2226) Phil Bronstein: Comedian or newspaper editor?

2227) Bennett Cerf: Financier or book publisher?

2228) Zoilo Versalles: Baseball player or Guatemalan general?

2229) Fulgencio Batista: Baseball player or Cuban dictator?

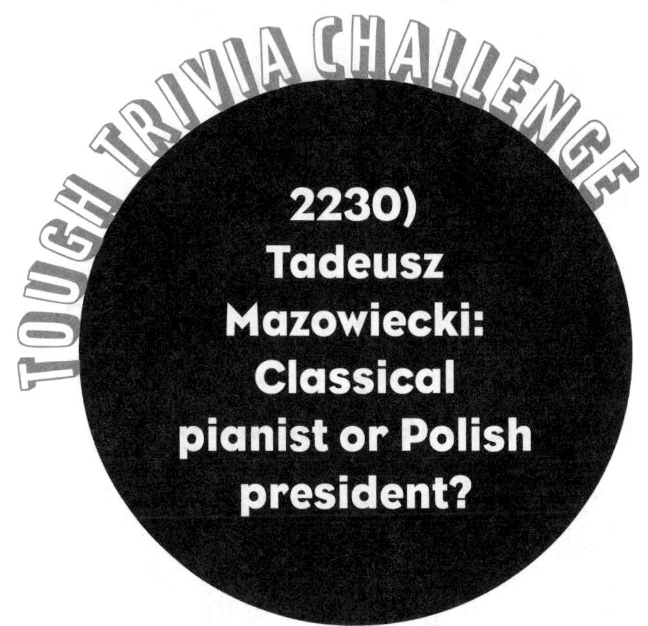

2231) T.C. Boyle: Artist or novelist?

2232) Milan Kundera: Mathematician or novelist?

2233) IMMANUEL KANT: PHILOSOPHER OR RELIGIOUS REFORMER?

2234) Sally Struthers: Actress or gossip columnist?

2207. theater critic, 2208. American politician, 2209. Batman creator, 2210. Watergate conspirator, 2211. mathematician, 2212. economist, 2213. assassin, 2214. artist, 2215. reality-show contestant, 2216. novelist, 2217. tennis player, 2218. Miss USA, 2219. French president, 2220. actress, 2221. actor-director, 2222. attorney, 2223. cartoonist, 2224. Craigslist founder, 2225. actress, 2226. editor, 2227. publisher, 2228. ballplayer, 2229. dictator, 2230. Polish president, 2231. novelist, 2232. novelist, 2233. philosopher, 2234. actress

IT'S ALL RELATIVE

2235) Are President Richard Nixon and actress Cynthia Nixon related?

2236) Are author Ernest Hemingway and actress Mariel Hemingway related?

2237) True or false: Novelist Nicholson Baker is actor Jack Nicholson's son.

2238) ARE ACTRESSES ROSALIND RUSSELL AND KERI RUSSELL RELATED?

2239) Are composers Johann and Richard Strauss related?

2240) Are civil rights leader Jesse Jackson and baseball Hall of Famer Reggie Jackson related?

2241) Are singer Dean and comedian Demetri Martin related?

2242) Are psychiatrist Sigmund Freud and artist Lucian Freud related?

2243) Are artists Claude Monet and Eduard Manet related?

2244) Are actresses Julia and Emma Roberts related?

2245) ARE ACTRESS JANE SEYMOUR AND HENRY VIII'S WIFE JANE SEYMOUR RELATED?

2246) Are basketball stars Reggie and Cheryl Miller related?

2247) Are singers Paul and Carly Simon related?

2248) Are actors Kirk and Michael Douglas related?

2249) Are composers Johann Sebastian Bach and P.D.Q. Bach related?

2250) ARE QUARTERBACK TOM BRADY AND FORMER TREASURY SECRETARY NICHOLAS BRADY RELATED?

2251) Are former baseball commissioner A. Bartlett Giamatti and actor Paul Giamatti related?

2252) Are actress Anne Hathaway and the Anne Hathaway who married William Shakespeare related?

2253) Are comedienne Carol Burnett and Survivor creator Mark Burnett related?

2254) Are Broadway composers Richard and Mary Rodgers related?

2255) Are authors Henry and William James related?

2235. no, 2236. yes, 2237. false, 2238. no, 2239. no, 2240. no, 2241. no, 2242. yes, 2243. no, 2244. yes, 2245. no, 2246. yes, 2247. no, 2248. yes, 2249. no, 2250. no, 2251. yes, 2252. no, 2253. no, 2254. yes, 2255. no

2256) Are author Charles Dickens and country star Little Jimmy Dickens related?

2257) Are actors Tom and Colin Hanks related?

2258) ARE FORMER TV NEWSWOMAN MARIA SHRIVER AND FORMER VICE-PRESIDENTIAL NOMINEE SARGENT SHRIVER RELATED?

2259) Are *Moby Dick* author Herman Melville and alt-rock musician Moby related?

2260) Are billionaire John D. Rockefeller and Vice President Nelson Rockefeller related?

2261) Are President Ronald Reagan and talk-show host Michael Reagan related?

2262) Are billionaire J. Paul Getty and actress Estelle Getty related?

2263) Are comedian David Spade and designer Kate Spade related?

2264) ARE ACTRESS OLYMPIA DUKAKIS AND FORMER PRESIDENTIAL CANDIDATE MICHAEL DUKAKIS RELATED?

2265) Are singer Tony Bennett and University of Virginia basketball coach Tony Bennett related?

2266) Are singers Frank and Nancy Sinatra related?

2267) Are civil rights leader Martin Luther King and actress Regina King related?

2268) Are actors John and Drew Barrymore related?

2269) Are singer Enrico Caruso and actor David Caruso related?

2270) Are director Cameron Crowe and actor Russell Crowe related?

2271) Are NBA Commissioner David Stern and radio shock jock Howard Stern related?

2272) ARE AUTHOR JAMES FENIMORE COOPER AND SHOCK-ROCKER ALICE COOPER RELATED?

2273) Are talk-show host Morton Downey Jr. and actor Robert Downey Jr. related?

2274) Are inventors Wilbur and Orville Wright related to architect Frank Lloyd Wright?

2275) Are actor George Clooney and singer Rosemary Clooney related?

2276) Are singer Katy Perry and Texas governor Rick Perry related?

2277) ARE SINGER PAUL MCCARTNEY AND DESIGNER STELLA MCCARTNEY RELATED?

2278) True or false: Nicolas Cage is director Francis Ford Coppola's nephew.

2279) Are Senators Joseph and Eugene McCarthy related?

2280) Are singers John and Julian Lennon related?

2256. no, 2257. yes, 2258. yes, 2259. yes, 2260. yes, 2261. yes, 2262. no, 2263. yes, 2264. yes, 2265. no, 2266. yes, 2267. no, 2268. yes, 2269. no, 2270. no, 2271. no, 2272. no, 2273. no, 2274. no, 2275. yes, 2276. no, 2277. yes, 2278. true, 2279. no, 2280. yes

2281) Are ventriloquist Edgar Bergen and actress Candice Bergen related?

2282) Are talk-show host Conan O'Brien and newswoman Soledad O'Brien related?

2283) Are Confederate general Jeb Stuart and Watergate conspirator Jeb Stuart Magruder related?

2284) True or false: *Lord of the Rings* actor Sean Astin is the son of *Addams Family* actor John Astin.

2285) TRUE OR FALSE: ACTRESS BRIDGET FONDA IS THE DAUGHTER OF JANE FONDA.

2286) True or false: Actress Anjelica Huston is director John Huston's daughter.

Match the presidential pairs to the correct relationship.

2287) The Adamses
2288) The Harrisons
2289) The Johnsons
2290) The Roosevelts

a) father and son
b) grandfather and grandson
c) cousins
d) not related

TILL DEATH DO US PART

2291) Kim Kardashian had a much-ridiculed 72-day marriage to what NBA player?

a) Baron Davis
b) Blake Griffin
c) Kris Humphries
d) Lamar Odom

2292) Garth Brooks is married to what fellow singer?

a) Patty Loveless
b) Kathy Mattea
c) Reba McEntire
d) Trisha Yearwood

2293) Vince Gill is married to what fellow singer?

a) Amy Grant
b) Norah Jones
c) Sarah McLachlan
d) Linda Ronstadt

2294) ELVIS COSTELLO IS MARRIED TO WHAT FELLOW SINGER?

A) DIANA KRALL
B) CLEO LAINE
C) PATTI SMITH
D) DUSTY SPRINGFIELD

2295) Blake Shelton is married to what fellow singer?

a) Miranda Lambert
b) Martina McBride
c) Jennifer Nettles
d) Carrie Underwood

2281. yes, 2282. no, 2283. no, 2284. true, 2285. false—Jane's niece, Peter's daughter, 2286. true, 2287. a, 2288. b, 2289. d, 2290. c, 2291. c, 2292. d, 2293. a, 2294. a, 2295. a

2296) Katy Perry was married to what comic actor?

a) Russell Brand
b) Jim Carrey
c) Steve Coogan
d) Ricky Gervais

2297) Kenny Chesney was briefly married to what actress?

a) Carey Mulligan
b) Winona Ryder
c) Kristen Wiig
d) Renee Zellweger

2298)Keith Urban is married to what actress?

a) Anna Faris
b) Kate Hudson
c) Angelina Jolie
d) Nicole Kidman

2299) Which actress has NOT been married to Tom Cruise?

a) Katie Holmes
b) Nicole Kidman
c) Annette O'Toole
d) Mimi Rogers

2300) DEF LEPPARD PRODUCER MUTT LANGE WAS MARRIED TO WHAT SINGER?

A) PAT BENATAR
B) JOAN JETT
C) MARTINA MCBRIDE
D) SHANIA TWAIN

2301) Paul Newman was married to what actress?

a) Audrey Hepburn
b) Katharine Hepburn
c) Geraldine Page
d) Joanne Woodward

2302) Coldplay lead singer Chris Martin is married to what actress?

a) Helena Bonham Carter
b) Kellie Martin
c) Gwyneth Paltrow
d) Kate Winslet

2303) Emma Thompson was married to what actor?

a) Kenneth Branagh
b) Stephen Fry
c) Michael Gambon
d) Hugh Laurie

2304) John Travolta is married to what actress?

a) Kirstie Alley
b) Swoosie Kurtz
c) Lori Loughlin
d) Kelly Preston

2305) ACTRESS RITA WILSON IS MARRIED TO WHAT ACTOR?

A) KEVIN COSTNER
B) ROBERT DUVALL
C) TOM HANKS
D) BILL MURRAY

2306) Robert Wagner was twice married to what actress?

a) Dyan Cannon
b) Jill Clayburgh
c) Goldie Hawn
d) Natalie Wood

2307) True or false: Frank Sinatra married Harpo Marx's daughter.

2308) Ernest Borgnine was briefly married to what actress?

a) Patti LuPone
b) Mary Martin
c) Ethel Merman
d) Dorothy Provine

2309) Model Gisele Bundchen is married to what quarterback?

a) Tom Brady
b) Peyton Manning
c) Aaron Rodgers
d) Tony Romo

2296. a, 2297. d, 2298. d, 2299. c, 2300. d, 2301. d, 2302. c, 2303. a, 2304. d, 2305. c, 2306. d, 2307. false—Zeppo Marx's ex-wife, 2308. c, 2309. a

2310) Model Brooklyn Decker is married to what tennis star?

a) James Blake
b) Jim Courier
c) Mardy Fish
d) Andy Roddick

2311) Model Miranda Kerr is married to what actor?

a) Orlando Bloom
b) Patrick Dempsey
c) Josh Lucas
d) Chris O'Donnell

2312) Ryan Reynolds was married to what fellow actor?

a) Drew Barrymore
b) Cameron Diaz
c) Scarlett Johansson
d) Maggie Q

2313) JENNIFER GARNER IS MARRIED TO WHAT FELLOW ACTOR?

A) BEN AFFLECK
B) GEORGE CLOONEY
C) MATT DAMON
D) BEN STILLER

2314) Sculptor Don Gummer is married to what actress?

a) Judi Dench
b) Jane Lynch
c) Vanessa Redgrave
d) Meryl Streep

2315) Julie Andrews was married to what director?

a) Robert Altman
b) Blake Edwards
c) Howard Hawks
d) Billy Wilder

2316) Actress Bridgette Wilson is married to what athlete?

a) Carl Lewis
b) Pete Sampras
c) Barry Sanders
d) Curt Schilling

2317) Humphrey Bogart was married to what actress?

a) Lauren Bacall
b) Ingrid Bergman
c) Ava Gardner
d) Katharine Hepburn

2318) MARILYN MONROE WAS MARRIED TO WHAT BASEBALL STAR?

A) MICKEY MANTLE
B) DUKE SNIDER
C) JOE DIMAGGIO
D) TED WILLIAMS

2319) Actress Ava Gardner was NOT married to which of the following?

a) Howard Hughes
b) Mickey Rooney
c) Artie Shaw
d) Frank Sinatra

2320) Julia Roberts was married to what singer?

a) Trace Adkins
b) Lyle Lovett
c) Aaron Tippin
d) Dwight Yoakam

2321) Mia Farrow was married to what singer?

a) Tony Bennett
b) Bing Crosby
c) Mick Jagger
d) Frank Sinatra

2322) TV newswoman Jane Pauley is married to what cartoonist?

a) Scott Adams
b) Bill Amend
c) Stephan Pastis
d) Garry Trudeau

2310. d, 2311. a, 2312. c, 2313. a, 2314. d, 2315. b, 2316. b, 2317. a, 2318. c, 2319. a, 2320. b, 2321. d, 2322. d

2323) Elizabeth Taylor was NOT married to:

a) Richard Burton
b) Albert Finney
c) Eddie Fisher
d) Senator John Warner

2324) Which actor was Meg Ryan married to, Dennis Quaid or Randy Quaid?

2325) Steven Spielberg is married to what actress?

a) Elizabeth Berkley
b) Kate Capshaw
c) Diane Keaton
d) Sissy Spacek

2326) HALLE BERRY WAS MARRIED TO WHAT BASEBALL PLAYER?

A) REGGIE JACKSON
B) DEREK JETER
C) DAVE JUSTICE
D) FRANK THOMAS

2327) Actress Jane Kaczmarek was married to what *West Wing* actor?

a) Rob Lowe
b) Joshua Malina
c) Richard Schiff
d) Bradley Whitford

2328) Isla Fisher is married to what comic actor?

a) Sacha Baron Cohen
b) Will Ferrell
c) Tom Green
d) David Spade

2329) Model Christie Brinkley was married to what singer?

a) Billy Idol
b) Billy Joel
c) John Mellencamp
d) Steven Tyler

TOUGH TRIVIA CHALLENGE

2330) Actress Felicia Farr was married to what actor?

a) Henry Fonda
b) Jack Lemmon
c) Walter Matthau
d) James Stewart

2331) Lee Majors was married to what fellow actor?

a) Farrah Fawcett
b) Kate Jackson
c) Cheryl Ladd
d) Jaclyn Smith

2332) CNN FOUNDER TED TURNER WAS MARRIED TO WHAT ACTRESS?

A) SALLY FIELD
B) JANE FONDA
C) GOLDIE HAWN
D) LANA TURNER

2333) Johnny Cash was married to what fellow singer?

a) Carlene Carter
b) Deana Carter
c) June Carter
d) Rosanne Cash

2334) Arnold Schwarzenegger was married to what TV newswoman?

a) Katie Couric
b) Soledad O'Brien
c) Maria Shriver
d) Paula Zahn

2335) Mary Steenburgen is married to what fellow actor?

a) Ted Danson
b) Kelsey Grammer
c) Woody Harrelson
d) George Wendt

2323. c, 2324. Dennis, 2325. b, 2326. c, 2327. d, 2328. a, 2329. b, 2330. b, 2331. a, 2332. b, 2333. c, 2334. c, 2335. a

2336) Ashley Judd is married to what racecar driver?

a) Dario Franchitti
b) Jimmie Johnson
c) Casey Mears
d) Tony Stewart

2337) Actress Donna Dixon is married to what *Saturday Night Live* star?

a) Dan Aykroyd
b) Chevy Chase
c) Dennis Miller
d) Bill Murray

2338) Andre Agassi is married to what fellow tennis star?

a) Martina Hingis
b) Monica Seles
c) Maria Sharapova
d) Steffi Graf

2339) Chris Evert has been married to all the following athletes EXCEPT:

a) John Lloyd
b) Rick Mears
c) Andy Mill
d) Greg Norman

2340) VIVIEN LEIGH WAS MARRIED TO WHAT FELLOW ACTOR?

A) MARLON BRANDO
B) HUMPHREY BOGART
C) CLARK GABLE
D) LAURENCE OLIVIER

2341) Beyonce is married to what fellow musician?

a) Babyface
b) Jay-Z
c) Li'l Wayne
d) Kanye West

TOUGH TRIVIA CHALLENGE

2342) Carole Lombard was married to what fellow actor?
a) Jack Benny
b) Clark Gable
c) Bob Hope
d) James Stewart

2343) Carly Simon was married to what fellow singer?

a) Bono
b) Mick Jagger
c) Billy Joel
d) James Taylor

2336. a, 2337. a, 2338. d, 2339. b, 2340. d, 2341. b, 2342. b, 2343. D

CELEBRITY NICKNAMES

2344) What baseball player is nicknamed A-Rod?

2345) WHAT BASEBALL PLAYER WAS NICKNAMED K-ROD?

2346) What NBA player was nicknamed T-Mac?

2347) What musician is nicknamed T-Bone?

2348) What NBA player was nicknamed K-Mart?

TOUGH TRIVIA CHALLENGE

2349) St. Louis Cardinals reliever Marc Rzepczynski is nicknamed after what game?

2350) What silent movie star was known as the Little Tramp?

2351) What baseball player was nicknamed D-Train?

2352) What actor, best known for westerns, was nicknamed the Duke?

2353) WHAT WAS WILLIAM CODY'S NICKNAME?

2354) Who was known as the Butcher of Baghdad, Saddam Hussein or Fidel Castro?

2355) Henry Clay was known as The Great...

a) Henry C
b) Complainer
c) Compromiser
d) Consolidator

2356) Joseph Rommel was known as the Desert...

a) Rat
b) Fox
c) Mouse
d) Beast

2357) MANFRED VON RICHTHOFEN WAS BETTER KNOWN AS...

2358) Louis Armstrong's nickname was...

a) Satchel
b) Satchmo
c) Salami
d) Scando

2359) What was Stonewall Jackson's real first name?

a) Timothy
b) Truman
c) Thomas
d) Theodore

2360) Who was known as Honest Abe?

2361) What was Ernesto Guevara's nickname?

2262) Was Billy the Kid's real first name William?

2363) True or false: Plato's real name was Arisocles.

2344.Alex Rodriguez, 2345. Francisco Rodriguez, 2346.Tracy McGrady, 2347.Joseph Burnett, 2348. Kenyon Martin, 2349. Scrabble, 2350. Charlie Chaplin, 2351. Dontrelle Willis, 2352. John Wayne, 2353. Buffalo Bill, 2354. Saddam Hussein, 2355. c, 2356. b, 2357.The Red Baron, 2358. b, 2359. c, 2360.Abraham Lincoln, 2361. Che, 2362. no, it was Henry, 2363. true

2364) BASEBALL GREAT WILLIE MAYS WAS KNOWN AS:

A) THE SAY HEY KID
B) THE SAY WHAT KID
C) THE SAY THERE KID
D) THE SAY SAY KID

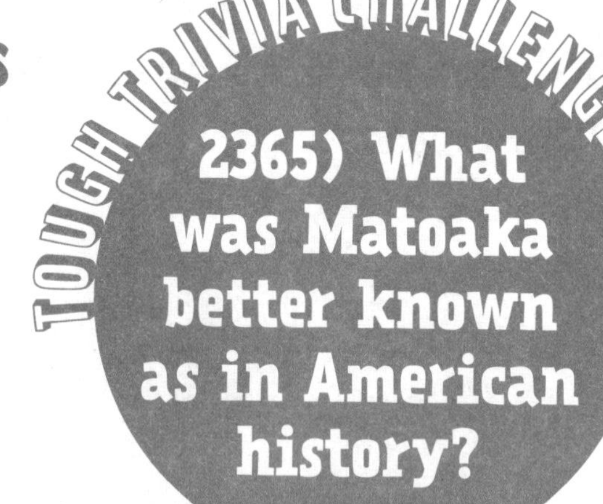

2365) What was Matoaka better known as in American history?

2366) Baseball great Joe DiMaggio was known as the ___________ Clipper.

a) Clippy
b) Yankee
c) Philly
d) Husky

2367) Basketball's Pete Maravich was known by what nickname:

a) Punky Pete
b) Piston Pete
c) Pistol Pete
d) Picky Pete

2368) Roman Emperor Gaius Julius Caesar Augustus Germanicus was nicknamed Caligula, which means...

a) Silly man
b) Large head
c) Little boots
d) Big brain

2369) Basketball's Karl Malone was known by what nickname:

a) The Milkman
b) The Mailman
c) The Minuteman
d) The Musketman

2370) Joe Namath was nicknamed after what street:

a) Broadway
b) Main Street
c) Broad Street
d) Avenue of the Americas

2371) WHAT AMERICAN WAS KNOWN AS THE FATHER OF HIS COUNTRY?

2372) What was boxer Mike Tyson's nickname?

a) Iron Mike
b) Mighty Mike
c) Steel Mike
d) Mikitimike

2364. a, 2365. Pocahontas, 2366. b, 2367. c, 2368. c, 2369. b, 2370. a, 2371. George Washington, 2372. a

2373) What was boxer Marvin Hagler's nickname?

a) Marvelous

b) Meticulous

c) Meteor

d) Master

2374) What was boxer Randal Cobb's nickname?

a) Mex

b) Tex

c) Lex

d) Flex

2375) What actor/wrestler is known as the Rock?

2376) What basketball player was nicknamed Sir Charles?

2377) Cedric Kyles is better known by what nickname?

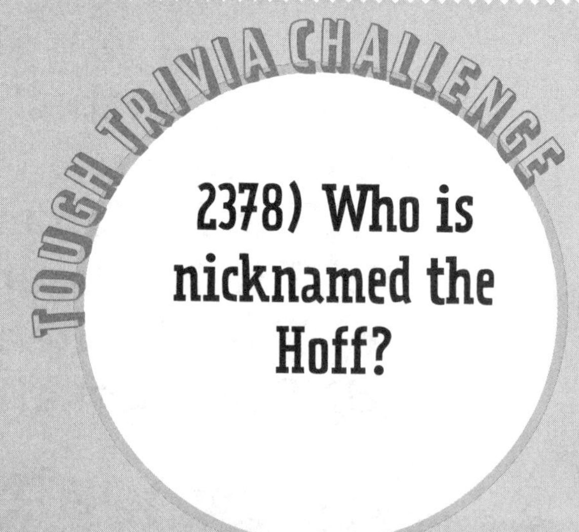

2378) Who is nicknamed the Hoff?

2379) Pirate Bartholomew Roberts was known by what name?

a) Black Bart

b) Brown Bart

c) Red Bart

d) Blue Bart

2380) What actor and former governor had the nickname the Governator?

2381) True or false:
Isabella of France was nicknamed She-Wolf.

2382) Anne Boleyn was known as Anne of ______ Days.

a) 100
b) 200
c) 1,000
d) 2,000

2383) WHAT WAS DESIGNER COCO CHANEL'S REAL FIRST NAME?

A) GABRIELLE
B) GERTRUDE
C) GILDA
D) GLINDA

2384) What band has a musician nicknamed the Edge?

2385) What band was nicknamed the Fab Four?

2386) Who is known as the King of the Blues?

a) B.B. King
b) C.C. King
c) D.D. King
d) G.G. King

2387) What band was nicknamed the Most Dangerous Band in the World?

2388) WHAT COUNTRY MUSIC GREAT WAS CALLED THE MAN IN BLACK?

2373. a, 2374. b, 2375. Dwayne Johnson, 2376. Charles Barkley, 2377. Cedric the Entertainer, 2378. David Hasselhoff, 2379. a, 2380. Arnold Schwarzenegger, 2381. true, 2382. c, 2383. a, 2384. U2, 2385. The Beatles, 2386. a, 2387. Guns N' Roses, 2388. Johnny Cash

2389) What was the nickname of jazz great Charlie Parker?

a) Fly
b) Bird
c) Bee
d) Bug

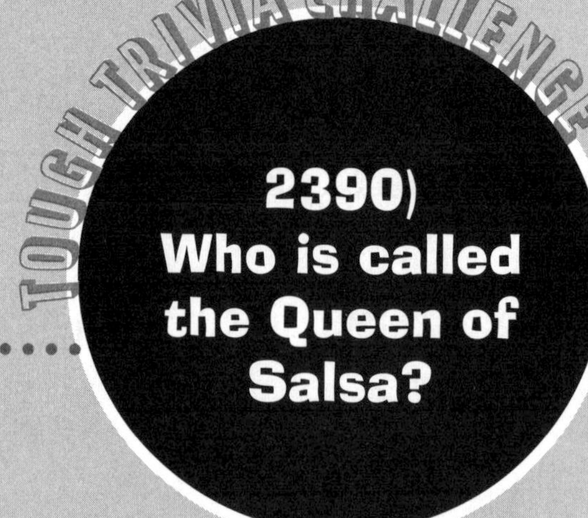

2391) What singer is known as the Motor City Madman?

2392) What was the name of the voice artist who, thanks to playing Bugs Bunny, Daffy Duck, and many others, was called the Man of a Thousand Voices?

a) Mel Smith
b) Mel Blue
c) Mel Blanc
d) Mel Jackson

2393) Whose nickname is J.Lo?

2394) What is Alfred Matthew Yankovic's nickname?

2395) True or false: Ziggy Marley's real name is David.

2389. b, 2390. Celia Cruz, 2391. Ted Nugent, 2392. c, 2393. Jennifer Lopez, 2394. Weird Al, 2395. true

CHAPTER 5

Comics & Animation

COMIC BOOKS

2396) True or false: a nineteenth-century publication by Histoire de M. Vieux Bois is considered to be the first comic book.

TOUGH TRIVIA CHALLENGE

2397) The first true American comic book is considered to be...
a) *Famous Funnies*
b) *Fractured Fairytales*
c) *Hero Comics*
d) *Classics Illustrated*

2398) True or false: The series that developed out of that first American comic book in the previous question cost two cents when it was first released.

2399) When was the term "graphic novel" first used to describe sophisticated comic books?
a) 1964 b) 1970 c) 1973 d) 1980

2400) Which came first, Detective Comics or Action Comics?

2401) Who came first, Superman or Mandrake the Magician?

2402) True or false: In 1946, comic books outsold traditional books.

2403) True or false: There were comic-book burnings in Chicago and New York in the 1960s by people who thought they were harmful to young people.

2404) WHEN DID THE U.S. POSTAL SERVICE HONOR COMIC BOOKS WITH A SERIES OF SUPERHERO STAMPS?

A) 1955
B) 1966
C) 1987
D) 2006

2405) True or false: **The U.S. Postal Service Superhero stamps did not include Batman.**

2406) When was the Comic Code Authority created?

a) 1954
b) 1960
c) 1964
d) 1971

2407) True or false: *Mad* magazine was first published as a comic book.

2408) True or false: DC is short for *Detective Comics.*

2396. true. 2397. a. 2398. false—it was a dime. 2399. a. 2400. Detective Comics. 2401. Mandrake. 2402. true. 2403. false—it happened in the 1940s. 2404. d. 2405. false. 2406. b. 2407. true. 2408. true

2409) WHAT ART SPIEGELMAN TWO-VOLUME ILLUSTRATED COMIC-BOOK MEMOIR EARNED CRITICAL AND MAINSTREAM ACCLAIM IN 1986?

A) *MORRIS*

B) *MAUS*

C) *MR. MOUSE*

D) *MESS*

2410) *Time* magazine's list of the 100 best English language novels from 1923 to 2005 included which comic book?

2411) True or false: A comic book was nominated for the 2006 National Book Awards.

2412) Which of the following films was not based on a comic book/graphic novel?

a) *Road to Perdition*

b) *Ghost World*

c) *Pulp Fiction*

d) *A History of Violence*

2413) True or false: About 50 comic books are added to the Library of Congress's collection every month.

2414) True or false: Popular British comic books have included *The Beano, The Dandy,* and *Viz.*

2415) In 1947, *Classic Comics* became known as what?

a) *Classics Comics*

b) *Classics Illustrated*

c) *Illustrated Classics*

d) *Comic Book Classics*

2416) True or false: According to the 1954 Comics Code, good always had to triumph over evil.

2417) ACCORDING TO THE COMICS CODE, ALL BUT THE FOLLOWING WERE NEVER ALLOWED TO BE PRESENTED DISRESPECTFULLY:

A) JUDGES

B) POLICEMEN

C) TEACHERS

D) GOVERNMENT OFFICIALS

2418) True or false: **The Comics Code forbade showing unique methods of concealing weapons.**

2419) True or false: According to the Comics Code, kidnappers always had to be punished.

2409. b, 2410. Alan Moore's *Watchmen*, 2411. true—Gene Yang's *American Born Chinese*, 2412. c, 2413. false—more like 200, 2414. true, 2415. b, 2416. true, 2417. c, 2418. true, 2419. true

2420) True or false: The Comics Code stated that the word "horror" couldn't be used in a comic book title.

2421) Did the Comics Code specifically restrict the ridicule of religion?

2422) TRUE OR FALSE: THE COMICS CODE STATED THAT DIVORCE COULD NEVER BE TREATED HUMOROUSLY.

2423) True or false: The Comics Code stated that monkeys should never be presented as pets.

2424) Did the Comics Code rule that tobacco couldn't be advertised in comic books.

2425) Did the Comics Code rule that politicians couldn't advertise in comic books.

2426) Did the Comics Code rule that sea monkeys couldn't be sold in comic books.

2427) Did the Comics Code rule that fireworks couldn't be sold in comic books?

2428) Which came first: DC or Marvel?

2429) True or false: Marvel was originally called Timely Comics.

SUPERHEROES

DC or Marvel?

2430) Spiderman
2431) Wonder Woman
2432) Super-Man
2433) The Hulk
2434) Batman
2435) Fantastic Four

2436) **True or false:** The Flash, Hawkman, and the Green Lantern were all introduced in the same year.

2437) What superpower does Sue Richards have?

2438) What superpower does Mr. Fantastic have?

TOUGH TRIVIA CHALLENGE

2439) Which came first, Spider-Man or the Human Torch?

2440) The Fantastic Four first appeared in...

a) 1941
b) 1961
c) 1971
d) 1981

2441) What is the superhero name for Johnny Storm?

2442) MATTHEW MICHAEL MURDOCK IS THE ALTER EGO NAME FOR WHAT SUPERHERO?

2420. false, 2421. yes, 2422. false, 2423. false, 2424. yes, 2425. no, 2426. no, 2427. yes, 2428. DC, 2429. true, 2430. Marvel, 2431. DC, 2432. DC, 2433. Marvel, 2434. DC, 2435. Marvel, 2436. True—1940, 2437. invisibility, 2438. he can stretch his body, 2439. Human Torch, 2440. b, 2441. Human Torch, 2442. Daredevil

2443) What is the superhero name for Ben Grimm?

2444) Who showed up in comics first, Captain America or Captain Marvel?

2445) WHAT IS THE SUB-MARINER'S NAME?

MATCH THE COMIC BOOK HERO TO HIS (OR HER) SECRET IDENTITY.

2446) Bruce Banner	a) Batgirl
2447) Billy Batson	b) Batman
2448) Betsy Braddock	c) Captain America
2449) Frank Castle	d) Captain Marvel
2450) Linda Danvers	e) The Flash
2451) Barbara Gordon	f) Green Lantern
2452) Dick Grayson	g) Hawkman
2453) Carter Hall	h) The Incredible Hulk
2454) James "Logan" Howlett	i) Iron Man
2455) Clark Kent	j) Plastic-Man
2456) Peter Parker	k) Psylocke
2457) Diana Prince	l) The Punisher
2458) Kyle Rayner	m) Robin
2459) Steve Rogers	n) Spawn
2460) Albert Simmons	o) Spider-Man
2461) Tony Stark	p) Supergirl
2462) Bruce Wayne	q) Superman
2463) Wally West	r) Wolverine
2464) Eel O'Brian	s) Wonder Woman

2465) What is the only way to defeat Mr. Mxyzptlk?

2466) Who killed Superman?

a) Doomsday
b) Lex Luthor
c) Scorpius
d) No one

MATCH THE VILLAIN TO HIS OR HER NEMESIS.

2467) Black Manta	a) Aquaman
2468) Bullseye	b) Batman
2469) Cheetah	c) Blade
2470) Deacon Frost	d) Captain America
2471) Deathstroke	e) Daredevil
2472) Dormammu	f) Ghost Rider
2473) Eivol Ekdol	g) Iron Man
2474) Jigsaw	h) Judge Dredd
2475) Judge Death	i) The Punisher
2476) Loki	j) Spawn
2477) Magneto	k) Spider-Man
2478) Malebolgia	l) Dr. Strange
2479) Mandarin	m) Superman
2480) Mephisto	n) Teen Titans
2481) Mr. Mxyzptlk	o) Teenage Mutant Ninja Turtles
2482) Dr. Octopus	p) Thor
2483) Red Skull	q) Wonder Woman
2484) The Shredder	r) X-Men

2443. the Thing, 2444. Captain Marvel, 2445. Prince Namor, 2446. h, 2447. d, 2448. k, 2449. l, 2450. p, 2451. a, 2452. m, 2453. g, 2454. r, 2455. q, 2456. o, 2457. s, 2458. f, 2459. c, 2460. n, 2461. i, 2462. b, 2463. e, 2464. j, 2465. trick him into saying his name backwards (Kltpzyxm), 2466. a, 2467. a, 2468. e, 2469. q, 2470. c, 2471. n, 2472. l, 2473. b, 2474. i, 2475. h, 2476. p, 2477. r, 2478. j, 2479. g, 2480. f, 2481. m, 2482. k, 2483. d, 2484. o

THE ADVENTURES OF TINTIN

2485) In what language did *The Adventures of Tintin* first appear?

a) English

b) Japanese

c) French

d) Italian

2486) The Adventures of Tintin was created by artist Georges Remi whose pen name was...

a) Hergé

b) Hugo

c) Huggy

d) Higgy

2487) What is Tintin's dog's name?

a) Snowy

b) Sonny

c) Ziggy

d) Slappy

2488) Tintin is a...

a) Hunter

b) Reporter

c) Police officer

d) Teacher

2489) In Tintin, what is Professor Calculus' physical challenge?

a) A wooden leg

b) He's hard of hearing

c) He's blind in one eye

d) He has three missing fingers

2490) True or false: **Until Steven Spielberg's film, Tintin has never been featured in a movie.**

2491) True or false: There are Tintin shops in Belgium and England.

TOUGH TRIVIA CHALLENGE

2496) Which came first, *Tintin in the Land of the Soviets* or *Tintin and Alph-Art?*

2492) IN WHAT YEAR DID TINTIN FIRST APPEAR?

A) 1912
B) 1929
C) 1938
D) 1941

2493) What is the merchant marine captain in Tintin named?

a) Captain Haddock
b) Captain Pike
c) Captain Grouper
d) Captain Flounder

2494) TRUE OR FALSE: THERE'S A TINTIN ADVENTURE CALLED CIGARS OF THE PHAROAH.

2495) True or false: Tintin once faced a villain named Musstler, named as a combination of Mussolini and Hitler.

2497) Where does Captain Haddock live?

a) Merlinspike Hall
b) The Merlinoplex
c) Chez Merlin
d) Merlin Acres

2498) True or false: In the Tintin adventures, Bianca Castafiore is an opera singer.

2485. c, 2486. a, 2487. a, 2488. b, 2489. b, 2490. false, 2491. true, 2492. b, 2493. a, 2494. true, 2495. true, 2496. *Tintin in the Land of the Soviets*, 2497. a, 2498. true

2499) Which of the following was not an actual Tintin adventure:

a) *Tintin in Tibet*
b) *Tintin and the Picaros*
c) *Tintin in the Congo*
d) *Tintin in New York*

Tintin in the Bowery

2500) In the Tintin adventures, which of the following is an insurance salesman:

a) Nestor
b) Jolyon Wagg
c) Kalish Ezab
d) Cutts

2501) TRUE OR FALSE: **THE STUDY OF TINTIN IS KNOWN AS TINTINOLOGY.**

2502) Did Tintin ever travel to the moon?

ARCHIE COMICS

2503) Archie Andrews first appeared in...

a) Pep Comics

b) Pop Comics

c) Plop Comics

d) Ploop Comics

2504) Who is Archie's best friend?

2505) Which one has black hair, Betty or Veronica?

2506) True or false: *Archie Comics* sued the band The Veronicas for infringing on its trademark.

2507) What is Archie's hometown?

2508) True or false: *Archie Comics* #1 set a record for the highest price paid for a comic book.

2509) TRUE OR FALSE: SABRINA THE TEENAGE WITCH IS A SPINOFF OF ARCHIE COMICS.

2510) True or false: The American pop/rock group the Monkees was first conceived as recurring characters in Archie Comics.

2499. d, 2500. b, 2501. true, 2502. yes, 2503. a, 2504. Jughead, 2505. Veronica, 2506. true, 2507. Riverdale, 2508. false—but it did set the record for highest price for a non-superhero comic book, 2509. true, 2510. false

2511) True or false: Josie and the Pussycats is a spinoff of Archie Comics.

2512) True of false: Archie has never appeared on a U.S. postage stamp.

2513) How many brothers and sisters does Archie have?

2515) Is Reggie in the band the Archies?

2516) True or false: The fictional band the Archies had an actual hit?

2517) What instrument does Jughead play?

2518) True or false: Jughead has a younger sister named Chrysanthemum.

2519) What letter does Jughead usually have on his sweatshirt?

2520) What is the name of the shop where the Archie crowd hangs out?

a) Pop Tate's Chok'lit Shoppe
b) Arnold's Drive In
c) Eat Here
d) The Peach Pit

2521) True or false: Josie was a character in Archie Comics for more than five years before she became leader of a band.

COMIC STRIPS

2522) THE COMIC BRENDA STAR WAS FIRST PUBLISHED IN 1940. WHAT WAS HER JOB?

A) FIREFIGHTER
B) SUPERHERO
C) REPORTER
D) PILOT

TOUGH TRIVIA CHALLENGE

2523) How many Katzenjammer Kids are there?

2524) True or false: One of the first comic strips was called *Little Nemo in Slumberland.*

2525) In a famous early comic, who was Mutt's sidekick?

2526) True or false: The comic *Krazy Kat* started as filler at the bottom of a comic called *The Dingbat Family.*

2527) WHAT WAS THE INNOVATION OF THE COMIC *GASOLINE ALLEY?*

A) SPLIT PANELS
B) ITS CHARACTERS AGED
C) NO MEN WERE FEATURED
D) IT HAD NO WORDS

2511. true, 2512. false, 2513. none, 2514. Veronica's, 2515. yes, 2516. true—"Sugar, Sugar", 2517. drums, 2518. false—her name was Forsythia, 2519. 5, 2520. a, 2521. true, 2522. c, 2523. two, 2524. true, 2525. Jeff, 2526. true, 2527. b

2528) Who is Blondie's husband?

2529) True or false: *Brenda Star* was created by a woman.

TOUGH TRIVIA CHALLENGE

2530) What is the last name of Terry in *Terry and the Pirates*?

a) Long
b) Lester
c) Lee
d) Luongo

2531) True or false: Tom Wilson worked at a greeting card company when he created Ziggy.

2532) What was the first comic strip to win a Pulitzer Prize for Editorial Cartooning?

a) *Pogo*
b) *Doonesbury*
c) *Hi and Lois*
d) *The Far Side*

2533) According to the comic character Cathy, the four basic guilt groups are Food, Love, Mother, and...

a) Home
b) Career
c) Movies
d) More Food

2534) WHICH LAUNCHED FIRST, *THE FAR SIDE* OR *BLOOM COUNTY*?

2535) Where did *The Far Side* first appear?

a) *The New York Times*
b) *The Philadelphia Inquirer*
c) *The Miami Herald*
d) *The San Francisco Chronicle*

2536) True or false: *Calvin and Hobbes* creator Bill Watterson didn't want any merchandise to be created based on his characters.

2537) Who created *The Boondocks*?

a) Aaron McGruder
b) Maron McAuder
c) Garry McMurtry
d) Ali McAllister

2538) Buck Rogers first appeared in the...

a) 1920s
b) 1930s
c) 1940s
d) 1950s

2539) Who appeared in comic strips first, Popeye or Dick Tracy?

2540) WHAT IS ALLEY OOP?

2528. Dagwood, 2529. true, 2530. c, 2531. true, 2532. b, 2533. b, 2534. *The Far Side*—but both were in 1980, 2535. d, 2536. true, 2537. a, 2538. a, 2539. Popeye, 2540. a caveman

2541) True or false: *Prince Valiant* has appeared in more than 3,500 comic strip episodes.

2542) What do most comic strips have that *Prince Valiant* doesn't?

a) Color
b) Multiple characters
c) Lines around the frames
d) Conversation and thought balloons

2543) True or false: Mussolini banned most American comic strips in Italy.

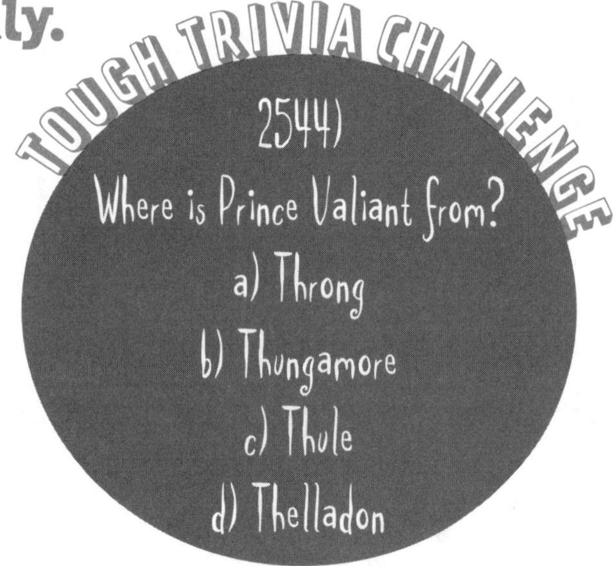

TOUGH TRIVIA CHALLENGE

2544) Where is Prince Valiant from?

a) Throng
b) Thungamore
c) Thule
d) Thelladon

2545) True or false: The same artist who created *B.C.* also co-created *The Wizard of Id.*

2546) What is Doonesbury's first name?

2547) Early *Doonesbury* comic strips were reprints of ones artist Gary Trudeau had created for what school's newspaper?

a) Harvard
b) Yale
c) Brown
d) University of Pittsburgh

2548) WHAT COLLEGE WAS THE CENTRAL LOCATION OF EARLY DOONESBURY COMICS?

A) WALDEN COLLEGE
B) WALDO COLLEGE
C) WIDENER COLLEGE
D) WILCO COLLEGE

2549) What is Garfield's owner's name?

2550) What is Garfield's owner's dog's name?

2551) True or false: Jim Davis is still the only illustrator of Garfield comics.

TOUGH TRIVIA CHALLENGE

2552) Where does Garfield artist Jim Davis live?
a) Ohio
b) New York
c) Pennsylvania
d) Indiana

2553) TRUE OR FALSE: IN THE ANIMATED TV SHOW THAT AIRED FROM 1982–1991, GARFIELD WAS VOICED BY LORENZO MUSIC.

2554) When was Garfield launched?

a) 1978
b) 1982
c) 1989
d) 1992

2555) What is Garfield's favorite food?

2541. true, 2542. d, 2543. true, 2544. c, 2545. true, 2546. Mike, 2547. b, 2548. a, 2549. Jon, 2550. Odie, 2551. false, 2552. d, 2553. true, 2554. a, 2555. Lasagna

..PEANUTS..

2556) What is the relationship between Linus and Lucy?

2557) Who is Snoopy's brother?

2558) Who is older, Charlie Brown or Sally Brown?

2559) WHAT IS LUCY'S LAST NAME?

2560) What is Linus's younger brother's name?

2561) True or false: Peppermint Patty's last name is Reichardt.

2562) What does Peppermint Patty call Charlie Brown?

2563) What color is Schroeder's hair?

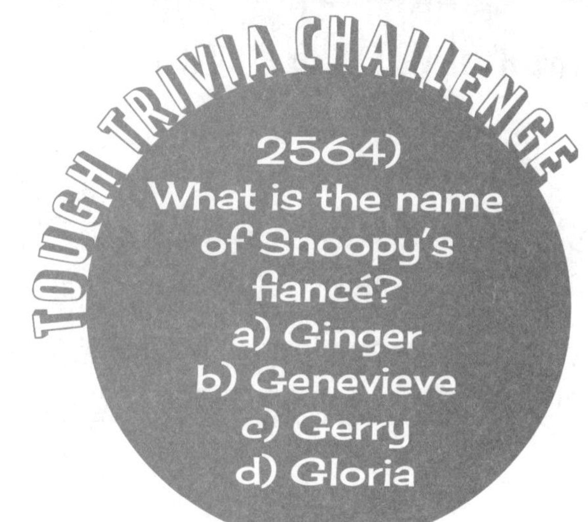

2564) What is the name of Snoopy's fiancé?
a) Ginger
b) Genevieve
c) Gerry
d) Gloria

2565) What position does Schroeder play on Charlie Brown's baseball team?

2566) True or false: Schroeder was first introduced as an infant in the *Peanuts* comic strip.

2567) In what month does Schroeder celebrate Beethoven's birthday?

2568) WHO IS IN LOVE WITH SCHROEDER?

2569) What does Marcy usually call Charlie Brown?

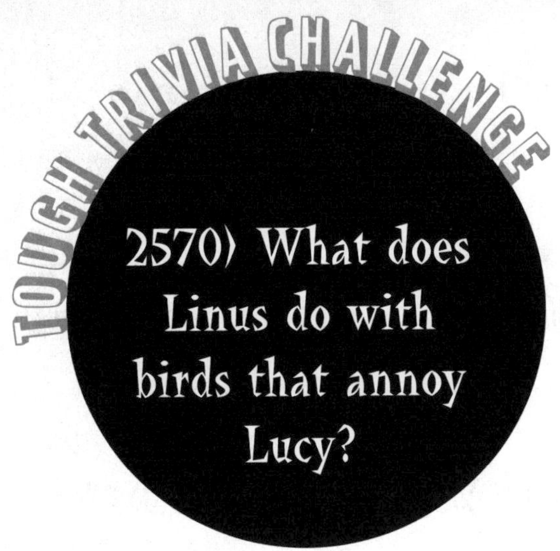

2571) What color hair does the girl who Charlie Brown has a crush on have?

2572) True or false: Charlie Brown's father is a chef.

2573) Is Charlie Brown's pen pal a boy or a girl?

2574) TRUE OR FALSE: SNOOPY HAS A BROTHER NAMED OLAF.

2575) True or false: Snoopy has a brother named Andy.

2576) True or false: Snoopy has a brother named Fred.

2577) True or false: Snoopy has a sister named Bette.

2578) True or false: Snoopy has a sister named Snippy.

2579) True or false: Snoopy has a brother named Marbles.

2580) True or false: Snoopy has a sister name Maybelle.

2581) True or false: Snoopy has a sister named Frances.

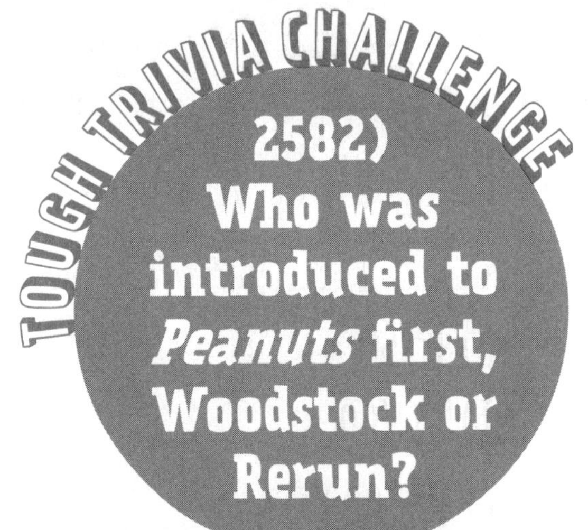

2556. brother and sister, 2557. Spike, 2558. Charlie Brown, 2559. Van Pelt, 2560. Rerun, 2561. true, 2562. Chuck, 2563. blonde, 2564. b, 2565. catcher, 2566. true, 2567. December, 2568. Lucy, 2569. Charles, 2570. pats them on the head, 2571. red, 2572. false—he's a barber, 2573. a girl, 2574. true, 2575. true, 2576. false, 2577. true, 2578. false, 2579. true, 2580. false, 2581. false, 2582. Rerun

2583) TRUE OR FALSE: SNOOPY HAS A BROTHER NAMED HENRY.

2584) Where was Snoopy born?
a) Del Ray Puppy Farm
b) Dense Hills Puppy Farm
c) Daisy Hill Puppy Farm
d) Daisy Way Puppy Farm

2585) Does Snoopy play on Charlie Brown's baseball team?

2586) True or false: Snoopy didn't always walk only on his hind legs.

2587) Charles Schulz created more than ___________ *Peanuts* strips.

a) 1,750
b) 17,500
c) 175,000
d) 50,000

2588) Who is Snoopy's enemy when he is fantasizing about being the World War I Flying Ace?

2589) WHAT DOES SNOOPY CALL HIS DOGHOUSE WHEN HE IS HAVING A WORLD WAR I FANTASY?

2590) What is Snoopy's nickname when he is wearing sunglasses?

2591) True or false: Snoopy became a mascot of the aerospace industry after the Apollo I fire.

2592) Who was introduced to *Peanuts* first, Sally or Peppermint Patty?

2593) **Who was introduced to *Peanuts* first, Schroeder or Lucy?**

2594) What is Frieda's defining physical feature?

2595) TRUE OR FALSE: **THE FIRST AFRICAN-AMERICAN CHARACTER IN THE *PEANUTS* COMICS, FRANKLIN, WAS INTRODUCED IN 1962.**

2596) **True or false:** A character named Shermy disappeared from the *Peanuts* strip in 1969.

TOUGH TRIVIA CHALLENGE

2597) What was Charles Schulz's nickname?

a) Sparky

b) Snoopy

c) Snarky

d) Pops

TOUGH TRIVIA CHALLENGE

2598) Anthony Rapp or Gary Burghoff: Which played Charlie Brown in the original off-Broadway version of the stage musical *You're a Good Man Charlie Brown?*

2599) True or false: **Franklin's father was a soldier in the Vietnam War.**

2600) **True or false:** Charles Schulz illustrated a book of letters to President Johnson.

2601) Which was not one of the original newspapers that carried the *Peanuts* comic strip in 1950:

a) *Washington Post*

b) *Philadelphia Inquirer*

c) *Denver Post*

d) *Seattle Times*

2583. false, 2584. c, 2585. yes, 2586. true, 2587. b, 2588. the Red Baron, 2589. Sopwith Camel, 2590. Joe Cool, 2591. true, 2592. Sally, 2593. Schoeder, 2594. her naturally curly hair, 2595. false—not until 1968, 2596. true, 2597. a, 2598. Burghoff, 2599. true, 2600. true, 2601. b

2602) WHO APPEARED FIRST IN *PEANUTS*, PIG-PEN OR FRIEDA?

2603) Is Charlie Brown bald?

2604) Do Charlie Brown and Peppermint Patty go to the same school?

2605) Did Charlie Brown's team ever win a baseball game?

2606) True or false: Lucy was the first person to pull a football away from Charlie Brown as he tried to kick it.

2607) WHICH WAS THE FIRST *PEANUTS* TV SPECIAL?

2608) Which came first at the movies, *Snoopy Come Home* or *A Boy Named Charlie Brown?*

2609) True or false: Charlie Brown doesn't go to France in *Bon Voyage, Charlie Brown.*

TOUGH TRIVIA CHALLENGE

2610) What was Snoopy's original owner's name?

a) Lala b) Layla

c) Lila d) Lily

2611) True or false: Sally wasn't in the original production of the stage musical *You're a Good Man Charlie Brown.*

2612) True or false: There was a stage musical sequel to *You're a Good Man Charlie Brown* called *Linus!*

2613) HOW MUCH DOES LUCY TRADITIONALLY CHARGE FOR PSYCHIATRIC HELP?

2614) TRUE OR FALSE: SNOOPY'S SONG "JOE COOL" FIRST APPEARED IN *IT'S VALENTINE'S DAY, CHARLIE BROWN.*

2615) True or false: A band called The Royal Guardsmen had a hit with a song called "Snoopy vs. the Red Baron."

2616) Has Pig-Pen ever appeared clean?

2617) Does Pig-Pen play an instrument in *A Charlie Brown Christmas?*

TOUGH TRIVIA CHALLENGE

2618) What is Linus' teacher's name?
a) Miss Omar
b) Miss Othmar
c) Miss Rothmear
d) Miss Rothenmeier

2619) Lucy's dress is usually what color?

2620) Did Lucy's pulling away of the football ever cost Charlie Brown's team a football game?

2621) True or false: Snoopy has never been licensed for a Nintento or Wii game.

2622) True or false: Lucy once put Linus's blanket through a paper shredder and spread the pieces across the Atlantic Ocean.

2623) What position does Lucy usually play on the Peanuts baseball team?

2602. Pig-Pen, 2603. no, not completely, 2604. no, 2605. yes, 2606. false—Violet did it first, in a 1951 comic strip, 2607. *A Charlie Brown Christmas*, 2608. *A Boy Named Charlie Brown*, 2609. false—but Lucy stays home, 2610. c, 2611. true, 2612. false—but there was one called *Snoopy!*, 2613. five cents, 2614. false—it was first used in *You're Not Elected, Charlie Brown*, 2615. true, 2616. yes, 2617. yes—the double bass, 2618. b, 2619. blue, 2620. yes, 2621. false, 2622. false, 2623. right field (sometimes center field)

COMPLETE THE TITLES OF THESE PEANUTS TV SPECIALS:

2624) *It's the Great ________, Charlie Brown*

2625) *You're in _____, Charlie Brown*

2626) *He's Your _____, Charlie Brown*

2627) *Play It _____, Charlie Brown*

2628) *You're Not ______, Charlie Brown*

2629) *There's No Time for ______, Charlie Brown*

2630) *It's the Easter ______, Charlie Brown*

2631) *Be My _______, Charlie Brown*

2632) *You're a Good ______, Charlie Brown*

2633) *It's Your First _______, Charlie Brown*

2634) *What a _______, Charlie Brown*

2635) *You're the _______, Charlie Brown*

2636) *She's a Good _______, Charlie Brown*

2637) *Life is a _______, Charlie Brown*

2638) *Someday You'll Find ____, Charlie Brown*

2639) *Is This ______, Charlie Brown*

2640) *Happy New _____, Charlie Brown*

2641) *It's the Girl in the Red _____, Charlie Brown*

2642) *Why, Charlie Brown, _____?*

2643) *It's Christmastime ______, Charlie Brown*

2644) *You're in the Super _______, Charlie Brown*

2645) *It Was the Best ________ Ever, Charlie Brown*

2646) *It's the Pied _____, Charlie Brown*

2647) *____ Must be Traded, Charlie Brown*

2648) *I Want a ___ for Christmas, Charlie Brown*

TOUGH TRIVIA CHALLENGE

2649) Which was not featured in an episode of the *This Is America, Charlie Brown* mini-series.

a) *The Mayflower voyage*

b) The Wright Brothers' flight

c) The first Thanksgiving

d) The building of the transcontinental railway

ANIME/MANGA

2650) Which is primarily marketed to girls, shonen manga or shojo manga?

Complete the names of these Hayao Miyazaki animated films.

2651) *Howl's Moving* _____

2652) *Spirited* _____

2653) _______ *Mononoke*

2654) *Kiki's Delivery* ______

2655) *My* _______ *Totoro*

2656) _______ *in the Sky*

2657) What was the name of the pioneer anime white lion who had his own TV show?

- **a) Kumbu**
- **b) Kamba**
- **c) Kimba**
- **d) Kongo**

2658) Which of the following was not an early anime/manga series that aired on American TV?

- *a) Tobor: The Eighth Man*
- *b) Gigantor*
- *c) Marine Boy*
- *d) Metroman*

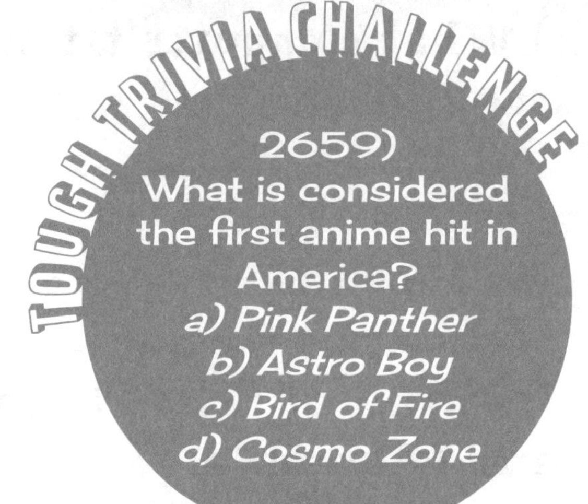

2660) Who was Speed Racer's girlfriend?

- **a) Sophie**
- **b) Trixie**
- **c) Angie**
- **d) Maizie**

2661) True or false: One of the landmark anime shows of the 1970s was called ***Mobile Suit Gundam.***

2624. Pumpkin, 2625. Love, 2626. Dog, 2627. Again, 2628. Elected, 2629. Love, 2630. Beagle, 2631. Valentine, 2632. Sport, 2633. Kiss, 2634. Nightmare, 2635. Greatest, 2636. Skate, 2637. Circus, 2638. Her, 2639. Goodbye, 2640. Year, 2641. Truck, 2642. Why, 2643. Again, 2644. Bowl, 2645. Birthday, 2646. Piper, 2647. Lucy, 2648. Dog, 2649. c, 2650. shojo manga, 2651. Castle, 2652. Away, 2653. Princess, 2654. Service, 2655. Neighbor, 2656. Castle, 2657. c, 2658. d, 2659. b, 2660. b, 2661. true

..PIXAR..

2662) What computer titan helped found Pixar?
a) Larry Ellison
b) Bill Gates
c) Steve Jobs
d) Steve Wozniak

2663) True or false: the villain in *A Bug's Life* is General Mandible.

Match the actor to the Pixar film in which he supplied the voice of a villain:

2664) Ned Beatty	a) *A Bug's Life*
2665) Steve Buscemi	b) *Cars 2*
2666) Ian Holm	c) *The Incredibles*
2667) Wayne Knight	d) *Monsters, Inc.*
2668) Jason Lee	e) *Ratatouille*
2669) Joe Mantegna	f) *Toy Story 2*
2670) Christopher Plummer	g) *Toy Story 3*
2671) Kevin Spacey	h) *Up*

2672) What fuel is manufactured by Monsters, Inc?

2673) WHAT FUEL DO THE MONSTERS EVENTUALLY DISCOVER IS MORE ENERGY-EFFICIENT?

2674) True or False: The voice of the little girl in *Monsters, Inc.* was supplied by the 2-year-old daughter of one of the animators.

2675) True or false: the only Oscars won by Pixar movies have been for Best Animated Feature.

2676) Did *Monsters, Inc.* win the Oscar for Best Animated Feature?

2677) Did *Finding Nemo* win the Oscar for Best Animated Feature?

2678) True or false: *Everybody Loves Raymond* co-stars Ray Romano and Brad Garrett both supplied the voices of fish in *Finding Nemo.*

2679) Did *The Incredibles* win the Oscar for Best Animated Feature?

2680) What is Mr. Incredible's occupation when not working as a superhero?
a) Advertising executive
b) Cook
c) Insurance adjuster
d) Truck driver

2662. c, 2663. false—Hopper, 2664. g, 2665. d, 2666. e, 2667. f, 2668. c, 2669. g, 2670. h, 2671. a, 2672. scream, 2673. laugh, 2674. true, 2675. false, 2676. no, 2677. yes, 2678. false—Garrett only, 2679. yes, 2680. c

2681) TRUE OR FALSE: HOLLY HUNTER WAS NOMINATED FOR BEST SUPPORTING ACTRESS FOR HER VOICE WORK IN *THE INCREDIBLES.*

2682) What is Mrs. Incredible's superheroine name?

2683) What is the superpower of the Incredibles' older son?
a) Mindreading
b) Super speed
c) Super strength
d) Throws lightning bolts

2684) What is the superpower of the Incredibles' daughter?
a) Bulletproof
b) Flying
c) Invisibility
d) None

2685) WHAT IS THE NAME OF THE MAIN VILLAIN IN *THE INCREDIBLES?*
A) FLATTOP
B) FROZONE
C) MR. GLASS
D) SYNDROME

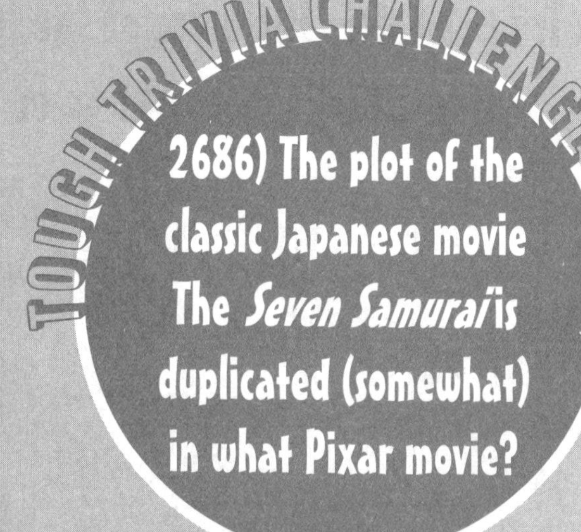

2686) The plot of the classic Japanese movie The *Seven Samurai* is duplicated (somewhat) in what Pixar movie?

2687) Did Cars win the Oscar for Best Animated Feature?

2688) The plot of the Michael J. Fox movie *Doc Hollywood* is duplicated (somewhat) in what Pixar movie?

2689) The plot of the 1991 action-comedy *If Looks Could Kill* is duplicated (somewhat) in what Pixar movie?

2690) Did *Ratatouille* win the Oscar for Best Animated Feature?

2691) Who supplies the voice of Colette, the chef who falls in love with the hero in *Ratatouille?*

- **a) Brigitte Bardot**
- **b) Juliette Binoche**
- **c) Catherine Deneuve**
- **d) Janeane Garofalo**

▲▲▲▲▲▲▲▲▲▲▲▲▲▲▲▲▲▲▲▲▲▲▲▲▲▲

2692) Which of these words rhymes with "ratatouille"?

- a) Feel
- b) Hooray
- c) Philly
- d) Phooey

▲▲▲▲▲▲▲▲▲▲▲▲▲▲▲▲▲▲▲▲▲▲▲▲▲▲

2693) DID *WALL-E* WIN THE OSCAR FOR BEST ANIMATED FEATURE?

2694) Did *Up* win the Oscar for Best Animated Feature?

▲▲▲▲▲▲▲▲▲▲▲▲▲▲▲▲▲▲▲▲▲▲▲▲▲▲

2695) Did *Toy Story 3* win the Oscar for Best Animated Feature?

▲▲▲▲▲▲▲▲▲▲▲▲▲▲▲▲▲▲▲▲▲▲▲▲▲▲

Put these Pixar films in the order of their initial theatrical release.

- 2696) *Ratatouille*
- 2697) *Finding Nemo*
- 2698) *Monsters Inc*
- 2699) *A Bug's Life*
- 2700) *Toy Story*
- 2701) *Toy Story 3*
- 2702) *The Incredibles*
- 2703) *Up*
- 2704) *WALL-E*
- 2705) *Cars*

▲▲▲▲▲▲▲▲▲▲▲▲▲▲▲▲▲▲▲▲▲▲▲▲▲▲

2706) WHAT YEAR WAS THE FIRST TOY STORY RELEASED IN MOVIE THEATERS?

- A) 1990
- B) 1993
- C) 1995
- D) 1998

2681. false, 2682. Elasti-girl, 2683. b, 2684. c, 2685. d, 2686. A Bug's Life, 2687. No, 2688. *Cars*, 2689. *Cars 2*, 2690. yes, 2691. d, 2692. d, 2693. yes, 2694. yes, 2695. yes, 2696-2705: Toy Story, A Bug's Life, Monsters Inc, Finding Nemo, The Incredibles, Cars, Ratatouille, WALL-E, Up, Toy Story 3, 2706. c

2707) True or false: Josh Whedon, creator of *Buffy the Vampire Slayer,* helped write the original Toy Story.

2708) Who is seen first in *Toy Story,* Woody or Buzz?

2709) What is the name of the pizza parlor/game room in *Toy Story*?

2710) In *Toy Story,* what kind of animal is Scud?

2711) True or false: *Toy Story* was Tom Hanks' fourth animated film.

2712) True or false: As originally written, *Toy Story's* Woody was going to be a ventriloquist dummy.

TOUGH TRIVIA CHALLENGE

2713) What is Sid's last name in *Toy Story?*
a) Johnson
b) Philips
c) Davis
d) Lasseter

2714) True or false: As originally written *Toy Story's* Buzz Lightyear was going to be a caveman.

2715) TRUE OR FALSE: G.I. JOE APPEARS IN TWO SCENES IN *TOY STORY.*

2716) What sitcom actor has supplied a voice in every Pixar movie?
a) David Foley
b) Brad Garrett
c) John Goodman
d) John Ratzenberger

2717) Who is the only actor to perform live (not animated) in a Pixar movie?

a) Tim Allen
b) Ed Asner
c) Tom Hanks
d) Fred Willard

2718) What is the name of the desk lamp that forms the "I" in the Pixar logo?

a) Edison
b) Lumen
c) Luxo
d) Sherlock

2719) WHAT IS THE PRIMARY INGREDIENT IN RATATOUILLE?

A) CABBAGE
B) CHEESE
C) EGGPLANT
D) RAT

2720) True or false: in *Toy Story 2*, Buzz Lightyear is kidnapped by the Evil Emperor Zurg.

2721) What is the name of Woody's horse in *Toy Story 2* and *Toy Story 3*?

2722) True or false: Dinoco, the much-coveted sponsor in *Cars*, operates a gas station seen in Toy Story.

2723) What is WALL-E's favorite musical?

a) Cats
b) Fiddler on the Roof
c) Hello, Dolly!
d) Singin' in the Rain

2724) In what small town does most of the action take place in *Cars*?

2725) Who wins the Piston Cup in *Cars*?

a) Francesco Bernoulli
b) Chick Hicks
c) Lightning McQueen
d) Strip "The King" Weathers

2707. true, 2708. Woody, 2709. Pizza Planet, 2710. dog, 2711. false—it was his first, 2712. true, 2713. b, 2714. false, 2715. false—Hasbro wouldn't give permission for him to be used at all, 2716. d, 2717. d, 2718. c, 2719. c, 2720. false, 2721. Bullseye, 2722. true, 2723. c, 2724. Radiator Springs, 2725. b

2726) Which real-life racecar driver does NOT voice a character in *Cars*?

a) Dale Earnhardt Jr.
b) Danica Patrick
c) Richard Petty
d) Michael Schumacher

2727) TRUE OR FALSE: THE LADYBUG IN A *BUG'S LIFE* IS MALE.

2728) Which city does NOT host a race in *Cars 2*?

a) Berlin
b) London
c) Rome
d) Tokyo

2729) True or false: former James Bond actor Timothy Dalton is the voice of superspy Finn McMissile in *Cars 2*.

2730) Which model of car is NOT among the "lemons" trying to destroy the racecars in *Cars 2*?

a) Gremlin
b) Pacer
c) Pinto
d) Yugo

2731) A statue of what car is at the center of town in *Cars*?

a) Edsel
b) Model T
c) REO Speedwagon
d) Stanley Steamer

2732) HOW MANY TIMES DID DOC HUDSON WIN THE PISTON CUP?

A) 0
B) 1
C) 2
D) 3

2733) What notorious destroyer of toys lives next door to Andy in *Toy Story*?

a) Bonnie
b) Charlie
c) Johnny
d) Sid

2734) By the time of *Toy Story 3*, Andy's neighbor has a job as what?

a) Busboy
b) Garbage man
c) Gas-station attendant
d) Paperboy

2735) What is Lightning McQueen's catchphrase?

a) Bazinga!
b) Ka-chigga ka-chigga!
c) Ka-chow!
d) Zoom zoom!

2736) In the Pixar short *Presto*, a magician's rabbit refuses to come out of the hat unless he gets what?

a) A carrot
b) A girlfriend
c) A raise
d) A vacation

2737) Actor and comedian Dan Whitney, a notable voice in two Pixar features and several shorts, is better known by what name?

2726. b, 2727. true, 2728. a, 2729. false—Michael Caine, 2730. c, 2731. d, 2732. c, 2733. d, 2734. b, 2735. c, 2736. a, 2737. Larry the Cable Guy

2738) Pixar made a series of shorts for the Disney Channel featuring Lightning McQueen and Mater under what umbrella title?

2739) What veteran songwriter and pianist had been nominated for 14 Oscars and lost them all before winning for the song "If I Didn't Have You" from *Monsters, Inc.*?

- **a) Elton John**
- **b) Diana Krall**
- **c) Alan Menken**
- **d) Randy Newman**

2740) *Cars* was inspired in part by the landscapes along what famous highway?

- a) I-95
- b) Pacific Coast Highway
- c) Route 66
- d) U.S. 40

2741) TRUE OR FALSE: PIXAR FOUNDER JOHN LASSETER WAS A JUNGLE CRUISE CAPTAIN AT DISNEYLAND.

2742) What was the name of John Lasseter's attention-getting early short film?

- *a) Luxo*
- *b) Luxo Jr.*
- *c) Luxo Sr.*
- *d) Mister Luxo*

DISNEY ANIMATION

2743) Put these five early Disney movies in order of their first theatrical release.

Pinocchio
Dumbo
Bambi
Snow White and the Seven Dwarfs
Fantasia

2744) In *Beauty and the Beast*, what is Belle's father's invention supposed to do?

2745) WHAT IS GASTON "ESPECIALLY GOOD AT"?

2746) Who is Chip's mother?

2747) True or false: *Beauty and the Beast* lost the Best Picture Academy Award to *Dances with Wolves*.

TOUGH TRIVIA CHALLENGE

2748) In *Beauty and the Beast*, what is the name of the clock?

2749) What color is Belle's dress she wears while in town?

2750) True or false: ***Beauty and the Beast*** **begins with the words "Once upon a time."**

2751) How many times did the Prince dismiss the beggar woman?

2752) The rose was enchanted to bloom until the Prince's ____ birthday?

2738. *Mater's Tall Tales*, 2739. d, 2740. c, 2741. true, 2742. b, 2743. *Snow White and the Seven Dwarfs*, *Pinocchio*, *Fantasia*, *Dumbo*, *Bambi*, 2744. chop wood, 2745. expectorating, 2746. Mrs. Potts, 2747. false—it lost to *Silence of the Lambs*, 2748. Cogsworth, 2749. blue, 2750. true, 2751. twice, 2752. twenty-first

2753) Who wrote the original story of *The Little Mermaid*?

a) The Brothers Grimm
b) Hans Christian Anderson
c) Edger Allen Poe
d) H.G. Wells

2754) WHAT SONG FROM *THE LITTLE MERMAID* WON THE ACADEMY AWARD FOR BEST SONG?

2755) Who says that the Prince in *The Little Mermaid* looks "kinda hairy and slobbery"?

2756) For how many days does the potion turn Ariel into a human?

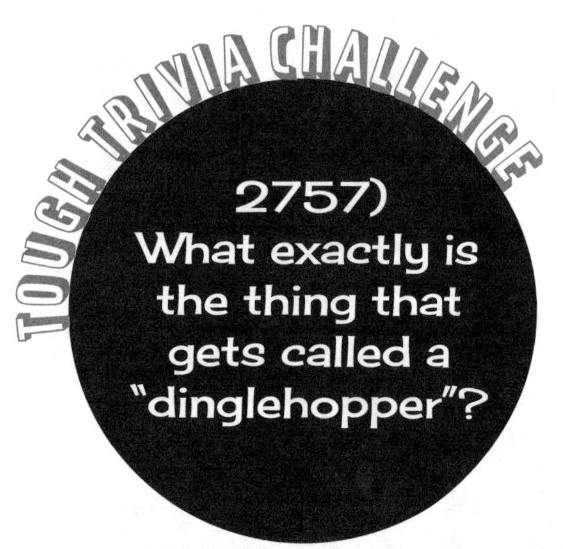

2758) True or false: A man voiced Ursula, the sea witch, in *The Little Mermaid*.

2759) WHAT IS THE NAME OF THE HUMAN THAT URSULA TRANSFORMS INTO?

2760) What is the name of the mouse in *Dumbo*?

2761) True or false: *Dumbo* was supposed to be on the cover of *Time* magazine in December of 1941 but that changed when Pearl Harbor was bombed.

2762) Does Dumbo ever talk?

2763) True or false: In *Disney's Cinderella*, the stepsisters are named Drizella and Ariella.

2764) True or false: In *Disney's Cinderella*, the prince is never named.

2765) Which song comes first in Disney's *Peter Pan,* "The Second Star to the Right" or "A Pirate's Life"?

2766) In the Disney film, which hand of Captain Hook's is a hook, left or right?

2767) **What are *Lady and Tramp* eating when "Bella Notte" is sung to them?**

2768) True or false: The Siamese cats in *Lady and the Tramp* are named Si and Am.

2769) In *Disney's Sleeping Beauty,* the title character is named Aurora. Is this her name in the German or the Italian version of the story?

2770) IN *THE FOX AND THE HOUND,* IS COPPER THE FOX OR THE HOUND?

2771) Is Vixey a fox or a hound?

2772) True or false:
The same actor voiced Thomas O'Malley in *The Aristocats,* Baloo the Bear in *Jungle Book,* and Little John in *Robin Hood.*

TOUGH TRIVIA CHALLENGE

2773) How many kittens does Duchess have in *The Aristocats?*

2753. b, 2754. "Under the Sea", 2755. Scuttle the seagull, 2756. three, 2757. a fork, 2758. false, 2759. Vanessa, 2760. Timothy, 2761. true, 2762. no, 2763. false—Drizella and Anastasia, 2764. true, 2765. "The Second Star to the Right", 2766. left, 2767. spaghetti and meatballs, 2768. true, 2769. Italian, 2770. the hound, 2771. fox, 2772. true—It was Phil Harris, 2773. three

2774) True or false: The same actress provided the singing voices for Mulan and Princess Jasmine.

2775) TRUE OR FALSE: *TANGLED* WAS ORIGINALLY GOING TO BE CALLED *RAPUNZEL UNBRAIDED.*

2776) What is the hero's name in *Tangled?*

a) Flint Riser

b) Flynn Rider

c) Frank Rymer

d) Fred Reisler

2777) True or false: Randy Newman wrote the songs for *Tangled.*

2778) *Disney's The Princess in the Frog* is set in the...

a) 1880s
b) 1920s
c) 1940s
d) 1960s

2779) Which of the following is not a character in *Brother Bear?*

a) Koda

b) Kenai

c) Sitka

d) Sakina

2780) Who is the father of *Hercules*?

2781) True or false: Susan Egan, who played the voice of Meg in Disney's *Hercules,* played Belle in Broadway's *Beauty and the Beast.*

TOUGH TRIVIA CHALLENGE

2782) How many of Greek mythology's nine muses were used in Disney's *Hercules?*

2783) TRUE OR FALSE: IN *HERCULES,* ZEUS' VOICE WAS CREATED BY COMPUTER AND DIDN'T USE AN ACTOR.

2784) What are the names of the two evil minions of Ares in *Hercules*?

a) Pain and Pleasure
b) Pain and Panic
c) Mean and Neasty
d) Hurt and Help

2785) Paul Shaffer, who played the voice of Hermes in *Hercules,* is bandleader for what late night TV show?

2786) Hercules' Roman numeral credit card says it expires in the year M BC. What year is that?

2787) What is Hercules' flying horse's name?

2774. true—it was Lea Salonga, 2775. true, 2776. b, 2777. false, 2778. b, 2779. d, 2780. Zeus, 2781. true, 2782. five, 2783. false, 2784. b, 2785. *Late Night with David Letterman*, 2786. 1,000 BC, 2787. Pegasus

2788) True or false: The talking statues in Disney's *The Hunchback of Notre Dame* were named after the author of the original novel?

2789) Which songs comes earlier in *The Hunchback of Notre Dame:* "God Help the Outcasts" or "A Guy Like You"?

2790) True or false: Belle from *Beauty and the Beast* makes a brief appearance in *The Hunchback of Notre Dame.*

2791) Stephen Schwartz wrote the music and lyrics for Disney's *The Hunchback of Notre Dame.* He also wrote the music and lyrics for a hit Broadway show about a witch. Name it.

2792) True or false: In The *Lion King,* Zazu has a different number of tail feathers depending on the scene.

2793) True or false: Elton John was an unknown songwriter when he wrote the score for *The Lion King.*

2794) James Earl Jones, who provided the voice for Mufasa in *The Lion King* also provided the voice for a villain in a non-animated film series. Name the series.

2795) True or false:

The same actor who voices adult Simba in *The Lion King* also starred in the movie *Inspector Gadget.*

2796) WHAT KIND OF ANIMALS ARE THE RESCUERS?

MATCH THE VILLAIN TO THE MOVIE.

2797) Cruella de Vil
2798) Dr. Facilier
2799) Frollo
2800) Gaston
2801) Hades
2802) Jafar
2803) Madame Medusa
2804) Maleficent
2805) Man
2806) Ratcliffe
2807) Professor Ratigan
2808) Scar
2809) Shan Yu
2810) Shere Khan
2811) Stromboli
2812) Sykes
2813) Ursula

a) *101 Dalmatians*
b) *Aladdin*
c) *Bambi*
d) *Beauty and the Beast*
e) *The Great Mouse Detective*
f) *Hercules*
g) *The Hunchback of Notre Dame*
h) *The Jungle Book*
i) *The Lion King*
j) *The Little Mermaid*
k) *Mulan*
l) *Oliver and Company*
m) *Pinocchio*
n) *Pocahontas*
o) *The Princess and the Frog*
p) *The Rescuers*
q) *Sleeping Beauty*

2814) What kind of cats menace Lady and the Tramp?

2815) What is the last name of the family befriended by Peter Pan?

2788. true—Victor and Hugo are named for Victor Hugo, 2789. "God Help the Outcasts", 2790. true, 2791. *Wicked*, 2792. true, 2793. false, 2794. *Star Wars*—he voiced Darth Vader, 2795. true—it was Matthew Broderick, 2796. Mice, 2797. a, 2798. o, 2799. g, 2800. d, 2801. f, 2802. b, 2803. p, 2804. q, 2805. c, 2806. n, 2807. e, 2808. i, 2809. k, 2810. h, 2811. m, 2812. l, 2813. j, 2814. Siamese, 2815. Darling

2816) What does Wendy sew back together for Peter Pan?

2817) What is the name of the Lion King at the beginning of the movie?

TOUGH TRIVIA CHALLENGE

2818) WHAT IS SLEEPING BEAUTY'S REAL NAME?

2819) By the end of the movie, who is the new Lion King?

2820) In the Disney version of *Robin Hood,* what kind of animal is Robin Hood?

Match the supporting characters in the Disney *Robin Hood* to the animal.

2821) Allan-a-Dale	a) Badger
2822) Friar Tuck	b) Bear
2823) Little John	c) Lion
2824) Prince John	d) Rooster
2825) Sheriff of Nottingham	e) Wolf

2826) What was the song made famous in Disney's 1933 "Three Little Pigs" cartoon?

2827) IN *PINOCCHIO*, IS HONEST JOHN A GOOD GUY?

Match the Disney princesses (and less royal Disney heroines) to their true love.

2828) Ariel
2829) Aurora
2830) Cinderella
2831) Esmeralda
2832) Jazmine
2833) Meg
2834) Nala
2835) Pocahontas
2836) Tiana
2837) Vixen

a) Aladdin
b) Prince Charming
c) Eric
d) Hercules
e) Naveen
f) Philip
g) Phoebus
h) Robin Hood
i) Simba
j) John Smith

2838) True or false: Mel Blanc, the voice of Bugs Bunny, was originally supposed to voice a character in *Pinocchio* but, after recording, it was decided to make the character mute.

2839) True or false: *Dumbo* was based on a book.

2840) What is the name of the mouse in *Dumbo*?

2841) True or false: Dumbo's mom's name is never mentioned.

2842) True or false: In the short, *Der Fuehrer's Face*, Donald Duck lives in Nazi Germany.

2816. his shadow, 2817. Mufasa, 2818. Princess Aurora, 2819. Simba, 2820. fox 2821. d, 2822. a, 2823. b, 2824. c, 2825. e, 2826. "Who's Afraid of the Big Bad Wolf?", 2827. no, 2828. c, 2829. f, 2830. b, 2831. g, 2832. a, 2833. d, 2834. i, 2835. j, 2836. e, 2837. h, 2838. true—it was Gideon, Honest John's sidekick, 2839. true, 2840. Timothy, 2841. false, 2842. true

2843) WAS DONALD DUCK OR MICKEY MOUSE PART OF THE THREE CABALLEROS?

2844) What is the mother cat's name in *The Aristocats*?

a) Duchess
b) Dainty
c) Daliah
d) Dorcett

2845) Which of the following Disney princesses was not a princess by birth?

a) Snow White
b) Belle
c) Jasmine
d) Aurora

2846) Which Disney princess never technically became a princess by bloodline or marriage?

a) Mulan
b) Ariel
c) Pocahontas
d) Belle

2847) Which princess has two living parents?

a) Cinderella
b) Ariel
c) Snow White
d) Mulan

2848) True or false: One of the Disney princesses was voiced by a man.

2849) Which of these Disney princesses wears a crown?

a) Belle
b) Cinderella
c) Ariel
d) Aurora

2850) Which Disney princess has a tiger as a sidekick?

2851) WHICH DISNEY PRINCESS HAS A HORSE AS A SIDEKICK?

2852) Which Disney princess has a hummingbird as a sidekick?

2853) Which Disney princess has mice as sidekicks?

2854) Which Disney princess has fish as sidekicks?

2855) What is Belle's father's name?

a) Mitchell
b) Michael
c) Maurice
d) Maury

2856) TRUE OR FALSE: DRIZELLA, FLORA, AND TREMAINE ARE THE FAIRIES THAT RAISE PRINCESS AURORA.

2857) Which Disney princess has the most siblings?

a) Cinderella
b) Jasmine
c) Ariel
d) Mulan

2858) Which Disney princess has a name that means "little mischief"?

2859) Which Disney Princess has the longest hair?

a) Jasmine
b) Aurora
c) Rapunzel
d) Mulan

2860) Which Disney princess sings "I want adventure..."?

2861) Which Disney princess sings "Up where they stay all day in the sun"?

2862) Which Disney princess sings "The dream that you wish will come true"?

2843. Donald Duck, 2844. a, 2845. b, 2846. a, 2847. d, 2848. false, 2849. d, 2850. Jasmine, 2851. Mulan, 2852. Pocahontas, 2853. Cinderella, 2854. Ariel, 2855. c, 2856. false, 2857. c, 2858. Pocahontas, 2859. c, 2860. Belle, 2861. Ariel, 2862. Cinderella

2863) Which Disney princess sings "the way you did once upon a dream"?

2864) Which Disney princess do we see as a baby?

a) Cinderella
b) Snow White
c) Aurora
d) Jasmine

2865) Where does *Princess and the Frog* primarily take place?

2866) True or false: *Tangled* is the first official Disney princess film without the proper name of a character in its title.

2867) In *Tangled*, how long is Rapunzel's hair at maximum?

a) 30 ft.
b) 50 ft.
c) 70 ft.
d) 90 ft.

2868) In Tangled, are there more animated thugs or townspeople?

2869) IN *THE PRINCESS AND THE FROG*, WHERE IS PRINCE NAVEEN FROM?

A) CALDONIA
B) MALDONIA
C) CARDODIA
D) FREEDONIA

2870) Louis the Alligator in *The Princess and the Frog* is a tribute to what trumpet player:

a) Louis Armstrong
b) Louie Prima
c) Louis Calhern
d) Louis L'Amour

2871) What kind of business does Tiana open at the end of *The Princess and the Frog*?

2872) What is the name of the firefly in *The Princess and the Frog*?

TOUGH TRIVIA CHALLENGE

2873) In *The Princess and the Frog*, what is Tiana's debutante friend's name?

a) Charlene
b) Charlotte
c) Charmaine
d) Charla

2874) In *The Princess and the Frog,* what is Dr. Facilier also known as?

a) The Shadow Man
b) Lord of Darkness
c) Beast of the Moon
d) The Man from Beyond

2875) True or false: In *The Princess and the Frog,* Mama Odie can't speak.

2876) True or false: Oprah Winfrey supplied one of the voices in *The Princess and the Frog.*

2863. Aurora, 2864. c, 2865. New Orleans, 2866. false, 2867. c, 2868. townspeople, 2869. b, 2870. a, 2871. a restaurant, 2872. Ray, 2873. b, 2874. a, 2875. false—but she is blind, 2876. true—she's Eudora, Tiana's mother

2877) WHAT DISNEY FILM INCLUDED THE SONG "GIVE A LITTLE WHISTLE"?

2878) What Disney film included the song "Once Upon a Dream"?

2879) What Disney film included the song "Bella Notte (This is the Night)"?

2880) What Disney film included the song "I'm Late"?

2881) What Disney film included the song "Baby Mine"?

2882) WHAT DISNEY FILM INCLUDED THE SONG "EVERYBODY WANTS TO BE A CAT"?

2883) What Disney film included the song "Candle on the Water"?

2884) What Disney film included the song "Friend Like Me"?

2885) What Disney film included the song "Can You Feel the Love Tonight"?

2886) What Disney film included the song "Go the Distance"?

2887) What Disney film included the song "Reflection"?

2888) What Disney film included the song "True Love's Kiss"?

2889) What Disney film included the song "Hawaiian Roller Coaster Ride"?

2890) WHAT DISNEY FILM INCLUDED THE SONG "MY FUNNY FRIEND AND ME"?

2891) What Disney film included the song "You'll Be in My Heart"?

2892) What Disney film included the song "Colors of the Wind"?

2893) What Disney film included the song "Part of Your World"?

2894) What Disney film included the song "Be Our Guest"?

2895) WHAT DISNEY FILM INCLUDED THE SONG "CRUELLA DE VIL"?

2896) What Disney film included the song "The Second Star to the Right"?

2897) What Disney film included the song "A Dream is a Wish Your Heart Makes"?

2898) What Disney film included the song "God Help the Outcasts"?

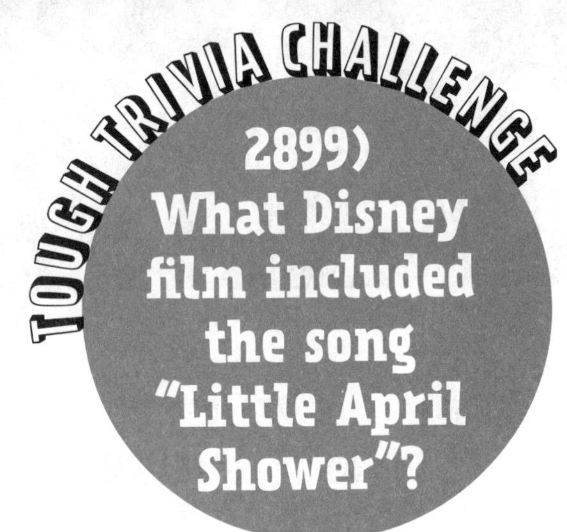

2900) What Disney film included the song "Trust in Me"?

2901) What Disney film included the song "I'm Wishing"?

2902) TRUE OR FALSE: *BEAUTY AND THE BEAST* AND *THE LITTLE MERMAID* WERE RELEASED THEATRICALLY IN THE SAME YEAR.

2903) Which of the following was not made at Disney Florida studio:

a) *Lilo and Stitch*
b) *Atlantic*
c) *Mulan*
d) *Brother Bear*

2877. Pinocchio, 2878. Sleeping Beauty, 2879. Lady and the Tramp, 2880. Alice in Wonderland, 2881. Dumbo, 2882. The Aristocats, 2883. Pete's Dragon, 2884. Aladdin, 2885. The Lion King, 2886. Hercules, 2887. Mulan, 2888. Enchanted, 2889. Lilo and Stitch, 2890. The Emperor's New Groove, 2891. Tarzan, 2892. Pocahontas, 2893. The Little Mermaid, 2894. Beauty and the Beast, 2895. 101 Dalmatians, 2896. Peter Pan, 2897. Cinderella, 2898. The Hunchback of Notre Dame, 2899. Bambi, 2900. The Jungle Book, 2901. Snow White and the Seven Dwarfs, 2902. false, 2903. c

LOONEY TUNES/ MERRIE MELODIES

2904) WHAT STUDIO CREATED LOONEY TUNES?

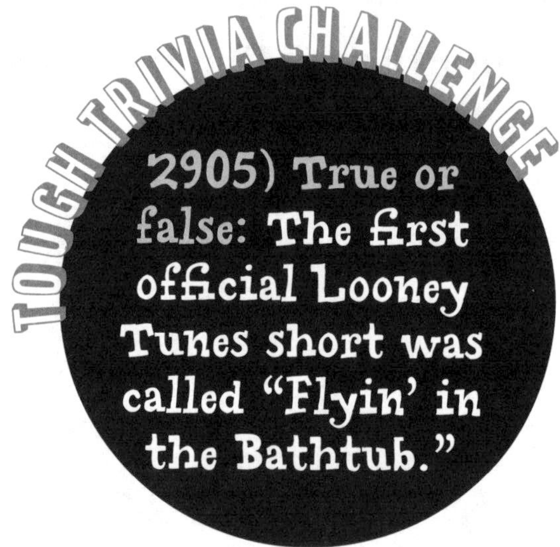

2906) Who is Porky Pig's girlfriend?

2907) Which were originally in black and white, Looney Tunes or Merrie Melodies?

2908) True or false: The Looney Tunes musical theme is called "The Merry-Go-Round Broke Down."

2909) True or false: Porky Pig was originally paired with a cat named Beans.

2910) Which came first, Daffy Duck or Bugs Bunny?

2911) TRUE OR FALSE: VIOLENCE IN SOME LOONEY TUNES SHORTS WAS EDITED OUT FOR TELEVISION VIEWING.

2912) Which came first, Porky Pig or Bugs Bunny?

2914) In what movie did Looney Tunes and Disney characters appear together?

2915) What was the name of the film where Michael Jordan appeared with Bugs Bunny?

2916) True or false: Some Looney Tunes shorts no longer air because they include racist stereotypes.

2917) WAS BUGS BUNNY CREATED IN THE 1930S OR THE 1940S?

2918) True or false: Bugs Bunny was made an honorary Marine.

2919) True or false: Bugs Bunny's name isn't used in "A Wild Hare."

2920) True or false: The first pairing of Bugs Bunny and Elmer Fudd, "A Wild Hare," was nominated for an Oscar for Best Animated Short.

2921) True or false: Bugs Bunny met Adolph Hitler in "Herr Meets Hare."

2922) Which of the following was not part of the "Duck Season/Rabbit Season" trilogy:

a) "Rabbit Seasoning"
b) "Duck! Rabbit, Duck!
c) "Rabbit Fire"
d) "Duck Under Class"

2923) What is the name of Marvin the Martian's hairy friend?

a) Hughie
b) Hugo
c) Hugio
d) Hungry-O

2924) TRUE OR FALSE: BUGS BUNNY HAS A STAR ON THE HOLLYWOOD WALK OF FAME.

2925) Who appeared first on a U.S. postage stamp, Bugs Bunny or Mickey Mouse?

2904. Warner Bros., 2905. false—it was "Sinkin' in the Bathtub.", 2906. Petunia, 2907. Looney Tunes, 2908. true, 2909. true, 2910. Daffy Duck, 2911. true, 2912. Porky Pig, 2913. bagpipes, 2914. *Who Framed Roger Rabbit*, 2915. *Space Jam*, 2916. true, 2917. 1930s, 2918. true, 2919. true, 2920. true, 2921. true, 2922. d, 2923. b, 2924. true, 2925. Bugs Bunny

2926) True or false: **Bugs Bunny never said "What's Up, Doc?"**

2927) Which did Bugs Bunny not tunnel his way to:

a) Mexico
b) Antarctic
c) The Arctic
d) The Himalayas

2928) True or false: Porky Pig is the only character to ever sign off Warner Bros. cartoons with "That's all, folks."

2929) What color are Bugs Bunny's gloves?

2930) WHO WAS THE VOICE OF BUGS BUNNY FROM 1940 TO 1989?

A) MEL CHEESE
B) MEL BLANC
C) MEL TORME
D) MEL MONET

Complete the Bugs Bunny short title with "hare," "rabbit," "bunny," or "wabbit."

2931) "The Heckling ________"
2932) "The _________ Who Came to Supper
2933) "The ______-Brained Hypnotist"
2934) "Tortoise Wins by a __________"
2935) "Little Red Riding __________"
2936) "_________ Force"
2937) "_________ Conditioned"
2938) "_______ Transit"
2939) "Hot Cross __________"
2940) "Buccaneer ___________"
2941) "_____________ Hood"
2942) "Hillbilly _______"
2943) "Lumber Jack __________"
2944) "Beanstalk ____________"
2945) "Wideo _________"

NON-DISNEY ANIMATION

TOUGH TRIVIA CHALLENGE

2946) Who was the non-singing voice of the title character in the animated film *Anastasia?*

a) Meg Ryan
b) Julia Roberts
c) Sandra Bullock
d) Melanie Griffith

2947) *Anastasia* concerns what country's royal family?

2948) True or false: John Cusack played all of the male parts in *Anastasia*.

2949) The prologue song in *Anastasia* is "Once Upon a ________."

2950) WHAT FAIRY TALE BALLET DO CHARACTERS IN *ANASTASIA* ATTEND?

2951) True or false: Kirsten Dunst is the voice of Young Anastasia in *Anastasia*.

2952) True or false: The song composer who wrote the score for *The Prince of Egypt* wrote the Broadway musical *Wicked*.

2953) Who is the voice of Miriam in *The Prince of Egypt?*

a) Meg Ryan
b) Julia Roberts
c) Sandra Bullock
d) Melanie Griffith

2926. false, 2927. c, 2928. false, 2929. white, 2930. b, 2931. Hare, 2932. Wabbit, 2933. Hare, 2934. Hare, 2935. Rabbit, 2936. Hare, 2937. Hare, 2938. Rabbit, 2939. Bunny, 2940. Bunny, 2941. Rabbit, 2942. Hare, 2943. Rabbit, 2944. Bunny, 2945. Wabbit, 2946. a, 2947. Russia, 2948. false, 2949. December, 2950. *Cinderella*, 2951. true, 2952. true—Stephen Schwartz, 2953. c

2954) Which of the following is not a voice in *The Prince of Egypt?*

a) Danny Glover
b) Ralph Fiennes
c) Meryl Streep
d) Steve Martin

2955) What language besides English is sung in *The Prince of Egypt?*

2956) True or false: *The Prince of Egypt* was rated PG-13.

2957) True or false: Boys II Men perform on the *The Prince of Egypt* soundtrack.

2958) TRUE OR FALSE: VAL KILMER PLAYS BOTH MOSES AND GOD IN *THE PRINCE OF EGYPT.*

2959) In *The Prince of Egypt,* is Moses adopted by the Pharaoh's daughter or his wife?

2960) What is Moses' wife's name?

a) Tzarah
b) Tzporah
c) Tzinnia
d) Tzorah

2961) How many quotes about Moses run after the final credits of *The Prince of Egypt.*

2962) Which is not a song in *The Prince of Egypt:*

a) "Through Heaven's Eyes"
b) "Pharaoh's Dream"
c) "Playing with the Big Boys"
d) "The Plagues"

2963) WHO SINGS WITH WHITNEY HOUSTON ON "WHEN YOU BELIEVE" ON THE SOUNDTRACK FOR *THE PRINCE OF EGYPT?*

A) MARIAH CAREY
B) ELLA FITZGERALD
C) MARTIN SHORT
D) BARBRA STREISAND

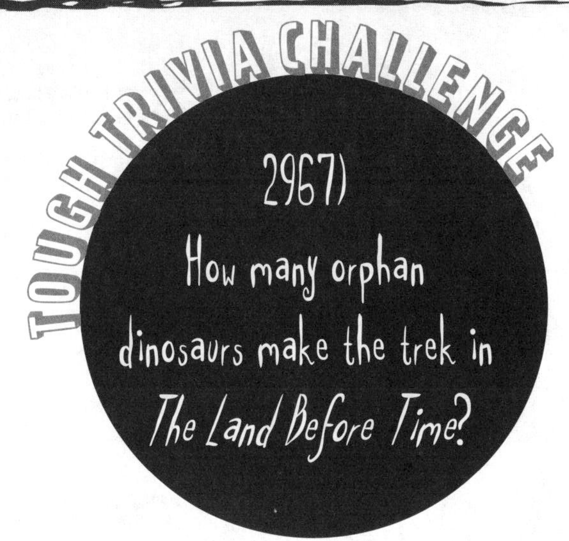

2964) True or false: Steven Spielberg directed *The Prince of Egypt.*

2965) When was the first *Land Before Time* film released?

a) 1976
b) 1982
c) 1988
d) 1991

2966) **True or false:** The actress who voiced Cera in *The Land Before Time* was five years old when the film was released.

2968) True or false: **Mark Hamill, from *Star Wars*, was the voice of Littlefoot in the first *Land Before Time* film.**

2969) True or false: In *The Land Before Time,* the same actor voiced Petrie and Rooter.

2970) True or false: Don Bluth, who created *The Land Before Time*, previously worked for Disney.

2971) WHICH DON BLUTH FILM CAME FIRST, *A TROLL IN CENTRAL PARK* OR *ALL DOGS GO TO HEAVEN*?

2954. c, 2955. Hebrew, 2956. false—just PG, 2957. true, 2958. true, 2959. his wife, 2960. b, 2961. three—from the Hebrew Bible, the New Testament, and the Qur'an, 2962. b, 2963. a, 2964. false, 2965. c, 2966. false—she was an adult, 2967. five, 2968. false, 2969. false, 2970. true, 2971. All Dogs Go to Heaven

2972) What kind of dinosaur are the longnecks?

a) Stegosaurus
b) Apatosaurus
c) Saurolophus
d) Triceratops

2973) True or false: *The Land Before Time* is a musical.

2974) What is *The Land Before Time* nickname for triceratops?

2975) In *The Land Before Time* what are "mountains that burn"?

2976) WHAT IS THE NAME FOR THE PLACE THAT THE LAND BEFORE TIME DINOSAURS ARE TRYING TO REACH?

2977) What is the name of the spiketail that the *Land Before Time* dinosaurs meet while on their journey?

2978) Where does Littlefoot see an image of his late mother?

2979) Which *The Land Before Time* sequel came first: *The Great Valley Adventure* or *The Time of the Great Giving*?

2980) What Disney film was released on the same day as *The Land Before Time?*

a) *The Jungle Book*

b) *The Rescuers Down Under*

c) *Oliver & Company*

d) *Robin Hood*

2981) True or false: Don Bluth and producers Steven Spielberg and George Lucas supervised twelve direct-to-video sequels for *The Land Before Time.*

2982) Which *The Land Before Time* sequel came first: *Journey Through the Mists* or *The Mysterious Island*?

2983) Which *The Land Before Time* sequel came first: *The Big Freeze* or *The Secret of Saurus Rock*?

2984) TRUE OR FALSE: *THE LAND BEFORE TIME X* IS CALLED *JURASSIC PRANKS.*

2985) Which *The Land Before Time* sequel came first: *The Wisdom of Friends* or *Invasion of the Tinysauruses?*

2986) True or false: **There was a TV series based on *The Land Before Time.***

2972. b, 2973. false—but its sequels are, 2974. three-horns, 2975. volcanoes, 2976. the Great Valley, 2977. Spike, 2978. in the clouds, 2979. *The Great Valley Adventure*, 2980. c, 2981. false—they were not involved at all, 2982. *Journey Through the Mist*, 2983. *The Secret of Saurus Rock*, 2984. false, 2985. *Invasion of the Tinysauruses*, 2986. true

2987) What does NIMH in *The Secret of Nimh* stand for?

2988) What is Fievel and his family's last name in *An American Tail.*

2989) WHAT DOES FIEVEL THINK THERE ARE NONE OF IN AMERICA?

2990) What song sung by Linda Ronstadt and James Ingram is sung over the end titles of *An American Tail?*

2991) What is the name of the sequel to *An American Tail*?

2992) True or false: A dog returns from the dead in *All Dogs Go to Heaven.*

2993) True or false: Burt Reynolds is the voice of Charlie B. Barkin in *All Dogs Go To Heaven.*

TOUGH TRIVIA CHALLENGE

2994) What is the name of the little girl in *All Dogs Go to Heaven?*

a) Anne-Marie
b) Alberta
c) Alyssa
d) Andrea

2995) Who is Charlie's dog buddy in *All Dogs Go to Heaven*?

a) Itchy
b) Scratchy
c) Patchy
d) Snuggly

2996) True or false: *All Dogs Go to Heaven* is set in the 1970s.

2997) WHAT KIND OF ANIMAL IS KING IN *ALL DOGS GO TO HEAVEN*?

2998) What kind of dog is Charlie in *All Dogs Go to Heaven*?

2999) True or false: Charlie Sheen voiced Charlie in *All Dogs Go to Heaven 2*.

3000) TRUE OR FALSE: IN *ALL DOGS GO TO HEAVEN 2*, CHARLIE'S DOG FRIEND CHOKES TO DEATH ON A CHICKEN DRUMSTICK.

3001) What animal is the human boy Edmond transformed into in *Rock-a-Doodle*?

a) A cow

b) A cat

c) A duck

d) A pig

TOUGH TRIVIA CHALLENGE

3002) *All Dogs Go to Heaven* was released in theaters on the same day as what Disney animated film?

a) *The Little Mermaid*

b) *Mulan*

c) *The Rescuers*

d) *The Aristocats*

3004) What kind of animal is the evil Grand Duke in *Rock-a-Doodle*?

3005) In *Thumbelina*, is Jaquimo a fish or a bird?

3006) What is the name of the Prince in *Thumbelina*?

3007) In *Thumbelina*, what kind of animal is Grundel?

3008) In *Thumbelina*, what kind of animal is Berkeley?

2987. The National Institutes of Mental Health, 2988. Mouskewitz, 2989. cats, 2990. "Somewhere Out There", 2991. Fievel Goes West, 2992. true, 2993. true, 2994. a, 2995. a, 2996. false—1939, 2997. an alligator, 2998. a German Shepherd, 2999. true, 3000. true, 3001. b, 3002. a, 3003. b, 3004. an owl, 3005. bird, 3006. Cornelius, 3007. a toad, 3008. a beetle

3009) True or false: The same actress who voiced Thumbelina also voiced Ariel in *The Little Mermaid* and Barbie in *Toy Story 2.*

3010) TRUE OR FALSE: BARRY MANILOW WROTE THE MUSIC FOR *THUMBELINA.*

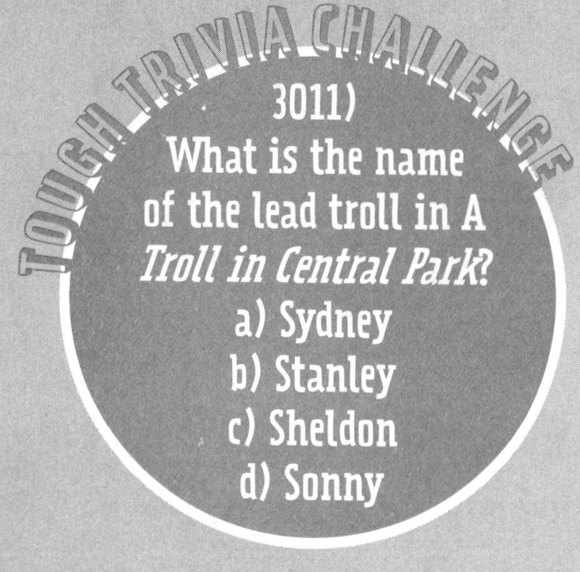

3012) What does Gnorga order done to the troll she catches making flowers grow in *A Troll in Central Park*?

a) Banished to Australia
b) Put in prison
c) Turned to stone
d) Set adrift in a lifeboat

3013) Who are the two children in *A Troll in Central Park*?

a) Gus and Rosie
b) Billy and Teddy
c) Sidney and Nancy
d) Eddie and Flo

3014) Is *The Pebble and the Penguin* set in the Arctic or the Antarctic?

3015) WHICH OF THE FOLLOWING IS NOT A MAIN CHARACTER IN *THE PEBBLE AND THE PENGUIN*?

A) HUBIE

B) MARINA

C) ROCKO

D) DAISY

3016) What kind of animal is Bartok, lead character in the *Anastasia* sequel *Bartok the Magnificent?*

3017) What does A.E. in *Titan A.E.* stand for?

3018) *Titan A.E.* is set in . . .

a) The 2000s

b) The 3000s

c) The 4000s

d) The 5000s

3019) True or false: Matt Damon is the voice of Cale in *Titan A.E.*

3020) True or false: Drew Barrymore is the voice of Akima in *Titan A.E.*

3021) True or false: ***Titan A.E.*** **was a major box office hit.**

3022) True or false: Don Bluth created animation for the *Dragon's Lair* video games.

3023) IN *ROBOTS*, DOES PAULA ABDUL VOICE WATCH OR CAPPY?

3024) True or false: In *Robots*, does Amanda Bynes voice Piper or Aunt Fanny?

3025) What is Rodney's metallic last name in *Robots*?

3026) What are the misfit robots called in *Robots*?

a) Outsiders

b) Rusties

c) Clankies

d) Boltless

3009. true—Jodi Benson, 3010. true, 3011. b, 3012. c, 3013. a, 3014. the Antarctic, 3015. d, 3016. a bat, 3017. After Earth, 3018. b, 3019. true, 3020. true, 3021. false—and it was the last film created by Fox Animation Studios for nine years, 3022. true, 3023. Watch, 3024. Piper, 3025. Copperbottom, 3026. b

3027) TRUE OR FALSE: MEL GIBSON IS THE VOICE OF ROCKY IN *CHICKEN RUN*.

3028) In what country is *Chicken Run* set?

TOUGH TRIVIA CHALLENGE

3029) What is the name of the studio that created *Chicken Run*?
a) Aardvark Animations
b) Oddbark Animations
c) Aardman Animations
d) Dreamworks

3030) In *Ice Age*, is Sid a wooly mammoth or a sloth?

3031) In *Ice Age*, what kind of animal is Diego?

3032) Which came first: *Ice Age: The Meltdown* or *Ice Age: Dawn of the Dinosaurs*.

3033) Which of the following didn't supply a voice for *Ice Age*:
a) Jack Black
b) Cedric the Entertainer
c) Ray Romano
d) John Stewart

3034) What color hat does the lead human in *Curious George* wear?

3035) IN *CATS DON'T DANCE*, IS DANNY TRYING TO BE A STAR ON BROADWAY OR IN HOLLYWOOD?

3036) The *Swan Princess* was adapted from:

a) An opera
b) A silent film
c) A ballet
d) A symphony

3037) True or false: The same person was the singing voice of the title characters in both *Anastasia* and *The Swan Princess.*

3038) Is Rothbart in *The Swan Princess* a sorcerer or a king?

3039) Which of the following is not a song in *The Swan Princess*?

a) "This is My Idea"
b) "Far Longer than Forever"
c) "Princesses on Parade"
d) "Truth is Never Easy"

3040) TRUE OR FALSE: THERE HAVE BEEN NO SEQUELS TO *THE SWAN PRINCESS.*

3041) Which came first, the animated or the live-action *Charlotte's Web*?

TOUGH TRIVIA CHALLENGE

3042) What is the name of the prince in *The Swan Princess*?

3027. true, 3028. England, 3029. c, 3030. sloth, 3031. a tiger, 3032. *Ice Age: The Meltdown*, 3033. d, 3034. yellow, 3035. Hollywood, 3036. c, 3037. true—Liz Callaway, 3038. Sorcerer, 3039. d, 3040. false—there have been two, 3041. animated, 3042. Derek

3043) True or false: Debbie Reynolds, who voiced Charlotte in *Charlotte's Web*, is the mother of Carrie Fisher, who played Princes Leia in *Star Wars*.

3044) In *Charlotte's Web*, what kind of animal is Wilbur?

3045) In *Charlotte's Web*, what kind of animal is Templeton?

3046) Did Popeye first appear in comic strips or on movie screens?

3047) What was Popeye's cinematic theme song?

3048) In the first Popeye cartoon, was his antagonist Bluto or Brutus?

3049) TRUE OR FALSE: BETTY BOOP APPEARED IN THE FIRST POPEYE CARTOON.

3050) In the 1937 short "Porky's Duck Hunt," was Porky Pig hunting Daffy Duck?

3051) True or false: There was a 1938 short called "Porky in Wackyland."

3052) Fleischer Studios, makers of Popeye cartoons, tried its hand at a feature film in 1939 with an animated movie based on what book?

a) *Dracula*
b) *The Swiss Family Robinson*
c) *Gulliver's Travels*
d) *Little Women*

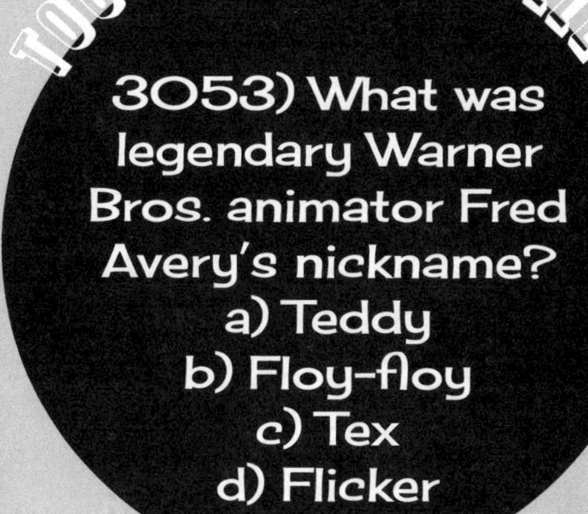

3053) What was legendary Warner Bros. animator Fred Avery's nickname?

a) Teddy
b) Floy-floy
c) Tex
d) Flicker

3054) DID ROBIN WILLIAMS VOICE *FERNGULLY: THE LAST RAINFOREST* BEFORE OR AFTER *ALADDIN*.

3055) Which came first, *Jimmy Neutron: Boy Genius* the movie or the TV show?

3056) Is the animated film *The Miracle Maker* about a sports team or based on a Bible story?

3057) What kind of animal is the title character in *Balto*?

3058) True or false: Anne Hathaway is the voice of Red Puckett in *Hoodwinked*.

3043. true, 3044. a pig, 3045. a rat, 3046. comic strips, 3047. "I'm Popeye the Sailor Man", 3048. Bluto, 3049. true, 3050. yes, 3051. true, 3052. c, 3053. c, 3054. before, 3055. TV show, 3056. a Bible story, 3057. a dog, 3058. true

3059) What is the name of the wolf in *Hoodwinked!*?

a) Wolfie Wolfsie
b) Wolf W. Wolf
c) James Wolfe
d) Virginia Wolfe

3060) Which of the following is not a suspect in *Hoodwinked*?

a) The Wolf
b) The Woodsman
c) Chief Grizzly
d) Granny

3061) True or false: The Oscar-winning animated short *Gerald McBoing-Boing* was based on a story by Dr. Seuss.

3062) The 1953 short in which Daffy Duck is tormented by his animator is called...

a) *Ducktastrophy*
b) *Friday the Duckteenth*
c) *Duck Amuck*
d) *Daffy Taffy*

3063) True or false: Mister Magoo was featured in a 1959 movie version of *Arabian Nights*.

3064) True or false: There was a 1966 animated feature film starring Huckleberry Hound.

3065) TRUE OR FALSE: THERE WAS A 1964 ANIMATED FEATURE FILM STARRING YOGI BEAR.

3066) What country created Astro Boy?

3067) Were the actual voices of the Beatles used in the 1968 animated feature *Yellow Submarine*?

3068) In what British city does the action of *Yellow Submarine* open?

3069) Which of these songs was written for *Yellow Submarine*?

a) "Revolution"
b) "Hey, Bulldog"
c) "A Hard Day's Night"
d) "Rocky Raccoon"

3070) True or false: There was a 1969 short film called *Bambi Meets Godzilla.*

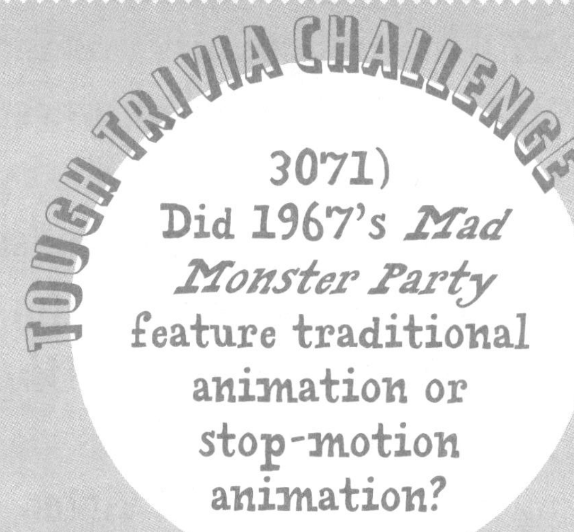

TOUGH TRIVIA CHALLENGE

3071) Did 1967's *Mad Monster Party* feature traditional animation or stop-motion animation?

3072) What Kingdom does Milo in *The Phantom Tollbooth* visit?

a) The Kingdom of Truth
b) The Kingdom of Wisdom
c) The Kingdom of Left Behind
d) The Kingdom of Krichton

3059. b, 3060. c, 3061. true, 3062. c, 3063. true, 3064. false, 3065. yes—*Hey There, It's Yogi Bear*, 3066. Japan, 3067. no, 3068. Liverpool, 3069. b, 3070. true, 3071. stop-motion animation, 3072. b

3073) In what country was the 1982 short *The Snowman* created?

3074) What band was the source of a partially animated film based on its album *The Wall*?

3075) True or false: Will Vinton, who earned national attention with his California Raisons commercials, took three and a half years to complete his 1985 claymation feature film *The Adventures of Mark Twain.*

3076) WHICH CAME FIRST, *AN AMERICAN TAIL* OR *A BUG'S LIFE*?

3077) In the Wallace and Gromit animated films, which one is the dog?

3078) What was the name of the other computer-animated insect movie that came out around the same time as *A Bug's Life*?

TOUGH TRIVIA CHALLENGE

3079) What was the name of the 2001 movie based on the *Final Fantasy* computer games?

3080) True or false: *The Iron Giant* was executive produced by The Who's Pete Townshend.

3081) True of false: In 1978 there was an animated theatrical feature film based on *The Lord of the Rings.*

3082) What was the 1985 Rainbow Brite animated film called:

a) *Rainbow Brite and the Curse of Darkness*
b) *Rainbow Brite and the Sun Stealers*
c) *Rainbow Brite and the Star Stealer*
d) *Rainbow Brite and the Dark Star*

3083) What was the name of the 1985 He-man and She-Ra animated feature film:

a) *He-Man and She-Ra: The Secret of the Sword*
b) *He-Man and She-Ra: The Secret of the Shield*
c) *He-Man and She-Ra: The Secret of the Mask*
d) *He-Man and She-Ra: The Secret of the Truth*

3084) True or false: There was a 1986 animated Transformers movie.

3085) Who voiced Sinbad in 2003's *Sinbad: Legend of the Seven Seas*?

a) George Clooney
b) Brad Pitt
c) James Marsden
d) Kevin Kline

3086) True or false: The Fantastic Mr. Fox was based on a book by the author of *Charlie and the Chocolate Factory.*

3087) TRUE OR FALSE: *9* WAS BASED ON AN AWARD-WINNING SHORT FILM.

3073. England, 3074. Pink Floyd, 3075. true, 3076. An American Tail, 3077. Gromit, 3078. Antz, 3079. *Final Fantasy: The Spirits Within*, 3080. true, 3081. true, 3082. c, 3083. a, 3084. true, 3085. b, 3086. true—Roald Dahl, 3087. true

3088) True or false: *9* was released the same year as the movie musical Nine.

Finish the title of these animated films:

3089) Little Nemo: Adventures in ________
3090) The ______ Unicorn
3091) _____ Upon a Forest
3092) We're _____! A Dinosaur's Story
3093) The ________ and the Goblin
3094) The _____ and the Cobbler
3095) Cat's Don't _______
3096) Doug's First _______
3097) The Road to El ________
3098) Joseph: King of ________
3099) Rugrats in ______
3100) Spirit: _______ of the Cimarron
3101) Hey ____! The Movie
3102) The ______ of Belleville
3103) The _____ of Kells

3104) Caroline was based on a book by what popular author?

a) Roald Dahl
b) J.R.R. Tolkein
c) Neil Gaiman
d) John Lithgow

3105) True or false: The movie *How to Train Your Dragon* was an almost scene-for-scene copy of the original novel.

3106) What is the Viking boy's name in *How to Train Your Dragon*?

3107) WHAT IS THE NAME OF THE ISLAND IN *HOW TO TRAIN YOUR DRAGON*?

A) BIRCH
B) BERK
C) BEACH
D) BLETCH

3108) In *How to Train Your Dragon*, Stoick the Vast is...

a) A rival chieftain
b) The dragon father
c) The Viking leader
d) A plot of land

3109) What is the nickname for the trained dragon in *How to Train Your Dragon*?

3110) In *How to Train Your Dragon*, Astrid is...

a) A boy dragon trainer
b) A girl dragon trainer
c) A rival kingdom
d) A dragon

3111) What does Gobber make for the hero of *How to Train Your Dragon*?

3088. true, 3089. Slumberland, 3090. Last, 3091. Once, 3092. Here, 3093. Princess, 3094. Thief, 3095. Dance, 3096. Vie, 3097. Dorado, 3098. Dreams, 3099. Paris, 3100. Stallion, 3101. Arnold, 3102. Triplets, 3103. Secret, 3104. c, 3105. false, 3106. Hiccup, 3107. b, 3108. c, 3109. Toothless, 3110. b, 3111. a prosthetic leg

CHAPTER 6

It Happened in . . .

• • 1988 • • •

3112) True or false: The leader of the Soviet Union in 1988 was Mikhail Gorbachev.

3113) Who was the vice president of the United States in 1988?

3114) In 1988, what was Anthony M. Kennedy appointed to?

3115) Where were the 1988 Winter Olympics held?

a) Soviet Union
b) Finland
c) Canada
d) United States

3116) Which of the following was not a Democratic presidential candidate in 1988?

a) Jesse Jackson
b) Richard Gephardt
c) Michael Dukakis
d) Evan Mecham

3117) What comic strip had its debut in 1988

a) FoxTrot
b) Doonesbury
c) B.C.
d) Hagar the Horrible

3118) What film won the 1988 Oscar for Best Picture?

a) Rain Man
b) Dangerous Liaisons
c) Mississippi Burning
d) The Accidental Tourist

TOUGH TRIVIA CHALLENGE

3119) In the Hebrew calendar, it was what year in 1988?

a) 5748-5749
b) 5750-5751
c) 5752-5753
d) 5754-5755

3112. true, 3113. George H.W. Bush, 3114. The Supreme Court, 3115. c, 3116. d, 3117. a, 3118. a, 3119. a

3120) What former pop singer became mayor of Palm Springs, California?

a) Bette Midler
b) Sonny Bono
c) Joni Mitchell
d) Judy Collins

3121) Where was the 1988 World Expo held?

a) Australia
b) Austria
c) England
d) Egypt

3122) What national park faced massive wildfires in 1988?

a) Grand Canyon
b) Great Smokey Mountains
c) Yellowstone
d) Yosemite

3123) WHAT FUTURE ONE-NAMED SINGER WAS BORN IN BARBADOS IN 1988?

3124) Who did George H.W. Bush defeat in the 1988 Presidential election?

3125) WHERE WERE THE 1988 SUMMER OLYMPICS HELD?

A) SOUTH KOREA
B) VIETNAM
C) JAPAN
D) CHINA

3126) What food company did Philip Morris buy in 1988?

a) Campbell's
b) Kraft
c) Kellogg's
d) Nabisco

3127) What future star of Arrested Development and Nick and Norah's Infinite Playlist was born in 1988?

3128) What Princess of York was born in 1988?

3129) What did Naguib Mahfouz win the Nobel Prize for in 1988?

a) Medicine
b) Physics
c) Literature
d) Peace

3130) Each of these was a #1 hit for Michael Jackson in 1988 EXCEPT:

a) "Bad"
b) "Dirty Diana"
c) "The Man in the Mirror"
d) "The Way You Make Me Feel"

3131) In 1988, the Supreme Court decided that the police didn't need one of these to look through thrown-out garbage?

3132) Each of these was a #1 hit for George Michael in 1988 EXCEPT:

a) "Father Figure"
b) "Kissing a Fool"
c) "Monkey"
d) "One More Try"

3133) True or false: Rick Astley's "Never Gonna Give You Up" was a #1 hit in 1988.

3134) One of the biggest hits of 1988, spending three weeks at #1, was what single by Poison?

a) "Every Rose Has Its Thorn"
b) "Nothin' But a Good Time"
c) "Talk Dirty to Me"
d) "Unskinny Bop"

3135) Guns 'n' Roses released what album in 1988?

a) Appetite for Destruction
b) Destruction Zone
c) Eve of Destruction
d) Self-Destruction

3120. b, 3121. a, 3122. c, 3123. Rihanna, 3124. Michael Dukakis, 3125. a, 3126. b, 3127. Michael Cera, 3128. Beatrice, 3129. c, 3130. a, 3131. search warrant, 3132. b, 3133. true, 3134. a, 3135. a

3136) True or false: **In 1988, the first computer worm was released.**

3137) WHO WAS REELECTED PRESIDENT OF FRANCE IN 1988?

A) JACQUES CHIRAC
B) VALERY GISCARD D'ESTAING
C) FRANCOIS MITTERRAND
D) NICOLAS SARKOZY

3138) The Soviet Union began pulling troops out of what country in 1988?

a) Afghanistan
b) Angola
c) Cuba
d) Poland

3139) What country ousted Janos Kadar as its leader after more than 30 years in power?

a) Czechoslovakia
b) East Germany
c) Hungary
d) Romania

3140) After eight years of war, Iraq agreed to a ceasefire with what country?

a) Iran
b) Kuwait
c) Saudi Arabia
d) United States

3141) What country became the first Muslim nation to be governed by a woman?

a) Indonesia
b) Jordan
c) Pakistan
d) Saudi Arabia

3142) Who was prime minister of Canada in 1988?

a) Kim Campbell
b) Jean Chretien
c) Brian Mulroney
d) Pierre Trudeau

Complete the titles of these novels published in 1988.

3143) Breathing __________
3144) The Cardinal of the __________
3145) Foucault's __________
3146) The Icarus __________

a) Agenda
b) Kremlin
c) Lessons
d) Pendulum

3147) What pitcher broke a record by ending the season with 59 consecutive shutout innings?

a) Roger Clemens
b) Dennis Eckersley
c) Orel Hershiser
d) Dave Stewart

3148) True or false: Kurt Vonnegut's novel Paris Trout was published in 1988.

3149) Who were the two stars of Rain Man, the winner of the Oscar for Best Picture?

3150) George H.W. Bush used what three-word phrase in vowing never to raise taxes if elected president?

3151) In 1988, who became the first tennis player in 18 years to win all four Grand Slam tournaments?

a) Andre Agassi
b) Stefan Edberg
c) Steffi Graf
d) Monica Seles

3152) Who recorded the 1988 hit song "Don't Worry, Be Happy"?

a) Bobby McFerrin
b) Bobby Brown
c) Bobby Brooks
d) Bobby Bacharach

3136. true, 3137. c, 3138. a, 3139. c, 3140. a, 3141. c, 3142. c, 3143. c, 3144. b, 3145. d, 3146. a, 3147. c, 3148. false—it's by Pete Dexter. 3149. Tom Cruise and Dustin Hoffman, 3150. read my lips, 3151. c, 3152. a

• • 1989 • •

3153) The Polish United Workers Party formed a labor union famously called...

a) Togetherness
b) One-for-all
c) Solidarity
d) Singleness

3154) GEORGE H.W. BUSH BECAME PRESIDENT OF THE UNITED STATES, REPLACING WHO?

3155) What was the name of the boat that spilled oil in the waters off Alaska?

a) Exxon Electra
b) Exxon Esso
c) Exxon Valiant
d) Exxon Valdez

3157) What was the site of protests in China?

a) Tiananmen Square
b) Tammarind Square
c) Beijing Square
d) Dragon Square

3158) What was the name of the Iranian leader who died in 1989?

a) Ayatollah Kommanchi
b) Ayatollah Kampchatka
c) Ayatollah Khomeini
d) Ayatollah Karmax

3159) What was the name of the hand-held system released by Nintendo in 1989?

3160) What baseball legend was banned from the game for allegedly gambling?

3156) Mikhail Gorbachev became the first Soviet ruler to visit this country since the 1960s.

a) United States
b) China
c) Japan
d) England

3161) WHAT SEGA SYSTEM IS RELEASED IN 1989?

3162) What was the name of the Hurricane that hit South Carolina in 1989?

a) Harold
b) Hugo
c) Herman
d) Henry

3163) Nicolae Ceausescu was overthrown as ruler of what country?

a) Hungary
b) Rumania
c) Turkey
d) France

3164) What race did Sunday Silence win in 1989?

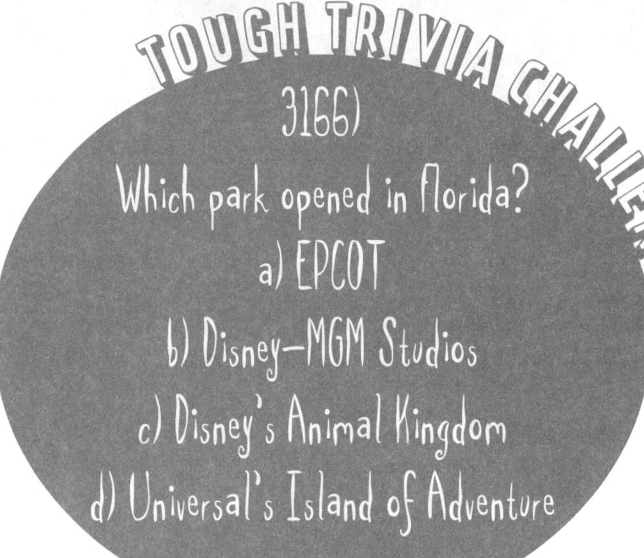

TOUGH TRIVIA CHALLENGE

3166)

Which park opened in florida?

a) EPCOT
b) Disney—MGM Studios
c) Disney's Animal Kingdom
d) Universal's Island of Adventure

3167) WHO WAS CONVICTED IN WHAT WAS KNOWN AS THE IRAN-CONTRA AFFAIR?

A) OLIVER WEST
B) OLIVER EAST
C) OLIVER SOUTH
D) OLIVER NORTH

3168) What was the name of the star of I Love Lucy who died in 1989?

3165) What book by Salman Rushdie led to Iran's leader putting a bounty on him?

a) The Satanic Purses
b) The Satanic Nurses
c) The Satanic Verses
d) The Satanic Curses

3153. c, 3154. Ronald Reagan, 3155. d, 3156. b, 3157. a, 3158. c, 3159. Game Boy, 3160. Pete Rose, 3161. Genesis, 3162. b, 3163. b, 3164. Kentucky Derby, 3165. c, 3166. b, 3167. d, 3168. Lucille Ball

3169) WHAT WAS TORN DOWN, BEGINNING ON NOVEMBER 9?

3170) What show won the Emmy Award for Outstanding Drama in 1989?

a) *St. Elsewhere*
b) *L.A. Law*
c) *NYPD Blue*
d) *Law and Order*

3171) Who was the great Shakespearian actor who died in 1989?

a) John Barrymore
b) Laurence Olivier
c) Edwin Booth
d) Marie Iaconangelo

3172) Which Jackson had a #1 hit in 1989, Janet or Michael?

3173) WHAT FUTURE TV PERSONALITY HAD THREE #1 HITS IN 1989?

3174) What duo had three #1 hits in 1989, but were stripped of the Best New Artist Grammy for the year after it turned out they'd been lip-syncing?

3175) Which country was the first to break free from the Communist bloc?

a) East Germany
b) Hungary
c) Lithuania
d) Poland

3176) What monarch died after 62 years on the throne?

a) King Abdullah
b) Queen Beatrix
c) Emperor Hirohito
d) King Hussein

3177) Cuban troops began a withdrawal from what nation in 1989?

a) Angola
b) El Salvador
c) Haiti
d) Mozambique

3178) Donald Trump bought the landing rights to operate a New York-to-Washington and New York-to-Boston air shuttle from what struggling airline?

a) Eastern
b) Northwest
c) Southwest
d) Western

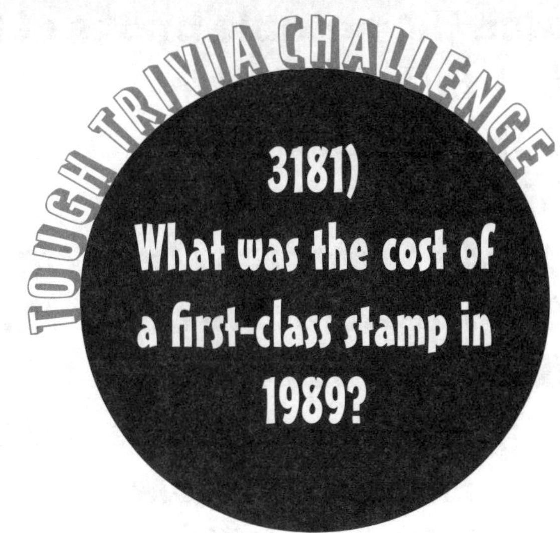

3179) Alfredo Stroessner was overthrown after 35 years as the dictator of what country?

a) Austria
b) East Germany
c) Liechtenstein
d) Paraguay

3182) Who became New York City's first African-American mayor?

a) David Dinkins
b) Carl McCall
c) David Paterson
d) Adam Clayton Powell

3180) U.S. troops invaded what nation in December, forcing out the country's president seven months after he ignored his loss in national elections?

a) Grenada
b) Haiti
c) Nicaragua
d) Panama

3183) The House passed, but the Senate rejected, a constitutional amendment to overturn a Supreme Court decision allowing what?

a) Free cigarettes
b) Flag burning
c) Gerrymandering
d) School prayer

3169. the Berlin Wall, 3170. b, 3171. b, 3172. Janet, 3173. Paula Abdul, 3174. Milli Vanilli, 3175. D, 3176. c, 3177. a, 3178. a, 3179. d, 3180. d,
3181. a quarter, 3182. a, 3183. b

Match the notable books of 1989 to their authors.

3184) *Billy Bathgate*
3185) *The Dark Half*
3186) *The Joy Luck Club*
3187) *A Prayer for Owen Meany*
3188) *The Remains of the Day*
3189) *The Russia House*
3190) *The Seven Habits of Highly Effective People*
3191) *A Time to Kill*

a) Stephen Covey
b) E.L. Doctorow
c) John Grisham
d) John Irving
e) Kazuo Ishiguro
f) Stephen King
g) John le Carre
h) Amy Tan

3192) Bristol-Myers merged with what pharmaceutical company?

a) Lilly
b) Merck
c) Squibb
d) Wyeth

3193) The Corcoran Gallery in Washington canceled a planned exhibition of the works of what controversial photographer?

3194) GEORGE HARRISON, BOB DYLAN, ROY ORBISON, TOM PETTY, AND JEFF LYNNE UNITED TO FORM WHAT SUPERGROUP?

3195) What interrupted the World Series for 11 days?

a) Earthquake
b) Flooding
c) Hurricane
d) Rioting

3196) What televangelist was sentenced to 45 years in prison for fraud?

a) Benny Hinn
b) Oral Roberts
c) Jimmy Swaggart
d) Jim Bakker

TOUGH TRIVIA CHALLENGE

3197) The term "wilding," meaning to go out on a crime spree, entered the language after a near-fatal assault on a jogger in what location?

3198) True or false: the actor who played Shoeless Joe Jackson in Field of Dreams played minor-league ball in the Chicago White Sox system.

3199) What hotelier was dubbed "The Queen of Mean" during her trial for tax evasion?

a) Lori Partridge
b) Leona Helmsley
c) Lisa Birnbaum
d) Leslie Stahl

TOUGH TRIVIA CHALLENGE

3200) William Bennett became the first person to hold what U.S. government post?

a) Drug czar
b) Secretary of Education
c) Secretary of Energy
d) Secretary of Homeland Security

3184. b, 3185. f, 3186. h, 3187. d, 3188. e, 3189. g, 3190. a, 3191. c, 3192. c, 3193. Robert Mapplethorpe, 3194. the Traveling Wilburys, 3195. a, 3196. d, 3197. Central Park in New York, 3198. false—though a namesake and relative of actor Ray Liotta did, 3199. b, 3200. a

1990

3201) What party gave up exclusive rule of the Soviet Union in 1990?

a) Democratic Party
b) Socialist Party
c) Communist Party
d) Whig Party

3202) Who was freed in South Africa after more than 27 years in prison?

3203) What country did Iraq invade in 1990, starting the Persian Gulf War?

a) Egypt b) Israel
c) Sudan d) Kuwait

3204) Did Margaret Thatcher resign and John Major become British Prime Minster or vice versa?

3205) Who was the vice president of the U.S. in 1990?

3206) What West Coast team beat Denver in the 1990 Super Bowl 55-10?

3207) Who won in the Men's Wimbledon battle between Stefan Edberg and Boris Becker?

3208) What long running animated TV series launched on Fox in 1990?

3209) What show business magazine began publishing in 1990?

a) *Entertainment Weekly*
b) *Variety*
c) *The Hollywood Reporter*
d) *TV Guide*

3210) THE X-RATING FOR MOVIES WAS REPLACED BY WHAT RATING IN 1990?

3211) What Washington D.C. landmark was completed in 1990?

a) The Smithsonian Air and Space Museum
b) The National Gallery of Art
c) The National Cathedral
d) The Vietnam Veterans Memorial

3212) What singer began her career with five straight #1 hits, with the first two topping the charts in 1990?

a) Mariah Carey
b) Paula Cole
c) Melissa Etheridge
d) Whitney Houston

3213) What was the name of the Muppet creator who died in 1990?

3214) Robert Van Winkle topped the charts under what stage name?

a) Gino Vannelli
b) Milli Vanilli
c) Vanilla Fudge
d) Vanilla Ice

3215) Michael Bolton re-recorded "How Am I Supposed to Live Without You?" and took it to #1, seven years after writing it for what singer?

a) Laura Branigan b) Janet Jackson
c) Joan Jett d) Dolly Parton

3201. c, 3202. Nelson Mandela, 3203. d, 3204. Thatcher resigned/Major became Prime Minister, 3205. J. Danforth Quayle, 3206. San Francisco 49ers, 3207. Edberg, 3208. *The Simpsons*, 3209. a, 3210. NC-17, 3211. c, 3212. a, 3213. Jim Henson, 3214. d, 3215. a

Match the author to his 1990 work.

3216) *Hocus Pocus*
3217) *An Inconvenient Woman*
3218) *Jurassic Park*
3219) *Vineland*

a) Michael Crichton
b) Dominick Dunne
c) Thomas Pynchon
d) Kurt Vonnegut

3220) What was the biggest box-office hit of 1990?

a) *Dances With Wolves*
b) *Ghost*
c) *Home Alone*
d) *Total Recall*

3221) "It Must Have Been Love" was a #1 hit off the soundtrack of what 1990 romantic comedy?

3222) Alannah Myles' single "Black Velvet" is about whom?

a) James Brown
b) Michael Jackson
c) Elvis Presley
d) Barry White

3223) Kevin Costner won an Oscar for 1990's *Dances With Wolves.* In what category?

a) Best Actor
b) Best Director
c) Best Original Score
d) Best Original Screenplay

3224) WHO STARRED IN TWO OF THE TEN BIGGEST BOX OFFICE HITS OF 1990?

A) HARRISON FORD
B) RICHARD GERE
C) ARNOLD SCHWARZENEGGER
D) BRUCE WILLIS

3225) What creator of Willy Wonka died in 1990?

3226) True or false: **North and South Yemen united in 1990.**

3227) True or false: East and West Germany united in 1990.

3228) Who created the TV series *Twin Peaks,* which debuted in 1990?

a) David Cronenberg
b) David Lynch
c) Martin Scorsese
d) Steven Spielberg

3229) On *Twin Peaks,* who killed Laura Palmer?

a) Her boyfriend
b) Her father
c) Her mother
d) Windom Earle

3230) True or false: North and South Vietnam united in 1990.

3231) True or false: North and South Sudan united in 1990.

3232) What talk show host guest-hosted *The Pat Sajak Show* in 1990, and had to clear the studio after a prolonged on-air argument with abortion-rights and gay-rights activists in the audience?

a) Glenn Beck
b) Sean Hannity
c) Rush Limbaugh
d) Bill O'Reilly

3233) True or false: **North and South Korea united in 1990.**

3234) True or false: East and West Pakistan united in 1990.

3235) General Motors introduced what ultimately unsuccessful car in 1990?

a) Chevette
b) Saturn
c) Trabant
d) Volt

3236) A 15-YEAR CIVIL WAR IN WHAT COUNTRY ENDED IN 1990?

A) IRAN
B) IRAQ
C) LEBANON
D) QATAR

3216. d, 3217. b, 3218. a, 3219. c, 3220. b, 3221. *Pretty Woman*, 3222. c, 3223. b, 3224. c, 3225. Roald Dahl, 3226. true, 3227. true, 3228. b, 3229. b, 3230. false, 3231. false, 3232. c, 3233. false, 3234. false, 3235. b, 3236. c

3237) What African nation declared independence in 1990?

a) Congo
b) Liberia
c) Namibia
d) Zambia

3238) Michael Milken, who went to prison for insider trading in 1990, pioneered the trading of what financial instrument?

a) Credit-default swaps
b) Derivatives
c) Junk bonds
d) Mortgage-based bonds

3239) Which man was NOT heavyweight champion of the world for part of 1990?

a) Buster Douglas
b) George Foreman
c) Evander Holyfield
d) Mike Tyson

3240) What was banned on U.S. airline flights in 1990?

a) Cell phones
b) Liquids
c) Weapons
d) Smoking

3241) What 1965 hit by the Righteous Brothers reentered the Top 20 in 1990, thanks to its use in the movie *Ghost*?

a) "Rock and Roll Heaven"
b) "Soul and Inspiration"
c) "Unchained Melody"
d) "You've Lost That Lovin' Feeling"

3242) What country won the 1990 World Cup?

a) Argentina b) Brazil
c) France d) Germany

3243) *Entertainment Weekly* made its debut in 1990, with whom on the cover?

a) Mia Farrow
b) Whitney Houston
c) k.d. lang
d) Oprah Winfrey

1991

3244) Who became the first freely elected president of the Russian Republic?

a) Georgy Malenkov

b) Alexei Kosygin

c) Leonid Brezhnev

d) Boris Yeltsin

3245) Who won the Duke vs. Kansas NCAA Basketball Championship in 1991?

3246) What Seattle band released the song "Smells Like Teen Spirit"?

TOUGH TRIVIA CHALLENGE

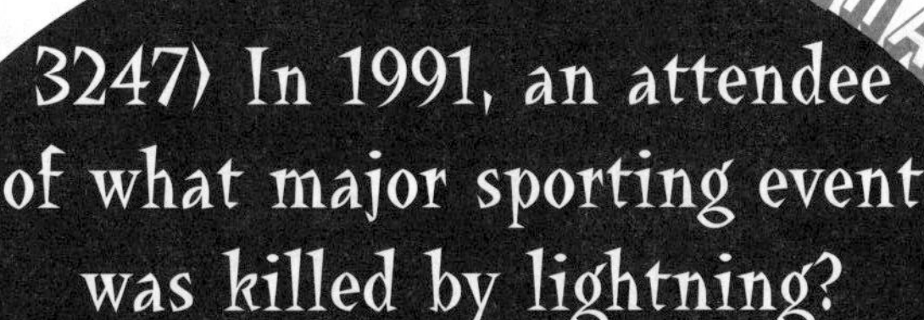

3247) In 1991, an attendee of what major sporting event was killed by lightning?

a) Super Bowl

b) World Series

c) U.S. Open

d) Kentucky Derby

3248) In 1991, a nuclear accident happened in what country?

a) United States

b) China

c) Yugoslavia

d) Japan

3249) What cable channel launched in 1991 after the merger of two rival channels, the Comedy Channel and Ha!?

3250) Which one dissolved in 1991 to be replaced by the other: The Supreme Soviet of the Soviet Union or the Congress of People's Deputies of the Soviet Union.

3237. c, 3238. c, 3239. b, 3240. d, 3241. c, 3242. d, 3243. c, 3244. d, 3245. Duke, 3246. Nirvana, 3247. c, 3248. d, 3249. Comedy Central, 3250. The Congress of People's Deputies of the Soviet Union dissolved

3251) Which of the following did not declare independence in 1991 after the dissolution of the Soviet Union?

a) Azerbaijan
b) Kyrgyzstan
c) Stanicole
d) Moldova

3252) What Governor of Arkansas declared his intentions of running for President?

3253) WHAT L.A. LAKERS STAR ANNOUNCED THAT HE HAD H.I.V.?

3254) What legendary jazz trumpeter, composer, and bandleader died in 1991?

a) Charles Mingus
b) Miles Davis
c) Duke Ellington
d) Louis Armstrong

3255) What airline shut down in 1991?

a) TWA
b) Pan-Am
c) Eastern
d) American TransAir

3256) *What song from the Robin Hood: Prince of Thieves soundtrack was the biggest hit of 1991, spending seven weeks at #1?*

3257) True or False: Michael Jackson had his final #1 hit in 1991 with "Black or White."

3258) What is the title of the #1 hit subtitled "Everybody Dance Now"?

3259) What Christian contemporary act's biggest mainstream hit was 1991's "Baby Baby"?

a) Amy Grant
b) Petra
c) Michael W. Smith
d) Stryper

3260) Germany moved its capital to Berlin from what city in 1991?

3261) Who began a 17-year run as host of *Meet the Press* in 1991?

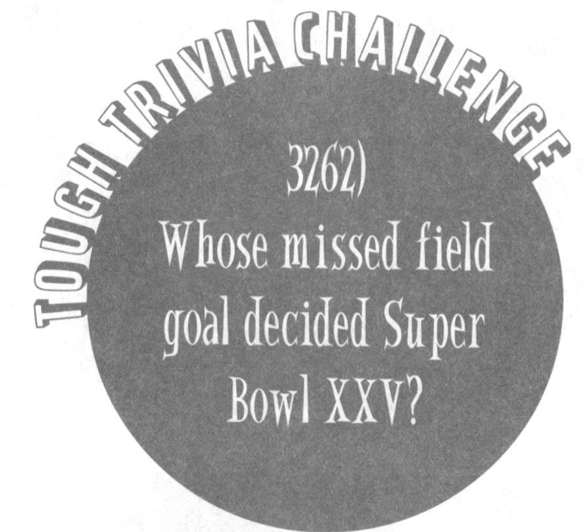

3263) The *Silence of the Lambs* won Oscars in each of these categories EXCEPT:

a) Best Picture
b) Best Actress
c) Best Supporting Actor
d) Best Director

3264) In the last gasp of the Soviet Union, Soviet troops staged a violent crackdown in what breakaway Baltic republic?

a) Estonia
b) Georgia
c) Latvia
d) Lithuania

3265) Who starred in two of the top ten moneymaking movies of 1991?

a) Kevin Costner
b) Anthony Hopkins
c) Arnold Schwarzenegger
d) Robin Williams

3266) What game show, which debuted in 1991, put young contestants in charge of tracking villains such as Sarah Nade and Patty Larceny?

a) *Brain Surge*
b) *Double Dare*
c) *Where in the World is Carmen Sandiego?*
d) *You Can't Do That on Television*

3267) What team defeated the Buffalo Bills in Super Bowl XXV?

a) Green Bay Packers
b) New York Giants
c) San Francisco 49ers
d) Tampa Bay Buccaneers

3268) What code name was given to the invasion of Iraq?

a) Operation Barbarossa
b) Operation Desert Storm
c) Operation Enduring Freedom
d) Operation Overlord

3269) A 1991 Douglas Coupland book coined what term for the generation that followed the Baby Boomers?

3251. c, 3252. Bill Clinton, 3253. Magic Johnson, 3254. b, 3255. b, 3256. "(Everything I Do) I Do It For You", 3257. false—"You Are Not Alone," 1995 3258. "Gonna Make You Sweat", 3259. a, 3260. Bonn, 3261. Tim Russert, 3262. Scott Norwood, 3263. c, 3264. d, 3265. a, 3266. c, 3267. b, 3268. b, 3269. Generation X

1992

3270) Where was President Bush when he threw up on camera at a state dinner?

a) Washington, D.C.
b) Japan
c) China
d) Mexico

3271) When the artists' boycott of South Africa ended, who was the first major musician to tour there?

a) Bruce Springsteen
b) Bono
c) Paul Simon
d) Elton John

3272) The 1992 Winter Olympics were held in Albertville...

a) France
b) Germany
c) Italy
d) Greece

3273) In 1992, Bill Clinton was elected the ______ President of the United States.

a) 39th b) 40th c) 41st d) 42nd

3274) Who did Princess Diana separate from in 1992?

3275) Riots caused death and damage in L.A. after four police officers were acquitted in the beating of who?

a) Rodney Allen Ripey
b) Rodney King
c) Rodney Dangerfield
d) Rodney Reynolds

3276) Anthony Perkins died in 1992. What horror movie was he most famous for appearing in?

a) A Nightmare on Elm Street
b) Psycho
c) Halloween
d) Friday the 13th

3277) Singer Sinead O'Conner caused controversy when she tore up a photo of who while she was a musical guest on *Saturday Night Live?*

a) Ronald Reagan
b) Pope John Paul II
c) Muhammad
d) Madonna

3278) What famous music hall in Paris, France, closed in 1992?

a) The Sorbonne
b) The Follies Bergere
c) The Ritz
d) Minsky's

3279) *Unforgiven* won Best Picture at the Oscars. What kind of film was it?

a) Musical
b) Comedy
c) Romantic drama
d) Western

3280) John Cage died in 1992. What was Cage best known as?

a) Basketball player
b) Politician
c) Zookeeper
d) Composer

3281) What monetary unit replaced the ruble in Estonia?

a) The krupa
b) The kroon
c) The carrot
d) The klam

3282) What *Twilight* actor was born in February of 1992?

3283) Which Disney park opened in 1992?

a) Disneyland Tokyo
b) EPCOT
c) Euro Disneyland
d) No Disney park opened in 1992

3270. a, 3271. c, 3272. a, 3273. d, 3274. Prince Charles, 3275. b, 3276. b, 3277. b, 3278. b, 3279. d, 3280. d, 3281. b, 3282. Taylor Lautner, 3283. c

1993

3284) Who was the Vice President of the U.S. in 1993?

3285) Was the population in 1993 greater or less than 5.5 billion?

3286) What East Coast team did Toronto beat in the 1993 World Series?

a) New York Yankees
b) Philadelphia Phillies
c) Washington Senators
d) Baltimore Orioles

3287) "Tears in Heaven" was named Record of the Year and Song of the Year at the Grammy Awards. Whose song was it?

a) Eric Clapton
b) Phil Collins
c) Sting
d) Paul McCartney

3288) Arthur Ashe died in 1993. What sport was Ashe famous for?

3289) True or false: Microsoft released Windows 95 in 1993.

3290) TRUE OR FALSE: ACTRESS AUDREY HEPBURN, WHO DIED IN 1993, WAS THE SISTER OF ACTRESS KATHARINE HEPBURN.

3291) What political office did Janet Reno hold?

a) Secretary of State
b) Attorney General
c) Speaker of the House
d) New York Senator

3292) How many days was the standoff between federal agents and the Branch Dividian group near Waco, Texas?

a) 22 days
b) 43 days
c) 51 days
d) 66 days

3293) True or false: Monica Seles was stabbed in the back in 1993 by a fan of another tennis star?

3294) True or false: In 1993, the leader of Israel and the leader of the Palestine Liberation Organization shook hands.

3295) What was Theodore John "Ted" Kaczynski better know as?

a) Donald Trump
b) Ice-T
c) The Unibomber
d) Benny Hill

3296) Andre the Giant died in 1993. What classic fantasy film did he appear in?

a) *The Wizard of Oz*
b) *The Princess Bride*
c) *The Neverending Story*
d) *Willow*

3297) The 1993 Tony winner for Best Play was *Angels in America: Millennium Approaches*. This was the first of how many Angels in America parts?

3298) Conway Twitty died in 1993. What was he best know as?

a) Baseball manager
b) Country singer
c) Southern congressman
d) Hotel owner

3299) True or false: The 1993 stage musical The *Who's Tommy* was about a pinball player who couldn't see, hear or speak.

3300) Bill Clinton signed the Brady Bill in 1993. What did it regulate?

a) Primetime television commercials
b) Overseas travel
c) Firearms purchases
d) Campaign contributions

3301) Ruth Ginsburg was named to the Supreme Court. What is her full name?

a) Ruth Barbara Ginsburg
b) Ruth Bader Ginsburg
c) Ruth Bilger Ginsburg
d) Ruth Buckingham Ginsburg

3302) What Bill Murray movie, released in 1993, concerns a man reliving the same day over and over again?

3284. Al Gore, 3285. greater, 3286. b, 3287. a, 3288. tennis, 3289. false, 3290. false, 3291. b, 3292. c, 3293. true, 3294. true, 3295. c, 3296. b, 3297. two, 3298. b, 3299. true, 3300. c, 3301. b, 3302. Groundhog Day

1994

3303) What later presidential primary candidate became Speaker of the House in 1994?

a) Haven Hamilton
b) Newt Gingrich
c) Stephen Breyer
d) Aldrich Ames

3304) What former football star was arrested for murder in California?

3305) Who won his first directing Oscar in 1994?

a) Chris Columbus
b) George Lucas
c) Steven Spielberg
d) Gerald R. Molen

3306) TRUE OR FALSE: THE WHITE HOUSE LAUNCHED ITS WEB PAGE IN 1994.

3307) What iconic 1969 peace, love, and music concert was reprised with a new list of performers including Green Day, Melissa Etheridge, and Metallica.

3308) NAFTA was established in 1994. What does it stand for?

a) North American Federation of Teacher's Aides
b) North American Free Trade Agreement
c) Nebraska Anti-Federalist Trade Association
d) No Arms for Turkey Association

3309) It was announced in 1994 that former President Reagan had what disease?

3310) It seems obvious, but what finally became Canada's official winter sport in 1994.

3311) Nancy Kerrigan's leg was clubbed in an attack in 1994. What sport did Kerrigan compete in?

3312) What did the Church of England do for the first time in 1994?

a) Ordained female priests
b) Allowed Irish to be clergy
c) Paid taxes
d) Established dioceses outside of the U.K.

3313) What future pop star, known for his music and his hair, was born in January of 1994?

3314) What did comet Shoemaker-Levy 9 collide with?

a) Mars
b) Jupiter
c) Earth
d) The Moon

3315) True or false: The New York Yankees beat the Houston Astros in the 1994 World Series.

3316) What famous painting was stolen and then recovered in 1994?

a) *The Mona Lisa*
b) *Nude Descending a Staircase*
c) *The Scream*
d) *The Last Supper*

1995

3317) Which grossed more at the box office in 1995, *Die Hard with a Vengeance* or *Toy Story*?

3318) Who is named President of France?

a) Jacques LeClerc
b) Jacques Damboise
c) Jacques Chirac
d) Jacques Indebox

3303. b, 3304. O.J. Simpson, 3305. c, 3306. true, 3307. Woodstock, 3308. b, 3309. Alzheimer's, 3310. hockey, 3311. figure skating, 3312. a, 3313. Justin Bieber, 3314. b, 3315. false—There was no World Series in 1994, 3316. c, 3317. *Die Hard with a Vengeance*, 3318. c

3319) What millionaire announced he would run for the Republican presidential nomination?

a) Bill Gates
b) Steve Forbes
c) Mark Zuckerberg
d) Donald Trump

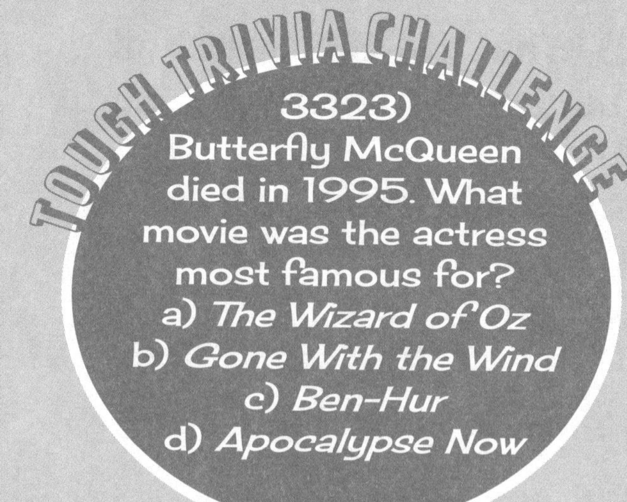

3323) Butterfly McQueen died in 1995. What movie was the actress most famous for?

a) *The Wizard of Oz*
b) *Gone With the Wind*
c) *Ben-Hur*
d) *Apocalypse Now*

3320) THE MILLION MAN MARCH WAS HELD IN 1995 IN WASHINGTON D.C. WHO ORGANIZED IT?

A) JON STEWART
B) AL SHARPTON
C) LOUIS FARRAKHAN
D) JAMES WATT

3324) Where did the Rock and Roll Hall of Fame open in 1995?

3325) THE GRAMMY FOR 1995 SONG OF THE YEAR WENT TO BRUCE SPRINGSTEEN'S "STREETS OF PHILADELPHIA." WHAT MOVIE WAS IT FROM?

3321) Where was Yitzhak Rabin assassinated?

a) New York City
b) London
c) Tel Aviv
d) Jerusalem

3326) Steve Fossett was the first person to do what solo?

a) Ski down Mt. Everest
b) Traverse the Sahara Desert
c) Cross the Pacific Ocean in a balloon
d) Compete on the Amazing Race

3322) Rose Kennedy died in 1995. What was her relation to John F. Kennedy?

a) Mother
b) Sister
c) Wife
d) Daughter

1996

3327) What was the name of the computer that beat champion Garry Kasparov?

a) Deep Red
b) Deep Green
c) Deep Purple
d) Deep Blue

3328) True or false: In 1996, Paula Abdul became the youngest person ever to win a Grammy for Album of the Year.

3329) WHO DID BILL CLINTON BEAT IN THE 1996 PRESIDENTIAL ELECTION?

3330) TRUE OR FALSE: THE MEDIAN HOUSEHOLD INCOME IN THE U.S IN 1996 WAS LESS THAN $40,000?

3331) What old school hotel in Las Vegas was imploded to clear space for the Venetian Hotel?

a) The Palms
b) The Sands
c) Caesar's Palace
d) The Trocadera

3332) The star of *Singin' in the Rain* died in 1996. He was...

a) Fred Astaire
b) Buddy Hackett
c) Gene Kelly
d) Rudolph Valentino

3333) What gangsta rapper was found shot and later died in 1996?

a) Ice-T
b) Ice Cube
c) Tupac Shakur
d) Talia Shire

3319. b, 3320. c, 3321. c, 3322. a, 3323. b, 3324. Cleveland, 3325. *Philadelphia*, 3326. c, 3327. d, 3328. false—but Alanis Morissette did, 3329. Bob Dole, 3330. true, 3331. b, 3332. c, 3333. c

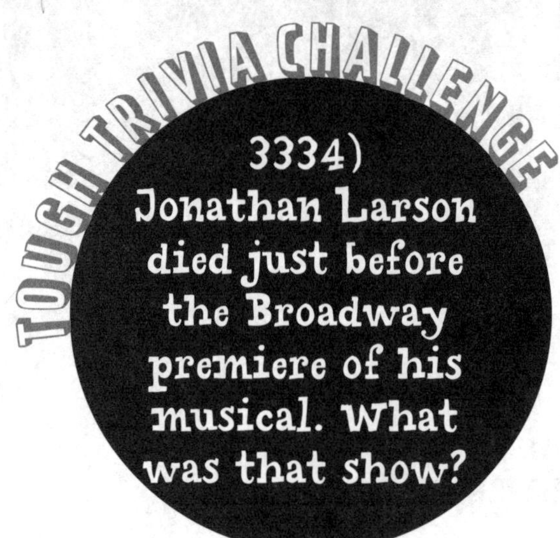

3335) Who was nominated to become the first female Secretary of State in 1996?
a) Ruth Bader Ginsburg
b) Madeleine Albright
c) Hillary Clinton
d) Ruth Buzzi

3336) Frank McCourt's bestselling book *Angela's Ashes* concerned growing up poor in what country?
a) Israel b) Egypt c) Ireland d) Poland

3337) In 1996, what percentage of American homes had a computer?
a) 33% b) 44% c) 55% d) 66%

3338) Who won the 1996 Emmy for Best Actor in a Comedy Series for his role in *3rd Rock from the Sun?*
a) John Lithgow
b) Rip Torn
c) Tim Conway
d) Dennis Miller

1997

3339) Who became Prime Minster of England in 1997?
a) Tony Scott
b) Tony Undershaft
c) Tony Blair
d) Tony Thatcher

3340) *IN JUNE OF 1997, DICTATOR POL POT FLED FROM HIS STRONGHOLD IN WHAT COUNTRY?*
A) *LAOS*
B) *CAMBODIA*
C) *SENEGAL*
D) *NIGERIA*

3341) What venerable department store folded in 1997?

a) F.W. Woolworth
b) P.J. O'Hullygully
c) G.W. Murphey
d) P.T. Barnum

3342) More than two million people around the world watched whose funeral in 1997?

3343) What movie, released in December 1997, became the highest-grossing movie in history—at least, until *Avatar* came along?

3344) What country opted to launch its own Parliament in 1997?

a) Spain
b) Australia
c) Scotland
d) Iran

3345) TRUE OR FALSE: THE FIRST HYBRID CAR TO GO INTO FULL PRODUCTION WAS THE TOYOTA PRIUS.

3346) Allen Ginsberg, who died in 1997, was famous for being a...

a) Speed skater
b) Mountaineer
c) Poet
d) Cartoonist

3347) True or false: In *The Terminator*, made in 1984, the nuclear war took place in 1997.

3348) The TV rating system debuted in 1997. What rating is between TV-PG and TV-M?

3349) Prince Michael Junior is born. Who is his famous father?

3334. Rent, 3335. b, 3336. c, 3337. b, 3338. a, 3339. c, 3340. b, 3341. a, 3342. Diana, Princess of Wales, 3343. Titanic, 3344. c, 3345. true, 3346. c, 3347. true, 3348. TV-14, 3349. Michael Jackson

1998

3350) The Unibomber pleaded guilty in 1998. Did he get a life sentence or the death penalty?

3351) Which grossed more at the box office, *Armageddon* or *A Bug's Life?*

3352) Which won the Oscar for Best Film, *Saving Private Ryan* or *Shakespeare in Love?*

3353) Britney Spears released her debut single in 1998. What song was it?

3354) WHO WON THE STANLEY CUP, DETROIT OR WASHINGTON?

3355) Who staged more nuclear tests in 1998, India or Pakistan?

3356) Where did the Athena probe find frozen water?

a) Mars
b) Venus
c) Mercury
d) The Moon

3357) What television sitcom, starring a famous comedian, aired its last episode in 1998 with about 76 million viewers watching?

3358) One of the world's most famous singers died in 1998 at the age of 82. Who was he?

3359) Who won the Olympic figure skating gold medal in 1998?

a) Tara Lipinksi
b) Holly Alexander
c) Oksana Baiul
d) Nicole Bobek

3360) Who broke Roger Maris's single-season home run record by hitting 70 in 1998?

3361) True or false: President Bill Clinton was impeached.

1999

3362) What is the name of the European currency that was established in 1999?

3363) Who became President of Venezuela in 1999?

a) Hugo Boss
b) Hugo Chavez
c) Hugo Victor
d) Hugo Castro

3364) What music sharing service had its debut—and caused controversy in the music business?

3365) WHO WON THE TOUR DE FRANCE IN 1999?

3366) BRANDI CHASTAIN SCORED THE GAME-WINNING POINT IN A BIG GAME AGAINST CHINA IN WHAT SPORT?

A) VOLLEYBALL
B) SOCCER
C) SOFTBALL
D) BASKETBALL

TOUGH TRIVIA CHALLENGE

3367) What two companies, primarily known for gasoline, merged in 1999?

a) Exxon and Shell
b) Mobil and Shell
c) Shell and Conesto
d) Exxon and Mobil

3350. life sentence, 3351. *Armageddon*, 3352. *Shakespeare in Love*, 3353. "…Baby One More Time", 3354. Detroit, 3355. Pakistan, 3356. d, 3357. Seinfeld, 3358. Frank Sinatra, 3359. a, 3360. Mark McGwire, 3361. yes—but did not have to leave office, 3362. the Euro, 3363. b, 3364. Napster, 3365. Lance Armstrong, 3366. b, 3367. d

3368) Who resigned as President of Russia

a) Boris Yeltsin

b) Vladimir Putin

c) Mikhail Gorbachev

d) Vladislav Surkov

3369) The son of what former president died in a plane crash.

3370) Who sang a 1982 song encouraging listeners to "party like it's 1999"?

3371) What is the name of the virus that raised concerns about possible massive computer breakdowns at the end of the year.

3372) Universal Music Group was formed in 1999 from the merger of what two record labels?

a) Universal and Polygram
b) Warner Bros. and Apple
c) K-Tl and Virgin
d) Polymer and Polygram

3373) WHAT ACTOR LEFT THE HIT SHOW *ER* FOR WHAT WOULD BECOME A VERY SUCCESSFUL MOVIE CAREER?

3374) What low-budget horror film went on to become the most profitable film of all time?

3375) What went over 150 million in 1999?

a) The number of cell-phone owners
b) The number of people in China
c) The number of Internet users around the world
d) The number of dogs in America

• • 2000 • • •

3376) In Florida, 6-year-old Elian Gonzalez made headlines after he was forced to return to his native country. What country?

a) El Salvador
b) Peru
c) Cuba
d) Russia

3377) A close presidential election in the U.S. brought attention to the voting cards used. What term was used to describe situations where votes weren't clear?

a) Muddy vote
b) Hanging chad
c) Vague vote
d) Partial confusion

3378) Who was Al Gore's running mate in the 2000 election?

a) Walter Mondale
b) Bob Dole
c) Joe Lieberman
d) John Kerry

3379) Who opted to leave the morning show program she co-hosted with Regis Philbin?

3380) Charles Schulz died in 2000. What is he best known for creating?

3381) What is the name of the magazine the Oprah Winfrey launched in 2000?

3382) Was 2000 a leap year?

3368. a, 3369. John F. Kennedy, 3370. Prince, 3371. Y2K, 3372. a, 3373. George Clooney, 3374. *The Blair Witch Project*—although that honor now belongs to the 2009 movie *Paranormal Activity*, 3375. c, 3376. c, 3377. b, 3378. c, 3379. Kathy Lee Gifford, 3380. the Peanuts comic strip and characters, 3381. O, 3382. yes

3383) Where were the 2000 Summer Olympics held?

a) China
b) Australia
c) Finland
d) South Africa

3384) Who became the first former first lady of the U.S. to be elected to a public office when she became a senator for New York?

3385) What won the Emmy Award for Outstanding Drama Series: *The West Wing* or *The Sopranos*?

3386) TRUE OR FALSE: IN 2000, AMERICAN ONLINE PURCHASED UNIVERSAL STUDIOS.

3387) Who won the St. Louis vs. Tennessee Super Bowl?

3388) Who won the Indiana vs. Los Angeles NBA Championship?

2001

3389) What number president did George W. Bush become when he took office in January of 2001?

3390) What fell into the Pacic Ocean in March of 2001?

a) An asteroid
b) The Russian Space Station Mir
c) Vice President Dick Cheney
d) A plane full of wild turkeys

3391) Junichiro Koizumi became prime minster of what country?

a) Japan b) Indonesia
c) Vietnam d) Cambodia

3392) What is the flight number of the plane that is brought down in Shanksville, PA, during the World Trade Center/Pentagon attacks?

a) Flight 90
b) Flight 91
c) Flight 92
d) Flight 93

3393) WHAT BAND PERFORMED THE 2001 GRAMMY-WINNING RECORD OF THE YEAR "BEAUTIFUL DAY"?

3394) In what month did the U.S. invade Afghanistan in response to the 9/11 attacks?

a) September
b) October
c) November
d) December

3395) What big Houston-based company filed for bankruptcy in December 2001?

a) Exxon b) Enderon
c) Enron d) Eldon

3396) In what year were both the movie and the novel *2001: A Space Odyssey* by Arthur C. Clarke, released?

a) 1960
b) 1968
c) 1972
d) 1978

3397) What long-running film series was launched on November 4, 2011?

a) *Star Wars*
b) *Lord of the Rings*
c) *The Fast and the Furious*
d) *Harry Potter*

3398) Isaac Stern died in 2001. What was he famous for playing?

a) Baseball
b) The piano
c) The violin
d) Basketball

3399) What powdered substance caused a scare when found in the U.S. mail?

a) Cocaine
b) Anthrax
c) Regolith
d) Titanium

3383. b, 3384. Hillary Clinton, 3385. *The West Wing*, 3386. false—it purchased Time Warner, 3387. St. Louis, 3388. Los Angeles, 3389. 43, 3390. b, 3391. a, 3392. d, 3393. U2, 3394. b, 3395. c, 3396. b, 3397. d, 3398. c, 3399. b

2002

3400) How many days did Pennsylvania miners spend trapped in a mine?

a) 44
b) 55
c) 66
d) 77

3401) Who won in the New England vs. St. Louis Super Bowl?

3402) Who won at Wimbledon when Venus Williams competed against her sister Serena Williams?

3403) Who won the World Cup, Brazil or Germany?

3404) True or false: The Osbournes won an Emmy for Best Reality Series.

3405) True or false: Denzel Washington was the first African-American to win the Oscar for Best Actor

3406) What New York mayor was given an honorary knighthood by the Queen of England?

a) Rudy Giuliani
b) Ed Koch
c) Michael Bloomberg
d) David Dinkins

3407) Dave Thomas died in 2002. What fast food franchise did he create?

3408) A woman burning a letter from her husband led to a wildfire that destroyed more than 130 houses in what state?

a) West Virginia
b) Colorado
c) Pennsylvania
d) California

3409) WHAT SUPERHERO WAS THE SUBJECT OF 2002'S TOP BOX-OFFICE GROSSING FILM?

3410) What country club, home of the Masters Tournament, came under fire for not admitting women as members?

a) Atlanta Springs
b) Georgia Pines
c) Augusta National
d) Oak Valley

3411) WHERE WERE THE 2002 WINTER OLYMPICS HELD?

A) SALT LAKE CITY
B) LOS ANGELES
C) CHICAGO
D) ATLANTA

3400. d, 3401. New England, 3402. Serena Williams, 3403. Brazil, 3404. true, 3405. false, 3406. a, 3407. Wendy's, 3408. b, 3409. Spider-man, 3410. c, 3411. a

..2003..

3412) What country joined the U.S. in launching a war against Iraq?

3413) In 2003, Palestine announced its first what?

a) Nuclear treaty
b) McDonald's
c) Prime minister
d) Symphony orchestra

3414) What space shuttle exploded as it reentered Earth's atmosphere?

3416) True or false: **Arnold Schwarzenegger was the first actor to become governor of California.**

3417) TRUE OR FALSE: BECAME THE FIRST MUSICAL EVER TO WIN AN ACADEMY AWARD FOR BEST PICTURE.

3418) Strom Thurmond died in 2003. He was a/an ___________.

a) Politician
b) Athlete
c) Wall Street trader
d) Restaurateur

3419) The supersonic jet the Concorde flew its last commercial flight in 2003. When was its first commercial flight?

a) 1964
b) 1969
c) 1976
d) 1982

3420) What angry-sounding disease effected cattle in Washington State?

3421) TRUE OR FALSE: AN EARTHQUAKE STRUCK THE IRANIAN CITY OF BAM.

3422) About 50 million Americans and Canadians lost power for two days because of power line failures in what state?

a) New York
b) Texas
c) California
d) Ohio

3423) Why did New York Times reporter Jason Blair resign?

a) Conflict of interest because of his website
b) He bought the paper
c) Plagiarism
d) None of the above

2004

3424) True or false: The United Nations declared 2004 the International Year of Rice.

3425) What country launched its first rocket into space?

a) Togo
b) Vatican City
c) Brazil
d) Peru

3426) WHO WON THE FORMULA ONE WORLD DRIVERS CHAMPIONSHIP FOR THE 17TH TIME?

A) MARIO ANDRETTI
B) MICHAEL SCHUMACHER
C) AL UNSER, JR.
D) TAKAI KATAI

3412. England, 3413. c, 3414. Columbia, 3415. Norah Jones, 3416. false—Ronald Reagan was also an actor, 3417. false, 3418. a, 3419. c, 3420. mad cow disease, 3421. true, 3422. d, 3423. c, 3424. true, 3425. c, 3426. b

3427) The largest cruise ship in the world at that time, the RMS *Queen Mary 2* ocean liner had its maiden voyage in 2004. How many decks did it have?

3428) The Boston Red Sox won the World Series in 2004. When was the last time they had won?

a) 1965 b) 1954
c) 1932 d) 1918

3429) The world's tallest bridge opens. Where is it located?
a) France
b) Italy
c) Spain
d) Germany

3430) Who resigned as U.S. Secretary of State in 2004?
a) Condoleezza Rice
b) Colin Powell
c) Hillary Clinton
d) Gus Giverson

3431) WHAT CONTROVERSIAL RELIGIOUS FILM WAS A BLOCKBUSTER HIT FOR DIRECTOR MEL GIBSON?

3432) What band had a 2004 hit with "Accidentally in Love"?

3433) Marlon Brando died in 2004. Which of the following was not one of his films.
a) *On the Waterfront*
b) *A Streetcar Named Desire*
c) *Viva Zapata!*
d) *Cat on a Hot Tin Roof*

3434) Because of the lockout, there was no Stanley Cup in hockey for the first time since what year?

a) 1919 b) 1925 c) 1945 d) 1950

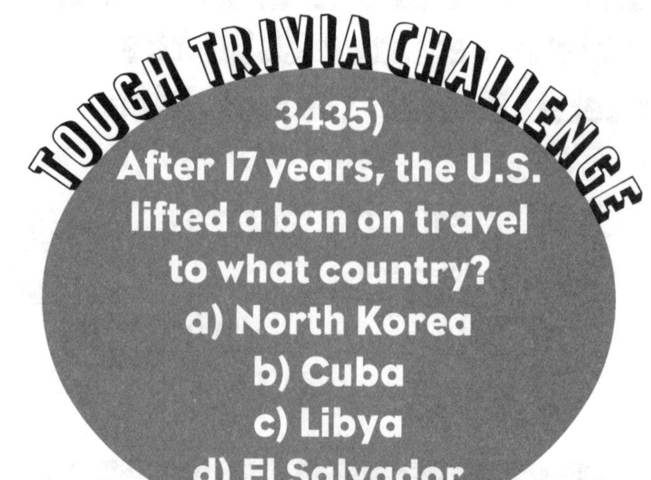

3435) After 17 years, the U.S. lifted a ban on travel to what country?
a) North Korea
b) Cuba
c) Libya
d) El Salvador

• • 2005 • •

3436) A 20-year civil war ended in what country?

a) Ethiopia
b) Sudan
c) Peru
d) Indonesia

3437) The international organization Group of Eight includes all the members of Group of Seven plus who?

a) Russia
b) China
c) Japan
d) The U.S.

3438) WHAT WAS THE NAME OF THE HURRICANE THAT CAUSED CONSIDERABLE DAMAGE TO THE GULF COAST?

3439) Who became the 17th Chief Justice of the Supreme Court?

a) John Jay
b) Robert James
c) John Roberts
d) Robert Johnson

TOUGH TRIVIA CHALLENGE

3440) After Pope John Paul died, Pope Benedict took over. What Roman number follows Benedict's name?

a) X
b) V
c) XV
d) XVI

3441) The 2005 Record of the Year "Here We Go Again" was a collaboration between Norah Jones and...

a) Tony Bennett
b) Ray Charles
c) Stevie Wonder
d) Steve Lawrence

3442) In 2005, which had a larger population, Europe or Africa?

3443) What replaced heart disease as the top cause of death for people under the age of 85?

3427. 17. 3428. d. 3429. a. 3430. b. 3431. *The Passion of the Christ*. 3432. Counting Crows. 3433. c. 3434. a. 3435. c. 3436. b. 3437. a. 3438. Katrina. 3439. c. 3440. d. 3441. b. 3442. Africa. 3443. cancer

3444) French surgeons performed the first human ______________ transplant.

a) Foot
b) Brain
c) Face
d) Double lung

3445) Who left his spot as anchor of the CBS Evening News in 2005?

a) Walter Cronkite
b) Dan Rather
c) Andy Rooney
d) Mort Crim

3446) TWO GREAT PLAYWRIGHTS DIED IN 2005, AUGUST WILSON AND ARTHUR MILLER. WHICH WAS OLDER?

3447) Women in what country were granted the right to vote?

a) Iraq
b) Iran
c) Kuwait
d) Sudan

..2006..

3448) Who declared that Pluto was not a planet?

a) The International Astronomical Society
b) The Committee for Astronomical Investigation
c) NASA
d) The International Planetary Society

3449) WHAT WAS THE FIRST NAME OF MARTIN LUTHER KING'S WIFE, WHO DIED IN 2006?

3450) What were the jobs of the main characters in the Christopher Nolan movie *The Prestige*, starring Hugh Jackman and Christian Bale?

3451) **Whose solo album *B'Day* went to number one on the Billboard charts?**

3452) WHO DID ST. LOUIS DEFEAT IN THE 2006 WORLD SERIES?

3453) How was Saddam Hussein executed in Iraq?

a) Firing squad
b) Electric chair
c) Hanging
d) Lethal injection

3454) Who did Pittsburgh defeat in Super Bowl XL?

3455) ***Who did Miami defeat in the 2006 NBA Finals?***

3456) What was the price of the record-setting sale of Jackson Pollock's *No. 5*, 1948?

a) $8 million
b) $18 million
c) $80 million
d) $140 million

3457) **Who did Italy defeat in the 2006 World Cup?**

3458) ***Jersey Boys*** **won the Tony Award for Best Musical. What singing group is the musical about?**

a) The Four Tops
b) The Four Freshmen
c) The Four Lads
d) The Four Seasons

3459) Where were the 2006 Winter Olympics held?

a) Austria
b) United States
c) Italy
d) Finland

3444. c, 3445. b, 3446. Arthur Miller, 3447. c, 3448. a, 3449. Coretta, 3450. magicians, 3451. Beyonce, 3452. Detroit, 3453. c, 3454. Seattle, 3455. Dallas, 3456. d, 3457. France, 3458. d, 3459. c

TOUGH TRIVIA CHALLENGE

3460) In 2007, archeologists in Japan found a 2,100-year-old what?

a) Apple
b) Melon
c) Orange
d) Banana

3461) WHAT BOOK, RELEASED IN 2007, BECAME THE FASTEST SELLING BOOK EVER?

3462) What group of Hollywood professionals went on strike in 2007?

a) Cinematographers
b) Actors
c) Writers
d) Editors

3463) Liz Claiborne died in 2007. What was her real first name?

a) Anne
b) Elizabeth
c) Liza
d) Elzebetha

3464) What former vice president of the United States won a Nobel Peace Prize in 2007?

a) Walter Mondale
b) Dan Quayle
c) Albert Gore Jr.
d) Spiro Agnew

3465) Nicolas Sarkozy beat Segolene Royal in what country's presidential elections?

3466) GORDON BROWN TOOK OVER FROM TONY BLAIR AS PRIME MINISTER OF WHAT COUNTRY?

TOUGH TRIVIA CHALLENGE

3467) Abdullah Gul became the president of what country?

a) Sudan
b) Turkey
c) East Timor
d) New Zealand

3468) Pervez Musharraf was reelected to a third term as president of what country?

a) Iraq
b) Afghanistan
c) Pakistan
d) Cambodia

3469) Who became the first woman speaker of the house in the U.S. in 2007?

3470) How much did the U.S. minimum wage go up to in 2007?

a) $4.45
b) $5.15
c) $5.85
d) $6.76

3471) Who did Indianapolis beat in Super Bowl XLI?

3472) True or false: It snowed in Buenos Aires in 2007.

3460. b, 3461. *Harry Potter and the Deathly Hallows*, 3462. c, 3463. a, 3464. c, 3465. France, 3466. Great Britain, 3467. b, 3468. c, 3469. Nancy Pelosi, 3470. c, 3471. Chicago, 3472. true

. . 2008 . .

3473) Who resigned as president of Cuba in 2008?

a) Raul Castro
b) Fidel Castro
c) Francis Castro
d) Charles Castro

3474) How many satellites did India send into orbit on one launch, setting a world record?

a) 5
b) 7
c) 10
d) 12

3475) How many gold medals did Michael Phelps win at the 2008 Summer Olympics?

3476) WHO WAS BARACK OBAMA'S VICE PRESIDENTIAL RUNNING MATE IN 2008?

3477) What state's senator was accused of trying to sell a U.S. Senate seat?

TOUGH TRIVIA CHALLENGE

3478) What country held its first general election in 2008?

a) Congo
b) Philippines
c) Mexico
d) Bhutan

3479) True or false: A leap second was added at the end of 2008.

3480) In 2008, proton beams were circulated for the first time around the main rings of the largest particle accelerator in the world, the Large Hadron Collider. What is the circumference of its main tunnel?

a) 2 miles
b) 5 miles
c) 11 miles
d) 17 miles

3481) In 2008, the ocean liner QE2 was retired. When did it launch?

a) 1965

b) 1969

c) 1976

d) 1981

3482) Arthur C. Clarke died in 2008. What kinds of books was he best known for?

a) Romance

b) Young adult fiction

c) Science fiction

d) Horror

3483) Charlton Heston died in 2008. Which of the following was not one of his movies:

a) *The Ten Commandments*

b) *Planet of the Apes*

c) *The Great Escape*

d) *The Omega Man*

3484) Which 2008 release grossed more at the box office, *Kung Fu Panda* or *Madagascar: Escape 2 Africa*?

3485) Who had a hit single in 2008 with "Bleeding Love"?

a) Link Larkin

b) Leona Lewis

c) Leslie Linkerson

d) Lewis Leonetti

3486) WHAT *SATURDAY NIGHT LIVE* CAST MEMBER FAMOUSLY IMPERSONATED VICE PRESIDENTIAL CANDIDATE SARAH PALIN?

3487) Whose boyfriend was arrested for stealing millions from investors?

a) Anne Hathaway

b) Shania Twain

c) Star Jones

d) Jennifer Aniston

3473. b, 3474. c, 3475. 8, 3476. Joe Biden, 3477. Illinois, 3478. d, 3479. true, 3480. d, 3481. b, 3482. c, 3483. c, 3484. *Kung Fu Panda*, 3485. b, 3486. Tina Fey, 3487. a

2009

3488) Who was reelected as president of Iran?

a) Ahmadda
b) Ahmadinejad
c) Achmallia
d) Aphaiadad

3489) What popular singer died on June 25, 2009?

3490) Thirty-two exoplanets were discovered in 2009. What is an exoplanet?

a) A plant with water
b) A planet outside of our solar system
c) A planet with an irregular orbit
d) A planet with no moons

3491) WHO WON THE NOBEL PEACE PRIZE IN 2009?

A) AL GORE
B) BARACK OBAMA
C) JAMES "THE REV" SULLIVAN
D) FRANCISCO AYALA

3492) Which grossed more at the box office in 2009: *Ice Age: Dawn of the Dinosaurs* or *Up*?

3493) A law was signed in 2009 banning federal employees from doing what?

a) Unionizing
b) Collecting overtime pay
c) Texting while driving
d) Smoking

3494) In 2009, Leon Panetta was named director of what?

a) Universal Studios
b) The CIA
c) The air traffic controller's union
d) The Cartoon Network

3495) OCTUPLETS WERE BORN IN 2009. HOW MANY BABIES IS THAT?

3496) *In 2009, all on board survived when a plane was forced to land in what river?*

a) Mississippi
b) Nile
c) Hudson
d) Ohio

3497) More than 450 people got sick in 2009 because of salmonella that was linked to what common product?

a) Milk
b) Peanut butter
c) Margarine
d) Soda

3488. b, 3489. Michael Jackson, 3490. b, 3491. b, 3492. *Ice Age: Dawn of the Dinosaurs*, 3493. c, 3494. b, 3495. 8, 3496. c, 3497. b

3498) Who was named Secretary of State in 2009?

a) Joe Biden
b) Madeleine Albright
c) James Baker
d) Hillary Rodham Clinton

3499) Which grossed more at the box office in 2009: *Sherlock Holmes* or *2012*?

3500) The last of the Kennedy brothers died. What was his name?

3501) What song did Susan Boyle sing on *Britain's Got Talent* that catapulted her to worldwide attention?

3502) What was the name of the sleeved blanket that became an "As Seen on TV" phenomenon?

TOUGH TRIVIA CHALLENGE

3503) What color was Michele Obama's coat at the swearing in of Barack Obama?

• • 2010 • •

3504) The tallest man-made structure in the world opened in 2010. Where is it?

a) Tokyo
b) Dubai
c) Paris
d) New York

3505) What country hosted the 2010 Winter Olympics?

3506) HOW DID THE PRESIDENT OF POLAND, LECH KACZYNSKI, DIE IN 2010?

A) PLANE CRASH
B) ASSASSINATION
C) CAR ACCIDENT
D) HEART ATTACK

3507) What was the name of the oil platform that exploded in the Gulf of Mexico?

a) Gulf Horizon
b) Deep Gulf
c) Deepwater Horizon
d) Deepwater Discoverer

3498. d, 3499. 2012, 3500. Ted, 3501. "I Dreamed a Dream", 3502. Snuggies, 3503. light green, 3504. b, 3505. Canada, 3506. a, 3507. c

3508) Who won the 2010 FIFA World Cup?

a) Brazil
b) Mexico
c) France
d) Spain

3509) Who leaked over 90,000 internal U.S. reports?

a) The FBI
b) The CIA
c) The website Wikileaks
d) The Kremlin

TOUGH TRIVIA CHALLENGE

3510) What flu epidemic was declared over in 2010?

a) H2N1
b) H1N2
c) H1N1
d) H2N2

3511) How many miners survived the accident in Copiapo, Chili?

a) 11
b) 22
c) 33
d) 44

3512) J.D. Salinger died in 2010. What was his most famous book?

a) *Animal Farm*
b) *Catcher in the Rye*
c) *Brave New World*
d) *East of Eden*

3513) For the 2010 presentation, the Academy Awards were changed to return to how many nominees for Best Picture?

3514) WHICH WON BEST PICTURE AT THE OSCARS, THE *HURT LOCKER* OR *AVATAR*?

3515) Which of the following did not perform in a tribute to Michael Jackson at the 2010 Grammy Awards?

a) Carrie Underwood
b) Janet Jackson
c) Usher
d) Jennifer Hudson

••2011••

3516) Terrorist leader Osama Bin Laden was killed in what country?

3517) WHAT TV STAR WAS FIRED FROM THE HIT SHOW TWO AND A HALF MEN?

3518) What was the last name of England's Princess Kate before she married Prince William?

3519) In 2011, an attempt was made to assassinate Congresswoman Gabrielle Giffords. What state does she represent?

3520) Big problems occurred in 2011 at the Fukushaima Dalichi ___________.

a) Movie studio
b) Nuclear facility
c) Japanese restaurant chain
d) Munitions plant

3521) What was the name of the New York-originated movement that had protesters living in tent cities around the country.

3508. d, 3509. c, 3510. c, 3511. c, 3512. b, 3513. Ten, 3514. *The Hurt Locker*, 3515. b, 3516. Pakistan, 3517. Charlie Sheen, 3518. Middleton, 3519. Arizona, 3520. b, 3521. Occupy Wall Street

3522) The space shuttle program ended in 2011. Which space shuttle flew the final mission?

3523) Steve Jobs died in 2011. What company did he lead?

3524) TRUE OR FALSE: THE UNITED NATIONS DECLARED 2011 THE INTERNATIONAL YEAR OF DENTISTRY.

3525) Who resigned in Egypt in February?

3526) Juno, a solar-powered spacecraft, took off for what planet?

3527) In December, the U.S. declared an end to what war?

3522. Atlantis, 3523. Apple, 3524. false, 3525. President Hosni Mubarak, 3526. Jupiter, 3527. the Iraq War

CHAPTER 7

Music

..POP & ROCK..

3528) True or false: The man credited with naming rock 'n' roll was a deejay in Chicago named Harvey Freed.

3529) True or false: Paul McCartney's actual first name is James.

3530) True or false: ABBA, representing Sweden, won the Eurovision song contest in 1974.

3531) True or false: One of the members of the band Fleetwood Mac is named Fleetwood.

3532) True or false: The first album released on CD was by Beethoven.

3533) TRUE OR FALSE: ONE OF THE MEMBERS OF THE BAND FLEETWOOD MAC IS NAMED MAC.

3534) True or false: The Beatles were once called the Quarrymen.

3535) True or false: Led Zeppelin was once called the Mugwumps.

3536) Which Beatles song came first, "Yellow Submarine" or "I Wanna Hold Your Hand"?

Match the one-named performer to his or her original name:

3537) Babyface
3538) Coolio
3539) Cher
3540) Hammer
3541) Ice-T
3542) Jay-Z
3543) Eminem
3544) Moby
3545) Sting

a) Gordon Sumner
b) Shawn Carter
c) Kenneth Edmonds
d) Tracy Morrow
e) Artis Leon Ivey Jr.
f) Cherilyn Sarskisian
g) Richard Melville Hall
h) Marshall Mathers
i) Stanley Kirk Burrell

3546) Which of the following is not a Beach Boys song?

a) "Goin' Surfin'"
b) "Surfin' USA"
c) "Surfer Girl"
d) "Surfin' Safari"

3547) True or false: In April of 1964, the Beatles had songs in all the top eight spots on the Billboard Hot 100 chart.

3548) Which of the Monkees resisted any reunion tours?

a) Micky
b) Michael
c) Davy
d) Peter

MATCH THE SONG TO THE BAND OR SINGER.

3549) "Yellow Submarine"
3550) "Do You Believe in Magic?"
3551) "Don't Worry Be Happy"
3552) "Feeling Groovy"
3553) "Daydream Believer"

a) The Lovin' Spoonful
b) The Beatles
c) Bobby McFerrin
d) The Monkees
e) Simon and Garfunkel

3528. false—it was a Cleveland deejay named Alan Freed, 3529. true, 3530. true, 3531. true—Mick Fleetwood, 3532. false—It was Billy Joel's *52nd Street*, 3533. false, 3534. true, 3535. false3536. "I Wanna Hold Your Hand", 3537. c, 3538. e, 3539. f, 3540. i, 3541. d, 3542. b, 3543. h, 3544. g, 3545. a, 3546. a, 3547. false—"only" the top five, 3548. b, 3549. b, 3550. a, 3551. c, 3552. e, 3553. d

Fill in the numeric blank in these song titles.

3554) "Tea for ______"
3555) "___ Tears"
3556) "____ Luftballoons"
3557) "______ Spanish Angels"
3558) "Pennsylvania 6-______"

a) Two
b) 96
c) 99
d) Seven
e) 5000

3559) Which of the following was not a song on Kelly Clarkson's *Thankful* album?

a) "Miss Independent"
b) "Low"
c) "A Moment Like This"
d) "Never Before"

TOUGH TRIVIA CHALLENGE

3560) *Which of the following is not a song on Regina Spektor's Songs album:*

a) "Samson"
b) "Delilah"
c) "Oedipus"
d) "Reading Time with Pickle."

3561) True or false: **"Dog Days Are Over" is on Florence and the Machine's "Ceremonials" album?**

3562) Which Eminem album came first, *Relapse* or *Recovery*?

3563) What is the name of Eminem's alter ego?

a) Slappy Sandy
b) Slim Shady
c) Slime Sally
d) Slum Sammy

3564) What legendary band was Robert Plant a part of?

3565) How many members are there in the Black Keys?

What are the first names of...

3566) Crosby
3567) Stills
3568) Nash
3569) Young

3570) HOW MANY MAMAS AND HOW MANY PAPAS WERE THERE IN THE MAMAS AND THE PAPAS?

3571) True or false: Singer Drake played one of the two leads in the TV series *Drake and Josh.*

3572) True or false: Big Boi was a member of OutKast.

3573) Vampire Weekend is originally from...

a) Scotland
b) United States
c) Australia
d) England

3574) True or false: Wilco grew out of a band called Uncle Tupelo.

3575) True or false: Arcade Fire got its name because its members worked in a Coney Island amusement arcade that burned down.

3576) Which of the following was not a song on the Train album *Train*?

a) "Meet Virginia"
b) "I Am"
c) "Iowa"
d) "Free"

3577) Which of the following artists did Kanye West not produce for?

a) Alicia Keys
b) Ray Charles
c) Ludacris
d) Janet Jackson

3578) True or false: Gnarls Barkley consists of Cee Lo Green and Mighty Mouse.

3554. a, 3555. b, 3556. c, 3557. d, 3558. e, 3559. d, 3560. b, 3561. false, 3562. *Relapse*, 3563. b, 3564. Led Zeppelin, 3565. two, 3566. David, 3567. Stephen, 3568. Graham, 3569. Neil, 3570. two each, 3571. false, 3572. true, 3573. b, 3574. true, 3575. false, 3576. c, 3577. b, 3578. false—Cee Lo Green and Danger Mouse

MATCH THE SONG TO THE ARTIST.

3579) "All My Ex's Live in Texas"
3580) "All My Rowdy Friends Are Coming Over Tonight"
3581) "Coal Miner's Daughter"
3582) "Crazy"
3583) "Deeper Than the Holler"
3584) "Elvira"
3585) "Flowers on the Wall"
3586) "Friends in Low Places"
3587) "The Gambler"
3588) "Gentle on My Mind"
3589) "Girls With Guitars"
3590) "He Stopped Loving Her Today"
3591) "I'm So Lonesome I Could Cry"
3592) "Independence Day"
3593) "Is There Life Out There?"
3594) "It's Only Make Believe"
3595) "Jolene"
3596) "Mountain Music"
3597) "Okie From Muskogee"
3598) "Only in America"
3599) "She's in Love With the Boy"
3600) "Sixteen Tons"
3601) "Stand by Your Man"
3602) "Ticks"
3603) "T-R-O-U-B-L-E"
3604) "Whiskey River"

a) Alabama
b) Brooks and Dunn
c) Garth Brooks
d) Glen Campbell
e) Patsy Cline
f) Tennessee Ernie Ford
g) Merle Haggard
h) George Jones
i) Loretta Lynn
j) Martina McBride
k) Reba McEntire
l) Willie Nelson
m) Oak Ridge Boys
n) Brad Paisley
o) Dolly Parton
p) Kenny Rogers
q) Statler Brothers
r) George Strait
s) Randy Travis
t) Travis Tritt
u) Conway Twitty
v) Hank Williams Sr.
w) Hank Williams Jr.
x) Tammy Wynette
y) Wynonna
z) Trisha Yearwood

3605) True or false: The band called Breaks is known in the U.S. as Brakesbrakesbrakes.

3606) Are the Avett Brothers (Scott, Seth, and Bob) actually all brothers?

3607) Which U2 album came first, *War* or *Achtung Baby*?

3608) HOW MANY BAND MEMBERS IN U2?

3609) Where does the band the Flaming Lips hail from?

a) Oklahoma
b) Florida
c) Texas
d) California

3610) True or false: Tegan and Sara, of the band of the same name, are identical twins.

3611) True or false: Mos Def is actually deaf.

3612) When was the first *Now That's What I Call Music!* CD released?

a) 1978
b) 1988
c) 1998
d) 2008

3613) Which of the following did not have a song on the first *Now That's What I Call Music* disc?

a) Hanson
b) Lenny Kravitz
c) Madonna
d) Imajin

3579. r, 3580. w, 3581. i, 3582. e, 3583. s, 3584. m, 3585. q, 3586. c, 3587. p, 3588. d, 3589. y, 3590. h, 3591. v, 3592. j, 3593. k, 3594. u, 3595. o, 3596. a, 3597. g, 3598. b, 3599. z, 3600. f, 3601. x, 3602. n, 3603. t, 3604. l, 3605. true, 3606. no—but Scott and Seth are, 3607. *War*, 3608. 4, 3609. a, 3610. true, 3611. false, 3612. c, 3613. c, 3614. false—1985

Match the member of Kiss to his facial make-up.

3615) Gene Simmons
3616) Paul Stanley
3617) Ace Frehley
3618) Peter Cris

a) Cat face
b) Stars around both eyes
c) Star around one eye
d) Wing-ish shapes around both eyes

3619) True or false: Katy Perry's real name is Katheryn Elizabeth Hudson.

3620) Who does not have a track on *That's What I Call Music 39* (released in 2011)?

a) Katy Perry
b) The Black Eyed Peas
c) Bruno Mars
d) Justin Bieber

3621) True or false: Katy Perry appeared in the movie *The Sisterhood of the Travelling Pants.*

3622) How old was Avril Lavigne when her album *Let Go* released?

3623) True or false: Avril Lavigne wrote theme songs for Tim Burton's *Alice in Wonderland, Charlie and the Chocolate Factory,* and *Planet of the Apes.*

3624) True or false: Lil Wayne and Busta Rhymes are both featured on Chris Brown's "Look at Me Now."

3625) TRUE OR FALSE: BRUNO MARS WAS RAISED IN HAWAII.

3626) True or false: In 1992, Bruno Mars appeared as a character named Little Elvis in the movie *Honeymoon in Vegas.*

3627) What country singer's name was the title of Taylor Swift's first hit single?

3628) True or false: Taylor Swift is the youngest person to be named Entertainer of the Year at the Country Music Association Awards.

3629) Who sang "Respect" (1967)?

3630) WHO SANG "WITH OR WITHOUT YOU" (1987)?

3631) Who sang "Hotel California" (1976)?

3632) Who sang "I Want It That Way" (1999)?

3633) Who sang "Where Did Our Love Go" (1964)?

3634) Who sang "Brown Sugar" (1968)?

3635) Who sang "Imagine" (1971)?

3636) Who sang "Superstition" (1972)?

3637) Who sang "Losing My Religion" (1991)?

3638) WHO SANG "BROWN EYED GIRL" (1967)?

3639) Who is featured with Katy Perry on the song "ET"?

3615. d, 3616. c, 3617. b, 3618. a, 3619. true, 3620. d, 3621. false, 3622. 17, 3623. false—just Alice in Wonderland, 3624. true, 3625. true, 3626. true3627. Tim McGraw, 3628. true, 3629. Aretha Franklin, 3630. U2, 3631. The Eagles, 3632. The Backstreet Boys, 3633. The Supremes, 3634. Rolling Stones, 3635. John Lennon, 3636. Stevie Wonder, 3637. R.E.M., 3638. Van Morrison, 3639. Kanye West

What musician is the subject of each of these biographical films.

3640) *Coal Miner's Daughter*
3641) *La Bamba*
3642) *Walk the Line*
3643) *Great Balls of Fire*
3644) *What's Love Got to Do With It*
3645) *Ray*
3646) *Sid and Nancy*
3647) *Why Do Fools Fall in Love*
3648) *Sweet Dreams*
3649) *Nowhere Boy*

a) Jerry Lee Lewis
b) Sid Vicious
c) Frankie Lymon
d) Richie Valens
e) John Lennon
f) Loretta Lynn
g) Ray Charles
h) Tina Turner
i) Johnny Cash
j) Patsy Cline

3650) Who sang "Oh, Pretty Woman" (1964)?
a) The Rolling Stones
b) The Who
c) Roy Orbison
d) Roy Acuff

3651) Who sang "What's Goin' On" (1971)?
a) Marvin Gaye
b) Michael Bolton
c) Mahalia Jackson
d) Michael Jackson

3652) Who sang "Go Your Own Way" (1976)?

3653) Who sang "When Doves Cry" (1984)?

3654) WHO SANG "BOHEMIAN RHAPSODY" (1975)?

3655) Who sang "(Sittin' On) The Dock of the Bay" (1968)?
a) Otis Day and the Knights
b) An Elevator Called Otis
c) Otis Redding
d) Helen Reddy

3656) Who sang "Born to Run" (1975)?

3657) Who sang "Waterfalls" (1995)?

3658) Who sang "Every Breath You Take" (1983)?

3659) Who sang "Dancing Queen" (1976)?

3660) Who sang "Jump" (1984)?

3661) WHO SANG "BYE BYE BYE" (2000)?

3662) Who sang "I Will Survive" (1978)?

a) Gloria Estefan
b) Gloria Gaynor
c) Laura Branigan
d) Gloria Stivik

3663) Who sang "Our Lips are Sealed" (1981)?

3664) Who sang "Just the Way You Are (1978)?

3665) Who sang "Papa Don't Preach" (1986)?

3666) WHO SANG "BENNY AND THE JETS" (1973)?

3667) Who sang "Time After Time" (1984)?

3668) Who sang "My Name Is" (1999)?

3669) Who sang "I Want to be Sedated" (1978)?

3670) Who sang "Let's Stay Together" (1971)?

3671) Who sang "Drops of Jupiter" (2001)?

3640. f, 3641. d, 3642. i, 3643. a, 3644. h, 3645. g, 3646. b, 3647. c, 3648. j, 3649. e3650. c, 3651. a, 3652. Fleetwood Mac, 3653. Prince, 3654. Queen, 3655. c, 3656. Bruce Springsteen, 3657. T.L.C, 3658. The Police, 3659. ABBA, 3660. Van Halen, 3661. 'N Sync, 3662. b, 3663. The Go-Go's, 3664. Billy Joel, 3665. Madonna, 3666. Elton John, 3667. Cyndi Lauper, 3668. Eminem, 3669. The Ramones, 3670. Al Green, 3671. Train

3673) Who sang "Breathe" (2000)?

3674) The Rolling Stones, the Beatles, the Doors, or the Who: "Hello, I Love You."

3675) THE ROLLING STONES. THE BEATLES. THE DOORS OR THE WHO: "SHE LOVES YOU."

3676) The Rolling Stones, the Beatles, the Doors or the Who: "Start Me Up."

3677) The president of Czechoslovakia named what American singer a special ambassador to the West?
a) Alice Cooper
b) Marilyn Manson
c) Bobby Vinton
d) Frank Zappa

3678) The Rolling Stones, the Beatles, the Doors or the Who: "Substitute."

3679) What folk singer wrote "This Land Is Your Land"?

3680) What band parodied the Beatles in two full-length mockumentaries, *All You Need Is Cash* and *Can't Buy Me Lunch*?

3681) Was *Cry of Love* released before or after Jimi Hendrix' death?

3682) Fake folk-music groups The Folksmen, Mitch and Mickey, and the New Main Street Singers are the subject of what mockumentary?

3683) David St. Hubbins, Derek Smalls, and Nigel Tufnel comprise what band?

3684) Who died first, James Brown or Johnny Cash?

3685) How many solo Top 40 singles did John Lennon have after his death?

a) 1 b) 2 c) 3 d) 4

3686) True or false: Buddy Holly was 22 when he died in a plane crash.

3687) True or false: More than 2 million Michael Jackson albums have sold since his death.

Match the bands to the rock documentaries.

3688) *Bring on the Night*
3689) *Don't Look Back*
3690) *The Kids Are Alright*
3691) *The Last Waltz*
3692) *Let It Be*
3693) *Rattle and Hum*
3694) *Shine a Light*
3695) *Shut up and Sing*
3696) *The Song Remains the Same*
3697) *Stop Making Sense*
3698) *Truth or Dare*
3699) *Year of the Horse*

a) The Band
b) The Beatles
c) The Dixie Chicks
d) Bob Dylan
e) Led Zeppelin
f) Madonna
g) The Rolling Stones
h) Sting
i) Talking Heads
j) U2
k) The Who
l) Neil Young

3672. Goo Goo Dolls, 3673. Faith Hill, 3674. The Doors, 3675. The Beatles, 3676. Rolling Stones, 3677. d, 3678. The Who, 3679. Woody Guthrie, 3680. The Rutles, 3681. after, 3682. A Mighty Wind, 3683. Spinal Tap, 3684. Johnny Cash, 3685. c, 3686. true, 3687. true, 3688. h, 3689. d, 3690. k, 3691. a, 3692. b, 3693. j, 3694. g, 3695. c, 3696. e, 3697. i, 3698. f, 3699. l

MATCH THE ALBUM WITH THE ARTIST.

3700) *5150*
3701) *Appetite for Destruction*
3702) *At Folsom Prison*
3703) *Back in Black*
3704) *Beauty and the Beat*
3705) *Dark Side of the Moon*
3706) *Electric Ladyland*
3707) *Graceland*
3708) *Highway 61 Revisited*
3709) *Hotel California*
3710) *Innervisions*
3711) *It Takes a Nation of Millions to Hold Us Back*
3712) *The Joshua Tree*
3713) *Let It Bleed*
3714) *Like a Prayer*
3715) *A Love Supreme*
3716) *Moondance*
3717) *Off the Wall*
3718) *Physical Graffiti*
3719) *Purple Rain*
3720) *Revolver*
3721) *The River*
3722) *The Stranger*
3723) *Superfly*
3724) *What's Going On*
3725) *Who's Next*

a) AC/DC
b) The Beatles
c) Johnny Cash
d) John Coltrane
e) Bob Dylan
f) The Eagles
g) Marvin Gaye
h) The Go-Go's
i) Guns 'n' Roses
j) The Jimi Hendrix Experience
k) Michael Jackson
l) Billy Joel
m) Led Zeppelin
n) Madonna
o) Curtis Mayfield
p) Van Morrison
q) Pink Floyd
r) Prince and the Revolution
s) Public Enemy
t) The Rolling Stones
u) Paul Simon
v) Bruce Springsteen
w) U2
x) Van Halen
y) The Who
z) Stevie Wonder

TOUGH TRIVIA CHALLENGE

3726)
How many Top 40 singles did the Beatles have after John Lennon's death?
a) 1
b) 2
c) 3
d) 4

SONG TITLES

3727) Are the words "Bohemian" or "Rhapsody" in Queen's song "Bohemian Rhapsody?

3728) Is the phrase "Sympathy for the Devil" in the Rolling Stones song "Sympathy for the Devil"?

3729) Is the word "Australia" in the Shins' song "Australia"?

3730) What is the parenthetical addition to the title for the Green Day song "Good Riddance"?

3731) What is the parenthetical addition to the title for the Bryan Adams song "I Do It For You"?

3732) What is the parenthetical addition to the title for the Simple Minds song "Don't You"?

3733) WHAT IS THE PARENTHETICAL ADDITION TO THE TITLE FOR THE JAMES TAYLOR SONG "HOW SWEET IT IS"?

3734) What is the parenthetical addition to the title for the Doors' song "Break on Through"?

3735) What is the parenthetical addition to the title for the Billy Joel song "Movin' Out"?

3736) What is the parenthetical addition to the title for the Offspring song "Pretty Fly"?

3700. x, 3701. i, 3702. c, 3703. a, 3704. h, 3705. q, 3706. j, 3707. u, 3708. e, 3709. f, 3710. z, 3711. s, 3712. w, 3713. t, 3714. n, 3715. d, 3716. p, 3717. k, 3718. m, 3719. r, 3720. b, 3721. v, 3722. l, 3723. o, 3724. g, 3725. y, 3726. d, 3727. no, 3728. no, 3729. no, 3730. (Time of Your Life), 3731. (Everything I Do), 3732. (Forget About Me), 3733. (To be Loved by You), 3734. (To the Other Side), 3735. (Anthony's Song), 3736. (For a White Guy)

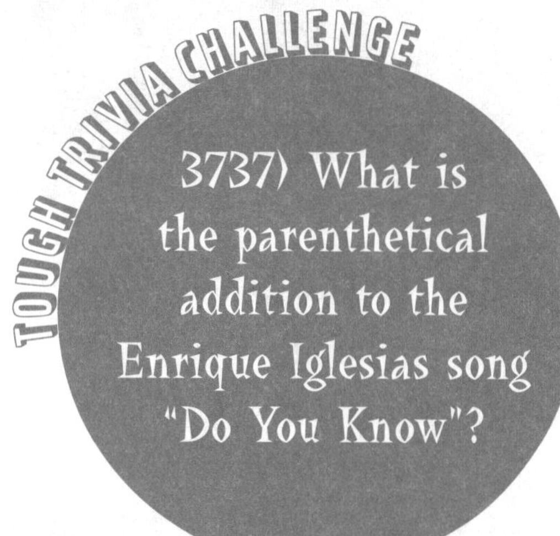

3738) What is the parenthetical addition to the title for Rolling Stones song "Satisfaction"?

3739) What is the parenthetical addition to the title for the R.E.M. song "It's the End of the World As We Know It "?

3740) WHAT IS THE PARENTHETICAL ADDITION TO THE TITLE FOR THE MICHAEL JACKSON SONG "P.Y.T."?

3741) What are the two parenthetical additions to the title for the Beastie Boys' song "Fight for Your Right"?

3742) What is the parenthetical addition to the title for Simon and Garfunkel's "The 59th Street Bridge Song"?

3743) What is the parenthetical addition to the title for the Whitney Houston song "Exhale"?

3744) What is the parenthetical addition to the title for Rupert Holmes song "Escape"?

3745) What is the parenthetical addition to the K.C. & the Sunshine Band song "Shake Your Booty"?

3746) DO THE WORDS "PIECE OF PIE" APPEAR IN THE STONE TEMPLE PILOTS SONG "PIECE OF PIE"?

3747) Are the Goonies mentioned in the Cyndi Lauper song "The Goonies R Good Enough"?

MATCH THE ARTIST TO THE SONG.

3748) "Be With You"
3749) "Boom Boom Pow"
3750) "Firework"
3751) "For Your Love"
3752) "Forget You"
3753) "Gold Digger"
3754) "Hey Soul Sister"
3755) "Hips Don't Lie"
3756) "Hot in Here"
3757) "Just Dance"
3758) "Just Kickin' It"
3759) "Legs"
3760) "Lose Yourself"
3761) "My Heart Will Go On"
3762) "New York State of Mind"
3763) "No Sleep"
3764) "Pretty Woman"
3765) "Pumped Up Kicks"
3766) "Rude Boy"
3767) "Saving All My Love for You"
3768) "Semi-Charmed Life"
3769) "Someone Like You"
3770) "Speed of Sound"
3771) "Superbass"
3772) "Vertigo"
3773) "Another One Bites the Dust"

a) Adele
b) Black Eyed Peas
c) Coldplay
d) Celine Dion
e) Eminem
f) Foster the People
g) Cee Lo Green
h) Whitney Houston
i) Enrique Iglesias
j) Jay-Z
k) Wiz Khalifa
l) Lady Gaga
m) Nicki Minaj
n) Nelly
o) Roy Orbison
p) Katy Perry
q) Queen
r) Rihanna
s) Shakira
t) Train
u) U2
v) Third Eye Blind
w) Kanye West
x) Xscape
y) The Yardbirds
z) ZZ Top

3737. (Ping Pong Song), 3738. (I Can't Get No), 3739. (And I Feel Fine), 3740. (Pretty Young Thing), 3741. (You Gotta), (to Party!), 3742. (Feelin' Groovy), 3743. (Shoop Shoop), 3744. (The Pina Colada Song), 3745. (Shake, Shake, Shake), 3746. no, 3747. no, 3748. i, 3749. b, 3750. p, 3751. y, 3752. g, 3753. w, 3754. t, 3755. s, 3756. n, 3757. l, 3758. x, 3759. z, 3760. e, 3761. d, 3762. j, 3763. k, 3764. o, 3765. f, 3766. r, 3767. h, 3768. v, 3769. a, 3770. c, 3771. m, 3772. u, 3773. q

WHOSE ALBUM?

3774) Bob Dylan or the Beatles: *Blonde on Blonde?*

3775) The Clash or Marvin Gaye: *London Calling?*

3776) The Rolling Stones or the Who: *Exile on Main Street?*

3777) The Monkees or the Beach Boys: *Pet Sounds?*

3778) Miles Davis or Elvis Presley: *Kind of Blue?*

3779) Jimi Hendrix or Janis Joplin: *Are You Experienced?*

3780) Bruce Hornsby or Bruce Springsteen: *Greetings from Asbury Park?*

3781) Nirvana or Coldplay: *Nevermind?*

3782) Morrissey or Van Morrison: *Astral Weeks?*

3783) CHUCK BERRY OR BARRY WHITE: *THE GREAT TWENTY-EIGHT?*

3784) Mac Davis or Fleetwood Mac: *Rumors?*

3785) David Bowie or Billy Joel: *The Rise and Fall of Ziggy Starudst and the Spiders from Mars?*

3786) B.B. King or Carole King: *Tapestry?*

3787) Loretta Lynn or Bjork: *Vespertine?*

3788) LED ZEPPELIN OR PINK FLOYD: *THE WALL?*

3789) Bob Marley or Little Richard: *Legend?*

3790) Simon and Garfunkel or Stevie Wonder: *Songs in the Key of Life?*

3791) Radiohead or the Jayhawks: *In Rainbows?*

3792) Jay-Z or Arcade Fire: *The Blueprint?*

3793) Iron & Wine or Coldplay: *A Rush of Blood to the Head?*

3794) Death Cab for Cutie or the Flaming Lips: *Transatlanticism?*

3795) THE SHINS OR THE DECEMBERISTS: *THE CRANE WIFE?*

3796) Vampire Weekend or Beck: *Sea Change*

3797) Rufus Wainwright or Amy Winehouse: *Back to Black?*

3798) Kanye West or Patty Griffin: *1000 Kisses?*

3799) The Avett Brothers or OutKast: *I and Love and You?*

3800) THE WHITE STRIPES OR RADIOHEAD: *ELEPHANT?*

3801) Sufjan Stevens or Wilco: *Yankee Hotel Foxtrot?*

3802) Which of the following is not a Beatles album?

a) *Revolver*
b) *Beatles for Sale*
c) *The Beatles '63*
d) *Rubber Soul*

3803) Which of the following is not an album by Sheryl Crow?

a) *C'mon C'mon*
b) *100 Miles from Memphis*
c) *Detours*
d) *All This and More*

3774. Bob Dylan, 3775. The Clash, 3776. The Rolling Stones, 3777. The Beach Boys, 3778. Miles Davis, 3779. Jimi Hendrix, 3780. Bruce Springsteen, 3781. Nirvana, 3782. Van Morrison, 3783. Chuck Berry, 3784. Fleetwood Mac, 3785. David Bowie, 3786. Carole King, 3787. Bjork, 3788. Pink Floyd, 3789. Bob Marley, 3790. Stevie Wonder, 3791. Radiohead, 3792. Jay-Z, 3793. Coldplay, 3794. Death Cab for Cutie, 3795. The Decemberists, 3796. Beck, 3797. Amy Winehouse, 3798. Patty Griffin, 3799. The Avett Brothers, 3800. The White Stripes, 3801. Wilco, 3802. c, 3803. d

3804) Which of the following is not an album by Beyonce Knowles:

a) *B'Day*
b) *I Am...Sasha Fierce*
c) *I Am... Yours*
d) *I Am...Tired*

3805) Which of the following is not an album by Jason Mraz?

a) *Mr. A-Z*
b) *Topics Unlimited*
c) *We Sing. We Dance. We Steal Things.*
d) *Waiting for My Rocket to Come*

3806) Which of the following is not an album by Christina Aguilera?

a) *My Kind of Christmas*
b) *Mi Reflejo*
c) *Back to Basics*
d) *Running Away*

3807) Which of the following is not an album by Ben Folds?

a) *You Don't Know Me*
b) *Rockin' the Suburbs*
c) *Songs for Silverman*
d) *Way to Normal*

3808) Which of the following is not an album by Cee Lo Green:

a) *Cee-Lo Green and His Perfect Imperfections*
b) *Cee-Lo Green Has It Down*
c) *Cee-Lo Green...Is the Soul Machine*
d) *The Lady Killer*

3809) WHICH OF THE FOLLOWING IS NOT AN ALBUM BY NELLY FURTADO:

A) *FOLKLORE*
B) *WHOA, NELLY!*
C) *LOOSE*
D) *NELLY'S DREAM*

3810) Which of the following is not an album by Kylie Minogue:

a) *Intimate and Live*
b) *Pop It*
c) *Aphrodite*
d) *Body Language*

RAP

3811) On what record label did Kanye West originally produce music for Jay-Z and Alicia Keys?

a) Roc-A-Billy Records
b) Roc-A-Fella Records
c) Roc-Da-House Records
d) Roc-N-Out Records

3812) When was Kanye West's first album released?

a) 1996
b) 2000
c) 2004
d) 2006

3813) Which Kanye West album came first, Graduation or The College Dropout?

3814) What record label, run by Kanye West, also recorded John Legend?

a) GREAT Music
b) GOOD Music
c) OKAY Music
d) COOL Music

3815) Where was Kanye West born?

a) Atlanta
b) Philadelphia
c) Washington, D.C.
d) Boston

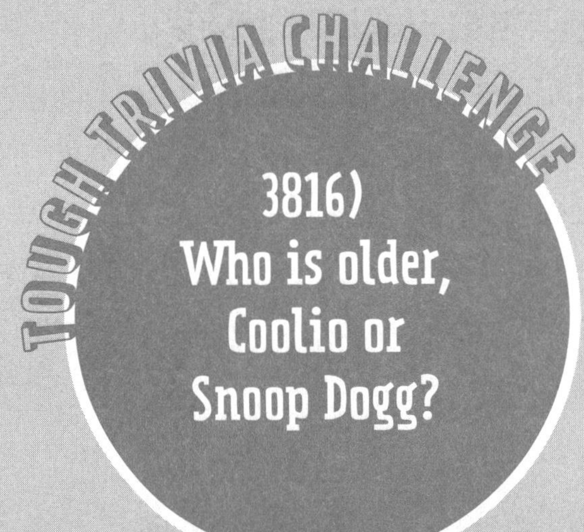

3804. d, 3805. b, 3806. d, 3807. a, 3808. b, 3809. d, 3810. b, 3811. b, 3812. c, 3813. *The College Dropout*, 3814. b, 3815. a, 3816. Coolio

3817) True or false: Coolio's "C U When U Get There" samples Pachelbel's "Canon in D."

3818) TRUE OR FALSE: KANYE WEST WAS FEATURED ON THE "GLOW IN THE DARK" TOUR.

3819) True or false: "Gangsta's Paradise" was written for the movie "Dangerous Minds."

3820) "Gangsta's Paradise" samples the song "Pasttime Paradise" by what artist?

a) Michael Jackson
b) Stevie Wonder
c) Ike Turner
d) Marvin Gaye

3821) True or false: MC Hammer's "U Can't Touch This" samples Rick James' "Super Freak."

3822) True or false: Ke$ha's "Right Round" samples Dead or Alive's "You Spin Me Round (Like a Record)."

3823) True or false: Kid Rock's "All Summer Long" samples "Warren Zevon's "An American Werewolf in London."

3824) True or false: Kid Rock's "All Summer Long" samples Lynyrd Skynyrd's "Sweet Home Alabama."

3825) True or false: Ludacris's "Coming 2 America" samples Mozart's "Requiem."

3826) True or false: Wycliff Jean attempted to become president of Haiti.

3827) What rapper created The Slim Shady LP?

3828) IN WHAT YEAR DID PUFF DADDY DECIDE TO BE RENAMED P. DIDDY?

A) 1995
B) 2001
C) 2003
D) 2005

3829) Who did Jay-Z face off with in a 2001 notorious rapping battle?

a) Nas
b) Nose
c) Nus
d) Nise

3830) What group was Lisa "Left-Eye" Lopes a part of?

a) TLC
b) Run-DMC
c) KRS-One
d) G-Unit

3831) True or false: Dr. Dre was punched in the face as he was about to receive a Vibe Lifetime Achievement Award.

3832) In 1990, a Florida record store owner was arrested over what 2 Live Crew album?

a) Move Somethin'
b) As Nasty As They Wanna Be
c) Banned in the U.S.A.
d) The Real One

3833) WHEN DID TUPAC SHAKUR DIE?

A) 1990
B) 1996
C) 1998
D) 2000

3834) Was *2pacalypse Now* released before or after Tupac Shakur's death?

3835) Was *Still I Rise* released before or after Tupac Shakur's death?

3817. true, 3818. true, 3819. false—but it was used in the film, 3820. b, 3821. true, 3822. true, 3823. false—the title of Zevon's song was "Werewolves of London", 3824. true, 3825. true, 3826. true, 3827. Eminem, 3828. b, 3829. a, 3830. a, 3831. true, 3832. b, 3833. b, 3834. before 3835. after

3836) Was *Me Against the World* released before or after Tupac Shakur's death?

3837) Was *All Eyez on Me* released before or after Tupac Shakur's death?

3838) Was *Loyal to the Game* released before or after Tupac Shakur's death?

3839) TRUE OR FALSE: THERE WAS A RAPPER NAMED MARZ BAR.

3840) True or false: There was a rapper named Lil' Scrappy.

3841) True or false: There was a rapper named Dreddy Kruger.

3842) True or false: There was a rapper named Messy Marv.

3843) True or false: Both Ludacris and Snoop Dogg are featured on Chingy's song "Holidae In."

3844) Who is not featured on Drake's song "Forever"?

a) Kanye West
b) Lil Wayne
c) Eminem
d) Snoop Dogg

3845) Who was featured on the Eminem hit "Love the Way You Lie"?

a) Rihanna
b) Dr. Dre
c) Missy Elliott
d) Mary J. Blige

3846) WHAT NUMERAL IS FEATURED TWICE IN THE TITLE OF AN MC HAMMER HIT?

Match the Ludacris-featured songs with their primary artist.

3847) "Break Your Heart"
3848) "Tonight (I'm Lovin' You)"
3849) "Unpredictable"
3850) "Oh"
3851) "Yeah!"
3852) "Gossip Folks"
3853) "Baby"
3854) "Glamorous"

a) Missy Elliott
b) Jamie Foxx
c) Taio Cruz
d) Fergie
e) Ciara
f) Enrique Iglesias
g) Justin Bieber
h) Usher

3855) Lil Wayne, Lil' Kim, or Lil Jon & The East Side Boyz: Who recorded "Yeah!"?

3856) Lil Wayne, Lil' Kim, or Lil Jon & The East Side Boyz: Who recorded "It's All About the Banjamins"?

3857) Lil Wayne, Lil' Kim, or Lil Jon & The East Side Boyz: Who recorded "Magic Stick"?

3858) Lil Wayne, Lil' Kim, or Lil Jon & The East Side Boyz: Who recorded "Down"?

3859) Lil Wayne, Lil' Kim, or Lil Jon & The East Side Boyz: Who recorded "Lillipop"?

3860) Lil Wayne, Lil' Kim, or Lil Jon & The East Side Boyz: Who recorded "Lovers & Friends"?

3861) Lil Wayne, Lil' Kim, or Lil Jon & The East Side Boyz: Who recorded "6 Foot 7 Foot"?

3862) WHO DID BUSTA RHYMES TEAM UP WITH ON "I KNOW WHAT YOU WANT"?

3836. before, 3837. before, 3838. after, 3839. false, 3840. true, 3841. true, 3842. true, 3843. true, 3844. d, 3845. a, 3846. 2—in the song "2 Legit 2 Quit", 3847. d, 3848. c, 3849. f, 3850. b, 3851. e, 3852. h, 3853. a, 3854. g, 3855. Lil Jon & The East Side Boyz, 3856. Lil' Kim, 3857. Lil' Kim, 3858. Lil Wayne, 3859. Lil Wayne, 3860. Lil Jon & The East Side Boyz, 3861. Lil Wayne, 3862. Mariah Carey

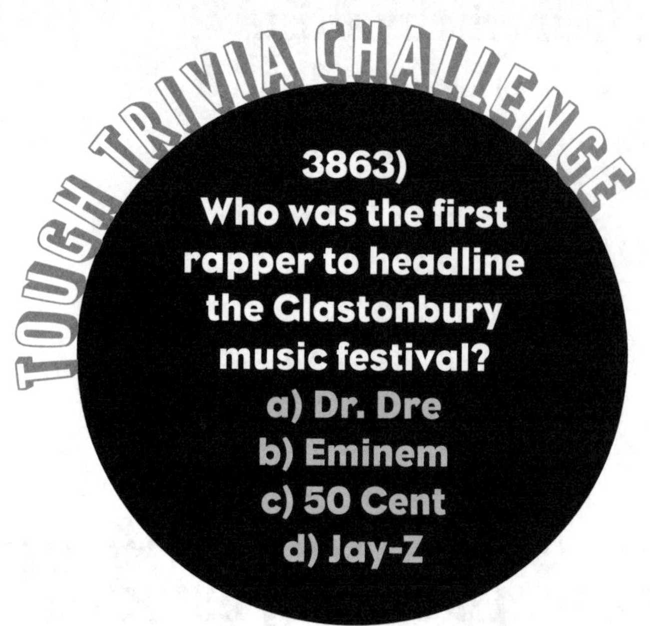

3864) Who gets "featuring" credit on Ludacris' "Runaway Love" and Method Man's "I'll Be There for You/You're All I Need to Get By"?

3865) Was "I'll Be Missing You" a Puff Daddy, P. Diddy, or Diddy song?

3866) Was "Come to Me" a Puff Daddy, P. Diddy, or Diddy song?

3867) WAS "I NEED A GIRL (PART ONE)" A PUFF DADDY, P. DIDDY, OR DIDDY SONG?

3868) Was "Bump, Bump, Bump" a Puff Daddy, P. Diddy, or Diddy song?

3869) Was "Last Night" a Puff Daddy, P. Diddy, or Diddy song?

3870) Was "Can't Nobody Hold Me Down" a Puff Daddy, P. Diddy, or Diddy song?

PATRIOTIC SONGS

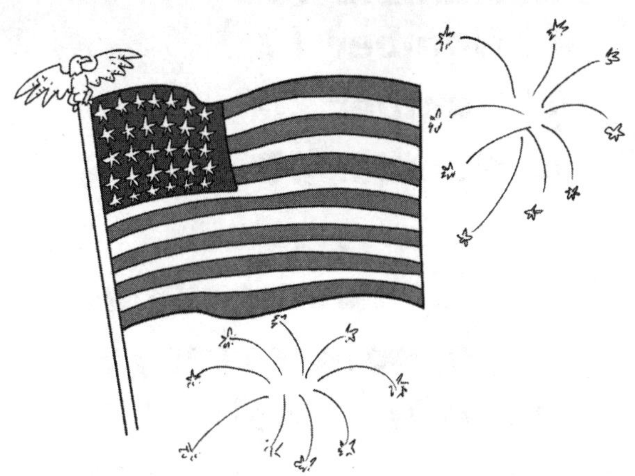

3871) True or false: **"God Bless America" was originally written to be part of a musical comedy revue.**

3872) **True or false:** "This Land in Your Land" was originally called "God Blessed America for Me."

3873) TRUE OR FALSE: **BRUCE SPRINGSTEEN RECORDED A VERSION OF "THIS LAND IS YOUR LAND."**

3874) **True or false:** The lyrics for "The Star Spangled Banner" were written by an 18-year old.

3875) True of false: **The lyrics for "The Star Spangled Banner" come from a poem called "Defense of Fort McHenry."**

3876) **True or false:** Francis Scott Key was a prisoner of war when he wrote "The Star Spangled Banner."

3877) What body of water does Fort McHenry overlook?

a) Delaware River
b) Chesapeake Bay
c) Atlantic Ocean
d) Gulf of Mexico

3878) TRUE OR FALSE: "MY COUNTRY, 'TIS OF THEE" HAS THE SAME MELODY AS THE BRITISH NATIONAL ANTHEM "GOD SAVE THE QUEEN."

3863. d, 3864. Mary J. Blige, 3865. Puff Daddy, 3866. Diddy, 3867. P. Diddy, 3868. P. Diddy, 3869. Diddy, 3870. Puff Daddy, 3871. true, 3872. true, 3873. true, 3874. false, 3875. true, 3876. false, 3877. b, 3878. true

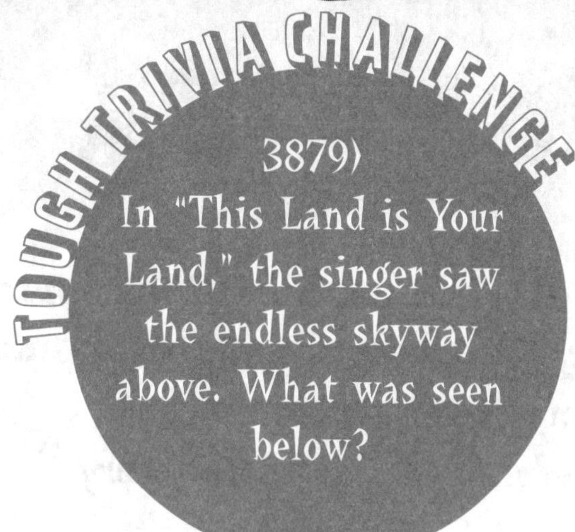

3880) True or false: **As a lawyer, Francis Scott Key successfully prosecuted Richard Lawrence, the first man to ever try to assassinate a U.S. president.**

3881) True or false: Francis Scott Key and author F. Scott Fitzgerald were distant cousins.

3882) True or false: **Francis Scott Key is not in the Songwriters Hall of Fame.**

3883) TRUE OR FALSE: **THERE IS ONLY ONE VERSE TO "THE STAR SPANGLED BANNER."**

3884) How high up the Billboard Hot 100 chart did Whitney Houston's 1983 version of "The Star Spangled Banner" climb?

a) **Number 6**
b) **Number 12**
c) **Number 20**
d) **Number 40**

3885) Which comedienne stirred up controversy when she spit after singing "The Star Spangled Banner" at a Padres baseball game?

a) **Lucille Ball**
b) **Roseanne Barr**
c) **Phyllis Diller**
d) **Sarah Silverman**

3886) Who messed up the lyrics to "The Star Spangled Banner" before Super Bowl XLV?

a) Christina Aguilera
b) Britney Spears
c) Fergie
d) Mama Cass

3887) True or false: "God Bless America" originally included the lyric "...to the right with a light from above."

3888) When did Jimi Hendrix begin performing his electric guitar version of "The Star Spangled Banner"?

a) 1964 b) 1966 c) 1968 d) 1970

3889) Which of the following parts of "The Star Spangled Banner" lyrics were used as the name of a movie:

a) *Twilight's Last Gleaming*
b) *Home of the Brave*
c) *So Proudly We Hail*
d) *Stripes and Bright Stars*

3890) TRUE OR FALSE: THE FIRST LINES OF "GOD BLESS AMERICA" ARE "GOD BLESS AMERICA/LAND THAT I LOVE."

3891) What hockey team, throughout the 1970s, played Kate Smith's version of "God Bless America" for the Broad Street Bullies and their fans?

3892) Who benefits from royalties for the song "God Bless America"?

a) Girl Scouts and Boy Scouts
b) Keep America Beautiful
c) The American Red Cross
d) The estate of Irving Berlin

3893) True or false: The same person who wrote "You're a Grand Old Flag" wrote "Yankee Doodle Dandy."

3894) True or false: Sales of "You're a Grand Old Flag" sheet music topped one million copies.

3879. "that golden valley", 3880. true, 3881. true, 3882. false—He was inducted in 1970, 3883. false, 3884. c, 3885. b, 3886. a, 3887. true, 3888. c, 3889. d, 3890. false—there's an intro section that begins "While the storm clouds gather far across the sea…", 3891. Philadelphia Flyers, 3892. a, 3893. true—George M. Cohan, 3894. true

3896) Who usually sings "God Bless America" at the beginning of the Indianapolis 500?
a) Florence Henderson (the *Brady Bunch* mom)
b) Shirley Jones (the *Partridge Family* mom)
c) Marion Ross (the *Happy Days* mom)
d) Esther Rolle (the *Good Times* mom)

3897) TRUE OR FALSE: "YOU'RE A GRAND OLD FLAG" WAS ORIGINALLY CALLED "YOU'RE A GRAND OLD RAG."

3898) True or false: "You're a Grand Old Flag" has the first reference ever to Uncle Sam.

3899) Daniel Rodriguez' post-9/11 version of "God Bless America" made it onto the Billboard Hot 100. What was Rodriguez's regular job?
a) Firefighter
b) Police officer
c) Ambulance driver
d) Construction worker

3900) True or false: The lyrics to "America the Beautiful" were originally written as a poem called "Pikes Peak."

3901) True or false: Katharine Lee Bates wrote the music and lyrics for "America the Beautiful."

3902) Where was Katharine Lee Bates a professor when she wrote the lyrics for "America the Beautiful"?
a) Princeton
b) Harvard
c) Wellesley
d) University of Delaware

Match the song to the artist.

3903) "American Pie"
3904) "Back in the USA"
3905) "Born in the USA"
3906) "God Bless the USA"

a) Chuck Berry
b) Lee Greenwood
c) Don McLean
d) Bruce Springsteen

3907) TRUE OR FALSE: "AMERICA THE BEAUTIFUL" DID NOT BECOME POPULAR UNTIL AFTER KATHARINE LEE BATES HAD DIED.

3908) Which of the following did not appear on the all-star country version of "America the Beautiful" that was recorded in 2001.

a) Toby Keith
b) Keith Urban
c) Billy Ray Cyrus
d) Trace Adkins

3909) Was the country-star version of "America the Beautiful" from the above question recorded before or after the 9/11 attacks?

3910) Who performed a duet with Ray Charles on "America the Beautiful" on his *Genius & Friends* album?

a) Martina McBride
b) Alicia Keys
c) Amy Winehouse
d) Cobie Caillat

3911) Where are people supposed to face if "The Star Spangled Banner" is playing and there is no flag visible?

3895. b, 3896. a, 3897. true, 3898. false, 3899. b, 3900. true, 3901. false—but she did write the lyrics, 3902. c—although she was teaching summer classes at Colorado College, 3903. c, 3904. a, 3905. d, 3906. b, 3907. true, 3908. c, 3909. before, 3910. b, 3911. toward the source of the music

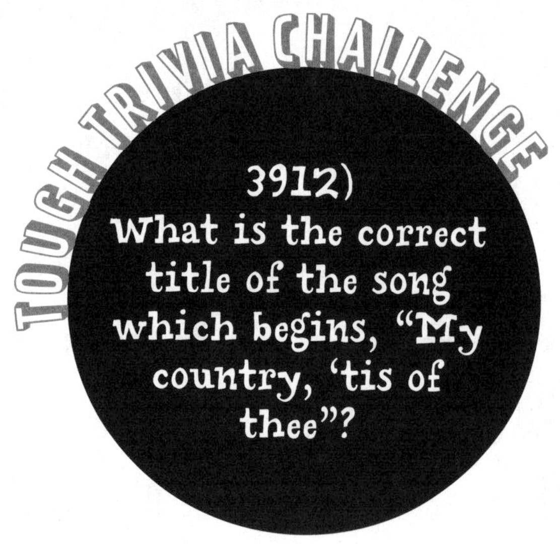

3913) What Broadway show featured the song "Yankee Doodle Dandy"?

a) *Show Boat*
b) *Oklahoma!*
c) *1776*
d) *Little Johnny Jones*

3914) **True or false:** The name of a Tom Cruise movie comes from the song "Yankee Doodle Dandy."

3915) In its original Broadway musical plot context, what is "Yankee Doodle"?

a) A solider
b) A horse
c) A statue
d A sports team

3916) TRUE OR FALSE: **PAUL JABARA RECORDED A DISCO VERSION OF "YANKEE DOODLE DANDY."**

3917) Who starred in the movie "Yankee Doodle Dandy"?

a) Humphrey Bogart
b) James Cagney
c) Edward G. Robinson
d) James Stewart

3918) Who wrote "Stars and Stripes Forever"?

MATCH THE POST-9/11 COUNTRY SONG TO THE ARTIST.

3919) "Courtesy of the Red, White and Blue"
3920) "Have You Forgotten?"
3921) "This Ain't No Rag, It's a Flag"
3922) "Where Were You When the World Stopped Turning?"

a) Charlie Daniels
b) Alan Jackson
c) Toby Keith
d) Darryl Worley

OPERA & CLASSICAL

3923) Which of the following opera titles are named for a character in it?

a) *Aida*
b) *La Boheme*
c) *Falstaff*
d) *La Traviata*
e) *Turendot*

3924) What was legendary soprano Beverly Sills' nickname?

a) Bongles
b) Bubbles
c) Baubles
d) Babbles

MATCH THE COMPOSER TO A FAMOUS WORK.

3925) Handel	a) "Rhapsody in Blue"
3926) Beethoven	b) "Brandenburg Concertos"
3927) Chopin	c) "The Minute Waltz"
3928) Tchaikovsky	d) "Appalachian Spring"
3929) Dvorak	e) "Bolero"
3930) Holst	f) "From the New World"
3931) Ravel	g) "The Planets"
3932) Stravinsky	h) "Messiah"
3933) Prokofiev	I) "The Firebird"
3934) Gershwin	j) "The Nutcracker"
3935) Copland	k) "Pastoral Symphony"
3936) Bach	l) "Peter and the Wolf"

3937) What composer is the subject of the play and movie *Amadeus*?

3912. "America", 3913. d, 3914. true—*Born on the Fourth of July,* 3915. b, 3916. true, 3917. b, 3918. John Philip Sousa, 3919. c, 3920. d, 3921. a, 3922. b, 3923. a, c, and e, 3924. b, 3925. h, 3926. k, 3927. c, 3928. j, 3929. f, 3930. g, 3931. e, 3932. i, 3933. l, 3934. a, 3935. d, 3936. b, 3937. Wolfgang Amadeus Mozart—and, actually, Antonio Salieri

In an orchestra, are each of the following to the conductor's left or right?

3938) First violins

3939) Cellos

3940) Violas

3941) Second violins

3942) True or false: In an orchestra, the tuba is positioned behind the violins.

3943) True or false: In an orchestra, the harp is positioned behind the bass clarinet and in front of the percussion.

3944) True or false: The first million-selling record was of an opera aria.

3945) HOW MANY PARTS MAKE UP WAGNER'S RING CYCLE?

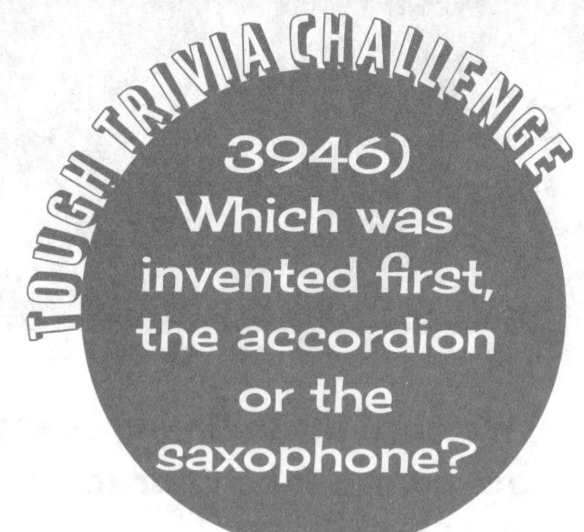

3946) Which was invented first, the accordion or the saxophone?

3947) "FIDELIO" IS THE ONLY OPERA BY BACH, BEETHOVEN, OR BRAHMS?

3948) Who wrote the opera *Carmen*?

a) Bizet

b) Beethoven

c) Brahms

d) Bach

3949) What Disney movie featured Moussorgsky's "Night on Bald Mountain"?

3950) Camille Saint-Saens wrote "Carnival of the ________"?

3951) A requiem is a piece of music written for what?

3952) Who wrote the music for "Peer Gynt"?

a) Grieg
b) Gregg
c) Grogg
d) Grugg

3953) A lot of orchestras play this Tchaikovsky work on the 4th of July, but it's not inspired by the American Revolution but by a different war. What's the work called?

3954) Which of the following was not one of opera's famed "Three Tenors"?

a) Jose Carreras
b) Luciano Pavarotti
c) Placido Domingo
d) Enrico Caruso

3955) True or false: "Angels We Have Heard on High" is based on a French carol.

3956) Rossini's "William Tell Overture" is well known as the theme song for what cowboy hero?

3957) What conductor of the New York Philharmonic also wrote the music for the Broadway musical *West Side Story*?

a) Leonard Bernstein
b) Richard Rodgers
c) Stephen Sondheim
d) Riccardo Muti

3958) What legendary Philadelphia symphony conductor led the orchestra in Disney's *Fantasia*?

a) Leopold Stokowski
b) Leonard Bernstein
c) Larry David
d) Lenny Bruce

3938. Left, 3939. Right, 3940. Right, 3941. Left, 3942. false, 3943. true, 3944. true—Enrico Caruso singing "Vesti la Giubba", 3945. 4, 3946. accordion, 3947. Ludwig van Beethoven, 3948. a, 3949. *Fantasia*, 3950. Animals, 3951. A funeral mass, 3952. a, 3953. *1812 Overture*, 3954. d, 3955. true, 3956. the Lone Ranger, 3957. a, 3958. a

HOLIDAY MUSIC

3959) IN "ANGELS WE HAVE HEARD ON HIGH," WHAT ARE THE ANGELS SINGING O'ER?

3960) "Away in a Manger" was first published in 1885 in...

a) Philadelphia
b) London
c) Paris
d) Rome

3961) True or false: "Decks the Halls" was originally called "Deck the Hall."

3962) According to "Deck the Halls," what should you join after striking the harp?

3963) True or false: As recorded by SHeDAISY, "Deck the Halls" made it to number 10 on the Billboard Hot 100.

3964) TRUE OR FALSE: "THE FIRST NOEL" WAS WRITTEN BY IRVING BERLIN.

3965) What Christmas carol is mentioned in Charles Dickens's *A Christmas Carol?*

a) "God Rest Ye Merry, Gentlemen"
b) "Jingle Bells"
c) "Frosty the Snowman"
d) "The Christmas Song"

3966) In "Good King Wenceslas," reference is made to the feast of Stephen. What day is that?

a) The day after Christmas
b) The day before Christmas
c) The twelfth day of Christmas
d) December 1st

3967) True or false: Wenceslas was never actually a king during his lifetime.

◆ ◆ ◆ ◆ ◆ ◆ ◆ ◆ ◆ ◆ ◆ ◆ ◆ ◆ ◆ ◆ ◆ ◆ ◆ ◆

3968) True or false: **The first line of "Hark! The Herald Angels Sing" was originally "Hark! How all the Welkin rings."**

3969) *IN* "HERE WE COME A-WASSAILING," WHAT COLOR ARE THE *LEAVES*?

3970) In "Here We Come A-wassailing," what is the first holiday mentioned?

◆ ◆ ◆ ◆ ◆ ◆ ◆ ◆ ◆ ◆ ◆ ◆ ◆ ◆ ◆ ◆ ◆ ◆ ◆ ◆

3971) The familiar tune of "Hark! The Herald Angels Sing" comes from what composer?

a) Beethoven
b) Brahms
c) Mendelssohn
d) Tchaikovsky

◆ ◆ ◆ ◆ ◆ ◆ ◆ ◆ ◆ ◆ ◆ ◆ ◆ ◆ ◆ ◆ ◆ ◆ ◆ ◆

3972) Was "It Came Upon the Midnight Clear" written in America or Europe?

3973) In "It Came Upon the Midnight Clear," what are the harps made of?

◆ ◆ ◆ ◆ ◆ ◆ ◆ ◆ ◆ ◆ ◆ ◆ ◆ ◆ ◆ ◆ ◆ ◆ ◆ ◆

3974) True or false: **Mariah Carey recorded a version of "Joy to the World" that combined the traditional carol with the pop song of the same name written by Hoyt Axton.**

◆ ◆ ◆ ◆ ◆ ◆ ◆ ◆ ◆ ◆ ◆ ◆ ◆ ◆ ◆ ◆ ◆ ◆ ◆ ◆

3975) True or false: "I Wonder as I Wander" comes from the opera *The Gifts of the Magi.*

◆ ◆ ◆ ◆ ◆ ◆ ◆ ◆ ◆ ◆ ◆ ◆ ◆ ◆ ◆ ◆ ◆ ◆ ◆ ◆

3976) "O Come All Ye Faithful" comes from the tune…

a) "Adeste Fideles"
b) "Odante Fieltes"
c) "Edente Edente"
d) "Adoni Eckles"

◆ ◆ ◆ ◆ ◆ ◆ ◆ ◆ ◆ ◆ ◆ ◆ ◆ ◆ ◆ ◆ ◆ ◆ ◆ ◆

3977) The lyrics to "O Little Town of Bethlehem" were written by a…

a) Catholic priest
b) Episcopal priest
c) Baptist minister
d) Lutheran minister

3959. the plains, 3960. a, 3961. true, 3962. the chorus, 3963. false—it only made it to 61, 3964. false—it's a traditional English carol, 3965. a, 3966. a, 3967. true—the title was given to him posthumously, 3968. true, 3969. green, 3970. New Year's, 3971. c, 3972. America, 3973. gold, 3974. true, 3975. false, 3976. a, 3977. b

TOUGH TRIVIA CHALLENGE

3978) Which of the following has not recorded "Go Tell It on the Mountain"?

a) Simon & Garfunkel
b) Toby Keith
c) The Blind Boys of Alabama
d) Bob Dylan

3979) The lyrics to "Joy to the World" are taken from...

a) Psalm 92
b) Psalm 98
c) Psalm 114
d) Psalm 122

3980) "Silent Night" was originally written in...

a) French
b) Italian
c) German
d) Spanish

3981) Which of the following has recorded "Silent Night"?

a) Elvis Presley
b) Christina Aguilera
c) Mariah Carey
d) All of the above

3982) In "The 12 Days of Christmas," what is the new item given on the sixth day?

3983) In "The 12 Days of Christmas," what are the people given on the eighth day doing?

3984) IN "THE 12 DAYS OF CHRISTMAS," WHAT ARE THE PEOPLE GIVEN ON THE ELEVENTH DAY DOING?

3985) True or false: According to the 2010 Christmas Price Index, the cumulative cost of all of the goods and services in "The 12 Days of Christmas" was over $23,000.

3986) True or false: "Up on the House Top" is considered the first holiday song to focus on Santa.

3987) Where does the comma belong in the song title "God Rest Ye Merry Gentlemen"—before or after "merry"?

3988) How high on the U.S. Adult Contemporary Chart did Kimberley Locke's 2005 version of "Up On the House Top" reach?

a) Number 1
b) Number 5
c) Number 10
d) Number 20

3989) Which was written first, "We Three Kings" or "We Wish You a Merry Christmas"?

3990) WHAT FAMILIAR TUNE IS "WHAT CHILD IS THIS" SUNG TO?

3991) What name was given to the all-star ensemble of British pop stars who recorded "Do They Know It's Christmas?"

TOUGH TRIVIA CHALLENGE

3992) In "Good King Wenceslas," what fountain does the peasant live near?

a) St. Andrews's fountain
b) St. Agnes' fountain
c) St. Stephen's fountain
d) St. Andrew's fountain

3993) Who plays drums on "Do They Know It's Christmas?"

a) Pete Best
b) Phil Collins
c) Mick Fleetwood
d) Ringo Starr

3994) True or false: Lionel Richie and Michael Jackson co-wrote "Do They Know It's Christmas?"

Match the Christmas song to the movie in which it was introduced.

3995) "Have Yourself a Merry Little Christmas"
3996) "Silver Bells"
3997) "Where Are You, Christmas?"
3998) "White Christmas"

a) *The Grinch*
b) *Holiday Inn*
c) *The Lemon Drop Kid*
d) *Meet Me in St. Louis*

3978. d, 3979. b, 3980. c, 3981. d, 3982. geese-a-laying, 3983. milking, 3984. piping, 3985. true, 3986. true, 3987. after, 3988. a, 3989. "We Wish You a Merry Christmas", 3990. "Greensleeves", 3991. Band Aid, 3992. b, 3993. b, 3994. false—Bob Geldof, 3995. d, 3996. c, 3997. a, 3998. b

3999) Eartha Kitt, Madonna, and Taylor Swift have all recorded what materialistic Christmas song?

4000) "Do They Know It's Christmas?" was released to raise money for famine relief in what African nation?

a) Ethiopia
b) Rwanda
c) Somalia
d) Sudan

4001) True or false: "Rudolph the Red-Nosed Reindeer" was first recorded by singing cowboy Roy Rogers.

4002) TRUE OR FALSE: THE FIRST MENTION OF RUDOLPH AS ONE OF SANTA'S REINDEER IS IN THE SONG "RUDOLPH THE RED-NOSED REINDEER."

4003) What is the most-played Christmas song?

a) "The Christmas Song"
b) "Do They Know It's Christmas?"
c) "Jingle Bells"
d) "Santa Claus Is Comin' to Town"

4004) What Christmas song is the best-selling single (Christmas or otherwise) in history?

a) "All I Want for Christmas Is You"
b) "Do They Know It's Christmas?"
c) "Do You Hear What I Hear?"
d) "White Christmas"

4005) TRUE OR FALSE: THE SONG "BLUE CHRISTMAS" ORIGINATED IN THE CHRISTMAS SPECIAL RUDOLPH THE RED-NOSED REINDEER.

4006) What is the proper title of the song that begins, "Chestnuts roasting on an open fire"?

4007) What satirist recorded the song "Green Christmas"?

a) Stan Freberg

b) Tom Lehrer

c) Bill Maher

d) Mort Sahl

4008) Leroy Anderson wrote the instrumental "Typewriter," which sounds like a typewriter. What Christmas-themed Anderson instrumental also seeks to replicate the sound of the activity described in its title?

4009) What singer wrote "The Christmas Song"?

a) Tony Bennett
b) Nat King Cole
c) Dean Martin
d) Mel Torme

TOUGH TRIVIA CHALLENGE

4010)
Who first recorded the gloomy Christmas song "Pretty Paper"?

a) The Beatles
b) Bob Dylan
c) Roy Orbison
d) Elvis Presley

4011) Who first recorded "Jingle Bell Rock"?

4012) What is the only lyric from "Jingle Bells" to be duplicated in "Jingle Bell Rock"?

a) Dashing through the snow
b) One-horse sleigh
c) Laughing all the way
d) What fun it is to ride

4013) How many separate times has "Jingle Bell Rock" hit the Top 40?

a) 2 b) 3 c) 4 d) 5

4014) WHAT IS THE SUBTITLE OF JOHN LENNON'S "HAPPY XMAS"?

3999. "Santa Baby." 4000. a. 4001. false—Gene Autry. 4002. true. 4003. a. 4004. d. 4005. false. 4006. "The Christmas Song." 4007. a.
4008. "Sleigh Ride." 4009. d. 4010. c. 4011. Bobby Helms. 4012. b. 4013. c. 4014. War Is Over

4015) What Broadway composer, best known for The Music Man, wrote "It's Beginning to Look a Lot Like Christmas"?

a) Alan Jay Lerner
b) Richard Rodgers
c) Stephen Sondheim
d) Meredith Willson

4016) WHAT ROCK AND ROLL HALL OF FAMER HIT THE TOP 20 WITH "ROCKIN' AROUND THE CHRISTMAS TREE" AT AGE 16?

A) CHRISTINA AGUILERA
B) LESLEY GORE
C) BRENDA LEE
D) BRITNEY SPEARS

4017) True or false: The same composer wrote "Rudolph the Red-Nosed Reindeer" and "Rockin' Around the Christmas Tree."

4018) What Broadway composer wrote "White Christmas"?

a) Harold Arlen
b) Irving Berlin
c) Jerry Herman
d) Richard Rodgers

4019) Every year at Christmas, David Letterman has Darlene Love as a guest on his show to sing what song?

4020) Who wrote the Spanish-English Christmas hit "Feliz Navidad"?

a) Vikki Carr
b) Jose Feliciano
c) Jose Greco
d) Carlos Santana

4021) What are you supposed to go tell on the mountain?

4022) What does "Gloria in Excelsis Deo" mean in English?

4023) True or false: The song "Santa Claus is Coming to Town" was originally written for the TV special of the same name.

4024) TRUE OR FALSE: RAY CHARLES, STEVEN TYLER, AND THE CHEETAH GIRLS HAVE ALL COVERED "SANTA CLAUS IS COMING TO TOWN."

4025) True or false: All recordings of "Santa Claus Is Coming to Town" by Bruce Springsteen are bootlegs.

4026) Besides "The Chipmunk Song," what Christmas song by Alvin and the Chipmunks hit the Top 40?

a) Let It Snow! Let It Snow! Let It Snow!
b) Rudolph the Red-Nosed Reindeer
c) Santa Claus is Comin' to Town
d) Winter Wonderland

4027) In "The Chipmunk Song," what present does Alvin really, really want?

4028) What movie star narrated the 1970 animated holiday special "Santa Claus is Comin' to Town"?

a) Gene Kelly
b) Donald O'Connor
c) Fred Astaire
d) Ginger Rogers

4015. d, 4016. c, 4017. true, 4018. b, 4019. "Christmas (Baby Please Come Home)", 4020. b, 4021. that Jesus Christ is born, 4022. Glory to God in the highest, 4023. False, 4024. true, 4025. true, 4026. b, 4027. a hula hoop, 4028. c

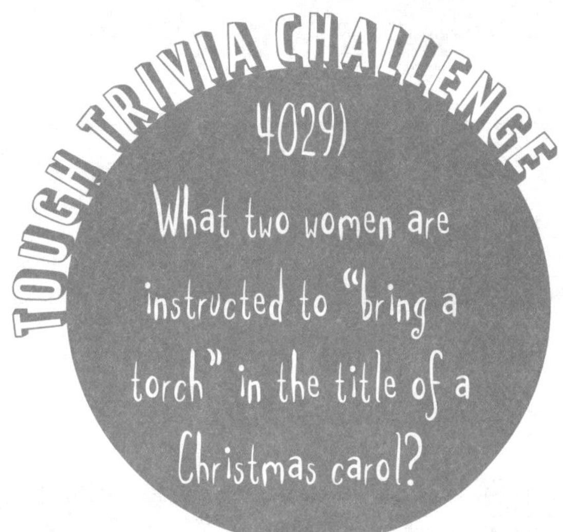

4030) How many times is Santa checking his list in the song "Santa Claus Is Comin' to Town"?

4031) Who played Kris Kringle in the animated "Santa Claus is Comin' to Town"?

a) Mickey Mantle
b) Mickey Rooney
c) Michael Murphy
d) Mitch Miller

4032) WHAT NUMBER REINDEER IS RUDOLPH?

4033) True or false: The character of Rudolph the Red-nosed Reindeer was created in the popular song of the same name.

4034) True or false: Gene Autry was the first to record "Rudolph the Red-nosed Reindeer."

4035) True or false: Lynyrd Skynyrd, Barry Manilow, and Dolly Parton all recorded versions of "Rudolph the Red-nosed Reindeer"

4036) True or false: In the original poem "A Visit from St. Nicholas," Donner was called Donder.

4037) WHAT CHRISTMAS SONG TITLE IS THE ENGLISH FOR THE LATIN "ADESTE FIDELES"?

4038) In what year did the TV special *Rudolph the Red-nosed Reindeer* premier on NBC?

a) 1964
b) 1968
c) 1971
d) 1975

4039) What misheard "Rudolph the Red-nosed Reindeer" lyric led to another best-selling children's holiday book?

4040) In the song "We Wish You a Merry Christmas," what treat do the singers demand?

a) Candy canes
b) Cookies
c) Figgy pudding
d) Wassail

Match the Christmas special to the narrator.

4041) Fred Astaire
4042) Jimmy Durante
4043) Burl Ives
4044) Boris Karloff

a) *Frosty the Snowman*
b) *How the Grinch Stole Christmas*
c) *Rudolph the Red-Nosed Reindeer*
d) *Santa Claus Is Comin' to Town*

4029. Jeanette, Isabella, 4030. twice, 4031. b, 4032. Nine, 4033. false, 4034. false, 4035. true, 4036. true, 4037. "O Come All Ye Faithful", 4038. a, 4039. "All of the other reindeer" misheard as "Olive, the Other Reindeer", 4040. c, 4041. d, 4042. a, 4043. c, 4044. b

CHAPTER 8

Big Screen/Little Screen

..MOVIES..

Match the movie comedy team to their film.

4045) The Marx Brothers
4046) Laurel and Hardy
4047) Abbott and Costello
4048) Hope and Crosby

a) *Sons of the Desert*
b) *Duck Soup*
c) *Buck Privates*
d) *The Road to Singapore*

Match the '80s movie teenager to his movie girlfriend.

4049) Ferris in *Ferris Bueller's Day Off*
4050) Daniel in *The Karate Kid*
4051) Ren in *Footloose*
4052) Blane in *Pretty in Pink*

a. Ariel
b. Ali
c. Sloan
d. Andie

Three films are tied for the records for most Academy Awards, with 11. Name the film that...

4053) Had a big scene involving a chariot race.
4054) Climaxed with the sinking of an ocean liner.
4055) Was the third film in a series.

4056) JULIE ANDREWS WON A BEST ACTRESS OSCAR FOR THE FIRST MOVIE SHE WAS IN. WHAT WAS THE MOVIE?

4057) Edith Head has won eight Oscars. What was her job in movies?

a) Costume designer
b) Cinematographer
c) Director
d) Screenwriter

4058) What is the name of the famous singer who made her movie debut in Funny Girl?

4045. b, 4046. a, 4047. c, 4048. d, 4049. c, 4050. b, 4051. a, 4052. d, 4053. Ben-Hur, 4054. Titanic, 4055. The Lord of the Rings: The Return of the King, 4056. Mary Poppins, 4057. a, 4058. Barbra Streisand

4059) Two movies were tied for being the first 3D movies to be nominated for Best Picture (in 2009). One was an animated Pixar movie. The other was a science fiction adventure. What were they?

4060) Jennifer Hudson won Best Supporting Actress for her first movie. What was the name of it?

4061) John Williams has the most Oscar nominations of any living person. What is his job?

- **a) Composing**
- **b) Directing**
- **c) Acting**
- **d) Costume design**

4062) True or false: A film critic named David Manning, quoted in ads for *A Knight's Tale, The Animal,* and other movies, was made up by the Sony marketing department.

4063) What does the rating PG stand for?

Complete the title of each of the following Mary-Kate and Ashley Olson movies.

4064) *It Takes* _________

4065) *Billboard* _________

4066) *Switching* _________

4067) *Passport to* _________

4068) *Our Lips are* _________

4069) *Winning* _________

4070) *Holiday in the* _________

4071) *Getting* _________

4072) *When in* _________

4073) *New York* _________

TOUGH TRIVIA CHALLENGE

4074) Justin Henry was the youngest actor ever nominated for an Oscar. How old was he in *Kramer vs. Kramer?*

Match the sports movie to the sport.

4075) *Rudy*	a) Bicycle racing
4076) *Miracle*	b) Track
4077) *The Bad News Bears*	c) Football
4078) *Chariots of Fire*	d) Basketball
4079) *Breaking Away*	e) Hockey
4080) *Rocky*	f) Baseball
4081) *Hoosiers*	g) Boxing

4082) Born in 1954 in Hong Kong, this actor, writer, producer, and director has been called the world's biggest non-Hollywood movie star. Who is this co-star of the remake of *The Karate Kid?*

4083) What is the last name of Shia LaBeouf's character in the Transformers movies?

a) Whitiker
b) Witwicky
c) Wochovsky
d) Wallenski

4084) Did Shia LaBeouf make the first Transformers movie before or after he played Mutt in *Indiana Jones and the Kingdom of the Crystal Skull?*

TOUGH TRIVIA CHALLENGE

4085) Put the following Lindsay Lohan movies in order of release: *Confessions of a Teenage Drama Queen, The Parent Trap,* and *Freaky Friday.*

4086) What is the full name of the second Transformers movie?

4087) What is the full name of the third Transformers movie?

4088) Put the following *Star Trek* films in order: *The Voyage Home, The Wrath of Khan, The Search for Spock, The Undiscovered Country, The Final Frontier.*

4059. Up and Avatar, 4060. Dreamgirls, 4061. a, 4062. true, 4063. Parental Guidance Suggested, 4064. It Takes Two, 4065. Billboard Dad, 4066. Switching Goals, 4067. Passport to Paris, 4068. Our Lips are Sealed, 4069. Winning London, 4070. Holiday in the Sun, 4071. Getting There, 4072. When in Rome, 4073. New York Minute, 4074. eight, 4075. c, 4076. e, 4077. f, 4078. b, 4079. a, 4080. g, 4081. d, 4082. Jackie Chan, 4083. b, 4084. before, 4085. The Parent Trap, Freaky Friday, Confessions of a Teenage Drama Queen, 4086. Transformers: Revenge of the Fallen, 4087. Transformers: Dark of the Moon, 4088. The Wrath of Khan, The Search for Spock, The Voyage Home, The Final Frontier, The Undiscovered Country

4089) According to *The Hollywood Reporter* in 2011, what is the most pirated movie of all time?

4090) Which *Mission: Impossible* film did J.J. Abrams, director of the *Star Trek* film, direct?

a) Mission: Impossible
b) Mission: Impossible II
c) Mission: Impossible III
d) All of the above

4091) How many Superman movies did Christopher Reeve star in?

4092) How many *Back to the Future* movies are there?

4093) What was the name of the Superman movie starring Brandon Routh and Kate Bosworth?

4094) WHO PLAYED CAROL FERRIS IN *THE GREEN LANTERN*?

4095) True or false: Peter Sarsgaard, from *The Green Lantern* and *Knight and Day*, was born in Norway.

4096) Besides *The Green Lantern*, what other superhero film was Ryan Reynolds in?

a) *X-Men Origins: Wolverine*
b) *Sky High*
c) *Thor*
d) *X-Men*

4097) What was the name of James Franco's character in *Spider-Man*?

a) Harry Harold
b) Harry Robertson
c) Harry Harris
d) Harry Osborn

4098) True or false: Three different actors played J. Jonah Jameson in the three Tobey McGuire *Spider-Man* films.

4099) True or false: Despite its title, *The Neverending Story* did end ... and had a sequel.

4100) In the Jim Carrey movie, how many penguins does Mr. Popper inherit?

4101) In *Lemony Snicket's A Series of Unfortunate Events*, who is the voice of Lemony Snicket?

a) Lemony Snicket
b) Jude Law
c) James Gandolfini
d) Johnny Depp

4102) How many Ace Ventura film did Jim Carrey star in?

4103) What Batman villain did Jim Carrey play in *Batman Forever?*

4104) Jim Carrey played Scrooge in 2009's *A Christmas Carol.* Who played the trio of ghosts?

4105) In 2009's *A Christmas Carol*, Gary Oldman voiced Bob Cratchit, Marley's ghost, and what other main character?

4106) What other superhero movies, besides *Superman Returns*, did Bryan Singer direct?

a) *X-Men* and *X2*
b) *Spider-Man 2* and *Spider-Man 3*
c) *The Green Hornet*
d) *None of the above*

4107) Bill Murray starred in a modern version of *A Christmas Carol* called __________?

a) *Scrooged*
b) *Marley and Me*
c) *Today's Carol*
d) *Merry Christmas, Mr. Scrooge*

4108) WAS THE 1951 VERSION OF *A CHRISTMAS CAROL* STARRING ALASTAIR SIM IN COLOR OR BLACK AND WHITE?

4089. *Avatar*, 4090. c, 4091. four, 4092. three, 4093. *Superman Returns*, 4094. Blake Lively, 4095. false—Illinois, 4096. a, 4097. d, 4098. false, 4099. true, 4100. six, 4101. b, 4102. 2, 4103. the Riddler, 4104. Jim Carrey, 4105. Tiny Tim, 4106. a, 4107. a, 4108. black and white

Match the movie to the opposing team.

4109) *The Mighty Ducks*

4110) *D2: The Mighty Ducks*

4111) *D3: The Mighty Ducks*

a) Team Iceland

b) The Hawks

c) The Varsity Warriors

4112) Who was the voice of Mr. Fox in *The Fantastic Mr. Fox?*

4113) Who was the voice of Mrs. Fox in *The Fantastic Mr. Fox?*

4114) The mean farmers in *The Fantastic Mr. Fox* are Boggis, Bunce, and ______

a) Bligh b) Bean c) Bunch d) Blech

4115) In the first film, what was the name of the team before changing its name to the Mighty Ducks?

a) District 1

b) District 5

c) District 9

d) District 14

4116) Which came first, the movie *The Mighty Ducks* or the hockey team the Anaheim Ducks?

4117) True or false: Wayne Gretzky appeared in a *Mighty Ducks* film.

4118) How many players appeared in all three Mighty Ducks films?

a) One

b) Two

c) Four

d) Seven

4119) What is the name of the girl who plays on the Mighty Ducks team in all three films?

a) Carol

b) Connie

c) Catherine

d) Cynthia

4120) True or false: Emma Stone appeared in the action/horror film *Day of the Dead.*

4121) Which of the following movies did not feature a song performed by Justin Timberlake on its soundtrack?

a) *Shark Tale*
b) *Bad Boys II*
c) *Love Actually*
d) *The Sandlot*

TOUGH TRIVIA CHALLENGE

4127) What was the title of the direct-to-video animated film that was madeup of the first three episodes of the *Mighty Ducks* TV series?

a) *Mighty Ducks the Movie: The First Face-Off*
b) *Mighty Ducks the Movie: Center Ice*
c) *Mighty Ducks the Movie: The Penalty Box*
d) *Mighty Ducks the Movie: Goal Tending*

4122) TRUE OR FALSE: JUSTIN TIMBERLAKE WAS THE VOICE OF BOO BOO IN THE MOVIE *YOGI BEAR*.

4123) True or false: Seth Rogan was one of the voices in *Kung Fu Panda*.

4124) What animal did Angelina Jolie voice in *Kung Fu Panda*?

4125) Which did Jack Black make first, *Nacho Libre* or *Year One*?

4126) True or false: The 2005 *King Kong* was the first time the 1930s classic film was remade?

4128) True or false: Naomi Watts played Ann Darrow in *King Kong*.

4129) Which came first, *Zombieland* or *Shaun of the Dead*?

4130) True or false: There's a movie called *The Incredibly Strange Creatures Who Stopped Living and Became Mixed-Up Zombies*.

4131) True or false: There's a movie called *Stop! Or My Mom Will Shoot!*

4109. b, 4110. a, 4111. c, 4112. George Clooney, 4113. Meryl Streep, 4114. b, 4115. b, 4116. the movie, 4117. true, 4118. d, 4119. b, 4120. false—but she was in *Zombieland*, 4121. d, 4122. true, 4123. true, 4124. a tiger, 4125. *Nacho Libre*, 4126. false, 4127. a, 4128. True, 4129. *Shaun of the Dead*, 4130. true, 4131. true

4132) True or false: There's a movie called *Operation Dumbo Drop.*

4133) True or false: There's a movie called *SSSSSSSsstutttterrrrer!*

4134) TRUE OR FALSE: THERE'S A MOVIE CALLED *PHFFFT!*

4135) True or false: There's a movie called: *Breakin' 3: Breakin It Old Skool.*

4136) True or false: There's a movie called *Leonard, Part 6.*

4137) True or false: There's a movie called *Santa Claus Conquers the Martians*?

4138) True or false: There's a movie called *Sorority House Massacre 2: Nightie Nightmare.*

4139) True or false: There's a movie called *Yikkity Yikes.*

4140) True or false: There's a movie called *Eegah.*

4141) True or false: There's a movie called *Blood on the Boardwalk II: Pier Pressure.*

4142) True or false: *Freaks and Geeks* was a movie before it was a TV show.

4143) Which was made first: *Teen Wolf* or *Not Another Teen Movie?*

4144) True or false: There's a movie called *Santa Claus Conquers the Martians II: The Elves' Revenge.*

4145) Which was made first: *Confessions of a Teenage Drama Queen* or *I Was a Teenage Frankenstein.*

4146) Which was made first: *17 Again* or *18 Again.*

Complete the titles of these Will Smith movies.

4147) *Bad* _____

4148) _____ *Day*

4149) *Wild Wild* _____

4150) *Enemy of the* _____

4151) *Men in* _____

4152) *Shark* _____

4153) *The* _____ *of Happyness*

4154) *I Am* _____

4155) *Seven* _____

4156) True or false: There's a movie called *Attack of the Killer Tomatoes.*

4157) True or false: There's a movie called *Jesse James Meets Frankenstein's Daughter.*

4158) True or false: There's a movie called *Killer Klowns from Outer Space*

4159) Have there been more *Rocky* movies or *Godzilla* movies?

4160) Have there been more *Child's Play* movies or *Nightmare on Elm Street* movies?

4132. true, 4133. false, 4134. true, 4135. false, 4136. true, 4137. true, 4138. true, 4139. false, 4140. true, 4141. false, 4142. false, 4143. Teen Wolf, 4144. false, 4145. I Was a Teenage Frankenstein, 4146. 17 Again, 4147. Boys, 4148. Independence, 4149. West, 4150. State, 4151. Black, 4152. Tale, 4153. Pursuit, 4154. Legend, 4155. Pounds, 4156. true, 4157. true, 4158. true, 4159. Godzilla, 4160. Nightmare on Elm Street

4161) What letter agent does Will Smith play in the *Men in Black films?*

4162) What letter agent does Tommy Lee Jones play in the *Men in Black films?*

MATCH THE CAST TO THE MOVIE.

4163) Chris Evans, Hayley Atwell, Tommy Lee Jones
4164) Chris Hemsworth, Natalie Portman, Anthony Hopkins
4165) Kristen Wiig, Maya Rudolph, Jessica St. Clair
4166) Amy Adams, Jason Segal, Chris Cooper
4167) Johnny Depp, Helena Bonham Carter, Anne Hathaway
4168) Leonardo DiCaprio, Joseph Gordon-Levitt, Ellen Page
4169) James McAvoy, Michael Fassbender, Jennifer Lawrence
4170) Anne Hathaway, Meryl Streep, Emily Blunt
4171) Logan Lerman, Pierce Brosnan, Sean Bean
4172) Will Farrell, Christina Applegate, Paul Rudd
4173) Jim Carrey, Morgan Freeman, Jennifer Aniston
4174) Christian Bale, Michael Caine, Katie Holmes
4175) Adam Sandler, Chris Rock, Kevin James
4176) Meryl Streep, Amanda Seyfried, Pierce Brosnan
4177) Eddie Murphy, Raven-Symone, Ossie Davis

a) *X-Men: First Class*
b) *The Muppet*
c) *Captain America: The First Avenger*
d) *Mamma Mia!*
e) *Percy Jackson and the Olympians: The Lightening Thief*
f) *Thor*
g) *Bruce Almighty*
h) *Grown Ups*
i) *The Devil Wears Prada*
j) *Bridesmaids*
k) *Batman Begins*
l) *Anchorman*
m) *Alice in Wonderland*
n) *Inception*
o) *Dr. Doolittle*

4178) Which of the following was not in *Get Smart*?

a) **Steve Carell**
b) **Nicole Kidman**
c) **Anne Hathaway**
d) **Alan Arkin**

4179) Which of the following was not in *Sisterhood of the Traveling Pants*?

a) Amber Tamblyn
b) Alexis Bledel
c) Rose McGowan
d) America Ferrera

4180) Which of the following was not in *The Chronicles of Narnia: Prince Caspian*?

a) George Henley
b) William Moseley
c) Anna Popplewell
d) Emily Blunt

4181) Which of the following was not in *Four Christmases*?

a) Will Farrell
b) Vince Vaughn
c) Reese Witherspoon
d) Jon Favreau

4182) True or false: **Alec Baldwin played Mr. Conductor in *Thomas and the Magic Railroad*.**

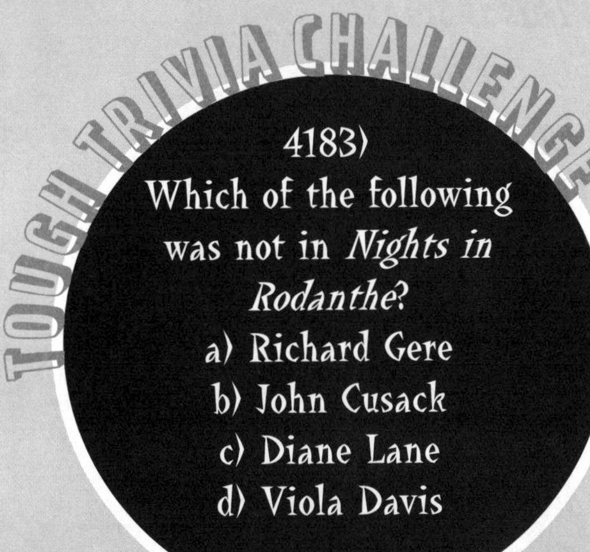

TOUGH TRIVIA CHALLENGE

4184) Have there been more *Land Before Time* movies or *Pink Panther* movies?

4185) The Library of Congress' National Film Registry selects up to 25 "culturally, historically or aesthetically signicant lms" each year. Which of the following was not among the initial group selected in 1989?

a) *Singin' in the Rain*
b) *Star Wars*
c) *The Wizard of Oz*
d) *Fantasia*

4186) True or False: ***Airplane!* is part of the National Film Registry.**

4161. J, 4162. K, 4163. c, 4164. f, 4165. j, 4166. b, 4167. m, 4168. n, 4169. a, 4170. i, 4171. e, 4172. l, 4173. g, 4174. k, 4175. h, 4176. d, 4177. o, 4178. b, 4179. c, 4180. b, 4181. a, 4182. true, 4183. b, 4184. *Land Before Time*, 4185. d, 4186. true

COMPLETE THE TITLES OF THESE FILMS, WHICH ARE ALL PART OF THE NATIONAL FILM REGISTRY.

4187) ________ *of the Sierra Madre*

4188) *How Green was my* ________

4189) *The Great Train* __________

4190) *All Quiet on the Western* ____

4191) *Lawrence of* __________

4192) *I Am a Fugitive from a Chain* ____

4193) *2001: A Space* _________

4194) *Bonnie and* _______

4195) *Birth of a* _________

4196) *Yankee Doodle* ________

4197) *Sweet Smell of* __________

4198) *One Flew Over the* ______ *Nest*

4199) *Blade* _______

4200) *An American in* _______

4201) *Meet Me in St.* ________

4202) *Invasion of the Body* _______

4203) *The African* _________

4204) *To Kill a* __________

4205) *North by* _________

4206) *The Last of the* _________

4207) *The Day the Earth Stood* ____

4208) ________ *Graffiti*

4209) *The Adventures of Robin* ____

4210) *The Outlaw Josie* _______

4211) *The Life and Times of Rosie the* _______

4212) *West Side* _______

4213) *How the West Was* ________

4214) *The Bridge on the* _____ *Kwai*

4215) *Easy* ________

4216) *The Ten* ____________

4217) *A Streetcar Named* ________

4218) *Raiders of the Lost* _______

4219) *Night of the Living* ______

4220) *Gunga* ___

4221) *Do the Right* ________

4222) *A Star is* _______

4223) *The Fall of the House of* ____

4224) *Apocalypse* _________

4225) *The Thing from Another* ____

4226) *The Sound of* _________

4227) *Planet of the* ________

4228) *All the King's* _______

4229) *This is Spinal* ____

4230) *In the Heat of the* ______

4231) *Boyz in the* _______

4232) *The* ________ *Stallion*

4233) ________ *and the Beast*

4234) *Young Mr.* _________

4235) *Butch Cassidy and the* _______ *Kid*

4236) *Seven Brides for Seven* ______

4237) *The Nutty* ___________

4238) *Jailhouse* __________

4239) *Going My* ________

4240) *The Rocky Horror Picture* ____

4241) *A Raisin in the* ________

4242) *Miracle on* ____ *Street*

4243) *The French* _________

4244) *Fast Times at* ________ *High*

4245) *Cool Hand* ________

4246) *Groundhog* ________

4247) *Blazing* __________

4248) *Wuthering* _______

4249) *The* ____ *Who Shot Liberty Valance*

4250) *Back to the* ___________

4251) *Close Encounters of the Third* ___

4252) *12 Angry* _____

4253) *The Perils of* _________

4254) *In Cold* _________

4255) *The 7th Voyage of* ________

4256) *The Story of G.I.* _____

4257) *The Muppet* ______

4258) *The Incredible* _______ *Man*

4259) *Dog Day* ___________

4260) *A Tree Grows in* ________

4261) *Saturday Night* ________

4262) *The Pink* ___________

4263) *The Empire Strikes* _______

4264) *All the* ________ *Men*

4265) ________ *X*

4266) *Sunset* _________

4267) *Some Like It* ____

4268) *Mr. Smith Goes to* ________

4269) *The Maltese* ________

4270) *High* ________

4271) *The Grapes of* _________

4272) *Citizen* ________

4273) *The Best Years of Our* _______

4274) *Rebel Without a* _________

4275) *Raging* _____

4276) *Duck* ______

4277) *Bringing Up* _____

4278) *All* _____ *Eve*

4279) *The* _________ *of Zenda*

4280) *My* __________ *Clementine*

4281) *King* ________

4282) *The* ______ *Rush*

4283) *Adam's* ______

4284) *A Night at the* ______

4285) *Lassie Come* ____

4286) *National* __________

4187. Treasure, 4188. Valley, 4189. Robbery, 4190. Front, 4191. Arabia, 4192. Gang, 4193. Odyssey, 4194. Clyde, 4195. Nation, 4196. Dandy, 4197. Success, 4198. Cuckoo's, 4199. Runner, 4200. Paris, 4201. Louis, 4202. Snatches, 4203. Queen, 4204. Mockingbird, 4205. Northwest, 4206. Mohicans, 4207. Still, 4208. American, 4209. Hood, 4210. Wales, 4211. Riveter, 4212. Story, 4213. Won, 4214. River, 4215. Rider, 4216. Commandments, 4217. Desire, 4218. Ark, 4219. Dead, 4220. Din, 4221. Thing, 4222. Born, 4223. Usher, 4224. Now, 4225. World, 4226. Music, 4227. Apes, 4228. Men, 4229. Tap, 4230. Night, 4231. Hood, 4232. Black, 4233. Beauty, 4234. Lincoln, 4235. Sundance, 4236. Brothers, 4237. Professor, 4238. Rock, 4239. Way, 4240. Show, 4241. Sun, 4242. 34th, 4243. Connection, 4244. Ridgemont, 4245. Luke, 4246. Day, 4247. Saddles, 4248. Heights, 4249. Man, 4250. Future, 4251. Kind, 4252. Men, 4253. Pauline, 4254. Blood, 4255. Sinbad, 4256. Joe, 4257. Movie, 4258. Shrinking, 4259. Afternoon, 4260. Brooklyn, 4261. Fever, 4262. Panther, 4263. Back, 4264. King's, 4265. Malcolm, 4266. Boulevard, 4267. Hot, 4268. Washington, 4269. Falcon, 4270. Noon, 4271. Wrath, 4272. Kane, 4273. Lives, 4274. Cause, 4275. Bull, 4276. Soup, 4277. Baby, 4278. About, 4279. Prisoner, 4280. Darling, 4281. Kong, 4282. Gold, 4283. Rib, 4284. Opera, 4285. Home, 4286. Velvet

TELEVISION

Match the winner to the show.

4287) Fantasia Barrino
4288) Yoanna House
4289) Alonzo Boddin
4290) Nick Lazzarini

a) *So You Think You Can Dance?*
b) *American Idol*
c) *Last Comic Standing*
d) *America's Next Top Model*

4291) True or false:
More people watched the final episode of the TV series M*A*S*H in 1983 then watched the Super Bowl that year.

Complete the title of each of these Disney Channel original movies.

4292) *Sharpay's Fabulous* ________
4293) *Lemonade* ___________
4294) *My Babysitter's a* __________
4295) *Camp Rock 2; The Final* _____
4296) *Princess Protection* ________
4297) *The Cheetah Girls: One* ______
4298) *Minute*___________
4299) *Wendy Wu: Homecoming* ____
4300) *High School* ___________
4301) *Stuck in the* ___________
4302) *Full-Court* __________
4303) *Cadet* ___________
4304) *Halloweentown II: Kalabar's* ___________
4305) *The Luck of the* __________
4306) *Phantom of the* __________
4307) *Zenon: Girl of the 21st* _______
4308) *Harriet the Spy: Blog* _______
4309) *16* ___________
4310) *Den* ___________
4311) *Phineas and Ferb The Movie; Across the 2nd* ___________

TOUGH TRIVIA CHALLENGE

4312
True or false: John Tartaglia, from the TV show *Johnny and the Sprites*, played Pinocchio in the Broadway musical version of Shrek.

4313) WHAT IS BOB THE BUILDER'S THREE-WORD ANSWER TO "CAN WE BUILD IT?"

4314) How old is Caillou supposed to be?

a) 2 b) 3 c) 4 d) 10

4315) What is Arthur the Aardvark's last name?

4316) Who had a TV series first, Dora or Diego?

4317) What was the first name of the first *Blue's Clues* host?

4318) Which Wiggle (or, at least, what color shirt Wiggle) left the band because of an illness?

4319) True or false: One of the most popular kids' TV shows of the 1950s featured a puppet named Howdy Doody.

4320) What is the name of the teacher on *The Magic School Bus?*

4321) LeVar Burton, the host of *Reading Rainbow,* also starred in a *Star Trek* TV series. Which one?

a) *Star Trek: The Next Generation*
b) *Star Trek* (the original series)
c) *Star Trek: Deep Space Nine*
d) *Star Trek: Voyager*

4287. b, 4288. d, 4289. c, 4290. a, 4291. true, 4292. *Sharpay's Fabulous Adventure,* 4293. *Lemonade Mouth,* 4294. *My Babysitter's a Vampire,* 4295. *Camp Rock 2: The Final Jam,* 4296. *Princess Protection Program,* 4297. *The Cheetah Girls: One World,* 4298. *Minutemen,* 4299. *Wendy Wu: Homecoming Warrior,* 4300. *High School Musical,* 4301. *Stuck in the Suburbs,* 4302. *Full-Court Miracle,* 4303. *Cadet Kelly,* 4304. *Halloweentown II, Kalabar's Revenge,* 4305. *The Luck of the Irish,* 4306. *Phantom of the Megaplex,* 4307. *Zenon: Girl of the 21st Century,* 4308. *Harriet the Spy: Blog Wars,* 4309. *16 Wishes,* 4310. *Den Brother,* 4311. *Phineas and Ferb The Movie: Across the 2nd Dimension,* 4312. true, 4313. "Yes we can" 4314. c, 4315. Read, 4316. Dora, 4317. Steve, 4318. Greg—yellow shirt, 4319. true, 4320. Miss Frizzle, 4321. a

4322) WHICH CAME FIRST, *H.R. PUFNSTUF* OR *SIGMUND AND THE SEA MONSTERS?*

4323) The first company to advertise on TV sold...

a) Food
b) Clothes
c) Watches
d) Cars

4324) Which of the following did not host the Nickelodeon Kids' Choice Awards

a) Jack Black
b) Tom Cruise
c) Justin Timberlake
d) Ben Stiller

4325) TRUE OR FALSE: SNOOP DOG WAS SLIMED AT THE 2011 NICKELODEON KIDS' CHOICE AWARDS

4326) The four former best friends on *Pretty Little Liars* are Spencer, Hanna, Aria and __________.

a) Emily b) Katie c) Maggie d) Jonah

4327) What are the evil robots called on *Mighty Morphin' Power Rangers* called?

a) Zods b) Zords c) Zens d) Zingas

4328) Which of the following was not a Degrassi series or special?

a) *The Kids of Degrassi Street*
b) *Degrassi: The Next Generation*
c) *Degrassi Takes Manhataan*
d) *Degrassi: Always Greener*

4329) Which of the following was not a cast member of *Freaks and Geeks*?

a) Seth Rogan
b) James Franco
c) Haley Joel Osment
d) Jason Segal

4330) Who does Jack McBrayer play on *30 Rock*?

a) Kenneth Parcell
b) Pete Hornberger
c) Frank Rossitano
d) Jack Donaghy

4331) What is the name of the TV show-within-a-show on 30 Rock?

a) *FYI with Tracy Jordan*
b) *PDQ with Tracy Jordan*
c) *TGS with Tracy Jordan*
d) *FAQ with Tracy Jordan*

4332) What is "30 Rock" short for?

4333) What show did Tina Fey leave to become a part of *30 Rock*?

4334) True or false: **In the original pilot for *30 Rock*, Jenna was played by Rachel Dratch.**

4335) Were there more episodes made of the original *Beverly Hills 90210* or the original *Hawaii Five-O*?

4337) WERE THERE MORE EPISODES MADE OF *HAPPY DAYS* OR *LAVERNE AND SHIRLEY*?

4338) Were there more episodes made of *Full House* or *Seinfeld*?

4339) Were there more episodes made of *The Cosby Show* or *X-Files*?

4322. H.R. Pufnstuf, 4323. c, 4324. b, 4325. true, 4326. a, 4327. b, 4328. d, 4329. c, 4330. a, 4331. c, 4332. 30 Rockefeller Plaza, 4333. *Saturday Night Live*, 4334. true, 4335. *Beverly Hills 90210* (296), 4336. Pennsylvania, 4337. *Happy Days* (255), 4338. *Full House* (192), 4339. *X-Files* (202)

4340) Were there more episodes made of *Lassie* or *Cheers*?

4341) Were there more episodes made of *Star Trek: The Next Generation* or *Star Trek*?

4342) Were there more episodes made of *Charmed* or *Bewitched*?

4343) Were there more episodes made of *Will & Grace* or *I Love Lucy*?

4344) Were there more episodes made of *Star Trek: Voyager* or *Star Trek: Deep Space Nine*?

4345) Were there more episodes made of *Stargate SG1* or *Mission: Impossible*?

4346) WERE THERE MORE EPISODES MADE OF *JAG* OR *M*A*S*H*?

4347) Were there more episodes made of *Little House on the Prairie* or *The Waltons*?

4348) Were there more episodes of *King of the Hill* or *The Flintstones*?

4349) Were there more episodes made of *Sabrina the Teenage Witch* or *Touched by an Angel*?

4350) Were there more episodes made of *Everybody Loves Raymond* or *Everybody Hates Chris*?

4351) WERE THERE MORE EPISODES MADE OF *FRIENDS* OR *MARRIED WITH CHILDREN*?

4352) Which was not a TV show in the 1950s?

a) *Toast of the Town*

b) *The Texaco Star Theater*

c) *You Bet Your Life*

d) *The Rube Goldberg Show*

4353) True or false: England had a children's TV series called *Mr. Noseybonk.*

4354) True or false: In Italy, a popular children's show was *Geppeppippeppipep's Garage.*

4356) True or false: One of the most popular children's shows in Latin America in the late 1980s was *Xou da Xuxa.*

4357) True or false: There was once a TV show called *When Things Were Rotten.*

4358) True or false: There was once a TV show called *The Secret Diary of Desmond Pfeffer.*

4359) TRUE OR FALSE: THERE WAS ONCE A TV SHOW CALLED *TODAY IS TOMORROW'S YESTERDAY.*

4340. *Lassie* (588), 4341. *Star Trek: The Next Generation* (178), 4342. *Bewitched* (254), 4343. *Will & Grace* (193), 4344. *Star Trek: Deep Space Nine* (176), 4345. *Stargate SG1* (214), 4346. *M*A*S*H*, 4347. *The Waltons* (213), 4348. *King of the Hill* (255), 4349. *Touched by an Angel* (212), 4350. *Everybody Loves Raymond* (210), 4351. *Married With Children* (259), 4352. d, 4353. true, 4354. false, 4355. true, 4356. true, 4357. true, 4358. true, 4359. false

4360) True or false: There was once a TV show called *Shasty McNasty.*

4361) True or false: There was once a TV show called *Albert Einstein, Boy Genius.*

4362) True or false: There was once a TV show called *It's Like, You Know.*

4363) True or false: There was once a TV show called *Dundee and the Culhane.*

4364) TRUE OR FALSE: THERE WAS ONCE A TV SHOW CALLED *JAKE AND THE FATMAN.*

4365) True or false: There was once a TV show called *Albonzo Good Morning.*

4366) True or false: There was once a TV show called *Holmes and Yo-Yo.*

4367) True or false: There was once a TV show called *Tenspeed and Brownshoe.*

4368) True or false: There was once a TV show called *Monday Night Hockey.*

4369) True or false: There was once a TV show called *Manimal.*

4370) True or false: There was once a TV show called *Superbrain.*

4371) True or false: There was once a TV show called *My Cave and Welcome to It.*

4372) True or false: There was once a TV show called *Pink Lady and Jeff.*

4373) TRUE OR FALSE: THERE WAS ONCE A TV SHOW CALLED *MY MOTHER THE CAR.*

4374) True or false: There was once a TV show called *The Ken Berry Wow Show.*

4375) TRUE OR FALSE: THERE WAS ONCE A TV SHOW CALLED *THE SHOW SHOW SHOW.*

Match the TV series to the city where it is set.

4377) *Bones* — a) Atlanta
4378) *Castle* — b) Burbank
4379) *Charmed* — c) Chicago
4380) *Chuck* — d) Indianapolis
4381) *CSI* — e) Las Vegas
4382) *Designing Women* — f) Los Angeles
4383) *Dexter* — g) Miami
4384) *The Dick Van Dyke Show* — h) Milwaukee
4385) *ER* — i) Minneapolis
4386) *Grey's Anatomy* — j) New Rochelle, N.Y.
4387) *Laverne and Shirley* — k) New York
4388) *The Mary Tyler Moore Show* — l) Sacramento
4389) *The Mentalist* — m) San Francisco
4390) *One Day at a Time* — n) Seattle
4391) *Private Practice* — o) Washington

4360. true, 4361. false, 4362. true, 4363. true, 4364. true, 4365. false, 4366. true, 4367. true, 4368. false, 4369. true, 4370. false, 4371. false, 4372. true, 4373. true, 4374. true, 4375. false, 4376. false, 4377. o, 4378. k, 4379. m, 4380. b, 4381. e, 4382. a, 4383. g, 4384. j, 4385. c, 4386. n, 4387. h, 4388. i, 4389. l, 4390. d, 4391. f

Match the fictional city to the TV show set there.

4392) Bedrock
4393) Cabot Cove, Maine
4394) Capeside, Massachusetts
4395) Cicely, Alaska
4396) Collinsport, Maine
4397) Dillon, Texas
4398) Fairview
4399) Genoa City, Wisconsin
4400) Gotham City
4401) Hooterville
4402) Mayberry, North Carolina
4403) Metropolis
4404) Neptune, California
4405) Orson, Indiana
4406) Pawnee, Indiana
4407) Port Charles, New York
4408) Quahog, Rhode Island
4409) Rome, Wisconsin
4410) Springfield
4411) Stars Hollow
4412) Stuckeyville
4413) Sunnydale, California

a) *The Andy Griffith Show*
b) *Batman*
c) *Buffy the Vampire Slayer*
d) *Dark Shadows*
e) *Dawson's Creek*
f) *Desperate Housewives*
g) *Ed*
h) *Family Guy*
i) *The Flintstones*
j) *Friday Night Lights*
k) *General Hospital*
l) *Gilmore Girls*
m) *Green Acres*
n) *Lois and Clark*
o) *The Middle*
p) *Murder, She Wrote*
q) *Northern Exposure*
r) *Parks and Recreation*
s) *Picket Fences*
t) *The Simpsons*
u) *Veronica Mars*
v) *The Young and the Restless*

4414) What does O.C. in *The O.C.* stand for?

4415) How many seasons did *The O.C.* last?

4416) True or false: Rooney was the first band to appear on *The O.C.*

4417) What is the name of the adopted son in *The O.C.*?

a) Robert
b) Ryan
c) Robin
d) Richard

4418) Which band did not appear on *The O.C.*?

a) Death Cab for Cutie
b) The Killers
c) The Thrills
d) Haircut 100

4419) WHAT DOES ESPN STAND FOR?

4420) What does CNN stand for?

4421) What does TCM stand for?

4422) What does CBS stand for?

4424) What does HBO stand for?

4425) WHAT DOES HGTV STAND FOR?

4426) What does DIY Network stand for?

4427) What does TLC stand for?

4428) What does BET stand for?

4429) What does GSN stand for?

4430) What language is Telemundo broadcast in?

4431) WHAT DOES OWN STAND FOR?

4392. i, 4393. p, 4394. e, 4395. q, 4396. d, 4397. j, 4398. f, 4399. v, 4400. b, 4401. m, 4402. a, 4403. n, 4404. u, 4405. o, 4406. r, 4407. k, 4408. h, 4409. s, 4410. t, 4411. l, 4412. g, 4413. c, 4414. Orange County, 4415. four, 4416. true, 4417. b, 4418. d, 4419. Entertainment and Sports Programming Network, 4420. Cable News Network, 4421. Turner Classic Movies, 4422. Columbia Broadcasting System, 4423. Comcast, 4424. Home Box Office, 4425. Home & Garden Television, 4426. Do-it-yourself Network, 4427. The Learning Channel, 4428. Black Entertainment Television, 4429. Game Show Network, 4430. Spanish, 4431. Oprah Winfrey Network

4432) Which network focuses primarily on the arts?
a) RFD-TV
b) Ovation
c) ION
d) Halogen

4433) What did AMC originally stand for?

4434) What does IFC stand for?

4435) What does CMT stand for?

4436) What did the VH in VH1 originally stand for?

4437) What does HLN stand for?

4438) True or false: There is a Pentagon Channel

4439) What does HSN stand for?

4440) Which of the following is not an ESPN channel?
a) ESPN Plus
b) ESPN2
c) ESPN-W
d) ESPN Classic

4441) WHAT DOES QVC STAND FOR?

4442) True or false: ARTN is the Armenian-Russian Television Network.

4443) True or false: There used to be a Lottery Channel.

4444) Which of the following is not a now-defunct premium channel.
a) Spotlight
b) Prism
c) Nightlight
d) Home Theater Network

TOUGH TRIVIA CHALLENGE

4445) WHAT DOES GAC STAND FOR?

4446) True or false: **MSNBC used to be called America's Talking.**

4447) True or false: **There is a Live Monkey Cam Channel.**

4448) TRUE OR FALSE: TRUTV USED TO BE COURT TV.

4449) What used to be the name of Nick Jr?

a) Nothin'

b) Noggin

c) Nudge

d) Origin

4450) True or false: SyFy used to be Sci-Fi.

4451) True or false: **NBC Sports Network used to be called Versus.**

4452) What network shares channels with Cartoon Network?

4432. b, 4433. American Movie Classics, 4434. Independent Film Channel, 4435. Country Music Television, 4436. Video Hits, 4437. Headline News, 4438. true, 4439. Home Shopping Network, 4440. c, 4441. Quality, Value, Convenience, 4442. true, 4443. true, 4444. c, 4445. Great American Country, 4446. true, 4447. false, 4448. true, 4449. b, 4450. true, 4451. true, 4452. Adult Swim

Match the actor to his show.

4453) Jon Cryer
4454) Larry David
4455) Billy Gardell
4456) Adrian Grenier
4457) Zachary Levi
4458) Joel McHale
4459) Nick Offerman
4460) Jim Parsons
4461) Jason Segel
4462) Eric Stonestreet

a) *Big Bang Theory*
b) *Chuck*
c) *Community*
d) *Curb Your Enthusiasm*
e) *Entourage*
f) *How I Met Your Mother*
g) *Mike and Molly*
h) *Modern Family*
i) *Parks and Recreation*
j) *Two and a Half Men*

Match the actress to her show.

4463) Alison Brie
4464) Kaley Cuoco
4465) Kat Dennings
4466) Zooey Deschanel
4467) Patricia Heaton
4468) Melissa McCarthy
4469) Amy Poehler
4470) Cobie Smulders
4471) Yvonne Strahovski
4472) Sofia Vergara

a) *2 Broke Girls*
b) *Big Bang Theory*
c) *Chuck*
d) *Community*
e) *How I Met Your Mother*
f) *The Middle*
g) *Mike and Molly*
h) *Modern Family*
i) *New Girl*
j) *Parks and Recreation*

4453. j, 4454. d, 4455. g, 4456. e, 4457. b, 4458. c, 4459. i, 4460. a, 4461. f, 4462. h, 4463. d, 4464. b, 4465. a, 4466. i, 4467. f, 4468. g, 4469. j, 4470. e, 4471. c, 4472. h

CHAPTER 9

Food

FRUITS & VEGGIES (PLUS SOME NUTS)

4473) True or false: Peach Melba was named after opera singer Nellie Melba.

4474) True or false: Waldorf Salad was named after Archduke Ferdinand Waldorf.

4475) Which is not a kind of apple?

a) McIntosh
b) Cortland
c) Volcanic
d) Brawley

4476) Which is not a kind of pear?

a) Anjou
b) Bartlett
c) Louise
d) Douglas

4477) WHICH IS NOT A KIND OF CHERRY?

A) BIGARREAU
B) BING
C) MORELLO
D) SULTAN

4478) Which of the following is not a kind of nut?

a) Cobnut
b) Hickory
c) Histon
d) Yeheb

4479) Which of the following is not a kind of grape?

a) Cabernet Franc
b) Cataba
c) Pinot Blanc
d) Waltham cross

4480) Which of the following is not a kind of tomato?

a) Big Boy
b) Moneymaker
c) Sandy
d) Shirley

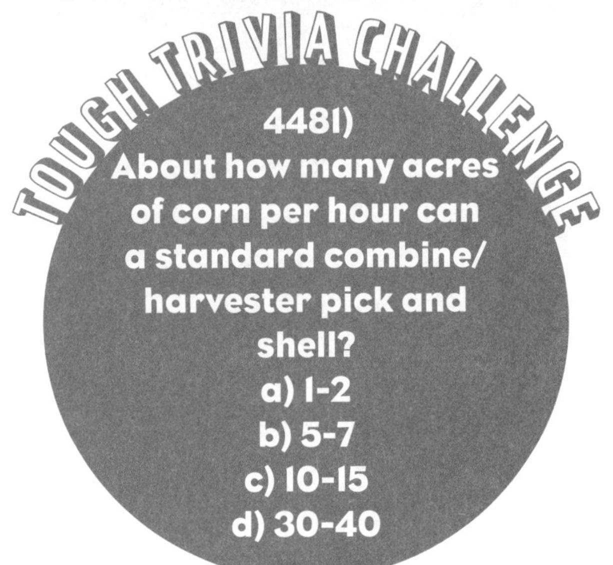

TOUGH TRIVIA CHALLENGE

4481) About how many acres of corn per hour can a standard combine/harvester pick and shell?

a) 1-2
b) 5-7
c) 10-15
d) 30-40

4482) True or false: Most corn grown in the 1800s in the U.S. only produced one large and two small ears.

4483) Which of the following is not a kind of corn?

a) Jersey Special
b) Texas Shoe Peg
c) Silver King Wisconsin
d) Reid's Yellow Dent

4484) TRUE OR FALSE: THE SPICIEST CHILI PEPPER IN THE WORLD IS THE TRINIDAD SCORPION BUTCH T.

4485) True of false: Apricot flowers are bright red.

4486) How hot is the hottest pepper in the world?

a) 1,700 Scoville heat units
b) 17,000 Scoville heat units
c) 146,300 Scoville heat units
d) 1,463,700 Scoville heat units

4487) True or false: There are more than 7,000 kinds of apples.

4488) Which of the following is not a kind of apple?

a) Fuji
b) Jonagold
c) Green Delicious
d) Winesap

4489) True or false: Avocado is native to Central Australia.

4473. true, 4474. false—it was named after New York City's Waldorf Hotel. 4475. c, 4476. d, 4477. d, 4478. c, 4479. b, 4480. c, 4481. c, 4482. true, 4483. a, 4484. true, 4485. false, 4486. d, 4487. true, 4488. c, 4489. false

MATCH THE FRUIT TO ITS LATIN NAME.

4490) Citrullius lanatus
4491) Rubes idaeus
4492) Cocus nucifera
4493) Malus sylvestris
4494) Prunus persica
4495) Phoenix dactylifera
4496) Ananas comosus
4497) Prunus armeniaca
4498) Citrus sinensis
4499) Rheum Rharbararum

a) Raspberry
b) Orange
c) Watermelon
d) Pineapple
e) Rhubarb
f) Apricot
g) Peach
h) Apple
i) Coconut
j) Fig

4500) HOW MANY SEEDS IN AN APRICOT?

4501) Do bananas grow on trees?

4502) True or false: Some cultures eat banana skins.

4503) True or false: fiber is the part of plant foods that our bodies digest.

4504) **True or false:** on a food label, high fiber means 20 grams or more per serving.

4505) Does avocado ripen on the tree or off the tree?

4506) Which has more carbs, apples or oranges?

4507) TRUE OR FALSE: A MAYAN LEGEND HAS IT THAT HUMANS ARE MADE FROM CORN.

4508) True or false: Mayans used to try to predict the future by reading kernels of corn.

4509) Which of the following is not a kind of orange:
a) Valencia
b) Blood
c) Cara Cara
d) Alphonso

4510) Which has more calories, blueberries or dates?

4511) WHICH HAS MORE CALORIES, FRESH COCONUT OR FRESH FIGS?

4512) Woody Allen directed a movie named after what fruit?

4513) Which has more calories, pears or plums?

4514) Which has more calories, peaches or prunes?

4515) Which has more calories, strawberries or grapes?

4516) Which has more calories, bananas or apricots?

4517) Which has more calories, grapefruit or mango?

4518) Which has more calories, papaya or passion fruit?

4519) WHICH HAS MORE CALORIES, RAISINS OR RHUBARB?

4520) Which has more calories, green beans or broccoli?

4521) Which has more calories, cucumber or eggplant?

4522) Which has more calories, horseradish or chives?

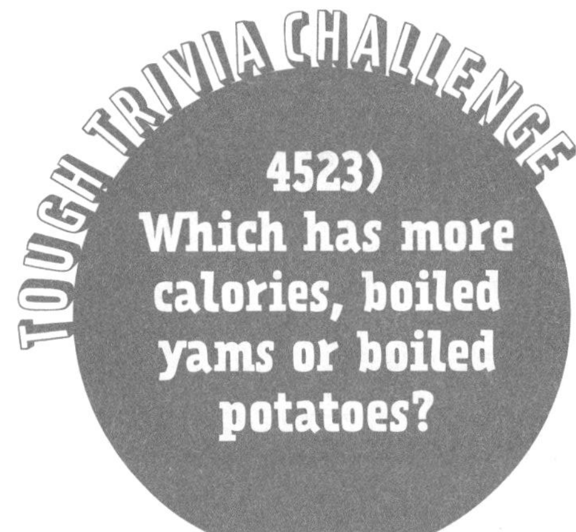

TOUGH TRIVIA CHALLENGE

4523) Which has more calories, boiled yams or boiled potatoes?

4524) Which has more calories, lettuce or kale?

4525) WHICH HAS MORE CALORIES, GREEN PEPPER OR RED PEPPER?

4526) Which has more calories, onion or parsley?

4490. c, 4491. a, 4492. i, 4493. h, 4494. g, 4495. j, 4496. d, 4497. f, 4498. b, 4499. e, 4500. one, 4501. no—but on very large plants, 4502. true, 4503. false—fiber is that part we can't digest, 4504. False—five grams or more, 4505. off the tree, 4506. apples, 4507. true, 4508. true, 4509. d, 4510. dates, 4511. coconut, 4512. bananas, 4513. pears, 4514. prunes, 4515. grapes, 4516. bananas, 4517. mango, 4518. papaya, 4519. raisins, 4520. green beans, 4521. eggplant, 4522. horseradish, 4523. yams, 4524. lettuce, 4525. red pepper, 4526. onion

AROUND THE WORLD

4527) True or false: All sushi includes shari (vinegared rice).

4528) Which had sushi first, China or Japan?

4529) DOES WASABI COME FROM A ROOT OR A LEAF?

4530) Which of the following is not a kind of western-style sushi?

a) Dynamite roll
b) Philadelphia roll
c) Seattle roll
d) Chicago roll

TOUGH TRIVIA CHALLENGE

4531)
The word "fajita" has been used to describe grilled meat and vegetables served in tortillas since 1744.

4532) Which of the following is an ingredient in California roll sushi?

a) Pineapple
b) Mango
c) Avocado
d) Peach

4533) What is the black seaweed wrap used in some sushi called?

a) Naan b) Nori c) Noni d) Nobi

4534) True or false: Soy sauce comes from soybeans.

4535) True or false: The Aztecs made guacamole.

4536) True or false: There is a Mexican cheese known as Chihuahua.

4537) What does salsa mean?

4538) TRUE OR FALSE: THE WORD ENCHILADA MEANS "IN TORTILLAS."

4539) True or false: **The Aztecs ate tamales.**

4540) Is flan a native Mexican dessert?

4541) Are churros fried or baked?

4542) What is a fried burrito called?

a) Quesadilla
b) Chimichanga
c) Tostada
d) Bunuelos

4543) WHAT DOES "CON CARNE," AS IN CHILI CON CARNE, MEAN?

4544) True or false: The word "mole" as it is used in Mexican cooking, comes from the same source as the animal mole.

4545) Were original quesadilla tortillas made from corn or flour?

4546) What does "queso" mean in Spanish?

4547) True or false: Aztecs used chocolate for religious and medical reasons, not for food.

4548) True or false: **Refried beans are traditionally fried twice.**

4549) ARE TRADITIONAL MEXICAN TACOS SERVED IN U-SHAPED SHELLS?

4550) True or false: A Virginia Chinese restaurant installed a bulletproof window because it was a favorite place for George W. Bush to eat.

4551) What part of China does Cantonese food come from?

a) North
b) South
c) East
d) West

4527. true, 4528. China, 4529. root, 4530. d, 4531. false—the term didn't see print until the 1970s, 4532. c, 4533. b, 4534. true, 4535. true, 4536. true, 4537. sauce, 4538. false—it means "in chili", 4539. true, 4540. no—it comes from Europe, 4541. fried, 4542. b, 4543. with meat, 4544. false, 4545. corn, 4546. cheese, 4547. true, 4548. false—the term actually comes from "frijoles refritos" or "well-fried beans", 4549. no, 4550. true, 4551. b

BREAKFAST

TOUGH TRIVIA CHALLENGE

4552) Which was not an original flavor of Pop-Tarts?
a) Strawberry
b) Brown sugar cinnamon
c) Apple currant
d) Cherry

4553) TRUE OR FALSE: IF YOU ONLY HAVE ONE, IT'S STILL POP-TARTS, NOT POP-TART.

4554) Which of the following is not a discontinued variety of Pop-Tarts?
a) Cheese Danish Pastry Swirls
b) Frosted Grape
c) Honey Nut
d) Hot Chocolate

4555) What company makes Pop-Tarts?

4556) Pop-Tarts were once advertised with a toaster character named...
a) Marvin b) Milton c) Muggsy d) Manny

4557) True or false: The original breakfast cereal—called Granola—was sold in blocks and needed to be chipped away by consumers and soaked in milk.

4558) True or false: Fruit Brute was originally one of the monster cereals.

4559) Cap'n Crunch was launched in...
a) 1963 b) 1968 c) 1972 d) 1979

4560) TRUE OR FALSE: THE SAME ANIMATOR WHO DEVELOPED ROCKY & BULLWINKLE ALSO DEVELOPED THE CAP'N CRUNCH CHARACTER.

4561) True or false: Punch Crunch had a boxer as a mascot.

4562) True or false: **The W.K. Kellogg Foundation was created in 1906 in an effort to help hospital patients digest food.**

4563) In what state is Battle Creek, home of Kellogg's?

4564) What company produces Cheerios?

a) General Mills
b) Kellogg's
c) Kashi
d) None of the above

4565) TRUE OR FALSE: KIX WAS THE FIRST PUFFED CEREAL.

4566) *In what year was Wheaties launched?*

a) 1890 b) 1912 c) 1924 d) 1957

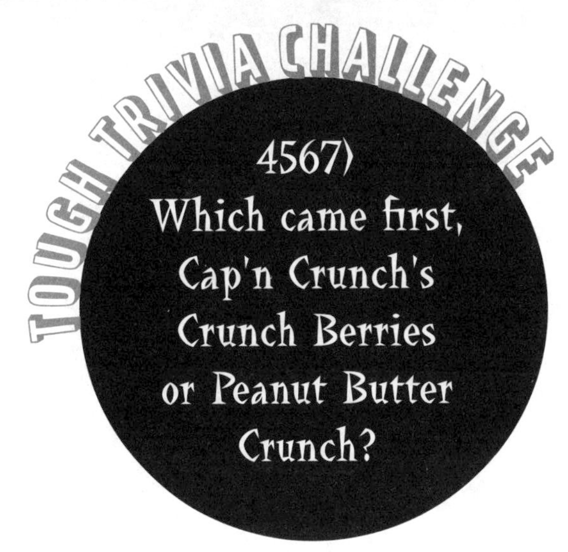

4568) What cereal has Tony the Tiger as a mascot?

4569) Is muesli made from cooked or uncooked rolled oats?

4570) Wheaties advertises itself as "The Breakfast of ___________."

4571) True or false: The first athlete to be featured on a Wheaties box was Babe Ruth.

4572) True or false: The first African-American athlete on a Wheaties box was Jackie Robinson.

4552. d, 4553. true, 4554. c, 4555. Kellogg's, 4556. b, 4557. true, 4558. true, 4559. a, 4560. true—Jay Ward, 4561. false—it was a hippo, 4562. true, 4563. Michigan, 4564. a, 4565. true, 4566. c, 4567. Crunch Berries, 4568. Frosted Flakes, 4569. uncooked, 4570. Champions, 4571. false—Lou Gehrig, 4572. false—Jesse Owens

TOUGH TRIVIA CHALLENGE

4573) Bob Richards, an early spokesperson for Wheaties, was a two-time Olympic champion in what sport?
a) Hurtles
b) Bobsled
c) Pole vault
d) Luge

4574) True or false: There wasn't a football player on the front of a Wheaties box until 1986.

4575) The first team to appear on a Wheaties box was the...
a) Minnesota Twins
b) Chicago Bills
c) U.S. Olympic basketball team
d) Philadelphia Flyers

4576) True or false: A women's sports team has never been on a Wheaties box.

4577) Who has been on more different Wheaties boxes: Tiger Woods or Michael Jordan?

4578) What popular breakfast cereal was originally called Apple O's?

4579) Which of the following was never a spokesperson for Wheaties?
a) Mary Lou Retton
b) Chris Evert
c) Tiger Woods
d) Willie Mays

4580) What cereal was advertised with the line "It's just like eating up the alphabet"?

4581) Bart's Peanut Butter Chocolate Crunch was a spin-off of what TV show?

4582) What cereal was advertised with the line "Kid tested, mother approved."

4583) True or false: There was a cereal called Bill & Ted's Excellent Cereal.

4584) Which of the following was not a Cheerio's variation:
a) Chocolate Cheerios
b) Yogurt Burst Cheerios
c) Cheerio Max
d) Banana Nut Cheerios

MATCH THE MASCOT TO THE CEREAL.

4585) Dig 'em
4586) Sam
4587) Snap, Crackle and Pop
4588) Sugar Bear
4589) Tony the Tiger

a) Froot Loops
b) Rice Krispies
c) Sugar Frosted Flakes
d) Sugar Smacks
e) Super Sugar Crisp

4590) True or false: Millenios were Cheerios that included pieces shaped like 2s.

4591) Which of the following was not a Chex variation?
a) Strawberry Chex
b) Honey Graham Chex
c) Cinnamon Chex
d) Yogurt-berry Chex

4592) In what decade was Cookie Crisp launched?
a) 1950s b) 1960s c) 1970s d) 1980s

4593) TRUE OR FALSE: CORN POPS WERE ORIGINALLY CALLED SWEETIE POPS.

4594) True or false: There were breakfast cereals based on Donkey Kong.

4595) What is the Cocoa Puffs' bird's name?
a) Kooky
b) Sonny
c) Socko
d) Wacko

4596) True or false: Corn Pops is different in the U.S. than it is in Canada.

4597) WHAT KIND OF BIRD IS THE FRUIT LOOPS MASCOT?

4598) Which of the following is not a Frosted Mini-Wheats variation?
a) Big Bite
b) Vanilla Crème
c) Blueberry Muffin
d) Chocolate Chip Muffin

4573. c, 4574. true—Walter Payton, 4575. a, 4576. false, 4577. Michael Jordan, 4578. Apple Jacks, 4579. d, 4580. Alpha-bits, 4581. The Simpsons, 4582. Kix, 4583. true, 4584. c, 4585. d, 4586. a, 4587. b, 4588. e, 4589. c, 4590. true, 4591. d, 4592. c, 4593. false—Sugar Pops, 4594. true, 4595. b, 4596. true, 4597. Toucan, 4598. d

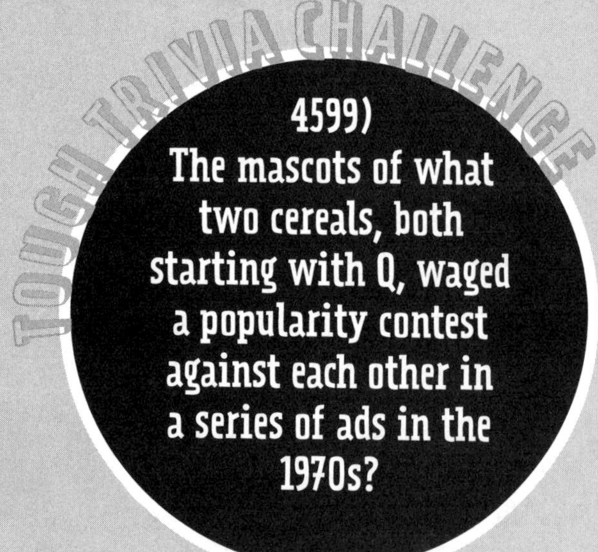

4599) The mascots of what two cereals, both starting with Q, waged a popularity contest against each other in a series of ads in the 1970s?

4600) What hot cereal's slogan was the basis for the later slogan, "I want my MTV"?

a) Cream of Wheat
b) Maypo
c) Postum
d) Quaker Oats

4601) What cereal, now a generic term, debuted at the Chicago World's Fair in 1893?

a) Corn flakes
b) Grape nuts
c) Raisin bran
d) Shredded wheat

4602) True or false: Grape-Nuts contains neither grapes nor nuts.

4603) The spiritual "Oh, Dem Golden Slippers" was reworked as an advertising jingle for what cereal?

4604) What was the name of the little boy used as a guinea pig to try Life cereal?

4605) WHAT CEREAL IS "NOT FOR SILLY RABBITS"?

4606) What cereal gets its name from the fact it has 100% of the recommended daily allowances of most necessary nutrients?

4607) What kind of creature is the mascot for Peanut Butter Crunch?

4608) WHAT PIRATE IS CONSTANTLY TRYING TO STEAL CAP'N CRUNCH?

4609) What is Cap'n Crunch's first name?

FAST FOOD

4610) Which of the following is not a discontinued McDonald's food item.

a) McDLT
b) Arch Deluxe
c) Hamburgler Supreme
d) Onion Nuggets

4611) TRUE OR FALSE: THE BURGER KING FISH SANDWICH USED TO BE CALLED THE BIG SWIMMER?

4612) True or false: Burger King was first known as Insta-Burger King.

4613) Which burger chain had the first deal with Lucasfilm to sell Star Wars glasses?

4614) The first McDonald's restaurant opened in ...
a) 1933 b) 1940 c) 1949 d) 1954

4615) True or false: The original McDonald's mascot was a chef named Speedee.

4616) Did McDonald's open first in Japan, France, or El Salvador?

4617) The first McDonald's PlayPlace playground opened in what year?
a) 1957 b) 1967 c) 1977 d) 1987

4618) True or false: McDonald's won a lawsuit that has kept the derogatory term McJob out of Merriam-Webster's Collegiate Dictionary.

4619) True or false: A copycat restaurant called MaDonalds opened in Kurdistan and sold Big Macks.

4620) The forerunner of Taco Bell, Bell's Drive-In, primarily served what food?

4599. Quisp and Quake, 4600. b, 4601. d, 4602. true, 4603. Golden Grahams, 4604. Mikey, 4605. Trix, 4606. Total, 4607. elephant, 4608. Jean Lafoote, 4609. Horatio, 4610. c, 4611. false—there was a Whaler and an Ocean Catch sandwich, but no Big Swimmer, 4612. true, 4613. Burger King, 4614. b, 4615. true, 4616. Japan, 4617. c, 4618. false—McDonald's did try suing, but the word still went in, 4619. true, 4620. hot dogs

MATCH THE CATCHPHRASE TO THE FAST FOOD CHAIN.

4621) Where's the beef?
4622) Eat fresh
4623) What you crave
4624) Home of the Whopper
4625) Finger lickin' good
4626) Think outside the bun
4627) I'm lovin' it.

a) White Castle
b) Burger King
c) KFC
d) Subway
e) Wendy's
f) Taco Bell
g) McDonald's

4628) Where is the Taco Bell Arena?

a) Boise, Idaho
b) Cleveland, Ohio
c) Springfield, Illinois
d) West Chester, Pennsylvania

4629) True or false: Taco Bell serves French fries in Spain.

4630) ALTHOUGH HIS IMAGE IS STILL ASSOCIATED WITH KENTUCKY FRIED CHICKEN/ KFC, COL. SANDERS SOLD THE COMPANY IN 1964.

4631) Col. Sanders' first name was...

a) Harry
b) Harrison
c) Henry
d) Harland

4632) True or false: Before he founded Wendy's, Dave Thomas helped create the spinning bucket sign for Kentucky Fried Chicken.

4633) Dave Thomas named Wendy's after his eight-year-old daughter, who was nicknamed Wendy. What was her real name?

a) Betty Lou
b) Melinda Lou
c) Annie Lou
d) Wanda Lou

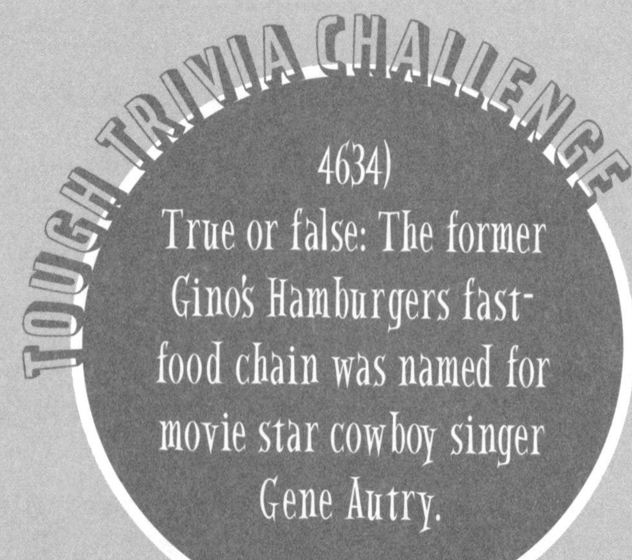

TOUGH TRIVIA CHALLENGE

4634) True or false: The former Gino's Hamburgers fast-food chain was named for movie star cowboy singer Gene Autry.

4635) Which former Beatle starred in a Pizza Hut commercial?

a) John b) Paul c) George d) Ringo

4636) Hardee's is a sibling of what other restaurant chain?

a) Bob's Big Boy
b) Carl's Jr.
c) Jack in the box
d) Rally's

4637) Which has more locations, Subway or McDonald's?

4638) True or false: Subway's BMT sandwich originally stood for Brooklyn Manhattan Transit.

4639) TRUE OR FALSE: SOME SUBWAY LOCATIONS ARE KOSHER.

4640) In what year did Subway begin offering $5 foot-long sandwiches?

a) 1978 b) 1988 c) 1998 d) 2008

4641) What school did "Subway diet" creator Jared Fogle attend?

a) Kansas State
b) University of Michigan
c) University of Southern California
d) Indiana University

4642) TRUE OR FALSE: THE FOUNDER OF PAPA JOHN'S PIZZA IS JOHN SCHLESSINGER.

4643) True or false: Domino's Pizza was originally called DomiNick's.

4644) True or False: In order to open the first Pizza Hut restaurant, co-owners Frank and Dan Carney borrowed money from their mother.

4645) True or false: The name Arby's comes from the R in roast and the b in beef.

4646) What kind of dog starred in a series of commercials for Taco Bell?

4621. e, 4622. d, 4623. a, 4624. c, 4625. b, 4626. f, 4627. g, 4628. a, 4629. true, 4630. true, 4631. d, 4632. true, 4633. b, 4634. false—it was for former Baltimore Colts' captain Gino Marchetti. 4635. d, 4636. b, 4637. Subway, 4638. true, 4639. true, 4640. d, 4641. d, 4642. false—John Schlatter, 4643. true, 4644. true, 4645. false—it comes from the Raffel brothers, the original owners. 4646. Chihuahua

4647) What boy was Burger Chef's assistant?

4648) McDonald's ads featured the Hamburglar. What rival chain used a similar character named Speedy McGreedy?

4649) True or false: Taco Bell gets its name from the mission-style architecture featuring a bell over the front door.

4650) The Taco Bell dog made an encore appearance in another company's ad, "auditioning" to be the spokesman for what insurance company?

a) Allstate
b) Geico
c) Prudential
d) State Farm

4651) True or false: Captain Kangaroo star Bob Keeshan was the first Ronald McDonald.

4652) Who is the mayor of McDonaldland?

4653) What was the Taco Bell dog's catchphrase?

4654) In what book does the character Long John Silver appear?

4655) WHAT WAS LONG JOHN SILVER'S JOB?

4656) What book is the source of the name "Starbucks"?

4657) What does Burger King call its coffee?

4658) True or false: Burger King restaurants used to have a giant king over the entrance.

4659) What fast food chain launched a disastrous ad campaign featuring a nerdy guy named Herb?

a) Burger King
b) McDonald's
c) Pizza Hut
d) Wendy's

4660) What presidential candidate swiped the slogan "Where's the beef?" to attack his main opponent in the Democratic primaries?

a) Bill Clinton
b) Michael Dukakis
c) Gary Hart
d) Walter Mondale

4661) What chicken restaurant chain is famously closed on Sundays?

a) Chick-Fil-A
b) Church's
c) KFC
d) Popeyes

4662) What California-based burger chain, with restaurants in just five states, is famous for a menu limited to the burger, the cheeseburger, and the double-double?

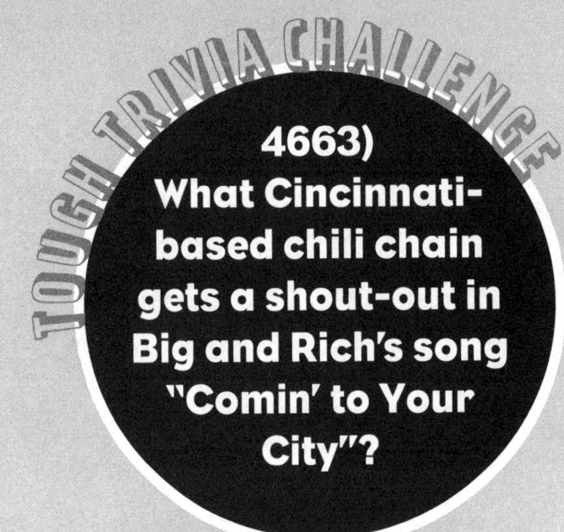

4663) What Cincinnati-based chili chain gets a shout-out in Big and Rich's song "Comin' to Your City"?

4664) Dennis the Menace did ads for what ice cream chain?

a) Baskin-Robbins
b) Dairy Queen
c) Haagen-Dazs
d) Tastee Freeze

4665) What name is given to the hamburger-and-hot-dog part of Dairy Queen franchises?

4666) What drive-in burger chain's signature items include limeade, tater tots, and foot-long chili dogs?

4667) TRUE OR FALSE: THE FOUNDER OF BROWN'S CHICKEN WAS ONCE THE GOVERNOR OF KENTUCKY.

4647. Burger Jeff, 4648. Hardee's, 4649. false—it was founded by Glen Bell, 4650. b, 4651. false—*Today Show* weatherman Willard Scott, 4652. Mayor McCheese, 4653. Yo quiero Taco Bell, 4654. *Treasure Island*, 4655. cook (of course), 4656. *Moby-Dick*, 4657. BK Joe, 4658. true, 4659. a, 4660. d, 4661. a, 4662. In-N-Out, 4663. Skyline, 4664. b, 4665. Brazier, 4666. Sonic, 4667. true

TOUGH TRIVIA CHALLENGE

4668) What Midwestern burger chain received an unsolicited testimonial from film critic Roger Ebert in a column, and posted it, in full, in the drive-thru lane?

4669) Who founded McDonald's?

a) Ray Buktenica
b) Ray Kroc
c) Ray Romano
d) Ray Stevens

4670) Detroit Red Wings owner Mike Ilitch owns what pizza chain?

a) Domino's
b) Little Caesars
c) Papa John's
d) Pizza Hut

4671) True or false: McDonald's Corp. owns Dominos Pizza.

4672) True or false: Coca-Cola owns Burger King.

4673) According to its ads, it takes two hands to handle what signature burger?

a) Big Jack
b) Wendy's Triple
c) Big Mac
d) Whopper

4674) The formula for what burger is "Two all-beef patties, special sauce, lettuce, cheese, pickles, onions on a sesame seed bun"?

4675) The owner of McDonald's also owned what Major League baseball team?

a) Milwaukee Brewers
b) San Diego Padres
c) San Francisco Giants
d) Texas Rangers

4676) In the song "Jack and Diane," the title characters are "sucking on a chili dog" outside what fast-food restaurant?

◆ ◆

4677) WHAT COWBOY STAR LENT HIS NAME TO A CHAIN OF ROAST BEEF RESTAURANTS?

◆ ◆

4678) True or false: 7-Eleven bought the Slurpee technology from the makers of Icee.

◆ ◆

4679) True or false: **A song called "Dance the Slurp" was given away at 7-Eleven stores in 1970.**

4681) *What city is considered the biggest consumer of Slurpees?*

a) Winnipeg, Canada
b) Chicago, Illinois
c) Atlanta, Georgia
d) Jackson, Mississippi

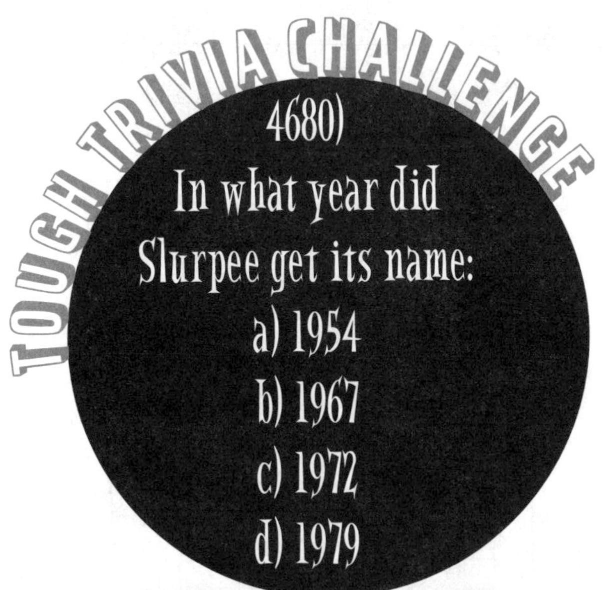

4680) In what year did Slurpee get its name:
a) 1954
b) 1967
c) 1972
d) 1979

4682) True or false: **Slurpees can only be sold at 7-Eleven.**

◆ ◆

4683) Which has not been a Slurpee flavor:

a) Super Sour Apple
b) Bruisin Berry
c) Dragon Fruit
d) Cap'n Crunch

◆ ◆

4684) In a promotion for The Simpsons Movie, what were Slurpees temporarily renamed?

4668. Steak-n-Shake, 4669. b, 4670. b, 4671. false— it owns Donato's, 4672. false, 4673. d, 4674. Big Mac, 4675. b, 4676. Tastee Freeze, 4677. Roy Rogers, 4678. true, 4679. true, 4680. b, 4681. a, 4682. false—they are also in some movie theaters, 4683. d, 4684. Squishees

4685) On what day do U.S. and Canada 7-Elevens offer free 7.11-ounce Slurpees?

4686) True or false: There have always been only twelve flavors of Slush Puppie.

4687) Which of the following has been used in the title of a Hollywood film?

a) KFC
b) White Castle
c) Papa John's
d) Burger King

4688) What shape are White Castle hamburgers?

4689) TRUE OR FALSE: WHITE CASTLE WAS FOUNDED IN WICHITA, KANSAS.

4690) What game has been used in Subway promotions?

a) Monopoly
b) Scrabble
c) Chutes and Ladders
d) Boggle

4691) What building was White Castle restaurants' architecture adapted from?

a) The Empire State Building
b) Westminster Abbey
c) Elsinore
d) Chicago Water Tower

4692) True or false: White Castle hamburgers are not flipped on the grill.

4693) True or false: All White Castle restaurants are in the U.S.

4694) True or false: You can buy stock in White Castle.

4695) HOW MANY WHITE CASTLE HAMBURGERS ARE IN A CRAVE CASE?

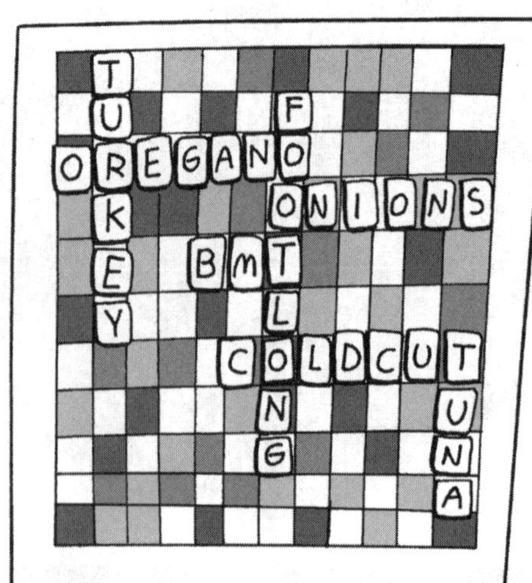

4696) What color are the words White Castle in the company's current logo?

4697) What color is the "way" in the Subway logo?

4698) What color is the "sub" in the Subway logo?

4699) Whose first store was in Hoboken, New Jersey: Blimpee or Subway?

4700) True or false: Jersey Mike's Subs was originally called Mike's Submarines.

4701) True or false: Jersey Mike's Subs was founded in Ohio.

4702) TRUE OR FALSE: PENN STATION'S FIRST RESTAURANT WAS IN OHIO.

4703) True or false: CiCi's Pizza does not offer takeout.

4704) What kind of animal is seen in most Chick-fil-A advertising?

4705) True or false: Chick-fil-A claims to have introduced the chicken nugget.

4706) What Atlanta-based bowl game has Chick-fil-A sponsored?

4707) Arthur Treacher's Fish and Chips was named after:

a) A British prime minister
b) An actor
c) A cricket player
d) A naval officer

4685. July 11, 4686. false, 4687. b, 4688. square, 4689. true, 4690. b, 4691. d, 4692. true, 4693. true, 4694. false—it's a private company, 4695. thirty, 4696. blue, 4697. yellow, 4698. white, 4699. Blimpee, 4700. true, 4701. false, 4702. true, 4703. false, 4704. cows, 4705. true, 4706. Peach Bowl, 4707. b

4708) ON WHAT HOLIDAY DOES NATHAN'S FAMOUS HOLD ITS ANNUAL HOT DOG EATING CONTEST?

4709) How many hot dogs did the 2011 winner eat?

4710) How much time do contestants in the Nathan's Famous hot dog eating contest have to eat as many hot dogs as they can?

4711) Do they have to eat the buns?

4712) Do women compete separately or with men in the Nathan's Famous hot dog eating contest?

4713) True or false: The original Long John Silver's location is now a McDonald's.

4714) Where is the Nathan's Famous hot dog eating contest held?

4715) True or false: The original Long John Silver's location was in a state without an ocean border.

4716) WHAT IS NEAR THE EXIT OF EVERY LONG JOHN SILVER'S RESTAURANT?

4717) What are the deep-fried cornmeal balls served at Long John Silver's called?

4718) True or false: Captain D's seafood restaurants were initially called Mr. D's.

4719) TRUE OR FALSE: POPEYES BEGAN AS A RESTAURANT CALLED CHICKEN ON THE RUN.

4720) What are chicken fingers or strips at Long John Silver's called?

4721) True or False: The owners claim Popeyes was named for the character Gene Hackman played in the movie The French Connection, not the cartoon character.

4722) TRUE OR FALSE: POPEYES LAUNCHED IN ALABAMA.

4723) Which of the following is not a Popeyes Signature Side?

a) Biscuits
b) Green Beans
c) Red Beans & Rice
d) Gumbo Bites

4724) True or false: In some foreign markets, Church's Chicken is known as Texas Chicken.

4725) True or false: Church's Chicken was so named because the first restaurant was housed in a former church.

4726) True or false: During the time it was owned by an Islamic venture capital firm, all pork products were removed from the Church's Chicken menu.

4727) Which of the following is not a Church's Chicken side dish?

a) Collard Greens
b) Okra
c) Mini-wings
d) Sweet Corn Nuggets

4728) Which of the following is not a sauce available at Church's Chicken?

a) White Gravy
b) Cocktail Sauce
c) Creamy Jalapeno Sauce
d) Tarter Sauce

4708. Independence Day, 4709. forty-three, 4710. ten minutes, 4711. yes, 4712. separately, 4713. true, 4714. Coney Island, New York, 4715. true—Kentucky, 4716. a bell, 4717. hush puppies, 4718. true, 4719. true, 4720. chicken planks, 4721. true, 4722. false—Louisiana, 4723. d, 4724. true, 4725. false—it's named for founder George W. Church, 4726. true, 4727. c, 4728. b

CHAIN RESTAURANTS

4729) True or false: The original Applebee's was called T.J. Applebee's Rx for Edibles & Elixirs.

4730) True or false: There are more than 3,500 Applebee's restaurants.

4731) Who voiced the Applebee's Apple?

a) Wanda Sykes

b) Wesley Snipes

c) Applebee's founder T.J. Palmer

d) Wayne Short

4732) In what state is Applebee's headquarters?

a) Missouri

b) Iowa

c) Kansas

d) Maine

4733) What does TGI Friday's claim the TGI stands for?

4734) What two color stripes are in the TGI Friday's logo?

4735) True or false: The first TGI Friday's was in New York.

4736) True or false: All TGI Friday's locations feature real Tiffany lamps.

4737) True or false: The original TGI Friday's was so popular as a bar that it needed ropes outside to help organize the line of patrons.

4738) Which of the following stadiums does not have a TGI Friday's Front Row Sports Grill?

a) Chase Field

b) Miller Park

c) Lucas Oil Stadium

d) Rangers Ballpark

4739) WHAT BRAND OF LIQUOR IS USED IN THE NAME OF SOME OF TGI FRIDAY'S GRILLED MENU ITEMS?

4740) Which is not a category of food at Noodles & Company?

a) Asian
b) African
c) Mediterranean
d) American

4741) True or false: In Cleveland, Panera Bread is know as Cleveland Bread Company.

4742) True or false: In St. Louis, Panera Bread is known as St. Louis Bread Company.

4743) TRUE OR FALSE: IN TRENTON, PANERA BREAD IS KNOWN AS TRENTON BREAD COMPANY.

4744) True or false: The company that is now Panera Bread used to be Au Bon Pain Co.

4745) True or false: Panera Bread owns Paradise Bakery & Café.

4746) True or false: Panera Bread still operates Au Bon Pain restaurants.

4747) Which of the following is not a Panera Artisan Bread?

a) Three Cheese
b) Three Seed
c) Triple Crust
d) Sesame Semolina

4748) Which of the following is not a Panera Specialty Bread?

a) Asiago Cheese
b) Tex-Mex
c) Tomato Basil
d) Honey Wheat

4749) True or false: There are no Le Peep restaurants in California.

4729. true, 4730. false—only around 1,500, 4731. a, 4732. c, 4733. Thank Goodness It's, 4734. red and white, 4735. true, 4736. false, 4737. true, 4738. c, 4739. Jack Daniel's, 4740. b, 4741. false, 4742. true, 4743. false, 4744. true, 4745. true, 4746. false, 4747. c, 4748. b, 4749. true

4750) WHAT MEAL DOES LE PEEP SPECIALIZE IN?

4751) Does the Bennigan's chain of restaurants have locations in Ireland?

4752) Does the Bennigan's chain of restaurants have a restaurant in Qatar?

4753) True or false: **the first Chili's location was in a former grocery store.**

4754) What color is the chili pepper in the Chili's logo?

4755) True or false: On The Office, the Dundie Awards were given out at a TGI Fridays.

4756) TRUE OR FALSE: THERE ARE CHILI'S LOCATIONS IN SINGAPORE AND KUWAIT.

4757) What meat entrée was famously celebrated by a do-wop group in an ad for Chili's?

4758) Chili's line of hamburgers are called...

a) Double Dipping Burgers

b) Big Mouth Burgers

c) Power Burgers

d) Brother Burgers

4759) True or false: The P.F. in the restaurant name of P.F. Chang's refers to an ancient Chinese dynasty.

4760) True or false: The first Cheesecake Factory was in Beverly Hills, California.

4761) True or false: **According to one study, the average sandwich at the Cheesecake Factory contained almost 1,400 calories.**

4762) Does the Cheesecake Factory serve omelets?

4763) Which of the following is not one of the Cheesecake Factory's Glamburgers?

a) Macaroni and Cheese Burger
b) Mashed Potato Burger
c) Farmhouse Cheeseburger
d) Memphis Burger

4764) TRUE OR FALSE: TEXAS ROADHOUSE IS BASED IN TENNESSEE.

4765) True or false: **The first Texas Roadhouse was in Indiana.**

4766) What is given free at every Texas Roadhouse table?

a) **Oyster crackers**
b) **Cheese balls**
c) **Peanuts**
d) **Popcorn**

4767) Was Texas Roadhouse founded in the 1980s or the 1990s?

4768) True or false: It's not uncommon to see the Texas Roadhouse wait staff line dancing.

4769) WHAT ANIMAL IS THE TEXAS ROADHOUSE MASCOT?

4770) True or false: **Olive Garden was founded in Italy.**

4771) True or False: General Mills launched Olive Garden.

4772) True or false: The décor in newer Oliver Garden restaurants is based on a specific house in Tuscany.

4773) The motto for Olive Garden is, "When you're here, you're ______."

4774) True or false: Maggiano's Little Italy restaurants were founded in Chicago.

4750. breakfast, 4751. no, 4752. yes, 4753. false—it was a post office, 4754. red, 4755. false—Chili's, 4756. true, 4757. Baby Back Ribs, 4758. b, 4759. false—it stands for owner Paul Fleming, 4760. true, 4761. true, 4762. yes, 4763. b, 4764. false—Kentucky, 4765. true, 4766. c, 4767. 1990s, 4768. true, 4769. armadillo, 4770. false, 4771. true, 4772. true, 4773. family, 4774. true

4775) **True or false:** The name Romano in Romano's Macaroni Grill is not taken from an actual person.

4776) True or false: Romano's Macaroni Grill is headquartered in Trenton, New Jersey.

4777) TRUE OR FALSE: JOHNNY CARRABBA CO-FOUNDED CARRABBA'S ITALIAN GRILL.

4778) Is Chicken Bryan served at Romano's Macaroni Grill or Carrabba's Italian Grill?

4779) Red Lobster is redesigning its restaurant in a style inspired by what state?

4780) True or false: Red Lobster founder Bill Darden opened his first restaurant when he was nineteen.

4781) True or false: The first Red Lobster restaurant was in Baltimore, Maryland.

4782) WAS RED LOBSTER FOUNDED IN THE 1960S, THE 1970S, OR THE 1980S?

TOUGH TRIVIA CHALLENGE

4783) WHERE DOES THE OUTBACK BOWL TAKE PLACE?

4784) True or false: Red Lobster's Crab Linguini Alfredo has more calories than four quarter-pound steamed lobsters.

4785) True or false: **Red Lobster calls its lower-fat choices LightHouse Selections.**

4786) True or false: There are Red Lobster restaurants in Japan.

4787) Which of the following is not a Darden restaurant?

a) Red Lobster
b) The Capital Grille
c) Olive Garden
d) Outback Steakhouse

4788) True or false: **Outback Steakhouse was founded in Texas.**

4789) True or false: There are no Outback Steakhouses in Australia.

4790) True or false: There are more than 100 Outback Steakhouses in South Korea.

4791) WAS OUTBACK STEAKHOUSE FOUNDED IN THE 1970S, 1980S, OR 1990S?

4792) True or false: There's over 1,800 calories in an Outback Steakhouse Bloomin' Onion.

4793) Which of the following is not an Outback side dish?

a) Garlic Mashed Potatoes
b) Grilled Asparagus
c) Walkabout Lima Beans
d) Sweet Potato Fries

4794) True or false: Outback owns two blimps.

4795) Which is the name of a breakfast platter at Cracker Barrel Old Country Store?

a) Grandpa Henry's Favorite
b) Uncle Herschel's Favorite
c) Cousin Hank's Favorite
d) Aunt Harriet's Favorite

4796) TRUE OR FALSE: YOU CAN BUY A ROCKING CHAIR AT CRACKER BARREL?

4797) True or false: Cracker Barrel sells its own brand of coffee.

4798) How many pegs in the peg game on the tables at Cracker Barrel?

4799) Which of the following is not a color peg in the Cracker Barrel peg game?

a) Yellow
b) Blue
c) Green
d) White

4775. false—the founder was Philip J. Romano, 4776. false—Dallas, Texas, 4777. true, 4778. Carrabba's, 4779. Maine, 4780. true—the Green Frog, 4781. false—Lakeland Florida, 4782. 1960s, 4783. Tampa, Florida, 4784. true, 4785. true, 4786. true, 4787. d, 4788. false, 4789. false, 4790. true, 4791. 1980s, 4792. true, 4793. c, 4794. true, 4795. b, 4796. true, 4797. true, 4798. fifteen, 4799. c

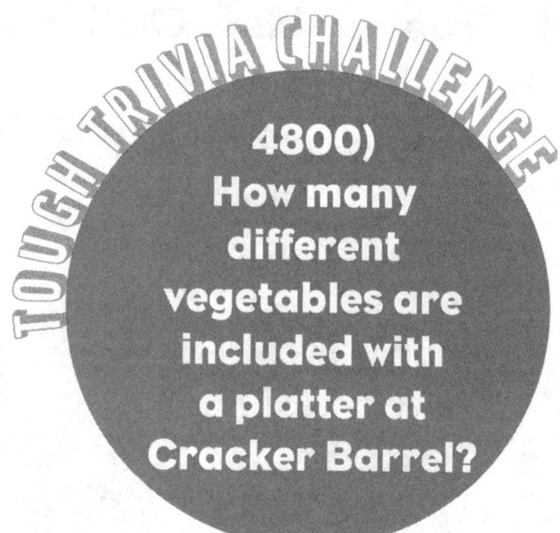

4801) What genre of music does Cracker Barrel primarily sell?

4802) TRUE OR FALSE: THE SAME COMPANY THAT OWNS RED LOBSTER OWNS RED ROBIN.

4803) True or false: Red Robin features fifteen different hamburgers.

4804) What is the name of the mascot for Red Robin?

4805) True or false: There are scrambled eggs on the Royal Red Robin Burger?

4806) True or false: Cracker Barrel has a Turkey special every Thursday.

4807) True or false: Red Robin offers half-price refills on its French fries.

4808) True or false: Red Robin started as Sam's Tavern.

4809) True or false: The name Red Robin comes from the song "When the Red, Red Robin (Comes Bob, Bob, Bobbin' Along).

4810) True or false: The original Red Robin is still open.

4811) True or false: Ruby Tuesday restaurants came before the Rolling Stones' song "Ruby Tuesday."

4812) True or false: All food is half price on Tuesdays at Ruby Tuesday.

4813) True or false: **The first Longhorn Steakhouse was in Atlanta.**

4814) Which of the following is an offering at Longhorn Steakhouse?

a) Fred's Filet
b) Frieda's Filet
c) Flo's Filet
d) Fern's Filet

4815) TRUE OR FALSE: LONGHORN STEAKHOUSE SERVES AN APPETIZER CALLED TEXAS TONION.

4816) What is the name of Golden Corral's bakery?

a) Brass Bell Bakery
b) Betty's Bakery
c) Bell's Big Bakery
d) Bill's Best Bakery

4817) Which of the following is not a regular item on the Golden Corral buffet?

a) **Pizza**
b) **Fudgy Brownies**
c) **Fried Oysters**
d) **Yeast Rolls**

4818) DOES GOLDEN CORRAL OFFER POT ROAST?

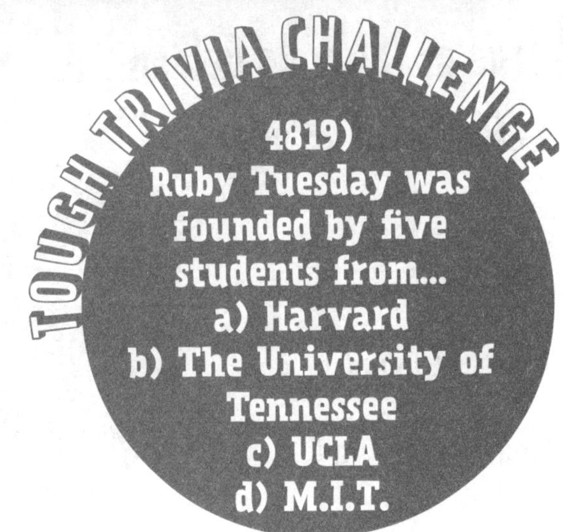

4819) Ruby Tuesday was founded by five students from...

a) Harvard
b) The University of Tennessee
c) UCLA
d) M.I.T.

4820) Where was the first Golden Corral?

a) South Carolina
b) North Carolina
c) South Dakota
d) North Dakota

4821) True or false: Golden Corral ads featured people getting hit in the head with frying pans.

4822) Did the first Golden Corral open in the 1960s, the 1970s, or the 1980s?

4800. 3, 4801. country, 4802. false, 4803. false—there are more than twenty, 4804. Red, the Red Robin, 4805. false—but there is a fried egg, 4806. true, 4807. false—fries get unlimited free refills, 4808. true, 4809. true, 4810. false, 4811. false, 4812. false, 4813. true, 4814. c, 4815. true, 4816. a, 4817. c, 4818. yes, 4819. b, 4820. b, 4821. true, 4822. 1970s

4823) **True or false:** No Golden Corrals offer food to go.

4824) True or false: Benihana was founded by a man named Benny Hana.

4825) **True or false:** The first Benihana was in New York City.

4826) True or false: **The Beatles ate at the original Benihana.**

4827) **True or false:** There are no Benihana restaurants in Japan.

4828) True or false: An episode of The Office featured a Christmas party at Benihana.

4829) **TRUE OR FALSE:** IT'S SOCIALLY ACCEPTABLE TO SIP FROM A SOUP BOWL AT BENIHANA.

4830) True or false: **There are more than 150 Big Boy Japan restaurants.**

TOUGH TRIVIA CHALLENGE

At Benihana, guests are given a wet towel called a...

a) Oshibori
b) Oxibori
c) Ushiburo
d) Ashaibarro

4831) **Before eating at Benihana, patrons are supposed to say "itadakimasu," which means:**

a) I'm hungry
b) Bless this food
c) I shall partake
d) Glory to Japan

4832) Did the first Big Boy restaurant launch before or after World War II?

4833) What are the two colors on the Big Boy overalls?

4834) TRUE OR FALSE: THERE WAS AN ADVENTURES OF BIG BOY COMIC BOOK.

4835) Big Boy restaurants go by many names. Which of the following states is not home to Bob's Big Boy?

a) Oregon
b) Maryland
c) California
d) Pennsylvania

4836) True or false: Before 1984, Shoney's featured the Big Boy statue.

4837) What color is Big Boy's hair?

4838) What color are Big Boy's eyes?

4839) What color are Big Boy's shoes?

4840) Where are you most likely to find a Black-eyed Pea restaurant?

a) Texas
b) Maine
c) Alaska
d) Florida

4841) BUBBA GUMP SHRIMP COMPANY WAS INSPIRED BY A REFERENCE IN WHAT OSCAR-WINNING FILM?

4842) True or false: **Most of the Bubba Gump Shrimp Company locations are in Malaysia.**

4843) **True or false:** There are recorded sounds in the restrooms of Buca di Beppo restaurants.

4844) True or false: **The first Buca di Beppo was in Minneapolis.**

4845) TRUE OR FALSE: BUCA DI BEPPO WAS ORIGINALLY CALLED BEPPO DI BUCA.

4846) How many people can sit at the Buca di Beppo Pope's Table?

a) 2 b) 5-8 c) 8-12 d) 12-18

4823. false, 4824. false, 4825. true, 4826. true, 4827. true, 4828. true, 4829. true, 4830. true, Un-numbered: a, 4831. c, 4832. before, 4833. red and white, 4834. true, 4835. c, 4836. true, 4837. black, 4838. blue with black pupils, 4839. black, 4840. a, 4841. *Forest Gump*, 4842. false, 4843. true, 4844. true, 4845. false, 4846. d, 4847. Black Angus Steakhouse

TOUGH TRIVIA CHALLENGE

4848) Which of the following is not one of the meat choices at Chipotle?

a) Barbacoa
b) Carnitas
c) Bison
d) Pork

4849) True or false: There are no California Pizza Kitchen restaurants in California.

4850) True or false: The original Chammps Americana restaurant was called Chapps.

4851) In what state are you most likely to find a Claim Jumper restaurant?

a) Arizona
b) West Virginia
c) Alabama
d) Florida

4852) Does the primarily-in-New Jersey Charlie Brown's Steakhouse chain have anything to do with the *Peanuts* comic strip?

4853) True or false: Jimmy Buffett gets a percentage of the profits from Cheeseburger in Paradise restaurants.

4854) Is there a Cheeseburger in Paradise restaurant in Key West?

4855) True or false: There's a restaurant in Hawaii called Cheeseburger in Paradise that is not part of the chain.

4856) Which of the following is not one of the "no's" at Baja Fresh?

a) No can openers
b) No freezers
c) No lard
d) No peppers

4857) Which burger chain owned Baja Fresh from 2002 to 2006?

a) McDonald's
b) Burger King
c) Wendy's
d) Hardee's

4858) Chipotle is named after...

a) A town in Mexico
b) Its founder
c) A pepper
d) None of the above

4859) Which burger chain was a majority investor in Chipotle from 1998-2006?

a) McDonald's
b) Burger King
c) Wendy's
d) Hardee's

4860) TRUE OR FALSE: THE FIRST CHIPOTLE WAS OPENED IN DENVER.

4861) TRUE OR FALSE: AS OF 2011, THERE WERE NO CHIPOTLES IN MONTANA.

4862) True or false: Chipotle doesn't advertise on television.

4863) True or false: Moe's Southwest Grill is not headquartered in the southwest.

4864) True or false: There are Denny's restaurants in Curacao.

4865) True or false: Denny's are open 24 hours.

4866) True or false: Every Chipotle restaurant is designed differently.

4867) True or false: The first of what would be Denny's restaurants was called Danny's Donuts.

4868) WAS DENNY'S FOUNDED IN THE 1940S, THE 1950S, OR THE 1960S?

4869) Which of the following is not part of a Denny's Grand Slam Breakfast?

a) Eggs
b) Sausage
c) Bacon
d) Home fries

4848. c, 4849. false, 4850. false—it was called Concourse 7, 4851. a, 4852. no, 4853. true, 4854. no, 4855. true, 4856. d, 4857. c, 4858. c, 4859. a, 4860. true, 4861. true, 4862. true, 4863. true—it's based in Atlanta, 4864. true, 4865. true, 4866. true, 4867. true, 4868. 1950s, 4869. d

4871) Denny's Allnighter eateries are all located:

a) In downtown urban locations
b) In waterfront locations
c) In college locations
d) Near federal penitentiaries

4872) True or false: The Seminole Tribe owns Hard Rock Café.

4873) True or false: The first Hard Rock Café was in New York City.

4874) True or false: All of the rock and roll memorabilia items at Hard Rock Cafés are donated.

4875) WHICH CAME FIRST: HARD ROCK CAFÉ OR PLANET HOLLYWOOD?

4876) Who was the first musician to donate a guitar to Hard Rock Café?

a) Bruce Springsteen
b) Eric Clapton
c) Pete Townsend
d) Getty Lee

4877) Where is the Hard Rock's museum, the Vault, located?

a) Orlando
b) London
c) Hollywood
d) New York

4878) Which of the following was not one of the original backers of Planet Hollywood?

a) Sylvester Stallone
b) Clint Eastwood
c) Demi Moore
d) Arnold Schwarzenegger

4879) Which of the following was not an unsuccessful spin-off of Planet Hollywood?

a) Cool Planet
b) Marvel Mania
c) Pizza Planet
d) Official All Star Café

4880) Is there a Planet Hollywood in Hollywood?

4881) If you are at a Hoss's Steak and Sea House are you more likely to be in Pennsylvania or North Dakota?

4882) True or false: Howard Johnson's was once the largest sit-down restaurants chain in America.

4883) How many flavors of ice cream did Howard Johnson's boast of having during its early days:

a) 12 b) 18 c) 28 d) 36

4884) WHAT COLOR, TRADITIONALLY, ARE THE ROOFS OF HOWARD JOHNSON'S?

4885) Which came first, Howard Johnson's restaurants or hotels?

4886) What is traditionally on top of a Howard Johnson's restaurant?

4887) True or false: There were once HoJos Campgrounds.

4888) True or false: There are no Howard Johnson's restaurants left west of the Mississippi River.

4870. c, 4871. c, 4872. true, 4873. false—it was in London, 4874. false, 4875. Hard Rock Café, 4876. b, 4877. b, 4878. b, 4879. d, 4880. no, 4881. Pennsylvania, 4882. true, 4883. c, 4884. orange, 4885. restaurants, 4886. a weathervane, 4887. true, 4888. true

4889) Which of the following is an iconic International House of Pancakes breakfast entrée?

a) Rough and Tumble Fresh 'n Funny

b) Rooty Tooty Fresh 'n Fruity

c) Really Tasty Fun 'n Fancy

d) Crisp and Crunchy Yum to my Tummy

4890) Did the International House of Pancakes rebrand itself as IHop in the 1970s, the 1980s, or the 1990s?

4891) IHOP'S SLOGAN WAS "COME HUNGRY. LEAVE ____________"

4892) Has IHop been around more or less than 50 years?

4893) True or false: Many of the jukeboxes at Waffle House restaurants feature songs about waffles.

4894) True or false: Joe's Crab Shack was founded in Maryland.

4895) What is the core food at Famous Dave's?

a) Hamburgers

b) Chicken

c) Tacos

d) Barbecue

4896) TRUE OR FALSE: JOE'S CRAB SHACK SERVES CRAB PUDDING FOR DESSERT.

..PIZZA..

4897) Which came first in the evolution of pizza, the cheese or the tomato sauce?

4898) Pizza as we know it is largely believed to have been conceived in...

a) **Naples**
b) **Verona**
c) **Rome**
d) **Cleveland**

4899) True or false:
Margherita pizza is named for Queen Margherita of Savoy.

4900) Are anchovies a salt-water or fresh-water fish?

4901) True or false: **Anchovies have no teeth.**

4906) True or false: Pizza Hut and Red Roof Inn are owned by the same company.

4907) WHAT MONTH IS NATIONAL PIZZA MONTH?

4908) True or false:
Pepperoni is the most requested topping on pizza.

Match the famous pizzerias to its city.

4902) De Lorenzo's
4903) Giordano's
4904) Ray's
4905) Regina Pizzeria

a) Chicago, Illinois
b) New York, New York
c) Trenton, New Jersey
d) Boston, Massachusetts

4889. b, 4890. 1970s, 4891. Happy, 4892. more, 4893. true, 4894. false—in Houston, 4895. d, 4896. false, 4897. the tomato sauce, 4898. a, 4899. true, 4900. salt water, 4901. false, 4902. b, 4903. a, 4904. b, 4905. d, 4906. false, 4907. October, 4908. false—cheese is

CONDIMENTS

4909) True or false: The name ketchup comes from Ke-chiap, a Chinese fish sauce.

4910) True or false: **It is against government standards to include vinegar in ketchup.**

4911) TRUE OR FALSE: ANOTHER NAME FOR KETCHUP USED TO BE TOMATO SOY.

4912) True or false: **Ketchup can be used to shine gold.**

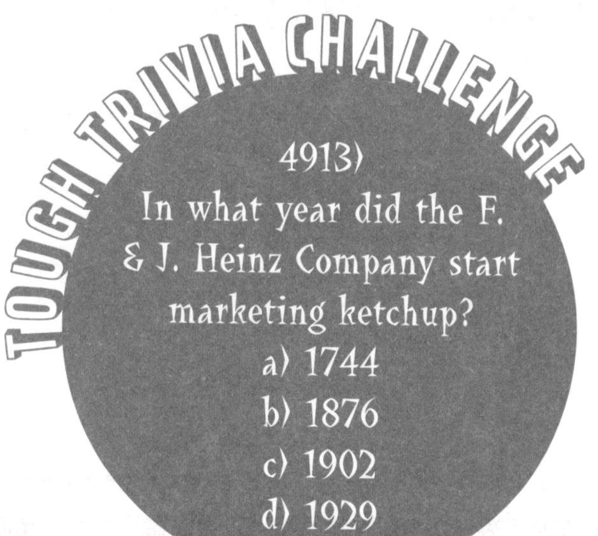

TOUGH TRIVIA CHALLENGE

4913)
In what year did the F. & J. Heinz Company start marketing ketchup?

a) 1744
b) 1876
c) 1902
d) 1929

4914) Does ketchup get darker or lighter when it's exposed to sun?

4915) True or false: Pope John XXII named his nephew as moutardier du pape or mustard-maker to the pope.

4916) Was mustard first considered a food or a medicine?

4917) DIJON IS A REGION OF WHAT COUNTRY?

4918) True or false: The flowers of a mustard plant are not edible.

4919) In Denmark, mustard seed is used to ward off werewolves.

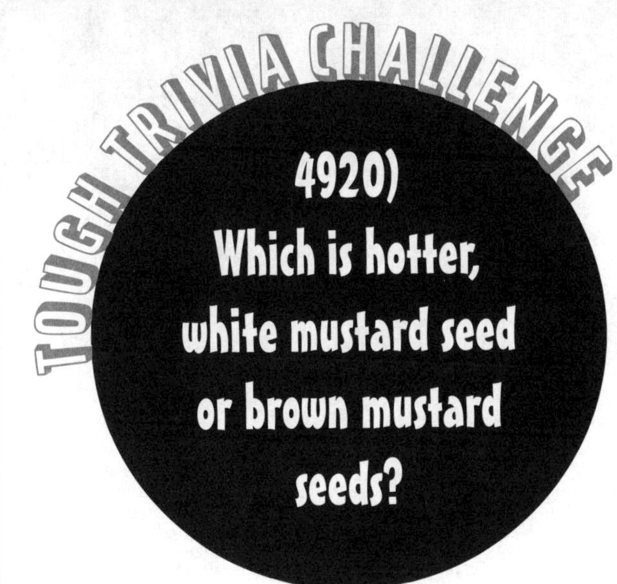

4921) Bordeaux mustard is made with...

a) Cheese
b) Dough
c) Tomato
d) Grape juice

4922) True or false: The mustard most used on hot dogs, American mustard or yellow mustard, was actually created in Egypt.

4923) True or false: there is a National Mustard Museum.

4909. true—Europeans later added tomatoes, 4910. false, 4911. true, 4912. false—but it can be used to shine copper, 4913. b, 4914. darker, 4915. true, 4916. medicine, 4917. France, 4918. false, 4919. false—although it is thought to help keep away evil spirits, 4920. brown, 4921. d, 4922. false—it was introduced by New Yorker George T. French at the 1904 St. Louis World's Fair, 4923. true—it's in Middleton, Wisconsin

SWEET STUFF

4924) True or false: Chewing gum makes an appearance in Mark Twain's *The Adventures of Tom Sawyer?*

4925) WRIGLEY'S JUICY FRUIT GUM FIRST APPEARED IN...

A) 1872 B) 1893
C) 1912 D) 1932

4926) True or false: In 1915, Wrigley sent gum to everyone listed in U.S. phone books.

4927) True or false: Pink became the standard color of bubble gum in 1952.

4928) True or false: Topps first combined baseball cards and bubble gum in 1971.

4929) True or false: Pez comes from the German word Phefferminz

4930) True or false: From the time it was launched, Pez candies included a dispenser.

4931) The first Pez dispenser sold in America featured what on top?

a) A Ford automobile
b) A Mickey Mouse head
c) Santa Claus
d) The White House

4932) In the movie *Stand By Me*, what flavor Pez does one character say is what he would pick if he could only have one food for the rest of his life?

4933) True or false: Snickers contains almonds.

4934) True or false: In Japan, Pez candy is white.

4935) Which of the following was not one of the historical figures who topped Pez dispensers in honor of the Bicentennial?
a) Betsy Ross
b) Paul Revere
c) Ben Franklin
d) Daniel Boone

4936) What yellow-wrapped, chocolate-covered peanut bar was Hershey's second product, after the Hershey bar?

4937) **True or false:** eBay was created as a way to make Pez-dispenser trading easier.

4938) ACCORDING TO MR. OWL, HOW MANY LICKS DOES IT TAKE TO GET TO THE CENTER OF A TOOTSIE POP?

4939) Before undergoing a name change, what were milk chocolate M&M's called?

4940) Which is not a variety of M&Ms?
a) Almond
b) Coconut
c) Crisped rice
d) Hazelnut

4941) What color of M&Ms was scrapped in 1975, and then reintroduced in 1987?

4942) Not counting special promotions, what color M&M was most recently added, in 1995?

4943) What candy was prominently featured in the movie "E.T."?

4944) BART SIMPSON HAS APPEARED IN COMMERCIALS FOR WHAT CANDY BAR?

4945) True or false: **the Oh Henry! Bar is named for Hank Aaron.**

4924. true, 4925. b, 4926. true, 4927. false—it happened in 1928, 4928. false—1951, 4929. true, 4930. false—it was sold for about 20 years without one, 4931. b, 4932. cherry, 4933. false—peanuts, 4934. true, 4935. c, 4936. Mr. Goodbar, 4937. false—that was only a marketing-created story, 4938. three, 4939. plain, 4940. d, 4941. red, 4942. blue, 4943. Reese's Pieces, 4944. Butterfinger, 4945. false—although he did do ads for it

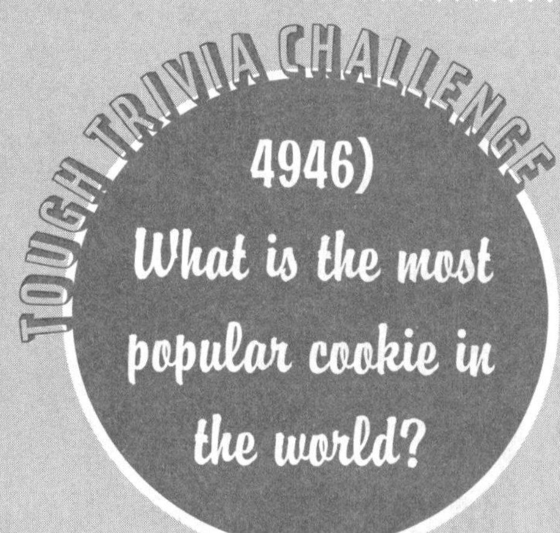

4947) True or false: Reggie Jackson once had a candy bar named after him.

4948) What company makes Oreos?

a) General Mills
b) Hershey
c) Keebler
d) Nabisco

4949) What ancestor of bowling is the name of a candy?

a) Kit Kat
b) Skittles
c) Starburst
d) Twix

4954) What candy bar is named after a novel by Alexandre Dumas?

4955) Appropriately, what candy company manufactures the Milky Way bar?

4956) What high-end chocolatier is headquartered on San Francisco Bay?

a) Fannie Mae
b) Frango
c) Ghirardelli
d) Godiva

4957) While several candy bars now have ice cream flavors, what candy bar was an ice cream brand first?

a) Dove
b) Reese's Pieces
c) Snickers
d) Symphony

Match the slogan to the candy.

4950) Gimme a break
4951) The Great American Chocolate Bar
4952) Melts in your mouth, not in your hand
4953) Sometimes you feel like a nut

a) Almond Joy
b) Hershey's
c) Kit Kat
d) M&M's

Match the slogan to the breath freshener.

4958) Brush your breath
4959) The curiously strong mints
4960) The 1 Calorie Breath Mint
4961) Two-two-two mints in one

a) Altoids
b) Certs
c) Dentyne
d) Tic Tac

TOUGH TRIVIA CHALLENGE

4962) What department store produces and distributes Frango mints?

a) Bloomingdale's
b) Filene's
c) Macy's
d) Neiman-Marcus

4963) WHAT BRAND OF BUBBLE GUM COMES WITH A COMIC STRIP INSIDE THE WRAPPER?

4964) What was the first Life Savers flavor?

a) Pep-O-Mint
b) Spearmint
c) Wild Cherry
d) Wint-O-Green

4965) What candy bar consists of peanuts around a caramel center?

a) Mr. Goodbar
b) Payday
c) Zagnut
d) Zero

4966) TRUE OR FALSE: HERSHEY'S KISSES WITH BOTH MILK CHOCOLATE AND WHITE CHOCOLATE ARE CALLED HUGS.

4946. Oreo, 4947. true, 4948. d, 4949. b, 4950. c, 4951. b, 4952. d, 4953. a, 4954. 3 Musketeers, 4955. Mars, 4956. c, 4957. a, 4958. c, 4959. a, 4960. d, 4961. b, 4962. c, 4963. Bazooka, 4964. a, 4965. b, 4966. true

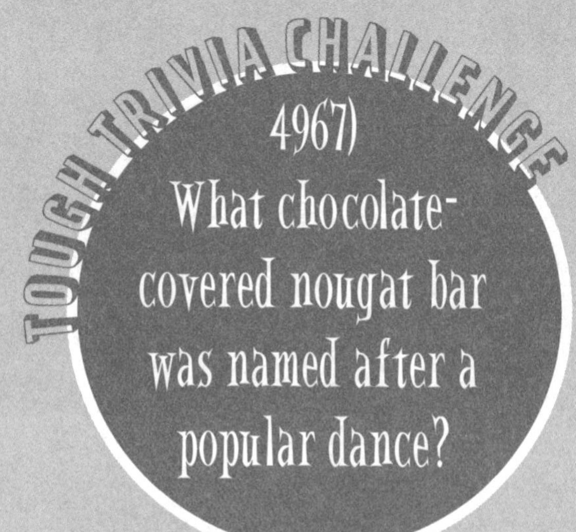

4968) True or false: Six people died from eating Pop Rocks candy combined with soda?

4969) What is the current name of the candy bar once called the $100,000 Bar?

4970) What candy bar features a bee on the wrapper?

4971) The name of what candy bar is short for "twin sticks"?

4972) What chewing gum has frequently advertised itself using twin sisters as spokesmodels?

4973) TRUE OR FALSE: BOTH CHOCOLATE AND VANILLA COME FROM BEANS.

4974) What do you get if you combine chocolate, marshmallows and graham crackers?

4975) What candy bar advertised itself as "thickerer"?

a) Chunky
b) Dove
c) Marathon
d) Whatchamacallit

4976) What chocolate company makes Quik instant cocoa?

a) Ghirardelli
b) Hershey
c) Mars
d) Nestle

4977) What provides the crunch in a Nestle Crunch bar?

a) Almonds
b) Peanuts
c) Rice
d) Walnuts

4978) True or false: A food can be called "sugar free" and still have some sugar in it.

4979) True or false: George Washington served ice cream to guests.

4980) True or false: **Ice cream was originally called iced cream.**

4981) WHAT MINERAL CONTROLS AND LOWERS THE TEMPERATURE OF INGREDIENTS DURING THE MAKING OF ICE CREAM?

4982) Soft ice cream involves increasing the amount of what?

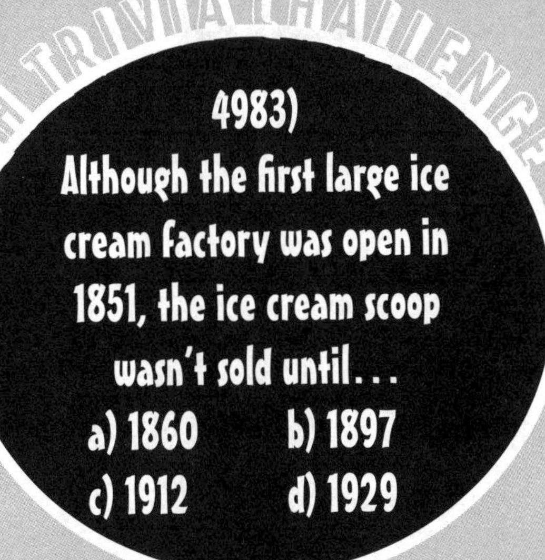

4983) Although the first large ice cream factory was open in 1851, the ice cream scoop wasn't sold until...

a) 1860 b) 1897
c) 1912 d) 1929

4984) What was introduced at the 1904 World's Fair in St. Louis?

a) The first ice cream sundae
b) Sprinkles/jimmies
c) Neapolitan ice cream
d) The edible cone

4985) True or false: **Haagen-Dazs is a Danish company.**

4986) Which of the following does not claim to be the place where the ice cream sundae was created?

a) Two Rivers, Wisconsin
b) Hoboken, New Jersey
c) Ithaca, New York
d) Evanston, Illinois

4967. Charleston Chew, 4968. false—it's an urban legend, 4969. 100 Grand, 4970. Bit-o'-Honey, 4971. Twix, 4972. Doublemint, 4973. true, 4974. S'mores, 4975. a, 4976. d, 4977. c, 4978. true—as long as it has less than .5 grams per serving, 4979. true, 4980. true, 4981. salt, 4982. air, 4983. c, 4984. d, 4985. false, 4986. b

4987) The chocolate-covered ice cream bar, the Eskimo Pie, was launched in 1934 in the city of Onawa. What state is Onawa in?

a) Ohio
b) Indiana
c) Iowa
d) Idaho

4988) Sherbet contains about what percentage of butterfat?

a) 1-2%
b) 3-4%
c) 5-6%
d) 7-8%

TOUGH TRIVIA CHALLENGE

4989) Ice cream and frozen custard each contain about what percentage of butterfat?

a) 2%
b) 10%
c) 15%
d) 21%

4990) The man who created the first chocolate bar was from...

a) England
b) France
c) Switzerland
d) China

SODA

4991) For a drink to be considered non-alcoholic, it cannot have more than what percent alcohol content:

a) .01%
b) .10%
c) .25%
d) .5%

4992) True or false: **Before 1899, soda bottles were hand blown.**

4993) Carbonated water is also called:

a) Soda water
b) High-fructose water
c) Waterlite
d) Diet water

4994) Carbonated water was developed in...

a) England
b) France
c) Germany
d) United States

4995) TRUE OR FALSE: PHOSPHATE SODA INCLUDES PHOSPHORIC ACID.

4996) When did soda vending machines initially appear.

a) 1900s
b) 1920s
c) 1940s
d) 1960s

4997) True or false: Coca-Cola used to contain cocaine.

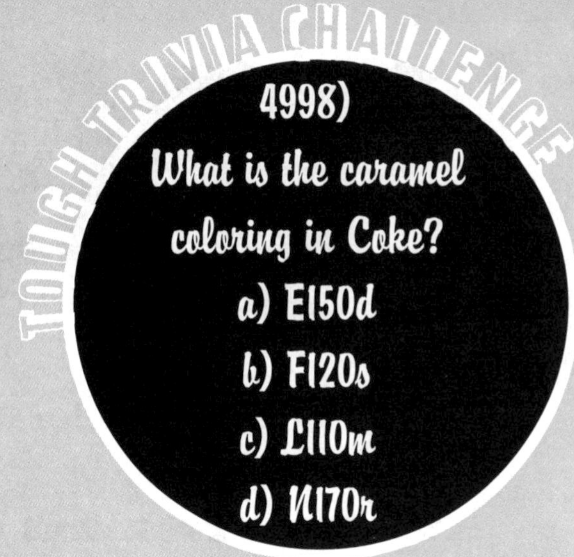

4999) When was Coca-Cola invented?

a) 1886
b) 1902
c) 1921
d) 1936

5000) True or false: Kosher for Passover Coca-Cola contains sucrose instead of high-fructose corn syrup.

4987. c, 4988. a, 4989. b, 4990. c—but that was for cooking, not eating, 4991. d, 4992. true, 4993. a, 4994. a, 4995. true, 4996. b, 4997. true, 4998. a, 4999. a, 5000. true.

ABOUT APPLESAUCE PRESS

What kid doesn't love Applesauce?

Applesauce Press was created to press out the best children's books found anywhere. Like our parent company, Cider Mill Press Book Publishers, we strive to bring fine reading, information, and entertainment to kids of all ages. Between the covers of our creatively crafted books, you'll find beautiful designs, creative formats, and most of all, kid-friendly information on a variety of topics. Our Cider Mill bears fruit twice a year, publishing a new crop of titles each spring and fall.

"Where Good Books Are Ready for Press"

Visit us on the web at
www.cidermillpress.com
or write to us at
12 Port Farm Road
Kennebunkport, Maine 04046

Other titles in this series:
The Biggest Joke Book Ever (No Kidding)
The Most Ginormous Joke Book in the Universe